9/11

W9-BYW-896

DEMCO

The Advertising Handbook

The Advertising Handbook is a critical introduction to the practices and perspectives of advertising. It explores the industry and those who work in it and examines the reasons why companies and organisations advertise; how they research their markets; where they advertise and in which media; the principles and techniques of persuasion and their effectiveness; and how companies measure their success. It challenges conventional wisdom about advertising power and authority to offer a realistic assessment of its role in business and also looks at the industry's future.

The third edition offers new material and a new organising framework, while continuing to provide both an introduction and an authoritative guide to advertising theory and practice. It is shaped to meet the requirements, interests and terms of reference of the most recent generation of media and advertising students – as well as taking account of some of the most recent academic work in the field, and, of course, contemporary advertising innovations.

This new edition includes:

*   fresh industry case studies
*   detailed profiles of and from advertising agencies and new media players
*   new and detailed workshop exercises to accompany each chapter
*   supplementary input from a range of contributors.

Helen Powell previously worked in the advertising industry and is currently Senior Lecturer and Programme Leader in Advertising at the University of East London. Her research interests and publications explore the changing role of cultural intermediaries, including celebrities, as informers of consumer choice across a range of media including lifestyle TV and advertising.

Jonathan Hardy is Senior Lecturer in Media Studies at the University of East London and also teaches political economy of media at Goldsmiths College, University of London. He is the author of *Western Media Systems* (2008).

Sarah Hawkin is Director for Continental Europe at JWT Education, is a frequent speaker at education conferences and has sat on adjudication panels for students at degree and masters level.

Iain MacRury is Principal Lecturer in Cultural Studies and Creative Industries and Director of the London East Research Institute at the University of East London. He is author of *Advertising* (2009), co-author of *The Dynamics of Advertising* (2000), and co-editor of *Buy this Book: Studies in Advertising and Consumption* (1997). He is also co-editor of *Olympic Cities: 2012 and the Remaking of London* (2008), and co-author of *The Secret Life of Cars* (2007).

Media Practice

Edited by James Curran, Goldsmiths College, University of London

The *Media Practice* handbooks are comprehensive resource books for students of media and journalism, and for anyone planning a career as a media professional. Each handbook combines a clear introduction to understanding how the media work with practical information about the structure, processes and skills involved in working in today's media industries, providing not only a guide on 'how to do it' but also a critical reflection on contemporary media practice.

The Newspapers Handbook 4th edition

Richard Keeble

The Radio Handbook 2nd edition

Carole Fleming

The Advertising Handbook 3rd edition

Helen Powell, Jonathan Hardy, Sarah Hawkin and Iain MacRury

The Television Handbook 3rd edition

Jonathan Bignell and Jeremy Orlebar

The Photography Handbook 2nd edition

Terence Wright

The Magazines Handbook 2nd edition

Jenny McKay

The Public Relations Handbook 3rd edition

Alison Theaker

The Cyberspace Handbook

Jason Whittaker

The Fashion Handbook

Tim Jackson and David Shaw

The New Media Handbook

Andrew Dewdney and Peter Ride

The Advertising Handbook

Third edition

Helen Powell, Jonathan Hardy,
Sarah Hawkin and Iain MacRury

Routledge
Taylor & Francis Group

LONDON AND NEW YORK

First edition first published 1995
by Routledge
Second edition first published 2002
by Routledge
This third edition first published 2009
by Routledge
2 Park Square, Milton Park, Abingdon, Oxon OX14 4RN

Simultaneously published in the USA and Canada
by Routledge
270 Madison Ave, New York, NY 10016

Routledge is an imprint of the Taylor & Francis Group, an informa business

First and second editions © 1995, 2002 Sean Brierley
Third edition © 2009 Helen Powell, Jonathan Hardy,
Sarah Hawkin and Iain MacRury
Individual chapters © Chapter contributors

Typeset in Times New Roman by
Florence Production Ltd, Stoodleigh, Devon

British Library Cataloguing in Publication Data
A catalogue record for this book is available from the British Library

Library of Congress Cataloging in Publication Data
The advertising handbook/[edited by] Helen Powell . . . [et al.]. – 3rd ed.
    p. cm. – (Media practice)
Rev. ed. of: The advertising handbook/Sean Brierley. 2nd ed. 2002.
    Includes bibliogaphical references and index.
1. Advertising – Handbooks, manuals, etc. I. Powell, Helen.
II. Brierley, Sean 1966–. Advertising handbook.
HF5823.B7273 2008
659.1 – dc22   2008047678

ISBN10: 0–415–42312–0 (hbk)
ISBN10: 0–415–42311–2 (pbk)

ISBN13: 978–0–415–42312–0 (hbk)
ISBN13: 978–0–415–42311–3 (pbk)

Contents

Illustrations

....

Figures

....

The following were reproduced with kind permission. While every effort has been made to trace copyright holders and obtain permission, this has not always been possible in all cases. Any omissions brought to our attention will be remedied in future editions.

Tables
....

Notes on contributors

Joseph Bassary is a Digital Project Manager with RMG Connect.

Andrew Blake is Associate Head of the School of Social Sciences, Media and Cultural Studies at the University of East London. He is interested in all aspects of contemporary culture and cultural policy, with a background as a saxophonist and composer who worked as a professional musician during the 1980s. Professor Blake's writings include several books on music, including most recently *Popular Music in the Age of Multimedia* (2007). He is also the author or editor of books on sport, consumer culture and fiction, including *The Irresistible Rise of Harry Potter* (2002), which has been translated into five languages.

Jacqueline Botterill is Assistant Professor in Communication, Popular Culture and Film at Brock University, St Catharines, Canada. She co-authored *The Dynamics of Advertising* (London: Routledge, 2000) with Barry Richards and Iain MacRury and *Social Communication in Advertising*, 3rd edn (New York: Routledge) with William Leiss, Stephen Kline and Sut Jhally. Her latest work, *Consumer Culture and Personal Finance* (London: Palgrave MacMillan) is forthcoming.

Tim Broadbent is the Regional Planning Director and Regional Effectiveness Director of Ogilvy & Mather Asia Pacific. He graduated in 1976 with two degrees in philosophy and has been an account planner since 1978, starting at BMP, the first agency built around planning. He is the only person to have twice won the Grand Prix in the IPA Effectiveness Awards, was the Convenor of Judges of the Awards in 2000 and editor of *Advertising Works 11*, and then served as Chairman of the IPA Value of Advertising Committee. His monograph, *Does Advertising Create Demand?* was published by WARC for the Advertising Association in 2007. Tim is a Fellow of the IPA and Visiting Professor of Marketing of the University of the Arts London. He lives in Beijing, China.

Julia Dane is a Lecturer in Advertising at the University of East London. Julia's postgraduate research interests concern girls' engagements with contemporary discourses of femininity. Her teaching practice specialises in gender representation in the media and research methods.

Jonathan Hardy is Senior Lecturer in Media Studies at the University of East London and also teaches political economy of media at Goldsmiths College, University of London. He is the author of *Western Media Systems* (Routledge, 2008).

Sarah Hawkin joined JWT in September 1998 in order to establish the agency in the education sector. She was instrumental in rapidly growing the account base, to the point where the agency is one of the leaders in its field. During 2004 Sarah – a bi-lingual French speaker – was responsible for building the client list on the Continent, and in January 2005 was appointed Director for Continental Europe, JWT Education. In this capacity she opened the agency's first dedicated office in Amsterdam. Sarah is a frequent speaker at education conferences and has sat on adjudication panels for students at degree and masters level.

Janet Hull joined the Institute of Practitioners in Advertising in September 2003 as Consultant Head of Marketing and Reputation Management, and is responsible for research, strategy and content development for IPA programmes aimed at key influencers on marketing investment and reporting decisions, including FTSE 350 companies, the City and Government. She has over 20 years' experience in account handling, strategy, business development and management roles in advertising (Abbott Mead Vickers and Young & Rubicam), public relations (Burson-Marsteller), and corporate and brand identity (Lewis Moberly). Janet is a member of the Marketing Society, the Worshipful Company of Marketors and Women in Advertising and Communications London. She also sits on the UK TI Marketing Strategy Board for the Creative Industries and is on the Advisory Board of the International Marketing Communications double degree between London Metropolitan University and ESCEM School of Business and Management in Poitiers. Janet has an MA in Modern Languages from St Anne's College, Oxford, a post-graduate diploma in European Marketing from Napier and a distinction in the IDM diploma.

Eleni Kasapi holds an MA in Mass Communications from the University of Leicester, and a PhD in Media and Advertising from the University of East London. She teaches in the School of Social Sciences, Media and Cultural Studies at UEL.

Stephen Kline is currently a Professor in the School of Communication at Simon Fraser University, Canada where he is Director of the Media Analysis Laboratory. He is author of *Out of the Garden* (Verso, 1995), as well as co-author of *Researching Audiences* (Arnold, 2003), *Digital Play* (McGill-Queen's University Press, 2003) and *Social Communication in Advertising* (3rd edn, Routledge, 2005). He has also been writing recently on media literacy, advertising visualisation, video gaming, children's food and toy marketing and children's consumer socialisation. Currently he is writing a book on the role of media in debates about lifestyle risks.

Darren Lilleker is Senior Lecturer in Political Communication at the Media School, Bournemouth University and Director of the Centre for Public Communication Research. His research focuses on the ways in which politicians interact with society and citizens. Recent publications include *Political Marketing in Comparative Perspective* (MUP, 2004), *The Marketing of Political Parties* (MUP, 2006), *Voters or Consumers* (CSP, 2007) and *Key Concepts in Political Communication* (Sage, 2006), as well as a number of journal articles. Dr Lilleker is also Chair of the PSA political marketing group.

Iain MacRury is Principal Lecturer in Cultural Studies and Creative Industries and Director of the London East Research Institute at UEL. He is author of *Advertising*

(Routledge, 2008), co-author of *The Dynamics of Advertising* (Harwood, 2000) and co-editor of *Buy this Book: Studies in Advertising and Consumption* (Routledge, 1997). He is also co-editor of *Olympic Cities: 2012 and the Remaking of London* (Ashgate, 2008) and co-author of *The Secret Life of Cars* (BMW, 2007). He has worked on a number of commercial branding and research projects for clients, including BMW, Motorola and HSBC.

Francisco J. Pérez-Latre is Professor of Advertising at the School of Communication of the University of Navarra, Spain. He is also Master of Arts in Marketing Communications/Advertising, Emerson College, Boston (1993) and has served as academic director at the Institute of Media and Entertainment in New York. He is the author of six books (in English he has written *Issues in Media and Entertainment*, Pamplona, 2006) and seventeen book chapters.

Helen Powell previously worked in the advertising industry and is currently Senior Lecturer and Programme Leader in Advertising at the University of East London. Her research interests and publications explore the changing role of cultural intermediaries, including celebrities, as informers of consumer choice across a range of media including lifestyle television and advertising.

Richard Scullion is a PhD candidate at the London School of Economics and Senior Lecturer in Advertising at the Media School, Bournemouth University. Richard specialises in marketing and political communications and his research has focused to date on political advertising and consumer behaviour, with a special interest in the concept of choice. He has published in a range of international journals and edited collections and is Secretary of the Political Marketing special interest group of the Academy of Marketing.

Hyunsun Yoon is a Lecturer in Media and Advertising at the School of Social Sciences, Media and Cultural Studies, University of East London. She has published articles on cross-cultural advertising.

Introduction: the advertising business

The editorial team

An advertising 'handbook' suggests a volume serving as a ready reference to a stable set of established practices and principles. This volume certainly provides such information. It is important to develop a perspective on the array of tasks and the know-how upon which the daily work of advertising is established. This handbook works precisely to support such a developed understanding of the contemporary advertising industry. However, at the same time it is crucial that any such perspective, on daily tasks and practices, also places advertising as an 'object-in-transition'.

Changing environments necessitate new practices. New circumstances challenge established principles. Advertising is operating in such shifting contexts, so that the handbook must also be an update; situating practices in the context of recent and rapid change. Indeed, the major challenge faced in the conception and production of an advertising handbook is the fact that the defining characteristic of the contemporary advertising industry can readily be understood as, from moment to moment, both constant evolution and radical reconfiguration.

As we write, already a number of emergent trends indicate further restructuring and reorganisation of the advertising industry; an industry already adapting to globalisation, new regulatory pressures and ever-changing audiences. These latest developments are addressed directly in this book and include shifts within the agency/client relationship, the changing media landscape, the haphazard yet relentless development of new media, the increased adoption of advertising by public sector organisations, changing ways of apprehending 'the consumer' and the ongoing rise of Integrated Marketing Communications (IMC). The interplay of advertising and branding, as connected but distinct areas of promotional practice, provides a backdrop to many of the chapters in the book – just as it does in the everyday workings of contemporary commercial communications.

In terms of the agency world itself, such evolutions – not to say 'revolutions' – continue to produce (and require) an ever-increasing number of specialists. The rapid revision and division of promotional labour creates new niches. New forms of expertise emerge, sometimes at the margins, to re-colonise and re-create the professional-practical advertising mainstream. Consider the centrality of e-based advertising to brand development strategies today. A minority interest has become pivotal in a matter of five years. Advertising is emerging in a space informed by dialogue: dialogue between old and new, real and virtual, strategy and serendipity.

Following this logic, and as the history of the advertising industry has revealed in recent decades however, formerly 'niche' practices, and the professional experts who develop, deploy and institute them, are likely to become ripe for takeover – from those network agencies (established big players working on a global scale) seeking to refresh and extend capacities and techniques. There is a permanent market for new inventions and re-inventions. Mega-agencies, with demanding shareholders, are alert to the potentially missed opportunity. Lack of expertise in any given area – especially if seen as 'cutting edge' – is often seen to represent a potentially missed business opportunity.

Specialisation is one current watchword. As Chapter 1 makes clear, we are beginning to see something of a regression in agency structures; with some agencies now re-describing themselves as 'full service agencies' (*Campaign*, 2008a). This is after a period where the received wisdom and the fact of the matter both highlighted disaggregated and 'unbundled' organisational structures in the industry. However, before we hark back to former times, this 're–invention' is most likely a return to the past as *label* and not as working-model.

Media planning is challenging as the primary 'creative' domain. Traditional 'creativity' – art direction and copy writing – are seemingly decentred in a broad-based re-conceptualisation of 'what really counts' in advertising communications. This is underscored by clients looking for innovative and subtle media solutions to deliver integrated campaigns that will work effectively across a number of platforms – not just press, but including virals, ambient ads, sponsorship tie-ins, cross brand promotions and so forth.

To support their response to this reconfiguration of clients' demands, agencies, still haunted by the spectre of unbundling, are turning to a number of innovative partnerships and alliances in order to assure and deliver increased service provision – as former disciplinary boundaries (e.g. between creative, media, planning, research, PR and Direct Marketing, etc.) become more fluid. For example, at WPP 'intra-disciplinary creative teams' are being established, merging the vision and creative expertise of teams from London and New York in advertising and linking direct marketing and interactive media (*WPP Annual Report*, 2006: 28). The range of ways in which agencies now describe themselves, 'full service digital', 'creative communications', 'full service advertising' and 'communications planning', is testament to the degree of diversification and rise of new typologies since the breakup of the full service agency – as the industry tries to negotiate and navigate a complex present by reaching, as it were, 'back to the future'.

Within the agency itself, the challenge of holding on to good staff is an obvious priority. This is expressed in a number of ways but is particularly demonstrated through the emphasis placed on individual staff development; whether in-house via language classes, or funding made available through extra-curricular activities of the employee's choosing. The constant (reflexive) evolution of advertising (going global, going virtual, going back to basics), as task and as industry, demands an alert and reflective professional – prepared to ask and answer questions – about this or that campaign, and about 'advertising' as an evolving commercial and cultural activity. This book aims to pose and re-pose some of these questions and to re-contextualise them with fresh and engaging examples.

So what are the more immediate challenges facing advertising agencies today? One major externality affecting agencies is the state of the global economy. Deeply influenced by economic cycles, advertising needs to respond to adjustments in client spending, especially as value for money is sought through added diversification in the marketing mix. The IPA's (Institute of Practitioners in Advertising) intervention, post the August 2007 'credit crunch', is testament to this with the launch of *The Little Book of Growth* sent out to every FTSE 350 company. Its function was to highlight the impact that advertising would have on businesses' market share, even in difficult economic climates, via 38 illustrative case studies (Whitehead, 2008: 4). As the US economic downturn gathered pace in 2008, the industry was able to counter its impact somewhat through the opportunities brought about by the Beijing Olympics. And while 2009 provides less cause for optimism, 2010 not only marks the completion of the first year in office of a new American president but also the Football World Cup in South Africa and the Winter Olympics in Vancouver. In the context of such recognised budgetary constraints, many clients have turned away from television in search of more cost-effective vehicles of promotion and agencies are now seen to be working harder as the econometric analysis of media investment is an increasingly prevalent client activity. An example of one such area that offers both challenges and opportunities is that of new media. As the number of new media platforms increase at a significant pace, informed by the influx of new technology, agencies must remain in tune with such developments and seek to harness them as more personalised, immediate and interactive communication opportunities. Such challenges function as a response to the increased difficulties in locating the targeted consumer in space and time, coupled with persistent media fragmentation and subsequent changes in media consumption. Many agencies have or are in the process of restructuring as they seek to come to grips with a digital offering. Social networking sites such as Facebook seems to have captured the public imagination to date and many brands, such as O2, have effectively recognised the potential of this space as a commercial entity without incurring any media spend. But how agencies will be remunerated in the context of the use of non-paid for media platforms is an interesting question.

In terms of content, the rise of the entertainment economy shapes and informs the advertising offer across all media as audiences demand more than simply being sold to. Indeed, Wolf (2000) has argued that it is the quest to entertain that justifies their use, with the function of creativity being to provide each commercial with what he terms the 'E-Factor' (Wolf, 2000: 27). As we each have greater choice over what we watch and how we choose to watch it, so advertising and other forms of promotion must battle for the consumer's attention. Nowhere is this more prevalent than with the rise of digital, which now accounts for 10 per cent of all adspend in developed markets, with Publicis Group predicting that by 2010 it will account for 25 per cent of its agency's revenue (*Campaign*, 2008a: 4). Indeed, 'for all agencies . . . the issue of how to reshape for a digital world remains top of the agenda' (*Campaign*, 2008a: 5).

Finally, it cannot be underestimated how advertising is a truly global business. While the first US and UK agencies initially ventured overseas in the 1920s, it was not until 50 to 60 years later that advertising significantly extended its global reach. The network model emerged as agencies opened up offices to match client's international needs and aspirations including the founding of WPP in 1985 and the 'Big Bang' that brought about the formation of Omnicom a year later. As brands continue to target new markets and the geographic scope of media proliferates, so agencies follow and as the complexities of meeting the client's ambitions increase so agencies continually need to restructure to meet such challenges. Functioning to 'decode the kaleidoscopic world into which its clients have been plunged' (Tungate, 2007: 264), WPP, Publicis Group, Omnicom, Interpublic and Havas merit the greatest share of advertising in 2007, based on billings (*Campaign*, 2008a: 12). The globalisation of the industry has seen the stronger get stronger as 'agency networks with the widest and strongest nets traditionally have caught the most fish.' (Banerjee, 2000: 19). Acquisition remains high on the agenda and targets are tracked on the basis of either their potential to extend geographic reach, with China and the burgeoning markets of Asia and the Indian sub-continent generating current interest, or the offer of new possibilities in an ever-changing media landscape, or both.

Reflecting on the immediate pressures facing the industry, as well as considering the longer-term evolution of advertising requires, above all, an account of change. Recent evolutions refracted through some of the most current challenges facing established institutional models and ways of thinking amount, arguably, to a paradigm shift; if not in advertising practice *per se*, then in the ideas and analyses which, daily and in part, constitute these practices. This third edition of *The Advertising Handbook* will continue the work of previous editions in articulating this shift in a clear, pragmatic and engaging way. It offers new material and a new organising framework featuring fresh industry case studies. A major change from the previous editions – aside from this edition's taking us forward five or so years – is that the collection brings together a range of contributing authors. The previous two editions of *The Advertising Handbook* were written, expertly, by one author – Sean Brierley.

The book differs, structurally, from the previous two editions (Brierley 1995; 2002) in that it is a collection of contributions. We have included chapters written by long established advertising professionals; we have chapters written by younger recruits to innovative agencies and we have chapters by experienced academic authors whose engagements with advertising have been primarily through teaching and theoretical research. However, the commitment remains the same; and like past editions the book aims to provide lucid accounts of various aspects of a multi-dimensional cultural and commercial entity: advertising. The aim: to continue to serve media and advertising students wanting to become more familiar with the practices of today's advertising industry.

The book is divided into three main sections and concludes with an in-depth analysis of the potential future of the industry. The first section, *Key issues and debates* (Chapters 1–5), provides the book's foundational material and adopts traditional headings as it examines the industry at the macro level.

Central to the advertising process, the industry's core institution, and the central locus of practice-in-transition, the advertising agency is the focus for Chapter 1. In this chapter Powell offers a critical examination of the agency/client relationship over time. Taking an historical overview of agency development, it explores how modern agency structures have been significantly informed by client demands, why relationships between these two parties are susceptible to frequent implosion, and the mechanisms available through which new partnerships might be forged. In particular, it dissects the advantages and disadvantages of the pitch process from both an agency and client perspective and seeks to understand why it remains the primary method of selection despite its flaws.

Agencies' work is often coordinated within the broader strategic and operational tasks of branding. The integration of promotional and commercial work with advertising is the major preoccupation of Chapter 2. Kline adopts a case study approach, to examine the ways in which McDonald's has sought to re-brand its image through the coordination of different modes of corporate communication. The chapter provides an illustrated account of a range of contemporary thinking, inflecting practical measures within corporate re-branding. In particular the work of Douglas Holt on cultural branding is explored. McDonald's provides a living case study reflecting in detail the challenges of a 'corporate responsibility make-over' delivered through the strategic utilisation of integrated marketing communication. As the chapter demonstrates, the effectiveness of such strategies can be impressive, as is clear from evidence of its success; in terms of the turn around in customer visits, global sales and profitability and, over the long term, the monetary value of the brand-equity as reflected in the stock price.

The agency is fundamental to making advertising. The brand is central to contemporary conceptions of commercial development. However, media is at the centre of advertising understood as *communication*. And media is also central to the transitions characterising contemporary advertising.

Indeed, media can legitimately lay claim to driving – and demanding – the greatest transformational impacts on the adverting industry, both in recent decades and throughout the history of advertising. As Pérez outlines, in the 1980s commercial television and radio expanded across most advanced economies. But it has been the 'media explosion' of the 1990s and beyond, propelled by digitalisation, media convergence, deregulation and commercialisation that has seen a massive expansion of media outlets and profound shifts in advertising expenditure, activity and in advertising formats across the media. Francisco Pérez examines the nature and implications of these pivotal shifts in media markets and in media and advertising relationships.

Relationships are at the heart of the advertising process. Knowledge is at the heart of many kinds of relationship. While research is something of a 'backstage' activity in the advertising industry, it has been central to the work of navigating the difficult 'conversation' between supply and demand, production and consumption, brand-image and consumer desire. As advertising seeks to negotiate and manage communications, it has turned to a wide array of techniques – entered into with the aim of knowing 'the consumer'. In Chapter 4, MacRury outlines some of these major research approaches and contextualises his account with reference to shifts and challenges emerging from the 'new' consumer, (globally) reconfigured market places, and from new advertising and e-commerce based technologies. As the interface between consumers and producers becomes more labile and flexible, a direct consequence of e-based technologies, the work of knowing, discovering and constructing 'the consumer' takes its place at the heart of brand building, relationship development and management. At the same time the contemporary consumer can turn the table on advertisers; the Web providing ever more sources and outlets for the consumer-as-researcher to operate.

Modes of advertising mediation are certainly shifting – and their attendant communications relationships along with them. However, one necessity remains in place; that advertising communications are regulated. This is a central and ongoing preoccupation for practitioners and industry critics alike. As Hardy outlines in detail, advertising regulation affects the day-to-day work of practitioners; it sets out 'rules' that advertisers, agencies and media need to recognise in their professional dealings and creative work. At another level it reflects ongoing struggles and debates in societies about how advertising is controlled, and by whom. In Britain, the principle of self-regulation, whereby the industry regulates its own behaviour, is now well-established and powerfully defended by the advertising industry. But advertising regulation is dynamic, with rules and approaches continually modified to address changes in technology, marketing, in politics and governance, in social attitudes and consumer behaviour. Regulation is a point of contact, very often collision, between the industry and other groups in civil society, addressing such questions as how marketers' 'freedom' to advertise should be balanced by consumer protection or wider social responsibility. These are the themes of Chapter 5, which explains how advertising is regulated in the UK and deals with controversies including food advertising to children and the integration of media content and advertising.

These initial chapters, outlining and updating ideas on some of the fundamental issues in the industry, provide a sense of the shifting baseline upon which advertising is operating today.

The second part, *Themed chapters* (Chapters 6–9), further examines the challenges facing advertising, refracted through some of the contemporary preoccupations facing advertising practitioners and highlighting the creative strategies adopted.

In Chapter 6, Dane and Yoon detail creative and media strategies employed by Lynx in its 20-year history and demonstrate both the evolution and reinvention of a highly popular youth brand as it has sought to address the challenges of 'lad culture'. Tapping into contemporary discourses around gender and identity and displaying the value of an on-going engagement with trends in popular culture, Lynx has now created not just brand loyalty in the 16–24 age group, but a unique brand experience fuelled by the potential and possibilities of advertising as online entertainment.

Indeed, as noted above, 'entertainment' is now understood to be a central element in some advertising strategies – as the lines between 'Madison and Vine' become blurred (Donaton, 2004). Celebrities serve as an interface – sometimes literally an inter-*face* – between advertising and entertainment cultures; famous faces serving brands' attempts, not only to build up 'product personalities', but to further destabilise boundaries between 'commercial communications' and 'cultural entertainment'.

This creative approach has a long history and reflects the way in which advertising has consistently drawn upon popular culture in the context of meaning making. But, as Powell documents in Chapter 7, there is a modern twist to the recent explosion of the branded celebrity. The chapter illustrates the merits and downfalls, in terms of ad effectiveness, of using celebrities as a conduit between the brand and the target audience. With examples from the last 10 years, the various stages of campaign development are set out in practical detail, charting choice of celebrity, legal considerations, costs, and the implications, both expected and unexpected, when stars' behaviour impacts upon a brand.

The 'face' of adverting remains a key preoccupation, inside the industry and for consumers and critics. The focus of Chapter 8 is on the ways in which race and gender inflect advertising, not only on page and screen, but in the making. How well does the advertising industry reflect the social composition of the society it serves? Is the white male dominance over creative execution and in leadership positions changing? How is the industry equipping itself to operate in multi-ethnic global environments? Blake assesses moves within the industry to articulate and institute the recognition of ethnicity and gender in the organisation and practice of advertising in the UK and in other countries. He assesses industry efforts to map and match consumer demand and diversity within the workforce and creative work – and in doing so introduces readers to some themes and approaches in the growing literature on cultural work. A traditional academic preoccupation meets a pressing industry concern: how are advertising agencies addressing questions of diversity and inclusivity in an era when multi-cultural and global are default conditions of brand communications?

In Chapter 9 Kasapi draws on detailed research with creative practitioners to provide an up-to-date picture of 'viral' advertising. When ads are formatted to enable rapid diffusion across web-based networks we witness, instance by instance, one exemplary conjunction of old and new. The attraction and entertainment of the advertising form is deployed (often in parodic ways) to induce consumers' engagement and affection. However, the medium is the message since, denuded of the commercial associations of TV ad placement, virals seem to enjoy a cultural status denied to traditional advertising by 'savvy' audiences. Kasapi shows the effectiveness of advertising operating in these new media environments; an effectiveness born of cultural engagement and community rather than by the traditional techniques of persuasion and targeting. The relationship between 'real' effectiveness and these virtual cultures remains unpredictable; nevertheless Kasapi is able to illustrate some important cross-over between new and traditional advertising impacts.

Written to reflect the topical issues for advertising agencies and new media players, the third section, the *Case studies* (Chapters 10–15), reflect a real depth of practical and analytic expertise in their illustration of continuing innovation and diversification of industry practice. The case studies also offer space for contextualising narrative history and detailed accounts of advertising in specific product sectors and the advertising issues confronting specialist advertisers.

The micro-niche virtual media relationship implicit in viral advertising dissemination has a counterpart and opposite: the global mega event. Mega events, such the Olympics, provide a challenge and an opportunity to advertising. Chapter 10 looks at sponsorship. Typically sponsorship has served to take brands' marketing expenditure away from traditional advertising in favour of the mass appeal of paid-for associations with a large national sporting event or (on a smaller scale) when a brand looks to engage specialist audiences or make a local impact using sponsorship as an alternative to advertising. However, and with the 2012 Olympics on the horizon and already promising a likely increased advertising spend in 2011 and 2012, to offset other pressures on the industry, it remains the case that the mass audiences guaranteed by global mega events offers a fillip to advertising – as advertisers seek to amplify the impact of sponsorships or, via 'ambush advertising', seek to diminish the associations attained by competitors sponsoring the event. This chapter looks in practical detail at one such event, the Olympics. In particular it outlines the complex work undertaken in relation to advertising and event mangers to defend the mega event as both brand and as 'channel', by managing the degree and kind of commercial exploitation.

Advertising is not always about glamorous global events, or immediately exciting consumer products. In Chapter 11 MacRury and Hawkin examine university advertising. University advertising is of interest because it is a special area and linked to certain 'not for profit' or otherwise 'public good' oriented sectors which are sometimes not considered in general discussions of advertising. University advertising is interesting because it represents a product sector where relationships to advertised products are especially complex and deep-seated. The chapter considers university advertising as an example of a kind of advertising where various 'stakeholders' might have conflicting views and where it takes on a role both in consumer communications but also, and in a secondary and inadvertent way, in rethinking and reconstituting the 'commodity' produced by the organisation.

Another product sector, often contrasted with education, is FMCG (Fast Moving Consumer Goods). Through an examination of FMCG advertising, Broadbent argues persuasively for the powerful role of branding in the advertising process. A detailed history of branding reveals how brands, functioning as a quasi-emotional marker of trust and authenticity, have come to define the consumer-product relationship – even for seemingly trivial goods. The careful exposition of case studies in Chapter 12 highlight how this function has evolved to now embody and exemplify the close proximity of brand choice and social identity.

Chapters 2 and 9 offer respectively general and particular media-related analyses to situate the impact of the Internet on advertising. Chapter 13 continues with a focus on this, perhaps the most pressing concern that the advertising world is currently facing. How can agencies (on behalf of eager and anxious clients) keep up with Internet developments? In particular, how can new technologies be used as a means of both targeting mobile consumers and delivering engaging brand messages – in ways that are both effective (in the traditional sense of enhancing clients' commercial performance) while being welcomed by and unobtrusive for net-empowered consumers? Charting the Internet's rise and evolution from Web 1.0 to 3.0, Bassary details the opportunities each successive phase has offered advertisers culminating in the present position which sees users as the *creators* of content that advertisers must now engage with   as selling and entertainment become closely aligned.

It was in Obama's campaign against Hilary Clinton for Democratic nomination for the 2008 Presidential candidacy, and his susequent campaign for the Presidency itself that saw the coming of age of Internet-communications in political advertising and campaigning. Obama's fundraising success was driven by e-commerce-style approaches, enabling voters to register support and donations on an unprecedented scale. These funds were then used to support both traditional advertising and a high stakes 30-minute 'infomercial' across the US TV networks. As Lilleker and Scullion in Chapter 14 demonstrate, the US presidential campaign links established and innovative techniques in a dramatic area of promotional political communications. Sophisticated branding techniques of engagement and mediation have become central to contemporary political life, with advertising only one component in a new political-marketing mix. Critical voices shocked at a President 'sold like a bar of soap' are seemingly consigned to history.

And it is with this history that the case studies are concluded. Fittingly Botterill takes the soap brand 'Lux' as her object of investigation in Chapter 15. This chapter charts the creative devices employed to embed a product into American popular culture, reminding us that while contemporary advertising and branding are often held up as distinctively subtle, early ads were also, in their time, quite ingenious in capturing consumers' attentions. This is demonstrated with specific reference to changes in copywriting styles and imagery. Botterill highlights the powerful cultural value of brand heritage as earlier advertising strategies have been rekindled in revised formats in recent campaigns to create new appeals – the brand history authenticating advertising of the present. The chapter is a highly relevant articulation of the way in which advertising says something significant about the socio-cultural environment in which it circulates, offering an insight into its values, concerns and sensitivities at any one moment in time.

Another conjunction of past and future brings us back to the advertising agency. The IPA and Future Foundation's joint initiative to examine the state of advertising and advertising agencies up to the year 2016 provides the impetus for the concluding chapter of this edition of the *Advertising Handbook*. Hull of the IPA considers models which agencies might develop in the light of the emergence of competing service providers, the prospects for future growth in the industry and where the potential for future media engagement lies. Drawing together some of the key themes of the book, including agency structures, agency/client relationships, the rise of FMCGs and new media, the overall conclusion is one whereby 're-invention is key to the agency of the future'. However, this is not to be feared but seized as an opportunity to find new ways to assert the added value agencies bring, while simultaneously examining new possibilities for both agency-client relationships and remuneration packages.

The Advertising Handbook will, we hope, continue to provide both an introduction and an authoritative guide to advertising theory and practice while being shaped to meet the requirements, interests and terms of reference of the most recent generation of media and advertising students – as well as taking account of some of the most recent academic work in the field and, of course, contemporary advertising innovations.

As noted above, the truism that 'advertising is in transition' has never been more widely repeated and acknowledged than it is today. Industry analysts continue to work to examine and evaluate the impacts of the Internet and new digital media on the practical and commercial work of the advertising business. At the same time the processes of globalisation and ideas about global media and marketing continue to inform and transform everyday practices and thinking, and the institutional frames through which advertising is managed and sold. Equally, and sometimes in the same breath, branding continues to provide a (shifting) focus for thinking through advertising practice, promotion and consumer research, as well as providing a spur to integration and synthesis across marketing disciplines and other sites of cultural production and distribution. Each chapter ends with a series of brief questions. Likewise, this introduction poses questions – to be considered now, but also in relation to each chapter:

- What is advertising?
- How is advertising changing?
- What is the relationship between advertising, marketing and branding?
- How is the relationship between advertising and media changing?
- What is the impact of new media on the advertising industry?
- How do advertising agencies manage creativity?
- How is advertising effectiveness managed?
- How are trans-national dynamics shaping advertising?

Part I

Key issues and debates

1 Advertising agencies and their clients

Helen Powell

Introduction

The advertising business comprises four sets of players: the advertisers, or clients, who purchase advertising to promote their business; the media, who receive around 90 per cent of the advertising budget to enable paid-for communication to be seen by a defined target audience; consumers who then see and might be influenced by advertising, and finally the advertising agencies themselves who produce advertisements to accommodate a growing number of media platforms. This chapter looks specifically at two of these parties: the client and the advertising agency and seeks to explore their working relationship. Taking an historical overview of agency development, it examines how modern agency structures have been significantly informed by client demands, why relationships between these two parties are susceptible to frequent deterioration and as a consequence the mechanisms available through which new partnerships might be forged. Underlining all these key themes is a particular set of power dynamics that positions the client as firmly in control in the majority of scenarios considered.

How the modern agency has been shaped by clients' demands

The history of the modern advertising agency is informed by a series of influences that involve the clients' evolving promotional needs, adaptation to ongoing technological developments, consistent media proliferation, the onset and development of globalisation, and as a response to economic cycles that impact businesses, client and agency-side. This history begins during the first wave of industrialisation and is driven by manufacturers' needs propelled forward by significant developments in industrial production, transportation and communication coupled with the rise of urbanisation and the expansion of mass literacy. The early advertising 'agent' did not work for a client but rather for a newspaper selling advertising space for a fee. The advertiser themselves produced the copy. However, as the number of newspapers increased the 'space seller' turned 'space broker' recognising the advantages to be gained in independent status, buying space in bulk from the newspapers and selling it on to an increasing number of clients (Leiss *et al.*, 2005: 132). This meant agents were no longer tied to one particular newspaper. This new flexible arrangement provided an opportunity to advise clients on media planning and on readership and circulation (in order to aid effective targeting) with agents benefiting from this specialist advisory position through maintaining media neutrality. Furthermore, he, and it was always a 'he', began to develop creative skills, facilitated by new printing technologies that allowed for the use of illustrations and was influenced creatively by the surfeit of outdoor posters. Thus not only did the agent advise on where to effectively place the advertisement but also how to fill up the space in terms of eye-catching design and layout. Hence, this is the first point, around 1880, at which the creative and media sides of advertising come together in one institution and which expands as the 'agent' begins to employ others, often freelancers, including artists and copywriters, as demand for his services increase. A client list emerges which ensures the agency's future and funds its development with business expanding significantly at the turn of the twentieth century, not only with the emergence of brands requiring national rather than local exposure but as a consequence of more new products coming to a mass market.

While this model of agency evolution dominates the literature, we must also note that 'a diversity of arrangements', especially at local level, also existed as opportunities for business arose (McFall, 2004: 110). However, by the 1920s, a specific modern agency model had consolidated in the US and was making its presence felt in London. Such an organisation offered clients a 'full service' based around the four pillars of creative work, research, media planning (print, radio, cinema and outdoor) and account management, the bridge in the relationship between client and agency. Tungate (2007) classifies J. Walter Thompson as the first agency to adopt this structure prior to its more widespread acceptance and implementation.

Following the Second World War, the US agencies consolidated their presence in London in two important ways. Not only did they dominate through a series of acquisitions of British agencies but also fuelled the quest for professionalisation which had begun much earlier overseas and which was taken up vociferously during this period by the IPA (Institute of Practitioners in Advertising). Such professionalisation became inextricably linked to the notion of specialisation; that in the context of the 'full service agency', now established in the UK, clients could gain specialist knowledge and expertise unavailable elsewhere: market research, account planning, media buying and in particular creativity. This gave potential clients a notable sense of added value in using an agency over in-house provision, especially in terms of dealing with the new medium of television. Professionalisation was inextricably linked to agency self-promotion. In response to this American domination, the British fight back did not come until the 1970s, a period characterised by a large number of agency formations in the UK often taking the founders' names. Two decades of celebrated copy ensued.

The end of the 1980s is an important turning point in British advertising history. Not only does it mark a point at which there was a noticeable proliferation of promotional culture, precipitated most famously a decade prior with the successful use of advertising in the election of Margaret Thatcher, but it would also herald the commencement in the UK of a major restructuring of the advertising landscape prompted by both external client demands and internal tensions between media and creative roles. What has been termed 'unbundling', the separation out of different agency functions, was driven client-side by calls for greater degrees of accountability and transparency in terms of expenditure, with requests for a more itemised approach to billing as recession began to set in following the stock market crash of 1987. Simultaneously a fundamental fissure, with roots dating back to the 1960s, began to run through the full service agency as the internal roles of media and creative split apart to go their separate ways. Henceforth the nature of client choices around service provision would need to be revised. While mass media dominated, creatives seemed to have the upper hand, as represented in the recent BBC series 'Mad Men' (BBC4, 2008). Valued as the 'face' of the agency through creative executions that the public recognised and the industry awarded, they brought kudos to the agency and raised their own personal career profiles. However, as mass media evolved into niche media the skills associated with media planning changed, emerging into its own creative art form as choice of media provision no longer remained simple. Demanding recognition against a backdrop of an increasingly complex media terrain, a break away ensued forming the major buying houses of today and more specialist media planning and later communication planning houses.

The fragmentation of the full service agency was followed by a period of intense merger and acquisition activity. The rise of the networks, functioning as holding companies for a range of specialist agencies, was testament to client demands that centred on a more focused and cheaper approach to agency provision. As a consequence the agency world was largely made up of a series of consolidated major players, who, post the period of unbundling, grew significantly in size by buying up other agencies, nationally and internationally, to form what is now termed global agency networks. The seeds of such bullish behaviour were planted earlier in the decade, when as early as 1986 Saatchi & Saatchi had already spent $1 billion acquiring 37 global companies (Tungate, 2007: 101). Networks had advantages in that they sought to accommodate client concerns over potential conflicts within a single agency by allowing different agencies, but sharing the same parent, to hold accounts within the same market sector. Secondly, they were able to provide an extended global reach that international brand managers now required. On the other hand, there was a plethora of smaller independent agencies, media and creative, which remained outside the network structure and which offered the client an alternative form of relationship and service. Finally, new players emerged in the gaps of agency provision, such as brand managers and the rise of public relations, all seeking to offer an alternative promotional response. The demise of the full service agency also brought an end to the range of in-house creative facilities. Photographers and television production, for example, were all turned over to freelancers or contracted out in the name of cost-effectiveness but interestingly have in themselves turned into an area of independent growth in terms of employment and diversification of provision.

From the mid-1980s to date the agency world has been characterised by reinvention as a response to changing client needs located within a context of new media, global brands and coupled with demands for higher degrees of accountability and transparency in relation to remuneration. The promotional world was accepted as being more complex than that in which the original full service agencies originated most significantly in terms of media opportunities and the requisite skills required to maximise their potential for clients. As a consequence, the power of media agencies has grown, operating beyond the parameters of the pricing and buying of spots to function on a more strategic basis and heralding the rise of communication specialists, such as the recently acquired Naked (by Australian marketing group, Photon). Creativity is no longer the preserve of creative agencies as this communications planning agency testifies, working with the client from a position of media neutrality to help determine the type of media and message that best informs their particular advertising problem.

The agency today

So what shape is the agency world in today? As the opening paragraph demonstrated, it is driven by the on-going expansion of media provision. As a consequence the buzzword of contemporary advertising is specialisation: either functioning as a division of a network or acting on the basis of an independent agency. Running parallel to these new structures is client demand for IMC, as a later chapter will document. Integrated marketing communications require greater degrees of cooperation between all parties concerned as the advertising message is facilitated and amplified by other communication forms. As a consequence we are seeing the development of partnerships, media and creative agencies working together in alliance or even seeing the return of some agencies calling themselves 'full service', as in the case of CHI & Partners (*Campaign*, 2008a: 14). These are few and far between and are not 'full service' in the original sense but owe their extended offer to a larger agency acting as a significant shareholder and hence often providing a media buying facility. As a result of such historical developments, the current agency landscape leaves a client with a proliferation of choice but which can be simplified into the duality of network versus specialist, always bearing in mind that a client can pick and choose which aspects of the network they wish to use. Ultimately, choice comes down to weighing up a series of advantages and disadvantages associated with both forms.

However, once the choice of agency or agencies has been made, the client must always be aware of the possible instability and disruption that might impact an agency as it is always potentially subject to either merger or takeover. From a client perspective, in this case Procter & Gamble, agency consolidation brings mixed responses. 'Among the disadvantages, when agencies merge, we must redouble our efforts to ensure we get the best from our agency partners while working with them to manage enormous organisational change. Among the advantages is the fact that we can eliminate duplication in many areas' (Stengel, 2002: 5).

Table 1.1   Working with a single network and specialist agencies

Working with a single network (example: WPP)

Advantages	Disadvantages
Will manage, plan and integrate every task facilitating overall synergy. Especially beneficial when operating a global campaign	Can be expensive compared with self-management as: a) you are paying for a major brand name and b) an integrated service
Saves the client time in terms of hiring and liaising with individual agencies as it provides an administrative hub	Client can feel a loss of control. Agency disinclined towards flexibility. Less time is often given to smaller clients.
Highly experienced	Can be creatively less exciting

Working with specialist agencies (example: Mother)

Advantages	Disadvantages
Offer expertise in specialised areas	Client has to manage the overall campaign and the different parties and personalities involved
Allows for greater client control as the client is managing all parts involved	Time consuming (especially in terms of the number of meetings held)
Client can pick and choose gaining the best agency from each discipline which can be more cost-effective	Ill-made choices in relation to any single specialist can impact the whole campaign

Adapted from Wright (2000: 107–8).

Pitching for business

The power and significance of the brand within contemporary consumer culture leaves few advertisers prepared to take risks through in-house advertising. This is reinforced by the IPA Effectiveness Awards established as a means to 'bolster the perception of advertising as an efficient commercial tool' (Cronin, 2004: 344). Before recruiting an agency, a client must initially decide exactly what it is that they want an agency to do for them as this will primarily inform the decision making process that ensues. That is to say, what exactly is the advertising problem? Once this has been determined, a mechanism by which a relationship can be established between agency and client is required. The most commonly used procedure is known as the pitch and is called by the client on account of one of the following. Firstly, it emerges out of a new business venture. Secondly, a client might be unhappy with their existing agency or it might lack the skill set necessary to take the campaign in a new direction, such as online. Thirdly, they may wish to test their existing agency against potential competition, particularly creatively. Finally, the pitch represents a significant change in personnel client-side, most frequently due to the introduction of a new marketing director and signifies a revised vision of the company's promotional needs.

There are a number of possible starting points for the pitch process. Firstly, through the role of the new business team within the agency contacts would have been made over time with potential future clients. As a result of such liaisons, an agency would become aware, directly or indirectly, when an account came up for review and interest would be registered. Clients also use the trade journal *Campaign* as a mechanism to announce they are looking for a new agency and to engender interest and this is also the means by which pitch wins and losses are circulated post resolution. While therefore some advertising agencies will express an interest directly to the client, it is the client's responsibility to draw up an initial long list of around 10 or 12 prospective contenders. This is often achieved through a variety of sources and influences: namely the involvement of the AAR (Advertising Agency Register), a consultancy that functions to facilitate agency selection (www.aargroup.co.uk); consideration of favoured current campaigns; reviewing annual lists of achievers (*Campaign*, 2008a). Past success is also deemed indicative of future performance, as noted by Maurice Saatchi who once reflected on the importance of industry ratings: 'Being the number one agency in this country was a passport on to pitch lists, because you are then too big and prominent to not make it on to a list for any serious piece of business which is moving.' (Fendley, 1995: 180). In terms of who might be included on this initial list, factors to be taken into consideration include: the size and previous experience of each agency; how well equipped it is in terms of skill sets to manage the task in hand; a judgement of the personalities involved and encountered at preliminary meetings, known as 'chemistry meetings'; a sense of compatibility in terms of businesses cultures; and finally, how an agency's creative style might fit in with the client's own vision for the brand or service in question.

From the chemistry meetings onwards, the pitching process is highly performative and many agencies often ironically struggle in the arena of their own self-promotion. As a result of these meetings, a shortlist emerges and the agencies selected (normally around 4 or 5) are given a specified period of time, usually anything between 2 to 8 weeks, to respond to the circulated client brief which they will address on the day of the pitch. The brief used is the same for all parties involved and often involves agreement to a security clause enforcing confidentiality concerning the business in question and its potential future developments. Who is involved agency side? The following personnel represent the typical make up a pitch team: a chief executive or managing director; an account team of approximately three people; a new business director and assistant; a lead strategy person; two planners; a creative director; two creative teams; a representative from traffic and a TV producer (Fisher, 2008: 24). In terms of pitching strategies, little detail is available, primarily on the basis that successful agencies are reluctant to share their winning formula. However, ultimately the majority of advertising pitches centre on a strategic and creative response to the client brief with clear demonstration of knowledge and insight into the business in question and the market sector in which it operates. The final selection is at the client's discretion and is arrived at through weighing up the criteria of each agency involved in relation to meeting the terms of the brief. Andy Law, founder of St Luke's, provides his own take on the rationale involved: 'Most clients cite poor and inconsistent service as their principal reason for leaving their current advertising agency (they cite 'creativity' as the main reason why they go to their new advertising agency).' (Law, 1998: 110).

In 2007, AMV claimed the most pitch wins with 14 successes out of 17 attempts; Fallon boasted a 100 per cent winning record (5 attempts and 5 wins); and CHI & Partners recorded the most new business without pitching (Cassidy, 2008). All agencies must decide exactly which pitches they should compete for, as such activity is both costly and demanding and other issues such as potential client conflict need to be factored in. In relation to conversion rates, Martin Jones, director of advertising at the AAR states: 'I think that the most significant observation is that the more selective agencies are in the number of pitches that they do, the more likely they are to be successful.' (Cassidy, 2008).

Overall problems identified with the pitch process

Agency critiques

Agencies have not held back when it comes to outlining their maltreatment by clients, during and after the pitch process. One issue concerns time: how agencies are given such a short period in which to respond to the client brief and prepare to pitch, but that often clients can take months to reach a final decision and then inform participants indirectly through the trade press. Time also has to be carefully managed in terms of ensuring that hours invested on a potential win are not hours neglected on an existing client account. In view of this BBH decided not to pitch at all in 2006 but rather to spend their time concentrating on building and extending relations with existing clients.

Perhaps the most controversial element to pitching is that of payment, or rather lack of it. 'It's estimated, when you factor in staff costs, that a typical UK pitch costs between £60,000 and £100,000 and an international one in excess of £500,000.' (Fisher, 2008: 24). Mapped out across the agency world this accrues approximately each year to a collective total of £32 million and 239 years spent on pitching (Bannister, 2006: 17). This is a cost that is not reimbursed. How much an agency decides to spend on a pitch is dependent on the size of the account. For example, when M&C Saatchi, JWT, BBH and DDB London pitched in 2005 for the British Airways account worth £60 million it was estimated that between them they spent £1 million on pitch activities (Beale, 2005: 23). More than simply the issue of staff costs, agencies feel aggrieved that their most valuable assets, their creative ideas, are expected to be presented for free to the prospective client and issues of plagiarism have arisen whereby while not winning the pitch the creative ideas presented have appeared in a campaign for the brand by another agency. The IPA has responded to this by allowing agencies to log pitch ideas with them so that if a client tries to use a creative idea that has not been paid for, then proof is available as to actual ownership (Bannister, 2006: 17).

The role of the incumbent (the agency in post) in the pitch process is the subject of much debate. Sources range between there being a 5–30 per cent chance of their retaining the business. Ultimately their main advantage over their competitors is superior knowledge of the business in question. However, when they lose they feel they were simply involved as a PR exercise, a mechanism to be let down gently, but when they win other agencies are quick to chastise the event as a sham, as simply an opportunity by the client to see what else is on offer, especially creatively.

Furthermore, some clients gain the reputation of being 'serial pitchers', holding a pitch year after year. Agencies are quick to identify such tendencies, recognising that what seems from the client's perspective to be essentially an advertising problem is more inherent, involving issues that lie at the core of the business and which cannot be resolved through any advertising solution that might be provided. However, there will always be those agencies that for a number of reasons will be eager to pitch, whatever the circumstances.

As a consequence of such critiques, the IPA (2006) in conjunction with other professional bodies has published a 'Best Practice Guide' that centres on the subject of agency selection (www.ipa.co.uk). In so doing it asks the client to consider carefully why they are undertaking a review and how to prepare for it. It provides guidelines on acceptable pitch practice including: the role and construction of the brief; appropriate timelines; drawing up the shortlist; informing agencies of the final decision; and appropriate feedback mechanisms.

Client critiques

While it may appear that the agency bears the brunt of disruption while pitching, clients too experience a sense of upheaval. This commences with the selection process and continues through beyond the final selection as the formation of a new set of relationships takes place. This can be an extremely anxious and reflective period for the client and marketing director in particular especially as he is likely to have called the pitch on the basis of a breakdown in an existing relationship. As has been established, compatibility of personalities is integral to agency selection and therefore perhaps the ultimate critique raised by clients involves the nature of the personnel representing the agency at the pitch. All too often, in order to raise the chances of winning, agencies develop an elite team of presenters. However, they will not necessarily be working on the account following any success and clients feel let down when the pitch team and the account team are not one and the same.

Alternatives to pitching

The pitch process encapsulates advertising as 'a business where the clients hold all the cards' (Tungate, 2007: 2) and in this over-supplied marketplace it is likely to remain the lifeblood of agency life. As accounts are lost for whatever reason then so this shortfall must be made up to balance the books and to allow for agency growth and development. For many in the agency such overt competition is both highly stimulating and motivating with any success quickly circulated throughout the agency world, which not only bolsters the egos of those involved but also the reputation of the agency as whole. However, the terms and conditions of pitching remain firmly in the prospective client's court. As such clients seem to demonstrate an ongoing preference for this method of selection, not only because they can clearly identify the differences between agencies in terms of their strategic insights into their advertising problem but also in terms of the comparative offers of creative solutions. In spite of the inherent weaknesses, when so many agencies compete for each account, start-ups especially will be prepared to present their ideas for free and indeed may even be prepared to negotiate on a final rate if it means overall selection. Thus despite the objectivity seemingly built into the pitch process, ultimately it can come down to costs in the last analysis. Alternatives to the pitch process have been mooted. These tend to centre on an approach favoured in the television series *The Apprentice* (BBC), giving selected agencies a brief to respond to at the start of a day-long event. On the other hand, a progressive selection process can take place whereby only the final two candidates need produce costly creative executions. Such initiatives, however, are rare as 'consensus on how the process can be made to work to everybody's satisfaction is as elusive as ever' (Tylee, 2007a).

Building a relationship and potential conflicts of interest

As noted, the number of pitches that take place each year indicate that few relationships have any sense of longevity beyond a few years, and in many cases are even shorter. However, there are examples that buck this trend. BBH and Levi's have worked together since the agency's inception and JWT's longstanding relationship with Lux dating back to 1915, for example, are worthy of note but are exceptions. Short-term relationships are not a new phenomenon, as identified in 1958 by Mayer in his summation of the US advertising industry at this time. He argues that a major problem is that 'advertising has not been able consistently to establish the long-term client relations, which are the economic foundations of professional practice' (Mayer, 1958: 329). Therefore the question needs to be asked, why do so many relationships break down? Ultimately it seems that the answer lies less in the disapproval of creative work by a client and more to do with a combination of the different cultures of working practice involved and the ultimate goals sought from any campaign, which are not necessarily the same for both client and agency.

What does a client want from an agency?

Involvement

Clients request to be involved in all stages of the advertising process, including allowances being made for their own input, where deemed appropriate. That is to say, they like to see where their money is going before it transpires into a final execution, while simultaneously mapping campaign development against the initial brief. Agencies have responded in different ways to this request. One of the most innovative approaches comes out of the creative agency St Luke's, which has developed the concept of 'brand rooms', a shared resource between agency and client and functioning as a spatial mechanism to service clients' needs more effectively. Each room represents the brand in the agency and Nixon (2003: 41) terms such an arrangement the 'business partner model' based on a feeling that each is integral to the other's success. In contrast, DLKW has developed the concept of a 'shared agenda' which they describe on their website as follows:

> Historically, agencies and clients have had separate agendas that they barter to make progress. Both client and agency waste a lot of time and energy trying to anticipate

the others' agenda – language such as 'how can we get this through the client', 'how can we get the agency to do this' being commonplace. We believe that if time is spent at the start of a relationship anticipating these issues, discussing working processes, explaining agendas, it's possible to align both agency and client together as one team behind a single set of objectives, values and working processes. We call this a 'shared agenda'. (www.dlkw.co.uk)

More generally, a common denominator across all agencies is the role of the account manager, a critical member of personnel who liaises primarily with a brand manager, client-side, to ensure both frequency and consistency of contact and communication. Cited often as functioning as 'the voice of the client in the agency', it is his or her responsibility to manage the campaign's development from the moment the client brief is brought into the agency through to final execution, on time and on budget, and beyond to the overall assessment of the campaign's effectiveness. Ultimately the account manager is a people person, brokering personalities and demands in-house with the client's needs and wishes, which are not always consistent and enduring. Finally, an important tool in allowing ongoing communication to be maintained is that of the agency 'intranet'. This has become essential as a live communications channel not only between agencies and their clients but also between the different agencies that might be involved in any one campaign.

Harmony

Where using a series of agencies to perform different functions, clients wish for harmonious cooperation during campaign development. Such a concern emerges on the basis of the range of services that a client can now enlist from multiple providers. Indeed, recent research has indicated that all parties involved like to have a shared sense of ownership of the strategic process and that 'relationships were more likely to break down when different agencies felt undermined, subjugated or in some way not afforded equal status' (Grant and McLeod, 2007: 429). Ultimately, such relationships will not manage themselves and the client must work hard in a mediating role. Indeed, one of the emerging new roles for the account manager in the context of the implementation of IMC is inter-agency liaison. That is, while in-house the agency might be working on a television campaign, he may also have to consult with, for example, outside digital specialists among others.

What does an agency want from a client?

A contract

Following success at the pitch, agencies require a written contract where not only is the scope of their responsibilities noted and agreed upon but also where the terms and conditions of remuneration are also marked out. This is an issue dating back to the 1950s when it was recognised that 'the ties between advertiser and agency are personal and often insecure (some agencies still do not have written contracts with their clients and most of the others rely on a single page which describes merely the bare bones of the relationship).' (Mayer, 1958: 40).

A detailed brief

At the start of any campaign, agencies look to the provision of a detailed brief that clearly and concisely provides not only the purpose of advertising but also how the effectiveness of the campaign is to be measured. Furthermore, the brief should define a company's corporate or brand position and describe its key business issues. In 2003 the IPA produced a set of best practice guidelines out of recognition that 'the brief is the most important bit of information issued by a client to an agency. It's from the brief that everything else flows.' (IPA, 2003). These guidelines were written with the objective that they would be disseminated across the client base with the ultimate goal of facilitating the client-agency relationship. Therefore, a good brief increases efficiency in the overall process of campaign development. So how should such a brief be structured? At the heart of the content is a clear definition of the client's business problem so that the designated lead agency might begin to consider its solution. The brief must be in writing so that it can be repeatedly referred to by all involved, especially where multiple agencies are involved, and should be followed by a verbal discussion which allows for points of clarification to be raised and responded to by all parties.

Regular contact

During campaign development, agencies look to the provision of regular and minuted meetings and conversations (call reports) with the client, so that all decisions can be recorded and necessary actions allocated to named account members. Call reports also provide a trail of campaign development that can allow for later reflection and assessment. In terms of day-to-day communication, account executives function to keep abreast of client developments and agency progress. Beyond this, account managers will speak or meet with the client on a weekly basis, and account directors on a monthly basis.

Such frequent contact can also avert potential problems as and when they arise. An example of good working practice is documented in relation to the global communications planning and implementation agency Mediaedge:CIA. In 2007 'MEC recorded a 100 per cent client retention rate and acted swiftly when there were issues with clients. For instance, it moved the Morrisons' planning and buying business from its Manchester agency to London and managed to stave off a predicted pitch process.' (Tylee, 2007b: 9).

Creative confidence

Finally, an agency wants their client to appreciate excellent advertising rather than advertising that is safe and ordinary, a route often taken client-side in the elimination of risk. However, what constitutes 'great' advertising is not subject to easy definition. While a client might want a campaign that is guaranteed to boost sales, many creatives view each campaign as an opportunity to win awards, new business and elevate their own kudos. Ultimately such disparate views often result in compromise. However, this is where the role of research has a critical part to play whereby 'agencies need to have formalised research processes because clients seek a degree of control over the uncertainties of creative production.' (Grant and McLeod, 2007: 427).

Conclusion

In summing up, we might agree that the character of the relationship between agencies and their clients is 'asymmetrical.' (Cronin, 2004: 341). The number of agencies courting each account primarily fuels this. As a result the changing structures and specialisations that have informed the modern agency have largely arisen as a response to clients' demands, especially more recently in relation to new media communications. In terms of the establishment of agency-client relationships, the pitch process continues its domination despite producing criticisms from both sides. While alternatives have been both considered and experimented with, it still remains the primary form for winning new business. AAR statistics record that only 5–10 per cent of new business moves without a pitch (Charles, 2008: 16). Clients not only draw up its terms and conditions, albeit with reference to IPA guidelines, but also its frequency. However, this is not to suggest that agencies themselves have no power, which in contrast to the client 'resides not in the actual production of goods but in the shaping or 'producing' of information about those goods.' (Malefyt, 2003: 140). The innovative ways in which agencies respond to this challenge can secure their future and their point of difference. However, in the future as the consumer becomes harder to reach, the agency and client must 'move closer together in terms of skill sets and working styles' if they are to combat this and other challenges (IPA/Future Foundation, 2006: 45) but instability has characterised client-agency relationships since their inception and will continue to remain a focal point of deliberation and discussion.

Questions for students

1. Why is the structure and organisation of an advertising agency never static?

2. Which factors do you consider as the most important in allowing for a good working relationship between an agency and its clients?

3. What suggestions might you put forward as an alternative to pitching? What advantages and disadvantages might they provide over the existing process?

4. How do you envisage the agency of the future?

2 Ronald's new dance: a case study of corporate re-branding in the age of integrated marketing communications

Stephen Kline

Introduction

The case study has a long and noble history in both the analysis of and teaching about marketing. In his book *Big Brands Big Trouble* American branding guru Jack Trout (2001: vii) proclaims: 'I have a better approach. Not only is learning from failure easier' but studying brand failures 'offers a more thorough analysis of what works and what doesn't.' According to Trout, frequently well considered marketing plans succumb when their managers fail to understand their brands are a 'percept', not a product. 'There is no objective reality. There are no facts. There are no best products. All that exists in the world of marketing are perceptions in the minds of customers or prospects. The perception is the reality. Everything else is an illusion'. From his analysis of 100 cases of brand failures, Haig (2005: 7) similarly argues that 'brands have also transformed the process of marketing into one of perception-building. That is to say that image is now everything. Consumers make buying decisions based around the perception of the brand rather than the reality of the product.' Both agree that the only way to avoid brand failure in today's dynamic markets is to understand the complex role of brand communication as the key element in the marketing mix.

Yet corporate branding remains one of the most slippery concepts in the marketing literature. The complexity of brand management lies in the fact that public perceptions depend not only upon the communication of the product's qualities and identity but on that of the corporation as well. Originally associated with the symbolic values projected in the advertising (Marchand, 1998; Leiss *et al.*, 2005) and public relations (Ewen, 1998; Davis, 2000), most corporations that produce and sell consumer products in the national marketplace employ strategies of corporate branding, which now encompass a variety of communication modalities through which they establish and consolidate the public's perceptions of their products, services and corporate ethos (Hansen and Christensen, 2003; Cornelissen, 2004; Christensen *et al.*, 2008). As Ind (1997: 80) states, contemporary corporate branding uses a combination of social communication modalities including community relations and word of mouth campaigns, PR and lobbying, social marketing and brand advertising and now web sites as the coordinated channels for communicating corporate values. Most corporate brands use more than one channel because each has its strengths and weaknesses. As Ind (1997: 80) argues, press coverage can be as important as advertising for the corporate brand: 'PR loses out to advertising in its controllability but it has the advantage over advertising in its ability to communicate more complex messages and in its credibility. The press coverage achieved through the media relationship activity has the appearance of neutrality.' Corporate communication has therefore become the coordinating office in most enterprises overseeing Advertising, Legal and PR.

Although integrated corporate communication is crucial to contemporary brand management, the limitations of a case study approach lie in the tendency of reading corporate communication in isolation of the changing cultural values and the media context through which they are communicated: what works at one moment may not when it is repeated or imitated. Moreover, brand wearout takes a serious toll on brand values as brand loyalty and involvement diminish, especially in sectors where innovation is prized. With the dramatic shifts in media cultures in mind, Holt (2004: xii) sets out to create a strategic language for brand management through a cultural case study approach, which analyses the most durable high profile brands 'historically to uncover the principles that account for their success'. His genealogies trace brand strategy to demonstrate how a brand's success is forged by the cumulative accretion of deep meaning in the mind of not only its customers, but of the culture as a whole. Looking at the advertising and marketing strategies of 20 market leaders, Holt stresses the importance of creative promotional communication which narrates the brand myths until 'iconic brands become the most compelling symbol of a set of ideas or values'. He points out that the brand's success depends not only on the weight of advertising and targeting of audiences but on the ability of the brand to crystallize 'a culturally situated desire or anxiety'.

It is through integrated marketing communications strategies that corporations not only project their core values but evolve within the dynamism of today's cultural contexts. Success, he argues, depends on how well the brand's myth adjusts to historical exigencies not by its consistency in the face of historical change but in their ability to keep their 'brand experiences' perpetually distinguishable from their competitors. 'The greatest opportunity for brands today is to deliver not entertainment, but rather myths that their customers can use to manage the exigencies of a world which increasingly threatens their identities . . . society's most vexing contradictions.' (Holt 2004: 221). This makes the process of brand renewal and re-branding one of the most crucial elements in contemporary marketing practice.

In what follows, these ideas about contemporary corporate branding will be explored through a historical case study of one of the most 'iconic' of all global brands – McDonald's. Today, McDonald's US holdings not only hover around 13,300 US franchised outlets that account for 43 per cent of total US burger sales, but with 30,000 restaurants in 121 countries, the brand dominates the fast-service restaurant market grossing four times Burger King's $11.3 billion and Wendy's 9.4 with its marketing muscle and brand savvy communication (Lang and Heasman, 2004). McDonald's triumphal ascent to and position as the world's leading restaurant chain, grossing $41 billion dollars annually, is a well-known American rags to global riches tale of an exemplary marketing savvy enterprise. The case of McDonald's corporate global brand management arguably proves illustrative for three simple reasons: firstly, because of its corporate commitment to promotional communication which has helped it become the ninth leading global brand; secondly, because its focus on corporate values not only fuelled its success but has inspired opposition which required constant corporate public relations efforts; and thirdly, because confronted by a cultural rejection of fast food culture at the turn of the millennium, McDonald's has been able to renew itself by an integrated corporate re-branding programme not only inspiring the 'i'm lovin' it' advertising campaign, but a corporate responsibility make-over that is expressed not only in its advertising campaign but in what its servers are wearing.

Ronald's Dance begins

The story of this American based marketing juggernaut is well known and much discussed in the marketing literature as well as the business press (Botterill and Kline, 2007). Established in California during the 1940s by two brothers, the McDonald's restaurant became a popular teen hangout in the first wave of post-war affluence. In an obvious marketing gesture to their loyal young customers, the brothers reduced the menu to the perennial favourite – hamburgers. More importantly, they experimented with applying assembly line efficiencies and Taylorist management techniques to food production. In order to reduce lines, the brothers developed their Speedee Service System, which allowed them to pre-stockpile the burgers for faster delivery and line control. Their profitability increased, allowing them to expand to four restaurants by 1953. Taking note of the brother's production innovations, in 1955, entrepreneur Ray Kroc bought the right to franchise the McDonald's fast food dining model. Renamed the McDonald's Corporation in 1960, Kroc shifted his branding strategy out of its original target of teens, choosing the family meal as the core of his restaurant business. Kroc's business credo – be efficient, be clean, be a good citizen – was the guiding principle which became deeply embedded in the McDonald's brand. Spending heavily on television advertising, which promoted the smiling clown face of its child-friendly brand mascot, Ronald McDonald, the McDonald's brand experience welcomed both parents and children into the warm glow of low cost eating. This brand formula worked well and the chain saw US profits increase in every consecutive quarter from incorporation to the dying days of the millennium.

For obvious reasons, McDonald's corporate growth has been closely followed by the public, the business community and by academics as an object lesson in corporate brand management (Boje, 2001). Noting how McDonald's refined the techniques of mass production and mass marketing of food to families, Ritzer (2004) holds up McDonald's as an exemplary capitalist enterprise – well worth studying for its general lessons about the adaptation of Fordist mass production principles to the food services industry. Ritzer underscores four key managerial principles of 'McDonaldization', which he argues exemplify the underlying dynamic of a 'rationalized' mass production and marketing approach. Foremost among these is the privileging of efficiency, as management focuses on delivering the product as quickly as possible at the least cost. Calculability is also central to the management system of rationalization, as the corporation uses systematic accounting, reporting and research to observe, measure, quantify and adjudicate corporate strategy. McDonald's managers focus on production control as the third pillar reducing the uncertainties of managing human labour by utilizing a system of production technologies wherever possible. And finally, Ritzer argues that predictability has become the central integrative tenet of global mass marketing, as McDonald's sets out to promote its brand experience by stringent quality control of product – which assures its consumers that a burger in Rangoon will taste the same as a burger in Seattle.

However, Ritzer's reading of McDonald's Fordist brand strategy has been criticized as an overly monolithic and inflexible mass marketing business model, which fails to acknowledge the cultural flexibility required for expansion into global markets where cultural tastes and changing lifestyles play an important role in forming relationships with unfamiliar products (Smart, 1999). Predictability therefore involves adaptation of menu to the brand's core marketing concept. Indeed, since 1971, when it began expansion into Europe and Asia, the McDonald's Corporation has also devoted considerable effort to new product innovation to enter new markets, to keep apace of changing tastes and to combat its competition in the fast food market. From egg McMuffins, McNuggets and McRibs to pizzas, tortias, sundaes and vegetarian burgers, McDonald's core menu is constantly being rewritten. More importantly it has developed brand adaptability into a system of planned cultural innovation, so that each product's sales are monitored religiously and evaluated according to profitability. In this sense, menu introductions have served the company well in their years of global expansion, enabling adjustments to varied palates and customs in the fluid global market. McDonald's willingness to adapt the basic product concept to suit local tastes (spicier chicken in China and mutton burgers in India) has helped the company avoid some of the costly cross-cultural marketing errors committed by other American global corporations throughout the 1990s.

One obvious oversight of Ritzer is that McDonaldization concerns not just the products or the management strategy which produces them, but the cumulative communication about the eating experience to the public. As data on McDonald's global and US ad spends reveal, the development of McDonald's brand has required significant ongoing investments in communications of all sorts to build the brand within diversified cultural contexts (BrandZ, 2008). What Ritzer overlooks is that the chain's rapid expansion from American suburbs to downtown Peking rested upon Kroc's glo-local projection of this family-oriented brand strategy: Love's (1986) corporate history portrays Kroc as the quintessential American marketing guru, who devoted himself largely to polishing McDonald's brand image at all times, and at all costs. Boje *et al.* (2005) argue that the clown motif associating the brand with the excitement of the circus was a consequential choice. It enchanted children while imbuing with a brand narrative grounded in the dynamic imagery of carnivalesque fun. Kroc understood that the hamburger was not the brand and that consumers' experiences of the restaurants were ultimately what mattered.

Kroc himself proclaimed that the astonishing success of the McDonald's chain was less due to the efficient delivery of low cost hamburgers, than to its unsullied corporate image and his own flair for 'show business'. But as the chain evolved, the core brand values inspired innovations: understanding the pressures of domestic lifestyles McDonald's innovated with the drive thru and with child-friendly promotions. Using bright primary colours, indoor playgrounds, Happy Meals featuring popular licensed toys and small-hand friendly food, McDonald's established itself as the family restaurant that made eating seem fun for kids and easy for Moms. Kroc's commitment to family-friendly brand values helped McDonald's become America's best known restaurant, with a larger share of the fast food market than the next four chains combined. But its successful brand strategy should not be read as dull and inflexible, even if the core brand values remain constant – because there is nothing rigid about good wholesome fun at a reasonable price.

According to *Advertising Age*, McDonald's ranks now among the top ten largest global brands, spending $1 405 million US dollars on its global advertising campaigns: more than Coke, Pepsi and Walt Disney. Backed by these enormous advertising spends, McDonald's brought the American burger culture to nations where it never existed before by dedicating itself to the idea of global branding the fast-hamburger restaurant concept. Its success therefore reminds us of the corporation's reliance on advertising as the main means of ensuring that the message of consistency and integration of the brand experience through a tightly managed global advertising campaign was at the heart of this expansion. As a result, only Santa Claus is better known to children around the world than Ronald McDonald.

Brand trouble and corporate re-branding

A host of critics pointing to community, labour and environmental issues associated with the McDonald's rationalizing business model have haunted the corporation's ascent to global stardom. Ritzer's analyse of McDonaldization points out that a corporation's marketing strategy can also be its greatest vulnerability: given the scale of its food empire, the decisions made by McDonald's can have profound impacts on local agriculture, the environment, labour markets and communities. With its many critics in mind, Ritzer argues that the 'irrationality of rationalization' should be thought of as the fifth dimension of this mass-marketing business model (Ritzer, 2004: 17). Arrangements and practices, which appear rational from the point of view of its price-cutting brand strategy, are not always in the interest of the customer, the workers, the communities in which they locate or the environment, he argues. Throughout its history, this corporation has been subjected to widespread public criticism in the press, films and street conversation until the McDonald's brand became synonymous with low paid McJobs, Amazon deforestation and American mass marketing. The media coverage of these issues has linked the McDonald's brand to public controversy as well as family fun. In response McDonald's has intensified its social marketing efforts focusing on Ronald McDonald House and a variety of children's charities.

Examining the mounting controversies found in its press coverage of the McDonald's corporation, Botterill and Kline (2007) draw attention to the important part played by public relations professionals in 'rationalizing the irrationalities' produced by the McDonald's brand strategy. As their review of news coverage indicates, McDonald's global ascent depends as much on smart lawyers and community relations negotiators, as on its advertising agents. The McDonald's brand has not only been burnished by a heavy investment in above the line media buys, but in corporate communications efforts more broadly conceived, including a vast squadron of corporate communications experts, including labour and community relations practitioners, political lobbyists, social marketers and lawyers, all who must be ready to respond to public discontents in its many guises. This cadre of corporate communication professionals earn their keep backstage by maintaining the legitimacy of the brand in the courts, in government hearings, and most problematically in the press, which informs an increasingly sceptical and risk adverse public.

Nowhere was the importance of integrated corporate communication more clearly revealed than in the 1989 McLibel court case. Against the backdrop of aggressive McDonald's expansion in Britain, a group of British Greenpeace activists decided to bring some of the problems associated with McDonaldization to public attention, distributing a leaflet entitled 'What's wrong with McDonald's?' that argued McDonald's quest for profit had extended American imperialism into the third world, encouraging labour exploitation and anti-unionism, devastated the environment and duped children into unhealthy diets. The leaflet encouraged consumers to boycott McDonald's, enjoy vegetarian diets utilizing home-grown vegetables and eat wholesome slow food together. Fiercely protective of its 'responsible' corporate ethos, McDonald's lawyers served writs on the five campaigners claiming libel. As the BBC (1997) reported, Paul Preston, chairman and chief executive of McDonald's in Britain declared: 'For the sake of our employees and our customers, we wanted to show these serious allegations to be false.'

The McLibel case became the longest trial in British history, lingering in the courts for 10 years as £10 million of McDonald's legal might battled two environmental advocates who defended themselves (with the help of a vast number of witness supporters) over their rights to publish criticism of the corporation. In 1997 the judge ruled in McDonald's favour on several counts and fined the plaintiffs £96,000, even though he found it was not libel to claim that McDonald's suppressed labour markets, made deceptive claims about its food, posed a health threat to its customers and exploited children's credulity with its promotions. If anything then, the court case only served to illustrate the activists' claims that this corporation used its position of global wealth and power to pummel those who would challenge its sanctimonious public image. The McSpotlight website, which originally posted the testimony, became the hub of a worldwide activist network, receiving 1.5 million hits per year revealing the growing importance of the Internet for brand management. Feeding a growing anti-corporate sentiment, especially in the youth market it targeted, the Golden Arches became a much reviled icon of the 'brand bullying' of the young (Gibbins and Reimer, 1999; Klein N., 2000; Crossley, 2002). World Trade Organization protesters targeted McDonald's at WTO meetings in Seattle, Montreal and Davos, as anti-globalization movements vented their frustration at the ascendant power of multinational corporations. The press coverage made McDonald's a worldwide target for protests: within hours of the US bombing raids on Afghanistan in 2001, angry Pakistan crowds protested by attacking McDonald's outlets in Islamabad and Karachi.

It is with McDonald's growing public relations problems in mind, that in his work *Tailspin* (2004), McCusker therefore labels the McLibel case, 'the world's biggest corporate PR disaster' with good reason: the real cost to the corporation was the negative brand effect accumulating during ten years, coverage of this Goliath vs. David fight with two British Greenpeacers. For this reason too, Haig (2005: 3) cites the McLibel case as one of the most stunning branding mistakes of all time: because brand values are lodged in perception they 'can become more valuable than their physical assets' but 'it also means they can lose this value overnight. After all, perception is a fragile thing. If the brand image becomes tarnished through a media scandal or controversial incident or even a rumour spread via the Internet then the company after a while can find itself in deep trouble'. That McDonald's had become a victim of its own success stems from press coverage which was neither sought nor wanted as well as the new digital distribution strategies through which advocacy communication takes place online. Public relations suits can craft press releases but not control the media smart advocacy movements and political consumerism that was mobilizing against them through networked alternative media.

The turn of the millennium saw new opposition mobilizing which also targeted McDonald's as the leading edge of the fast food industry's incursion into the global diet. The World Health Organization's (WHO) public declarations of a globesity crisis fuelled criticism of fast food culture (Lang and Heasman, 2004): McDonald's was typically mentioned first – a price of its success as the most visible fast food brand. Given its market leader status and super-sized marketing budgets, children became the 'canaries in the coalmine' of the globesity crisis debates (Kline, 2004a,b) as campaigning journalists around the world condemned McDonald's for its excessive marketing to children (Schlosser, 2001; Linn, 2003; Critser, 2003). McDonald's not only found itself having to defend its right to advertise to children in the UK, but in the US crusading lawyer Hirsh brought forward a law suit on behalf of the parents of two overweight teenagers who claimed their children were not aware that McDonald's food was fattening. Filed in August, the suit claimed that McDonald's, and two of its restaurants in the Bronx, failed to clearly and conspicuously disclose the ingredients and effects of its food, including high levels of fat, salt, sugar and cholesterol, to the girls. Hirsh argued that McDonald's franchises are therefore negligently selling risky products and should be held accountable for the girls' obesity, heart disease, diabetes, high blood pressure and elevated cholesterol. US District Court Judge Robert Sweet, however, dismissed this case on January 22, because he felt the plaintiffs failed to show that McDonald's food was 'dangerous in any way other than that which was open and obvious to a reasonable consumer' (Wald, 2003). In February Hirsh filed a revised complaint accusing the fast food giant of making misleading nutritional claims citing McDonald's for 'deceptive practices in the advertising, processing and sale of foods, including Chicken McNuggets, Filet-O-Fish, Chicken Sandwich, French fries and hamburgers.' In his 46-page complaint, Hirsch alleged that McDonald's does not make its nutritional information 'adequately available' and that numerous claims made by the fast-food chain are misleading and untrue (Findlaw, 2002). McDonald's quickly responded calling the lawsuit 'senseless' and 'frivolous', since it was parents, not the fast food industry's fault, if kids are eating improperly and are not active enough. The court agreed with McDonald's, noting that it was reasonable to assume that even teens were aware that McDonald's food was fattening (Wald, 2003). The release of a documentary (*Supersize Me*, 2004), in which filmmaker Morgan Spurlock willingly damages his health by eating nothing but McDonald's food for a month, revealed that the courts were an unpredictable place to defend their brand values.

McDonald's was becoming aware of the extent of its mistake. The cumulative weight of negative publicity, coupled with burger fatigue, and stiff competition from Subway and Starbucks (both of which offered healthy sandwich options) was showing up on the bottom line of the McDonald's Corporation. From 1997 McDonald's noticed a decline in customers and profits revealing the changing tastes and lifestyles that were impacting the entire food sector. Between 1998 and 2002, McDonald's experienced declining rates of growth and its actual share of the fast food market fell more than 3 per cent. Sales had been stagnant since 2000 and plummeted 2.8 per cent in 2002, amid the growing concern about child obesity, representing the first ever decline in the corporation's history. In Europe too, stiff competition from other fast-food chains and anti-McDonald's sentiments began to affect the bottom line. After 30 years of phenomenal growth in Britain, the McDonald's Corporation, which directly controls two-thirds of the 1,235 UK restaurants, reported a 61 million pound decline in their profits from the previous year. But most tellingly, McDonald's stock lost about 70 per cent of its value between late 1999 and mid-2003. The question began to be asked, was McDonald's equipped for the twenty-first century? The brand seemed to be having serious trouble.

The Emperor's new clothes
....

McDonald's pyrrhic victory in the courts did little to blunt the growing moral panic about the global fast food culture generally and McDonald's in particular, as its leading exponent. Internal research showed that their Golden Image, polished by billions of dollars of paid advertising and corporate relations, was now seriously tarnished. Kids were now making fun of the company in the playgrounds. Even in the *International Journal of Advertising to Children*, consultants were suggesting that it was time for the food industry to take some responsibility for the globesity epidemic (Nixon, 2004). Plagued by these concerns, and facing shareholder dismay at its declining profitability, McDonald's Corporation decided on a major re-branding. The head office charged its communications specialists to respond to the changing consumer tastes and the mounting anxiety about child globesity. This McDonald's did with great fanfare, devoting billions of dollars in a global corporate re-branding, intended to blunt McDonald's association with junk food and unhealthy lifestyles. Charlie Bell's, the CEO of McDonald's, 'Plan to Win' approach was a revival of the five Ps of marketing: price, people, product, place and promotion. But promotion was the guiding principle, steering the corporation away from fighting losing image battles in the courts and backrooms, towards acknowledging and addressing consumers' growing concerns. In their UK print and outdoor campaigns, a golden question mark now replaced the reviled Golden Arches explained by the tagline 'McDonald's. But not as you know it'. The question mark represented a series of re-design initiatives at the operational level, as McDonald's stores were to be given new interiors to suit different locations, staff uniforms and packaging were revamped, a greater focus was to be given to cleanliness and, most importantly of all, new menu items have been introduced (McDonald's press release, 2008).

In keeping with their promises of 'responsibility' McDonald's also set up a 13 member nutrition advisory team, who advised that they add salads, fruit and sandwiches to their menu, phase out the super size and reduce trans fats by changing the cooking oil. The panel argued parents should not be charged extra to substitute milk for soda in their children's Happy Meals (which contains roughly 470 calories and 18 grams) and that more fibre should be added to their burger buns. New products such as the Salad Plus, porridge and bagels were introduced, aimed at winning back young women and mothers. Yoghurts and fruit bags are also now available in Happy Meals and the super size option was no longer available. UK CEO Light pledged £7.4 million in initiatives designed to help parents choose healthier options at McDonald's and included new Happy Meal menus that included carrots, fruit jelly, chicken grills and apple juice. This message is conveyed in ads which show lots of vegetables and remind parents of the importance of keeping their kids healthy in today's risky world (*Business Week*, 2007).

However, menu changes alone could not achieve the turnaround, so McDonald's also developed a two-pronged global branding strategy. On one hand they decided to sidestep the child market by targeting teens rather than children, ironically returning to the burgers' original fans. Their first ad in the global youth campaign featured global pop star Justin Timberlake singing its new 'i'm lovin' it' strapline. This youth campaign focus unfolded with growing sponsorship of MTV show *Advance Warning* followed by ads employing hip yet dynamic teen icons such as skater legend Tony Hawks to speak to its new youthful targets based around four core areas: music, sport, fashion and entertainment. Their child and family ads now featured active kids having fun who rarely were shown actually eating. How could they, they never sat down.

Threatened with an advertising ban in the UK and new regulations of children's time advertising around the world, children's marketers re-assessed the importance of the perception of corporate responsibility for their brands: while Coke was banned from school corridors and voluntarily moved to restrict its advertising directed at kids, McDonald's argued for a different conception of its responsibility. From now on it would use advertising to teach kids about how to achieve healthy lifestyles promoting a balanced diet and lots of exercise to counteract their obesogenic lifestyles. At the annual conference of the Society for British Advertisers, UK CEO Light, cited in the *Guardian*, said: 'We do not need less communication to children: we need more. If we want to educate children to eat right and be active, we need effective marketing communications that are responsive and responsible. Advertising for the 3.6 million pound launch of the new healthy happy campaign, with the tagline 'it's what i eat, and what i do' will highlight fruit and vegetables.' Over £1 million was invested in designing and publicizing a 'nutrition education' package for a media literate British Youth hosted by Ronald, which introduced the 'Yum Chums' to teach about eating five a day fruit and vegetables (Yum Chums, 2008). The linking of online and schools promotional material into above the line promotion brings the UK into alignment with the US, where Channel One provides corporate access to young audiences by integrating satellite and online communication into the marketing mix. Not only did McDonald's choose the still unregulated 'online' location for the Yum Chum's media education effort, but drew regulators' attention to the problem of online advertising as the next battle ground for critics of children's marketing (*Sustain*, 2008).

Conclusion

The historical case study of McDonald's has been chosen because it exemplifies the flexible idea of branding that is currently practised by leading brand managers in the global marketplace. Although above the line marketing remains at the heart McDonald's communication of brand values and brand personality it has also learned the hard way that the blow back from even successful defenses of its responsibility in the courts can prove costly to a brand. Their re-branding effort under the 'i'm lovin' it' theme illustrates how the coordination of different modalities of corporate communication can bring into re-alignment the above the line promotion of child-friendly family values with the backstage defense of corporate ethos. The result has been a corporate turn around for the brand in terms of customer visits, global sales and profitability, and most importantly in the monetary value of the brand as exemplified in the stock price.

McDonald's re-branding became necessary because of the oppositional forces arising in the maturing consumer culture among consumers themselves – and their changing anxieties and concerns. However, consumers are revolutionary, argues Douglas Holt, 'only insofar as they assist entrepreneurial firms to tear down their old branding paradigms and create opportunities for companies that understand emerging new principles'. Building on Thomas Frank's 'cooption model', Holt (2002: 88) argues that 'Revolutionary consumers helped to create the market for Volkswagen and Nike and accelerated the demise of Sears and Oldsmobile. They never threatened the market itself. What has been termed "consumer resistance" is actually a form of market–sanctioned cultural experimentation through which the market rejuvenates itself'. Whereas in the 1950s brand strategies were dominated by what he calls a 'cultural engineering paradigm', in which brands sought to establish credibility in speaking to the dilemmas of consumer choice, these strategies evolved in the 1970s into a post-modern branding paradigm where products became symbols which provided social belonging and personal identity. It was, therefore, through their willingness to re-articulate their brand narratives within consumers' constant lifestyle experimentation, quest for individual uniqueness and social diversity, that brand durability was achieved.

But in the new millennium, marketers were confronted with growing opposition to globalization, fragmenting media, environmental concerns and a wariness of marketing itself (Cohen, 2003; Micheletti *et al.*, 2003). In response they once again looked to re-brand themselves in the face of politicized consumerism that sought stability and comfort in risky global markets. Holt sees the emergence of a 'post-postmodern branding paradigm', which recognizes that both the anxieties about markets, and the demands for corporate responsibility, are real. Holt believes that for iconic brand managers 'cultural disruptions lead to the creation of new myths': brand trouble will only be problematic in the future if the corporation refuses to acknowledge or continues to ignore the challenges, whether they be ethical, environmental or cultural issues. To this end Holt (2004: 220) advises corporations to transform themselves into post-postmodern organizations by cultivating a brand management which is:

> organized around developing identity myths that address emerging contradictions in society; a company organized to collaborate with creative partners to perform myths that have the charisma and authenticity necessary to attract followers: a company that is organized to understand society and culture, not just consumers; and a company that is staffed with managers who have ability and training in these areas.

Perhaps McDonald's has been showing the way.

Questions for students

1a What do you understand by the term 'Integrated Marketing Communications' (IMC)?

1b Why do you believe it has become significant as a marketing strategy?

1c Provide examples of brands that are, in your opinion, using IMC effectively. Draw up a chart that indicates the various points of interaction that the consumer has with these brands.

2   Is there a future for above-the-line advertising? If so by whom will it be used and in what ways?

3   Consider both the advantages and disadvantages of corporations using the Internet to manage their corporate image.

3 Advertising fragmentation: the beginning of a new paradigm?

Francisco J. Pérez-Latre

Introduction: advertising-funded industries in transition

The media and entertainment industries are undergoing rapid transformation prompted by changes in technology, regulation, markets and audiences. One authoritative source, the VSS Communications Industry Forecast 2007–11, projects continuing growth in the communications industry over the next five years, with Internet advertising, including pure play websites and digital extensions of traditional media, replacing newspapers as the largest ad medium by 2011. And advertising follows audiences.

Audience usage patterns seem to be in a profound transformation: 'because of the high demand for quick updates and short news briefs readily available on the web, [US] consumers now rely less on 30-minute broadcast or cable TV news shows and spend less time reading the Sunday paper, dropping time with ad-supported media by 6.3 per cent' (Tan, 2007). Advertising finance has tended to move from mass to targeted media. Some clients are less inclined to pay for broadcast TV advertising based on interruption. That is why authors such as Briggs and Stuart (2006) have argued that targeted media appear to be more effective. The publishing, broadcasting and advertising industries are more affected than other media and entertainment industries. In this context:

> we must address the old saw that new media don't destroy old media. Radio didn't kill newspapers; television didn't kill radio, and so on. That is true ... so far. But some new media are so disruptive that they force older media to change themselves radically in order to stay in business. Those that decide to circle the wagons and refuse to change, refuse to reinvent themselves, are almost certainly going to struggle to survive. (Cappo, 2003: 72)

A paradigm shift appears to be on the horizon.

This chapter concentrates on some of the market changes. However, traditional media still account for the greatest share of advertising expenditure. As we look into the transformations we must not forget that the Internet's share of advertising expenditure is below 10 per cent in most countries. Traditional media have an enduring attraction for advertisers and agencies. Marketers have increasingly pursued multimedia advertising campaigns across both 'old' and 'new' media. Media conglomerates have also sought to offer cross-platform advertising packages across their media holdings, providing a source of income, leverage and market power, as they restructure their business operations, try to offset losses from some media holdings and take advantage of developing ones. For advertisers and media, much has been made of efforts to run multimedia campaigns, to try to migrate audiences/users from one platform to another (i.e. from broadcast TV to the Internet).

In the current market situation there is a rather complex interaction between the old and the new. Therefore, the market changes covered in this chapter should not be understood as a linear transition from old to new, but as a more complex situation in which 'old' and 'new' media are combined in various ways and where both are in a state of flux. Corporate, technological, market and cultural convergence gives us some clues to interpret the emergence of a new paradigm (Murdock, 2000; Jenkins, 2006). Digitalization and all the allied changes in markets, consumers and regulation bring profound challenges for certain media forms and the business models on which they have been based. Advertising-financed TV is threatened by declining viewing across most linear channels. But television is still the most consumed medium. It is being distributed and reshaped across a variety of modes of distribution and consumption (Grey, 2008; Palmer, 2006; Spigel and Olsson (eds), 2004). The effort to find viable new economic models is driving changes in media, advertising and in the relationship between media and advertising.

In this chapter, the transformation of advertising and media is examined as a process involving, and often mixing, old and new. First, the paradigm shift in advertising is explored, taking a special look at television spots and new forms of advertising. Second, we consider how advertising agencies, that used to have full control of the business, face fresh competition from Internet portals that have the capacity to skip the agencies' intermediary role. We continue with a section on social networks and online video, media that shape new ways to interact with audiences. Finally, we look at the changes in advertising media share in the last decade in some key Western markets.

The paradigm shift in advertising

In an era defined as the 'post-television age' (Cappo, 2003), the way advertising works is changing (Auletta, 2005). Traditional advertising is said to be losing ground to viral marketing, gaming, on-demand viewing, long-form content and other 'new marketing' (Jaffe, 2005). The idea itself of 'advertising's death' is present in several major titles. Ries and Ries (2002) argue that the future for brands is in public relations and not in advertising. Zyman (2002) warns about the end of advertising as we know it. Both books claim that advertising agencies are selling clients short. In these books, when death is mentioned, the authors are describing more a transformation than an end. But they want to underline what they see as unprecedented levels of change. Life after traditional advertising is the topic of another set of books. New marketing techniques, including Internet advertising, video gaming and product placement are the focus of works by Jaffe (2005) and Galician (2004). The synergies achieved between entertainment and advertising through product placement are also examined by Donaton (2004).

The strength of online advertising and its cost-effectiveness is discussed in a variety of works that explain how search engines such as Google are changing current advertising strategies, adding the Internet to the media mix. Marketing without the operational use of agencies has also become a frequent topic in both the academic and managerial debate. Nyren (2005) suggests that there is no longer any need to work with an advertising agency.

Advertising-funded media and entertainment industries seem to be in transition (Farrell, 2007). Today, consumers of media are more in control of how, where and when they receive their messages. A broadcaster's ability to dictate when certain shows are watched or heard is somewhat diminished. There will always be demand for live television and radio, to deliver breaking news, as well as sporting events, awards shows and so on, but the drive towards more consumer control will likely continue. An equally strong revolution is happening in content-creation. Blogs, cellphone movies and social networking sites are contributing to an explosion of user-generated content. Bradley and Bartlett (2007: 1) address some media strategy implications of the new landscape: 'with the establishment of the Internet in the late 1990s, marketers began to use the web to *supplement* their offline campaigns. Eventually the convergence of widespread broadband, mobile technology, portable devices and user-generated content created a world which propelled marketers to new outlets such as rich media, podcasts, online videos and blogs'.

Brands are no longer built *solely* around the 30-second commercial: consumers' alienation with cluttered media and 'wearout', an expression that describes consumers' feelings of being exposed too often to too many messages, have become important factors. For Cappo (2003: 151):

> That simple solution to advertising doesn't exist anymore. Television is not as dominant as it once was. A whole world of cable and satellite channels is now available to smart marketers. One must devote more time to media evaluation and selection, and it can produce more effective advertising. That is exactly what clients are looking for – more answers to their marketing problems. And aside from the proliferation of television, cable and satellite signals, there has been a substantial growth in all other forms of marketing – sales promotion, direct marketing, sponsorship, not to mention the Internet.

The '2005 Best Global Brands', a *Business Week* special report, described what was increasingly seen as an industry turnaround:

> the best brand builders are also intensely creative in getting their message out. Many of the biggest and most established brands, from Coke to Marlboro, achieved their global heft decades ago by helping to pioneer the 30-second TV commercial. But it is a different world now. The monolithic TV networks have splintered into scores of cable channels, and mass-market publications have given way to special-interest magazines aimed at smaller groups. Given that fragmentation, it's not surprising that there's a new generation of brands, including Amazon.com, eBay, and Starbucks that have amassed huge global value with little traditional advertising. They've discovered new ways to captivate and intrigue customers. Now the more mature brands are going to school on the achievements of the upstarts and adapting the new techniques for themselves. (*Business Week*, August 1, 2005).

This trend seems to be growing. According to Brand Channel's 2006 Reader's Choice survey, the top five brands in the world were Google, Apple, YouTube, Wikipedia and Starbucks, with Skype also in the top 10. Some of these salient contemporary brands have been built with little help from traditional advertising. In this context there is an increasing premium for innovation in advertising media. Thanks to the Internet, advertising might be going through what could be considered as its first true paradigm shift since the advent of television half a century ago. The Internet attracts an increasing amount of national advertisers, 'offline' media companies are redoubling their online efforts and advertising agencies and media buyers are scrambling to cope. Advertising remains a very powerful economic force and advertisers spend more than ever. But much of the growth occurs in California, in the headquarters of companies such as Google and Yahoo.

Integration is considered a major driving force in the transformations, as advertisers explore new avenues. Outdoor advertising is being used in innovative ways. Out-of-home advertising – including poster sites, billboards, ambient and even some 'guerrilla' street actions – was long considered a backwater for the advertising industry, but it is getting tougher to ignore as it branches out beyond the old-fashioned billboard. New technologies tend to transform outdoor ads, a sector which includes ads on buses and trains and now even coasters in bars. As advertisers find it harder to reach certain customers through television and radio, such as AB social class who tend to be light consumers of ad-financed TV and radio, the increasing array of advertising vehicles is looking more attractive.

Another area of growth is 'branded entertainment', where advertisers and broadcasting executives thoroughly plan television shows and movies to achieve maximum brand impact. The stated goal is to avoid traditional advertising's pitfalls, tightly weaving a brand or product into media content, trying to counter consumers' growing habit of *zapping*, *zipping* or otherwise avoiding traditional commercial pitches. *Business Week* echoed similar developments in 2005:

> some marketers have worked to make their brand message so enjoyable that consumers might see them as entertainment instead of an intrusion. When leading brands are seen on TV they're apt to have their own co-starring roles (. . .) rather than just lending support during the commercial breaks. All are trying to create a stronger bond with the consumer (*Business Week*, August 1, 2005).

Word-of-mouth and viral marketing are also mainstreaming. They have become 'an increasingly potent force, capable of catapulting products from obscurity into runaway commercial successes' (Dye, 2000: 139). Dye has explained the dynamics of buzz: 'people like to share their experiences with one another [. . .] and when those experiences are favourable, the recommendations can snowball, resulting in runaway successes' (Dye, 2000: 139; Gladwell, 2002). Brands experiment with the brave new world of the Web 2.0 and user-generated content, using blogs and social networking sites such as MySpace, Facebook or Twitter. Virtual reality outlets such as Second Life and the video game industry have also proved increasingly attractive destinations for marketers.

Throughout advertising history, commercial communication has often been a one-way street. Marketers advertised and disseminated messages, and customers were a passive target. Lack of audience interest turned into widespread consumer scepticism: we watch many advertisements but we totally ignore the majority of them. Major brands still spend billions telling customers what they don't want to hear. Among other authors, Jaffe (2007) argues that marketers must adapt to the world of the Internet, social networks, user-generated content, blogs and podcasts. It is a world of powerful conversations, where dialogue, participation and community are paramount (Tapscott and Williams, 2006). Such accounts urge marketers to get to know users as persons, not just as faceless and silent members of a demographic segment. The goal is promoting conversations, to talk with consumers, not at them, and get them talking about products, services and issues.

Mass media advertising has also suffered from accountability problems. Many clients, advertising practitioners and researchers complain about the inability to determine the return on investment from advertising spending. More than two centuries of advertising in media has not brought a significant improvement in that regard. Although the problem is already well known, advertising's lack of effectiveness has been the subject of considerable research in recent times. From the classic work by Franzen et al. (1999), there have been some interesting works on the topic, such as Fletcher (2008), Shaw and Merrick (2005), Kotler and Calder (2008) and Vollmer (2008). The conclusion could be summed up by saying that a significant proportion of advertising messages are not contributing to sales as expected. According to Briggs and Stuart (2006), as much as 37 per cent of overall advertising expenditures are a complete waste. Marketers don't seem ready to lose that much and increasingly turn to more direct ways of communicating with consumers. However, the appeal of mass media advertising remains strong as a cost-efficient means to reach target consumers. As TV audiences fragment and decrease, the value increases for the diminishing proportion of programmes with high ratings and audience profiles attractive to advertisers, such as big, live TV events. NBC advertising slots for the Super Bowl 2009, for instance, are selling for as much as $3 million for 30 seconds. Vranica (2007) discussed some implications of Super Bowl advertising, broadcast by Fox in 2008:

> [Fox] has only two spots left for Super Bowl XLII to be played February 3, which is giving Fox the upper hand in negotiations. Demand for Super Bowl spots is being driven, in part, by renewed interest among movie studios this year as well as the lack of TV programs that get big ratings nowadays, according to media buyers. Rates for 30-second spots have topped $2.7 million for this season's final game, according to media buyers, up from as high as $2.6 million last year. Before it is all over, some of the final slots for the championship game could sell for as much as $3 million.

Bradley and Bartlett (2007) have studied the implications of the new landscape for media strategies and explain that with the Internet's continued strength during the 1990s, advertisers started to use it to complement their offline campaigns. Later on, broadband improvements, mobile phone technologies, portable devices and user-generated content have created a world that leads advertisers to use such new vehicles as podcasts, online videos and blogs.

New competitors: the advertising industry meets Silicon Valley

Advertising media are changing. And advertising agencies also face new competition. The purchases of MySpace by News Corporation in 2005 and YouTube by Google in 2006 extended to new arenas the battle for audiences and their time, with increasing use of word-of mouth, 'buzz' and viral marketing, all Internet-based communication strategies. In April and May 2007, a new battle erupted between the Internet giants headquartered in the US West Coast (Microsoft, Google and Yahoo) and some of the largest advertising companies (WPP, Publicis, Interpublic) that do not want to lose their share of the creative revolution taking place on the web (Steel, 2007b). Google's search engine has become the vehicle for generating vast profits from advertising, as well as from charging for sponsored links in search results. Google's market share and the increasing sophistication of ad placement, poses a major threat to advertising and media agencies: it skips the classic intermediary role agencies have played. Google's recent deal to let Yahoo adopt its contextual advertising capability means Google could command as much as 90 per cent of the web's contextual advertising.

As the use of online strategies by advertising grows, the struggle to control the income generated is intensifying. The wave of acquisitions in online advertising was inaugurated in April 2007, when Google bought online advertising agency DoubleClick for $3.1 billion.

In May 2007, Microsoft acquired aQuantive, a company specialized in online advertising. At $6 billion this was the most expensive purchase in Microsoft's history, and it follows the pattern of similar acquisitions by Google, Yahoo and several advertising agencies. The online ad market has rapidly consolidated to become an oligopoly, with a handful of global companies dominating sales of the ads users watch on their Internet searches. There is a business model here based on search, online video downloads or banners in news and entertainment sites. But there is also a more novel form pioneered by Google using automated methods of advertising location that is playing a determinant role in the way advertising is planned in media such as television, radio and newspapers.

The day before Microsoft's announcement, advertising 'megagroup' WPP had announced a new acquisition: 24/7 Real Media was bought for $649 million. This company places ads near online searches by users. Industry experts consider that WPP was trying to counter DoubleClick's purchase. It has been the most aggressive move by the advertising industry to get close to the technological side of the business. For some executives, the ad business cannot afford to limit itself to creativity and media planning. Meanwhile, Yahoo bought Right Media for $680 million. In a similar operation, Digitas, a digital marketing agency, was acquired by the giant advertising group Publicis for $1,300 million in January 2007. In April, Interpublic bought Reprise Media, a company specialized in search tools. Yahoo made another move acquiring closely held online advertising company Blue Lithium for about $300 million in September 2007. Blue Lithium was founded in January 2004 and operates an online advertising network that buys graphical display ad slots, such as banners, on about 1,000 sites owned by other web publishers and resells the slots to advertisers (Delaney, 2007).

Advertisers have traditionally trusted agencies for their media placement and accepted their role as intermediaries. The advertising industry is concerned with the fact that companies such as Google, Microsoft and Yahoo are positioning themselves in the advertising market and consider it a 'Silicon Valley invasion'. The largest advertising agencies have increased their interest in the online world. Some advertising budgets have migrated from traditional media to the Internet. According to TNS, a leading advertiser such as General Motors has increased its Internet expenditure by 16 per cent, but has decreased 60 per cent in newspapers and 15 per cent in television. The industry is reluctant to lose the opportunities that come with the online world and it is determined to avoid giants such as Google, Yahoo or Microsoft taking control of the Internet advertising business. But Google has started to challenge those rules, placing ads next to online searches presenting an alternative model to advertising agencies. aQuantive, the company recently acquired by Microsoft, was established in 1997 and includes several online advertising businesses, including Avenue A/Razorfish, considered one of the largest Internet advertising agencies. The expected income for aQuantive in 2007 is as high as $615 million. Microsoft traditionally did not want to play a role in the advertising business. Its technological culture resisted some previous initiatives in the online advertising space. However, since 2005, Microsoft has increased its number of employees in this field and has turned online advertising into a priority. Top executives believed that in spite of some remarkable investments the company was losing market share to its more direct rivals, Google and Yahoo. Besides, Google beat Microsoft in the fight to purchase DoubleClick (Steel, 2007a).

The acquisition spree might be an indication of growth in the online advertising market. Search-related advertising already accounts for 40 per cent of total Internet advertising expenditures, which account for 7.4 per cent of the overall advertising expenditures in the US in 2006 (Table 3.1). There are only seven countries in the world where Internet advertising was above 7 per cent of total advertising expenditure in 2006, in spite of the medium's impressive growth. However, it is significant that three of those seven are among the four top advertising markets worldwide (US, Japan and the UK; the others being Denmark, Sweden, Norway and Canada). Internet advertising's share is already similar to such established media as radio and outdoor. But experts and industry insiders are impressed with its rate of growth.

Figures show US online advertising spending is poised to overtake radio advertising for the first time in 2009, but online is also an opportunity for radio:

> US radio ad spending is expected to inch up 1.5 per cent in 2007, to $20.4 billion, short of online ad expenditures of $21.7 billion, which will be up 22 per cent from last year (. . .). Over the next several years, radio station websites and online audio advertising will be the principal drivers for radio advertising growth (Hau, 2007b).

> Radio companies such as Clear Channel, CBS and Cox Radio continue to have massive audiences, but consumers are spending less time listening to radio than they do surfing the Internet or watching TV. Besides, only 17 per cent of US consumers consider radio the 'most' essential medium, down from 26 per cent five years ago, according to a study released by Arbitron and Edison Media Research (Hau, 2007b).

The rise of online video

Online video advertising is turning into an alternative for the 30-second spot. Some industry insiders believe it gives more depth and visibility to some campaigns, for half the price. According to them, the website is replacing the 30-second spot as the central expression of a brand. Marketers are showing increasing sophistication in their use of online video to create not just linear presentations that look like TV commercials, but interactive, virtual experiences. But many are also careful not to overstate the transition. The 30-second spot is weakened and threatened, but remains a successful and attractive mode of advertising. It is the enduring features of TV that makes the TV spot still so important: most audience segments are still engaged with TV. Online allows for a richer relationship for some key target audiences but this must be seen in the context of who is online and active. There is a debate between those who think that the web 'will never be a replacement for TV's reach and ability to create interest' and those who underline 'the depth of experience a website allows' (Klaassen and Mcilroy, 2007). At the same time, the significance of multimedia campaigns running across old and new media cannot be underestimated.

Google's acquisition of YouTube also highlighted online video. Nearly 10 months after the purchase, 'the video sharing website is rolling out its first approach for selling ads within videos [. . .] Resembling a popular ad model cropping up on a number of other video sites, YouTube's new format is a semitransparent ad that appears in the bottom 20 per cent of the video. The ad shows up after a video plays for 15 seconds, and disappears up to 10 seconds later if the viewer chooses to watch the ad; the main video pauses until the commercial stops' (Steel, 2007b). The format is a first step towards standardization in online video advertising and reflects concern to avoid online advertising that can be considered intrusive. YouTube:

> plans to sell these ads only on videos from its select content partners, whose original videos include professionally produced videos and user-generated content. The partners will earn a share of ad revenue. The system is similar to Google's AdSense network, which matches ads to the content of a network of web sites, and gives those sites a cut in the profits. (Steel, 2007b)

Online advertising takes advantage of the increasing interest in advertising that travels along the Internet as good-quality entertainment. Elliott (2007) comments on this trend: 'for generations, advertising interrupted the entertainment that Americans wanted to read, hear or watch. Now, in a turnabout, advertising is increasingly being presented as entertainment – and surprisingly, the idea of all ads, all the time, is gaining some favour'. The proliferation of Internet broadband connections makes it easier for computer users to download or watch video clips, and that is enabling media companies, agencies and marketers to create websites devoted to commercials and other forms of advertising as entertainment or amusement. YouTube has also shown the popularity of *good television commercials* on the Internet. That is the reason behind the launch of advertising websites such as veryfunnyads.com (Time Warner's TBS cable network), didja.com (NBC Universal's USA Network) and honeyshed.com (Publicis advertising agency). It is interesting to note that, as Elliott (2007) says:

> oddly, the trend runs counter to another powerful impulse among consumers: the growing desire to avoid advertising. TV viewers for instance, are spending millions of dollars a year for TiVo and other digital video recorders that help them zip through or zap commercials, and click-through rates for banner web ads are declining. (Elliott, 2007)

Still, for all its promise, online video generates only a very small share of advertising revenue. Viewership has exploded: around 135.5 million Americans watch online video at least once a month, up 19 per cent from last year according to eMarketer (2008). The online video advertising market is expected to surge to 89 per cent in 2008 to $75 million, but that will account for just 3.6 per cent of overall Internet ad expenditures. By 2011, the market is expected to expand more than fivefold to $4.3 billion, which would still only add up to slightly less than 10 per cent of total online advertising spending (Hau, 2007a). Advertising from streaming video and audio totalled about $1.37 billion last year, up 38 per cent from 2006. According to AccuStream iMedia Research, there were about 2.1 2.7 billion views of streaming or progressive-download content a month at ad-supported or free content areas on the web in 2007, excluding user-generated videos. Ads shown before streamed television shows are expected to grow substantially.

Web video has a long way to go before it rivals search marketing (not to mention TV commercials or print ads), much less the huge numbers achieved by television commercials. Besides, professionally produced programming remains the biggest potential draw for advertising dollars, also on the Internet. Online video shapes a different vehicle where a new type of dialogue with audiences takes place:

> most early attempts at online video advertising involved simply attaching a 30-second TV ad to the front of a video clip. But the industry quickly recognized that recycling an ad format originally meant for a half-hour or hour-long TV programming didn't work well for online clips that were often barely longer than the ad itself. (Hau, 2007a)

Social networking: markets as conversations?

Social networks are another promising venue for advertising as the most relevant social networking sites try to monetize their huge and growing user base. Social networks are a source of opportunities for advertisers, as they enjoy massive increases in participation, audience and time. Their ability to create and foster communities is also attractive to advertisers that look for trust. There are still limits to the use of promotional messages in social networks. A social networking website does not guarantee loyal viewership. Content cannot be controlled by marketers, since many users will say what they want; in addition, trust cannot necessarily be monetized. At the same time, critical scholars highlight the increasing reach of commercial communications into formerly non-commodified spaces and new opportunities for 'manipulation' as promotional messages are integrated into online communications (Chester, 2007; McChesney, 2004). So we can see how in advertising message distribution social networks are a source of opportunities and also challenges.

Clemons (2007) has defined four conditions for marketing communications to achieve loyalty with social networks. They need to be personal (interesting personally for the participant); participatory (providing opportunities for interaction); plausible and believable (online interactions have to follow some plausible rules); there has to be the possibility of physical transition (the ability to actually go from the online world to the real world is a plus). Three advertising venues are considered promising in this context: placing traditional ads on a website; using paid content placement (for example, paying to have Second Lifers, the virtual reality community members, wearing certain clothes or drinking certain beverages); and word-of-mouth advertising (e.g., paying a Facebook user to recommend your product).

How media shares are changing

In general, traditional media retain the highest share of advertising expenditure, but their share of media audience and advertising markets is declining. Looking at advertising expenditure by medium (Tables 3.1–3.3), we can analyse what has been happening in the last decade in the largest advertising market in the world (US), the two largest European Union markets (Germany and the UK), and the European Union at large.

Paid-for daily newspapers are losing ground, threatened by free newspapers and online news outlets. Terrestrial television now competes for a share with cable and satellite. By 2006, cable television's share of advertising expenditure in the US was over 12 per cent (Table 3.1). Digital Terrestrial Television (DTT) is successful in some quarters and in the UK, Freeview has the largest, and growing, share of the digital television market, in 38 per cent of UK homes' main TV sets compared to 34 per cent share for pay satellite (Ofcom, 2008: 211). However, the share of advertising across the analogue terrestrial television channels fell between 1995 and 2006 (Table 3.2). In Germany television's total share grew in the same period. Radio and outdoor advertising tend to remain stable or grow in the three markets (Tables 3.1–3.3). Growth has been strongest for Direct Mail and the Internet (Tables 3.1–3.3). In the case of the Internet, some have argued that expenditure tends to be underestimated when online display advertising is the only consideration, as this fails to take into account search-related advertising and the role some websites are playing as contact points for brands.

In Western Europe, among EU-15 (Table 3.4), print media's share of advertising has continued to decline over the period 1994–2006. Television has increased slightly, mostly because of the expansion of commercial television following deregulation of broadcasting markets. Radio and outdoor advertising have tended to remain stable or improve share. The Internet has emerged as a significant player confirming the trends apparent in the largest markets.

The proportion of total advertising expenditure allocated to radio varies considerably from country to country. Radio advertising's share has remained stable. North American markets are especially strong:

Table 3.1   Advertising expenditures by medium in the US (1995–2006)

	1995	2000	2006	Change 1995–2006 (%)
Dailies	34.1	29.8	24.9	–9.2
Magazines	11.2	10.3	9.1	–2.1
Broadcast TV	30.2	25.3	23	–7.2
Cable TV	5.3	8.6	12.3	7
Radio	10.2	11.2	10.5	0.3
Outdoor	1	2.6	2.9	1.9
Internet	0	4.2	7.4	7.4

Source: The European Advertising and Media Forecast, July 2006.

Table 3.2   Advertising expenditures by medium in the UK (1995–2006)

	1995	2000	2006	Change 1995–2006 (%)
Dailies	38.4	37.6	30.9	–7.5
Magazines	16.2	15.1	12	–4
Terrestrial TV	28.2	25.5	18.9	–9.3
Cable/Satellite TV	2	4.1	6.8	4.8
Radio	3.1	4	3.2	0.1
Outdoor	4.3	5.2	6.1	1.8
Internet	0	1.1	13.3	13.3

Source: The European Advertising and Media Forecast, July 2006.

Table 3.3   Advertising expenditures by medium in Germany (1995–2006)

	1995	2000	2006	Change 1995–2006 (%)
Dailies	45.9	43.2	39.9	–6
Magazines	18.5	17.7	16.6	–1.9
Television	20.9	24.1	24.6	3.7
Radio	3.7	3.7	4.1	0.4
Outdoor	3.3	3.8	4.7	1.4
Internet	–	0.8	3	3

Source: The European Advertising and Media Forecast, July 2006.

Table 3.4   EU-15 media share 1994–2006

Medium	1994	2006	Change (%)
Newspapers	37.8	31.4	–6.4
Magazines	17	14.5	–2.5
Television	27.8	29.5	2.1
Internet	–	5.7	5.7
Outdoor	4.6	5.4	0.8
Radio	4.3	5	0.7

Source: The European Advertising and Media Forecast, July 2006.

in 2006 Canada and the US attracted 12.4 per cent and 11 per cent respectively of all display advertising expenditure. This is partly due to the strength of media markets in North America generally, but also the popularity of radio and the high number of radio stations. By comparison, UK radio advertising takes a 3.4 per cent share, similar to Japan (. . .). Radio markets which have a higher level of public funding generally have a lower share of the advertising market. For example, in Germany, 80 per cent of radio funding came from public sources while the radio sector had a 4 per cent share of all advertising. (Ofcom, 2007: 4)

These shifts in the distribution of advertising indicate a profound challenge to the business models of some key media industries. Increasing competition also encourages media to build stronger brand identities, to achieve differentiation, to be relevant to their audience and get into advertisers' media plans Audiences have more choices and options and advertisers face an ever more diversified and fragmented media landscape, which is changing the ways in which media plans are devised. Traditional media do not risk being replaced immediately, but they are challenged. The fact that free newspapers already account for 11.8 per cent of total advertising spending in Germany or 9.6 per cent in France cannot be ignored (Table 3.5). The Internet is already a significant player in the overall market. Table 3.6 lists the countries where Internet advertising's share is above 2 per cent.

In general, print advertising is declining. The Internet 'is taking an increasing share of advertising [. . .]. The online share is largest in the UK at 14.4 per cent' (Ofcom, 2007: 2). However, it is still far from the levels achieved by print or television. In broadcasting, advertising spending is moving from terrestrial broadcasting to multichannel cable, satellite and DTT, as take-up in countries approaching digital switchover (The European Union has recommended a switchover of all television sets from analogue to digital by 2009) begins to accelerate: 'multichannel viewing in the UK increased from 20 per cent in 2001 to 33 per cent in 2006, rising faster than its European neighbours. Multichannel share in Germany stood at 30 per cent in 2006, while in France, Italy and Spain it ranged from 10 per cent to 14 per cent' (Ofcom, 2007: 3). As audiences go multichannel, advertising tends also to move from terrestrial to cable or satellite. Radio and outdoor tend to remain stable.

In such a media landscape, an adjustment to media planning practices is called for. Media planning will need to adapt to a media environment where *ratings*, *shares*, *GRPs* or *CPT* are less relevant. Instead, planners will need to track ever more complex and changeable patterns of media consumption and use.

Table 3.5   Free papers advertising expenditure as a percentage of total advertising expenditures in selected countries (2006)

	Free papers total advertising share (%)
Germany	11.6
France	10.1
Sweden	6.2
Finland	4.9
Denmark	2.5

Source: The European Advertising and Media Forecast, September 2007.

Table 3.6 Countries where Internet advertising is above
2 per cent in overall expenditures (2006)

	Internet advertising as per cent of overall expenditures
United Kingdom	13.3
Denmark	12.8
Sweden	12.4
United States	9.5
Norway	9.3
Japan	7.8
Canada	7.8
Netherlands	6.1
Hungary	4.7
Finland	3.5
France	3.2
Germany	3
Belgium	2.8
Czech Republic	2.8

Source: The European Advertising and Media Forecast, September 2007.

Conclusion

Both the media and advertising industries are undergoing momentous changes worldwide. The crisis of the 30-second spot and the weakening performance of traditional advertising-supported media such as terrestrial television, print and radio are having a profound influence. Advertising follows consumers. And consumers seem to be talking loud. They enjoy good ads, which travel increasingly around the Internet. But they do not like excess: 'overmarketing' is considered a danger. The increasing availability and expectation of on-demand media makes it increasingly difficult for advertising to appear as an interruption: increasingly consumers tend to be more in control, at least of their choice of when, and what, to consume. This is a situation brand managers should read correctly: it does not mean the end of advertising, but it is a whole new context, with significant implications for the way in which messages are conceived and media space is sold and planned. A better audience understanding will help companies in those industries to develop advertising strategies that are relevant to consumers. The emergence of new online advertising formats, innovative out-of home solutions and 'branded entertainment' will continue to draw researchers' and industry attention. This situation calls for new creativity and flexibility in the way advertising media plans are laid out.

4 Advertising research: markets, methods and knowing consumers

Iain MacRury

With thanks to Paul Cook, Managing Director
of Insight Bridge Limited, for his assistance

A stilted conversation

> Scientific advertising follows the laws of psychology. The successful
> advertiser . . . must understand how the human mind acts. He must
> know what repels and what attracts. (Dill-Scott, 1908:5)
>
> Know your brand: know your customer. (Lance and Woll, 2006: 17)

The principal means of market information for manufacturers or service providers is money or, rather, 'price'. The most frequent way consumers 'tell' producers what they think or feel about products or services is either by buying or by choosing not to do so. But price is typically a crude medium for communication. Poor sales, empty shelves or weakened profits do not easily direct producers or providers towards *how* better to adapt to changes in consumer demand (except by lowering or increasing prices). From a consumer's perspective, walking away from a shop empty handed does not fully express the detailed character of specific dissatisfactions; nor can non-purchase communicate any sense of what this or that consumer might have been prepared to pay for. If all we know or are concerned about in our relationship to a product is the price, then 'choice' becomes a perfunctory act.

Pricing is important but, on its own, it provides, at best a stilted 'conversation' between producers and consumers. Most kinds of consumer-market relationship can benefit from additional, more flexible and more animated forms of mediation and management than that provided by price alone.

Consumer research is one component in the work of mediating and managing market relationships; especially in relation to consumer goods and services but also, lately, in relation to other areas of provision such as social services, including health and education. Consumer research shares its intermediary role (connecting consumption to provision/production) in common with the other advertising functions, that is, distribution of product advocacy via selected media, advertisement design and brand development.

Consumer research inhabits, opens up and structures notional 'spaces' in the market place; spaces for various kinds of producer-consumer 'dialogue' – feedback, analysis, exchange and adaptation. This is a crucial complement to the price and profit information gathered by any business.

One further and highly relevant 'currency' in the transactions between producers and consumers is regularly measured by ongoing research. *Attention* (Davenport and Beck, 2001) is crucial to marketing communications. A major research agenda tracks how many people might see which ads how many times – as registered, for example, in relation to readership, circulation and broadcast audience figures. This is important knowledge, provided in detail by joint media and advertising bodies (Figure 4.2). Media research attempts to record and audit estimates of the *quantity* of audience attention. For TV this is rated in terms of opportunity to see (OTS) figures. For print ads this is tracked in relation to circulation and readership figures (provided by Audit Bureau of Circulation and JICNARS).

Advertising research is a component of the consumer research 'dialogue' and a contributory element to consumer-market research more generally. Research supporting advertising communications develops, elaborates and extends analyses of consumers, media and products to better inform communications and mediation. From one important perspective, advertising research opens up a kind of meta-analysis of the consumer–producer dialogue. As well as adding ideas about what consumers think and feel, advertising research offers answers to the question: How is the (brand) conversation going?

Such figures give a relatively accurate snapshot view, one which nevertheless does not extend to include other information: the thoughts, feelings and ideas that circulate around advertised products and brands. Considering the *quality* of attention paid to advertising – precisely who is watching, how they watch and what these various audience segments might think or feel, etc. requires more detailed examination. These are the preoccupations of much consumer and advertising research.

Research in everyday life: '8 out of 10 cats . . .'

The classic 'Eight out of Ten Cats prefer . . .' slogan has become part of the folkloric culture surrounding consumer research; not least in the title of a currently popular UK comedy quiz show.[1] The long-standing currency of this phrase registers a casual, widespread and slightly mocking familiarity with certain ideas about (consumer) research; a cultural familiarity inevitable after over half a century[2] of market surveys, consumer interviews and advertised product claims. It suggests that research is interested in basic questions: 'Which products?' and 'How many consumers?'

The many and major other kinds of consumer related research undertaken to support advertising (and adjunct promotional work) are only infrequently foregrounded[3] and certainly not in such a way as to produce data cited directly in ad slogans – as in the famous instance above.[4] Research is in fact largely a 'backstage' or, in some accounts, a 'hidden' operation.[5]

Nevertheless, 'research' has become an acknowledged and not infrequently encountered component of contemporary commercial-promotional culture. People contribute actively to consumer research, for instance by participating in occasional telephone or online surveys, or in on-street interviews – sometimes in return for a (small) incentive: part of the researchers' attempts to offset the sense of 'intrusion' into private space and personal time – and to gain trust.

In addition to research requiring active consumer engagement, there is a good deal of background monitoring and processing of consumer-related information. This 'data mining' requires little or no deliberate input (or detailed consent) from the individuals being tracked; for instance, when online or when supermarket customers use a Clubcard or other similar EPOS (Electronic Point of Sale) database-linked loyalty schemes or with some credit card transactions. A negative sense of 'surveillance' is sometimes provoked by such methods (Arvidson, 2004). Research companies collating and selling such data are successful in finding markets for such information. Often incentives are a part of the transaction, with miscellaneous personalised vouchers and reward 'points' allocated.

Online consumer-related activities are traced and tracked by 'cookies'; programmes allowing Internet activity to be recorded via the server that hosts the website. Useful data can be generated about web–based consumption by tracking a web-browsing consumer 'landing' on a page. This works especially well if the particular consumer has an account and is identifiable over numerous visits to a 'host' site.[6] It is possible to follow navigations from and through host and subsequent sites – and on to a purchase or other action (or inaction). Anderson (2006: 12) highlights the increasing research relevance of 'terabytes of user behaviour data' providing online marketers with vital clues about future consumer behaviour – especially in relation to e-commerce and entertainment cultures.

Some privacy issues attaching to this type of data capture come have under review (*Economist*, 2008). Web users, for instance, on social networking sites such as Facebook, become anxious about information collection – especially where it is understood that such data are sold on. The potential to gain detailed and quite intimate data means that there are large incentives for marketers tracking online data. The promise is a fuller grasp of 'mass' data from millions of users, but at levels of detail affording insights to an almost individual level. The purportedly immense commercial value of online social networking sites is in part related to the persuasiveness of claims about the value of consumer and market data. The quick and accurate measurement of online advertising effects – as clicks are tracked back to behaviour and purchase – offers a challenge to other forms of advertising where effects are less readily quantified.

Inside the agency: research and the advertising process

Some types of consumer and advertising research are less frequently encountered by the general population. The main aims, methods and practices of consumer and advertising research are rarely considered in any detailed way by advertising audiences, or by shoppers and service users. However, knowledge production and management functions are central to the advertising industry (Hackley, 2003). Carefully planned research has been pivotal in many successful campaigns (Green, 2005). Knowledge about consumers is systematically gathered by a growing research industry and is produced and represented in various forms.[7] Large-scale quantitative analyses enable agencies to re-envision shifting populations and predict consumer trends. Informal qualitative insights (might) spark a new advertising idea to help develop a client's brand.

Research is undertaken before, during and after most advertising campaigns. Research of various kinds is integral to most advertising processes and is a way of producing and managing information likely to be useful to advertising clients. It is equally useful to agency teams, for example in creative idea development or media planning. Media owners undertake research towards making evidence based claims for the efficacy of advertising via their particular medium or publication. This research helps encourage and justify media buyers' and clients' (further) advertising expenditures.

Research is used to better understand consumers; consumers grouped in sectors and niches and who are routinely conceived as mysteriously resistant to, or bored by advertising. 'The consumer', in all his or her variety, is typically conceived and apprehended as 'changing' – becoming older or adopting new 'lifestyle' patterns. Understanding consumers better can help with ideas about representing products more creatively and more acceptably in relation to specified niche target markets and can foster a kind of cultural attunement – the marketing equivalent of empathy – between producers and consumers.

A research client invests in the potential of a premium return for getting an 'edge' over competitor brands. An imaginatively placed ad or a well-tuned product claim might tap hitherto unthought-of consumer desires. Such 'edge' can be gained from an approach discovered via rigorous or innovative investigation of consumer cultures and media use. The attempt is to defeat market rivals – not to mention capturing consumers' cash. Research promises to find out something new and place the commissioning client ahead of the game.

For instance, a research-based advertising strategy for John Smith's bitter (Broadbent and Best, 2006) in the 1980s lead to a rejuvenation of the brand's image among an important group of young consumers. Research findings inspired a youth-friendly campaign to beat off competition from lagers and hand-pumped bitters. This 'contributed to a revenue increase of £5m in the pub trade alone . . . in a declining market' (Broadbent and Best, 2006: 102). The campaign helped John Smith against competitors who did not beat the market slump. Research laid the foundation for developing campaign ideas but also for tracking and presenting successful campaign outcomes.

Pre-testing and ad effects

Research is an ongoing part of ad agency work. It can be used to gather up general lessons – with some agencies maintaining knowledge banks – reference archives reflecting industry knowledge and, perhaps, reflecting the 'style' and success of the agency. Ideally, an advertising agency will maintain a system to gather insights and ideas in relation to a particular product sector or advertising approach to support new brand strategies or in advance of a new business pitch. This work can add credibility to an agency's claims to the client that:

- We know your business best
- We know your market best
- We know the media best
- We know advertising best
- We know the consumer best

Before a new campaign, or as a campaign is developed in a new way, the agency pre-tests ad ideas in order to try and assess what may or may not work.[8] Mock-up drawings might be shown to a sampled target group. For example, established users of the brand/product, or non-users who, it is hoped, will change their view of the brand because of the new advertising direction. Computer-based animated mock-ups can provide a more finished pre-test prompt – and with the same ends. The aim is to avoid making the finished ad (at some expense) only to discover, once broadcast, that audiences are indifferent to, or put off by the ad.

Pre-testing in contrived settings is open to the charge that they do not allow a real measure of real audience attention. In a 'focus' group we might pay attention to the ad. In among the media clutter, it could sink without trace. Attempts to test ads in the real media environment rely on limited 'localised' launches, for example, by means of local radio or TV channels or in regional press. These serve as pilot tests and are undertaken in advance of risking and investing in a national or international media roll out. There are pitfalls here too. Local conditions can intervene to skew results. What plays well in Newcastle might fail in London and vice versa. International variations provide yet more uncertainty. The validity of conclusions drawn about national audiences based on local evidence cannot be guaranteed. International audiences provide, of course, yet more variability.

The Internet offers a recent further alternative. Pre-releasing ads online can yield useful information about audience responses. This can support decisions about extending main media dissemination and encourage higher volume investment in main media ad space – with the pre-release viral spread serving as an *ad hoc* pre-test. This cannot easily predict impacts on some effectiveness measures, such as sales, but can give a sense of popularity and indicate potential 'cult' appeal.

In 2007 Cadbury attributed some sales and profits success to an unlikely advertisement featuring a man in a gorilla-suit and playing a drum kit to the tune of Phil Collins' song *In the Air Tonight*. The ad was launched on TV during the final episode of cult youth TV show, *Big Brother*. This decision was reached after the ad had generated interest on sites such as YouTube.

Pre-testing to assess real market effects on sales or brand preference can be quite inaccurate. However, testing can assist in ensuring a very bad idea or a bad execution is amended. Pre-tests can reassure the client that it has not commissioned something useless or damaging for the brand. As with other kinds of research there is a twofold aim:

- to find out what does or does not 'work' with a creative idea and as measured against more or less formal objectives (e.g. audiences liking the ad, changing attitudes to the brand, etc.).
- to provide some limited reassurance that investment in ad production and media space will not be wasted.

Once any ad is released, monitoring, testing and research continue. Effects research is used by advertisers – in cooperation with the contracted ad agency – to track and monitor campaign outcomes. Various measures of effectiveness are used to answer questions such as:

- Have more people (in this market) bought the product since we began advertising in this new way?
- Are younger people expressing positive attitudes about the brand following the new ads (placed online)?

As with any kind of audit or target-based system of evaluation, there can be doubts about the validity of analysis; especially regarding selection of the indices of success and failure, such as sales, ad recall or a shift in expressed brand preference among representatives of a target group. Sophisticated statistical methods and acute estimates are required to disentangle advertisement-related effects from other significant variables – such as weather, competitors' marketing activity, prevailing economic conditions and, where relevant, cultural and promotional events – such as PR-based product exposure, the Olympics or World Cups. Having disaggregated such contributory factors (e.g. the negative impact of a wet summer to barbeque sales, an Olympic Gold medal rush on bicycle purchases or the contribution of World Cup success to the home lager market) an assessment is made of a particular campaign's impacts. By reducing advertising outcomes to one or two measurable indices (e.g. sales or recall), and as advertising agencies might argue, there is, however, a likelihood that other longer-term and deferred effects, such as brand building for the next generation, might be undervalued. This can limit creativity and so, arguably, stunt more deep-seated advertising-based contributions to brand development, with agency teams encouraged to go for the tactical hit – with a high impact memorable ad – rather than developing more sophisticated and longer lasting communications interventions. On the other hand, where there is little measurable immediate ad impact it can be hard to argue that future positive effects will nevertheless accrue.

From a client point of view, it is important to be able to identify value for money in relation to advertising communications strategy – to make judgements about how to apportion marketing and promotional budgets. Effectiveness research is a means for translating the complex and ineffable potential impacts of an advertising campaign back into a quantifiable set of outcomes, such as actual sales, brand image recall, propensity to buy, preference shifts, etc. Such research diminishes advertising creatives' sense of themselves as 'artists' by tightly contextualising advertising creativity in commercial marketing discourses. This is one source of a traditional negativity towards research within the industry. Creativity-oriented advertising agencies and their staff seek to highlight the diffuse and intangible 'impacts' of their work. Research emphasises mainly those benefits that can be captured and credibly represented to the client. The tension between 'art' and 'the bottom line' structures much advertising industry discourse and strategic debates about brand strategy (Nixon, 2003)

There can be tensions and conflicts over a given advertising strategy. A client Marketing Director may object to a particular image or line of copy: a talented creative might insist on the centrality of this or that stylistic choice to 'the vision of the brand'. Research and dialogue can sometimes productively inform the context of such debates and disagreements. For example, advertising pre-tests might affirm the 'just rightness' of a particular creative direction: however, this without necessarily determining final decisions.

The high cost of media-based advertising campaigns ensures that advertising clients will seek to invest only where it is clear that credible steps are taken to offset the risk that an advertising campaign might fail. In this case clients pay for various kinds of 'defensive' research; to monitor, assure or enhance the effectiveness of their investment in an advertising strategy; or else they suggest that the advertising or media agency offer such monitoring as part of the campaign package. This is a central part of the dynamics of client-agency accountability and partnership. Such formal types of performance-related accountability became especially popular in the late 1980s and 1990s, when financial directors and accountants typically began to influence decisions on the client side and within advertising agencies.

Online advertising offers new opportunities to those seeking close analysis of ad effectiveness – and checks of return on advertising investment. With click through and search–engine based advertising, such as provided by Google, the links between advertisements, behaviour and sales effects are more readily traceable. Advertising research is returned to its origins via such online technologies which mimic a traditional research process recommended in 1910 by Claude Hopkins.[9] He suggested that the best way to test and monitor newspaper advertising effects was to ensure that readers were invited to return a cut-out coupon to the advertiser. By counting coupon returns it was possible for advertisers to estimate the success or failure of advertising copy (Hopkins, 1910/1966: 231–2) and act accordingly – to improve future performance. The opportunity to measure correlations between some online advertising interventions and consumer behaviours directly is contributing to the relative success of online advertising in attracting clients' marketing expenditure.

Within the advertising agency[10] the research function is typically carried through by an account planner, someone who operates to better interlink clients', creatives' and con-sumers' preoccupations and priorities. Planners are described as specialist 'intermediaries' or 'interlocutors' (Hennion and Meadel, 1989), producing creative dialogues between different participants and moments within promotional processes and strategies – helping to maintain dialogue between producers (advertisers) and consumers (audiences). This role emerged in the late 1960s. Planners have been credited with providing a perspective and a resource within agencies that has enabled advertising to develop creatively – while benefiting from some of the rigours and insights afforded by various kinds of useful research.

Figure 4.1   Research linking production and consumers has been a feature of the advertising industry's offer to its clients since the early decades of the twentieth century. Courtesy of the J. Walter Thompson Company.

Production and consumption: 'A thing, but destined for someone'

Advertising emerged both as a consequence of and as a response to the changing geographical structure of consumer markets (Presbrey, 1929). As factory based mass production increased, and as populations moved increasingly to live in cities, the close link between local production and local consumption was severed in many product sectors – from food to clothes and so on. Later, and as scientific and industrial progress enabled high volume production of new technologies (washing machines, TVs, cars, PCs and mobile phones among many others) yet more product sectors came to market from distant factories.[11] Concurrently, the globalisation of trade in agricultural and manufactured products had further widened the distributive gap between the place of production and the place of consumption.

One consequence has been that in modern society producers and consumers are structurally relatively *anonymous* to one another. Just as we do not know a great deal about the origins of products (except through packaging and media-based information), so producers are conscious of knowing less than they would like to about the nationally and globally distributed consumers who are the 'destination' for what they have made.

Nineteenth-century economist Walter Bagehot highlighted the following principle in relation to the relationship between producers and consumers:

Table 4.1   Overview and summary: major functions, general types and broad aims/
approaches in advertising research

Main aims and focus	*Main intended research outcomes*	*Typical information sources and research methods*
Product/brand analysis: i.e. finding out the main relevant characteristics of product or brand image	• Increased understanding of the changing product sector and broad shifts in brand image or position	• Briefings from client research can be supplemented by product and market sector analysis (e.g. MINTEL, TGI or ONS panel data) • Coverage in relevant trade and consumer press provide further background
Competitor analysis	• Improved grasp of the 'field' of similar products and more detailed sense of similarities and differences between competitors. Sense of competitors' relative strengths and weaknesses	• Analytic audit of competitor advertising using press cutting or online resources such as 'Creative Club' • Comparative product and market sector analysis (e.g. via MINTEL, TGI data) • Formal or informal comparative brand-image / product analysis can be incorporated into consumer research work
Consumer research (general)	• Increased and updated knowledge and understanding of the ongoing and changing needs, desires and preferences of relevant consumers – especially as related to the product / service at hand • Broad brush trends and shifts apprehended • More intimate experiences/ thoughts captured and recorded • Contributions to developing ideas to capture consumer attention and interest in subsequently developed advertising communications – perhaps inspiring or affirming a new approach / direction • Getting 'underneath' everyday rationalisation and conventional explanations of motives and choices to find out about other more compelling motivations, desires or anxieties	• Quantitative consumer survey data (TGI, MINTEL, etc.) helps to track shifts in consumers' purchasing patterns and attitudes to the brand / product • Past advertising evaluation and effectiveness can be reviewed e.g. using awareness studies • Formal and informal qualitative research, such as interviews or focus groups, involving various responses to visual and other prompts can provide instances of the consumer 'voice' or provoke arresting idiosyncratic stories relevant to the brand • The implicit motivations and dispositions driving consumer habit and choice can be articulated by consumers and captured using sensitive and attentive practices of active 'listening' to gently guided individual or group conversations • Projective techniques invite respondents respond to prompts – often, in descriptions of other people, scenes or images reveal interesting aspects of respondent's relationship to the product/service at hand

Continued over the page . . .

Table 4.1   Overview and summary – *continued*

Main aims and focus	Main intended research outcomes	Typical information sources and research methods
Advertisement/ Pre-testing: i.e. showing ad to a sample audience	• Finding out how audiences might respond to the advertisement and trying to predict the impact such responses might have in reality once the ad is finally broadcast/ circulated • Testing general specific measures of ad effect and impact • Providing insight to help adjust/ improve, re-edit or re-shoot ad elements	• Local real tests: Here an ad is broadcast in the 'real' market place but in a limited area – say a small local TV or radio broadcast region. Local assessments are of the ad's impact on sales and/or attitude and extrapolated to the wider target audiences • Laboratory / theatre tests: sample audiences watch the ad in closed conditions • Concept testing: ad elements are mocked up – prior to production – and assessed with input from sample audience members, e.g. in focus groups
Media research	• Establishing the best media mix • Ensuring ad is seen in the right times/places and by selected target groups	• ABC figures for press provides circulation data • Joint industry and media bodies assure audience / readership data • Media owners commission and disseminate research about their audience composition and profile Planners and media buyers need to evaluate and assess these research claims • Consumer research will suggest affinities between target groups and new media options • These can be cross referenced with TGI data
Advertising effectiveness measures	• Establishing if a campaign has given value for money as defined by pre-agreed measures • Assessing if the agency has done a good job • Informing changes and new strategies or justifying the status quo (i.e. carrying on as before)	• Analysing sales data to track impact on price and sales cross referenced with ad spend, campaign 'bursts' and 'drips' • Qualitative work with small target groups to gain detailed sense of changing attitudes and propensities to buy/recommend the advertised product • Street or telephone surveys to test levels of attention, recall and attitude shifts • Online brand image monitoring using online surveys
Zeitgeist / 'spirit of the times'/ futures research	• Capturing key new features characterising a generation or an era defined with a specific focus on technological developments, emerging social changes ('the 'me' generation or 'tweens' i.e. youths aged between 8–12 years) • Prophesying future trends to 'get ahead of the game' • Such work might convince clients that agencies are imaginative, forward looking and able to grasp dynamic change	• Various kinds of future trends analysis, from 'cool hunters' picking out future 'from the street' trends using ethnographic observation to culturally inspired predictions drawing on niche literatures of the recent past/present (cyberpunk) to help characterise future social scenarios • Detailed quantitative projections and extrapolations using statistical data to chart and anticipate changing familial compositions, household structures, population peaks and troughs

. . . as every producer is mainly occupied in producing what others want, and not what he wants himself, it is desirable that he should always be able to find, without effort, without delay, and without uncertainty, others who want what he can produce. (Lombard Street, Walter Bagehot, Chapter 6)

This principle is basic to questions of logistical distribution, inventory management and marketing. It is useful too in understanding advertising and consumer research, which is an investment in knowledge designed to minimise the effort in 'finding others who want' what is produced. Overcoming this anonymity is the goal of much consumer and advertising research and is linked to three main advertising and branding functions:

- building trust
- providing information
- optimising distribution

Hennion and Meadel (1989) characterise the advertising agency as 'a laboratory of desire'. By combining creativity and applied consumer, media and product insights, the agency re-produces the advertised product in re-presentations as 'a thing, *but destined for somebody*' (Hennion and Meadel, 1989: 175, emphasis added). The agency develops image-based characterisations of the product or appropriate 'brand personalities' via engagement with research.

Sifting knowledge and insights relating to the product to be advertised can require detailed research; perhaps involving detailed manufacturers' briefings, visits to manufacturing plants, product sampling and analyses of the symbolic meanings and 'position' of competitor brands. Of equal importance is accurate and intimate knowledge of consumers; knowledge about people who might buy, use or desire the object advertised – the 'someone' for whom the product is 'destined' (Hennion and Meadel, 1989: 175). Research aims, in many cases, to help agencies answer quite concrete questions. For instance:

- 'Which combinations of media offer the best opportunities to capture the attention of male school-leavers?'
- 'What celebrities might be credible endorsers for finance products aimed at women aged 18–21?'
- 'What day-time TV programme would be good for a growing client (e.g. a new adventure travel company) to sponsor?'

Research is managed within individual agencies and across holding corporations' businesses to enhance the general and specific knowledge base of the corporation. Likewise advertising clients, media agencies and owners – the industry as a whole – depend upon research to inform but also to promote new ideas and new activities. Thus the IPA, the Advertising Association in the UK, ESOMAR[12] in Europe and WARC (The World Advertising Research Centre) worldwide, are among the bodies working to generate a corpus of advertising and research-based knowledge.

This institutional structure and the body of knowledge attached to it provides a degree of legitimacy in relation to claims made by the research industry, i.e. that its component agencies have rigorous and professional skills and that these are deployed ethically in relation to the industry's primary functions: the provision of rigorous data to assist clients in the navigation and management of consumer demand.

The Market Research Society works in the UK to maintain and disseminate standards and principles guiding consumer researchers' professional conduct and practice. The

Table 4.2   Some key UK bodies producing media and advertising related research

Audit Bureau of Circulations (ABC)
UK circulation auditing body for press, exhibitions, databases and electronic media

Broadcasters Audience Research Board (BARB)
Research body providing facts and figures on TV advertising

Cinema and Video Industry Audience Research (CAVIAR)
Audience research survey for the UK cinema industry

National Readership Surveys (NRS)
Research body providing readership data for newspapers & magazines

POSTAR
Research body providing data on poster advertising

PPA Marketing
Provides information on advertising in consumer magazines

PPA Professional
Provides information on business-to-business magazines

Radio Advertising Bureau (RAB)
Research body providing facts and figures on radio advertising

Radio Joint Audience Research (RAJAR)
Provides audience research data for radio

Thinkbox
Marketing body for the UK commercial television industry.

UK Association of Online Publishers
Promotes the online publishing industry

World Advertising Research Centre (WARC)
A global online database for advertising, marketing and media professionals

As outlined by the Advertising Association http://www.adassoc.org.uk/html/uk_websites.html

MRSs work to minimise instances of poorly designed, poorly conducted and inaccurately presented research. This body maintains commitments to protocols regarding respondent anonymity and helps to minimise sharp practices, such as SUGGING (selling under the guise of research), instances of which harm the reputation of the research industry – an industry which, from its centres in the UK and US, is now extending globally.

As a field of enquiry 'consumer research' and its various adjuncts and offshoots – examining media use, attitudes to brands and products, purchase behaviours and habits – is united primarily by its objectives (marketing and brand building) and its central objects (consumers and consumption). The aim is to know the consumer: to understand, map and navigate 'demand' and 'desire'. It is this rather than any common philosophy or method that lends coherence to the consumer-research endeavour taken as a whole. The range and richness of such work emerges from the interplay of approaches drawing on and linking to academic traditions and methods as diverse as ethnography and neuroscience (Du Plessis, 2005), semiotics and behavioural psychology, social policy and creative writing.[13] Equally, however, scepticism can undermine confidence in research pursued – sometimes very rapidly and to order – on behalf of powerful clients in a sometimes tense commercially focused environment this, especially, when there is such variety in the methods and theories called upon to frame and validate researchers' conclusions. This is of particular relevance in relation to the global extension of markets – and attendant research practices.

Changing markets: growing glocal

There are two major changes in the structure of markets that have direct consequences for research practice in the twenty-first century. One is the Internet. This appears to shrink distances. The gap between producer and consumer seems in many ways to have been reduced to a click. Consumers are seemingly less remote and less anonymous. The second is globalisation. This process means that wider geographical gaps between producers and consumers emerge. The networks linking marketplace to marketplace and manufacturer to consumer seem, however, to become closer and denser. These new terrains require navigation. Consumer researchers – working for growing global corporations – offer up valuable knowledge of global and local consumers.

In September 2008, the world's top marketing, advertising and opinion researchers met to discuss and share ideas at a conference themed 'Frontiers'.[14] With over 1,000 delegates from 60 nations, the conference included 100-plus speakers from 20 countries. The event, one of numerous such conferences, is testimony to the scale and reflective productivity of a research industry whose global annual turnover was US$24,618m in 2006 (Boyce, 2008: 1). Projected continued consumer-research expenditure growth[15] will be stimulated by rapid expansion in new market economies, notably in China, India and also in Latin America and Eastern Europe (Boyce, 2008: 2).

There is a powerful wish, particularly on the part of global corporations and their investors, to better understand consumers across the globe. Research companies, for instance Mintel and TNS,[16] operate within and across national markets. These very large research operations work – at times on a global scale – to help marketers understand and engage local consumers. Market research of various kinds serves the globalisation project.[17]

Advertisers, media and brand owners continue to commission various kinds of work to better help understand consumers – including, lately, a good deal of anthropologically inspired research worldwide (Sutherland and Denny, 2007). There is an increasing investment in looking at and listening to the significant minutiae of the global-everyday. Global marketers and advertisers, whether promoting a new banking service, a rock band on tour or a shampoo, confront a basic dilemma: how to manage the tension between global standardisation and local adaptation (Kjeldgaard and Askegaard, 2006: 524). Research offers to play a useful role here.

One global brand marketer preoccupied with the global vs local consumer dilemma – in the context of selling Johnson and Johnson's products – suggests:

> Global advertising is not trivial stuff nor is it for the fainthearted penny-pinchers. It calls for consumer insights from ongoing market research, to the testing of commercials . . . Incorporating appropriate consumer feedback early on is an investment that saves a lot of grief later, and protects many a brand. (Kumar, 2003)

Such pleas (and the attendant advice) are persuasive to advertisers and marketers anxious about making investments in international markets. Consumers are unpredictable and complex in any market. Developing successful communications with consumers in new markets depends upon a confident grasp of local specificities, to avoid costly errors. Knowing consumers means to know them in contexts, of culture, geography and economy. Good consumer research aims to address the gaps in knowledge of new markets and to test the assumptions upon which acknowledged advertising and marketing practices are based.

There is some significant and credible analysis (Kemper, 2003; Mazzerella, 2003) that raises a number of questions about the applicability of research techniques and assumptions about 'the consumer' (taken as an abstracted and unitary category) when applied wholesale across international borders and cultural boundaries, that is, across some of the 'Frontiers' highlighted by the ESOMAR conference. Mazzerella (2003) illustrates this by contrasting the fortunes of two well-known global brands marketing in India in the 1990s: Coke and Pepsi. Coca Cola attempted to sell its product on the back of a version of its then current global campaign – based on a mistaken premise, that 'global teens' were, at base more or less, and in relevant respects 'the same'. This was an assumption extrapolated from a global research approach, investigating the 'global teen'. The resultant ads were bland. They privileged the general over the specific. Globally appealing imagery featured instead of imagery touching local teenagers' concerns.

At the same time, Pepsi, like Coke a well-known, competitive global brand, had entered the market. Their informal research had prompted them to use Indian celebrities to lead a spectacular campaign (Mazzerella, 2003: 219–20) better attuned to its local contexts. In working to balance a global brand with a local market, as Mazzarella reports, 'Pepsi's scrappy, localised approach appeared to have got the equation right' (Mazzarella, 2003: 220).

Kumar (2003) and Mazzarella (2003) write from slightly different perspectives. Both highlight one important point. Applying demographic and lifestyle categories originating in the UK or US, in India or China or Venezuela, can lead to misconstruction of local demand. Globally-oriented work, if it is to yield real insights, requires complex local negotiations in interpretation of data and in the implementation of research. Globally validated research practices can be adapted to produce locally relevant knowledge. However, it is important that theoretical ideas and working assumptions about 'the consumer' are rethought in the context of concrete practices; real, local, market and consumption contexts and priorities.

In the longer established consumer marketplaces, notably the US and UK, and as with advertising expenditure more generally (Advertising Association/WARC, 2007; MacRury, 2009a), there has been slower growth in expenditure on consumer research. That said, over 70 per cent of all global expenditure on advertising and market research takes place in Europe and North America. It is in such 'saturated' consumer marketplaces that the researchers' promise to provide clients with a 'competitive marketing advantage' is taken as a convincing rationale for further investments in understanding the consumer. The novelty of online modes of research, along with anxieties connected to operating within the relatively newer virtual marketing terrain, have together provided further favourable conditions for those companies providing this type of research in particular. Globalisation, e-commerce and the Internet have necessitated some reflection and revision in the theory and practices of consumer research.

Researching consumers: people and populations

Consumer research does two different things in order to address contemporary large-scale, widely distributed and highly variegated consumer market places. Researchers work to understand *populations*. They want, also, to understand *people*. These are not unrelated tasks. The distinction between people and populations marks separate but connected conceptions. Populations are aggregated and statistical constructions – of groups of people – generated from the collation and comparison of quantitative facts (such as age and income) about individuals, as well as from a number of conventional categorisations, notably ethnicity and social class. Many such measures are probabilistic. This means that they provide only a sense of the likelihood that there will be a correlation between one variable (e.g. age) and others (e.g. the propensity to express a preference for a particular brand, to read a newspaper and to earn a certain amount of money per month).

'People' denotes a more human scale in thinking about consumers.[18] The distinction (from population) highlights a focus aimed at the research-driven exploration and articulation of individual differences – registered at a more personal level; this rather than in the abstracted and aggregated language of statistical representation. These two broad orientations have lead to the adoption and adaptation of different types of research, notably quantitative and qualitative methods. These research methods are tailored to different conceptions of the consumer, to different conceptions of the market and to different versions of how advertising operates.

Typically different methods and approaches are used in complementary and synthetic ways. Some elements of a research programme will use quantitative methods in describing the bigger picture using statistical measures, for example, to compare variations in consumer habits across populations. Another qualitative research element in the same research programme might focus on more specific explorations of selected individuals to provide deeper, unanticipated and more idiosyncratic conceptions of consumers' various needs, wants and desires.

Segmentation: describing and constructing the aggregated consumer

A key research objective for media and consumer research is segmentation. Identifying market segments informs advertising practice at every level. While the consensus in much social theory is that population segments are dispersed and fragmenting in a society that has changed radically in recent decades, it is also the case that advertising and consumer research practices continue to be guided by conventional social categorisations. Thus, media and other market-place analyses – and guiding discourses – continue to respect long-standing and conventional population segmentation. Table 4.3 is a helpful outline of the broad level groupings of the UK population in 2003 as presented by one influential consumer research provider, Mintel.

In working practices, and notwithstanding limitations in such categorisations, consumers are understood to represent and to be represented in such categories. These reflect measures of socio-economic class, but also of age, gender and region. Such demographic segmentations are used to help advertisers differentiate groups, for example, when selecting media. Media audiences are described largely in terms of such segments. Thus, *Cosmopolitan* is largely read by 'ABC1 females'.

Consumers: people, neighbourhoods and places

The UK's single largest source of research data comes from the Census, which is conducted every 10 years (last conducted in 2001), the completion of which is a legal requirement for the whole population. It provides the benchmark 'base data' for the majority of proprietary consumer segmentation tools. It also provides the most accurate base-line for predictions of population growth by geography.

The immense volume of available data lends itself to robust research analysis of even the smallest geographic areas, the uses of which are both diverse and sophisticated including sizing target audiences, optimising store location placement, profiling campaign respondents, setting localised store ranges and assessing appropriate local media.

The inherent nature of neighbourhoods and the concept that 'birds of a feather flock together' means that it is now easy to understand the relationship between geography and people.

In the past, researchers had to rely on aggregated information relating to large areas (perhaps 500–1,000 households) that inherently offered, at best, only a mediocre level of generalisation. Marketers seeking to both analyse and target very specific customer groups now have a huge array of proprietary consumer classifications including geodemographics

Table 4.3   Major demographic research categories for UK population segmentation (2003)

GB population profile, by demographic group, 2003
Base: adults aged 15+   *(%)*

Total	100
Men	49
Women	51
Age group	
15–19	7
20–24	8
25–34	18
35–44	19
45–54	16
55–64	13
65+	19
*Socio-economic group**	
AB	24
C1	28
C2	21
D	18
E	10
Television regions	
London	20
South	9
Anglia/Midlands	24
South West/Wales	11
Yorkshire/North East	16
North West	12
Scotland	9
Working status	
Working	52
Not working	26
Retired	22
Marital status	
Married	63
Not married	37
Presence of children	
Children 0–15	28
No children	72

Note: Data may not equal totals due to rounding
*MINTEL offers a useful definition of these heavily used demographic categories:
Socio-economic group
Socio-economic groups are based on the head of household or chief income earner and are defined as follows:
Socio-economic group   Occupation of chief income earner
A   Higher managerial, administrative or professional
B   Intermediate managerial, administrative or professional
C1   Supervisory or clerical, and junior managerial, administrative or professional
C2   Skilled manual workers
D   Semi and unskilled manual workers
E   All those entirely dependent on the state long term, through sickness, unemployment, old age or other reasons
Retired persons who have a company pension or private pension, or who have private means are graded on their previous occupation.
Source: Mintel.

(e.g. Mosaic, ACORN and Cameo), lifestyles (e.g. Personicx), plus an ever increasing array of individual lists with approximately 300 + variables relating to an individuals' product and service consumption patterns (e.g. Acxiom's Lifestyle Universe or Experian's Canvasse Lifestyle).

These tools enable targeting at household and even person level, having become vital information sources for advertisers, retail planners, door-to-door and target marketing companies, and are central to much consumer analysis.

Experian's Mosaic UK, one of the most widely used of these tools, uses a variety of Census, lifestyle, property, shareholding, credit and geographic data to classify each of the 24 million UK households into one of 11 groups, 61 types and 243 segments. It describes each of these distinct household types taking into account their financial, media, purchasing and lifestyle behaviours.

Many of these classifications are used to aid store location planning within large retailers and are commonly held as additional fields on databases for the purposes of relationship marketing, campaign selection and customer profiling.

The central premise behind many of these tools is that people who live in the same neighbourhoods will share some of the same needs, desires, purchasing motivations and lifestyle habits. However, it is important to note that much of the household level used in these tools is modelled (inferred) on the basis of patterns established in 'similar' areas – i.e. because one neighbourhood area acts in a particular way, it is inferred that similar areas might also act in this way.

Quantitative data of this type does not seek out the truth about each and every household or individual. Instead, such tools try to predict the most accurate and reliable probability-based 'picture' of the characteristics most prevalent within the neighbourhood, postcode or household. Quantitative research such as this provides valuable consumer insight supported by large sample sizes (a common downfall of qualitative research), and provides the ability to both analyse and target each and every household with the appropriate advertising message.

These segmentations are also incorporated into a wide variety of advertising and media planning tools, and can be used to profile respondents found on surveys such as TGI, NRS, MORI and Hitwise.

Surveys: monitoring and understanding trends

As well as understanding the connection between consumer preferences and geography, it is also vital to monitor changes in consumer's habits, motivations and attitudes over time. One way to do this is to use longitudinal data, i.e. data gathered over long periods of time using regularly repeated questions and approaches. The Family Expenditure Survey and the National Food Survey are both large-scale, consumption-related longitudinal studies carried out by the UK government. They include data from large numbers of respondents and are updated regularly. This allows for rigorous analysis of shifts in behaviour over time.

The FES is primarily a survey of household expenditure on goods and services, and household income. It provides an invaluable supply of economic and social data to central government, to other public and commercial organisations and to researchers in universities and independent research institutions.

The basic unit of the survey is the household and in 2000–2001, 6,637 households took part in the FES. The response rate was 59 per cent in Great Britain and 56 per cent in Northern Ireland.

Data is collected throughout the year to cover seasonal variations in expenditures. In addition to expenditure and income data, the FES collects information on socio-economic characteristics of the households, e.g. composition, size, social class, occupation and age of the head of household. (Family Expenditure Survey ONS)

For instance, in 2003, Weetabix, a well-known breakfast cereal, was considering its brand strategy. The role of large-scale quantitative data is made clear in the following excerpts for a post campaign effectiveness report:

Fundamental changes in consumer attitudes and behaviour were threatening the long-term commercial value of family staple breakfast cereals and ushering in dramatic growth for so-called 'Repertoire Brands'. The Weetabix brand faced a very real challenge in sustaining its longer-term commercial value, let alone moving ahead to become market leader. (Alford *et al.*, 2004: 1)

This diagnosis, identifying a specific problem facing the product sector, was validated by consulting large-scale quantitative measures. Recognition of negative impacts on the Weetabix brand's growth was understood with reference to ONS data. This revealed that:

By 2003 Family Food Panel measured that single sitting breakfast only accounted for 66 per cent of all breakfast occasions.

And that,

The Office of National Statistics [had] counted 6.86 million single-person households in 1998 and estimated this to grow to 7.42 million by 2003. (Alford *et al.*, 2004: 1fn)

These facts supported the following strategic analysis:

The fragmentation of single-sitting family breakfasts meant that repertoires [e.g. cereal bars eaten on-the-go] were growing to meet the individual needs of a family often eating breakfasts apart. For a brand the scale of Weetabix the fragmentation of the family breakfast posed a considerable threat and meant that the brand had to re-assert a role that worked across the modern family. And beyond the family, the rise of single person households likewise posed a threat to a family staple cereal traditionally positioned around family consumption. (Alford *et al.*, 2004: 1)

This strategic insight, perhaps also a matter of intuition linked to a developed sense of the Zeitgeist, could only be validated in relation to large-scale research. This was done successfully and assisted in developing some effective ads. Campaign effectiveness reports outlined the impact that these insights made to a change in brand and advertising strategy. The ensuing campaign:

. . . helped establish Weetabix as the number one in value sales for the first time in its . . . 70-year history; and, in so doing, [it]will have generated an estimated £31.46 million in extra revenues by the end of July 2005. (Alford *et al.*, 2004)

There are further and more focused quantitative data sources, which are tailored more closely to the specifics of product and market sectors. For instance, reports produced by Mintel, Keynote, Verdict or Datamonitor offer detailed and timely data designed to be valuable to the marketing industry. A recent report (Mintel, 2008) is characteristic of insightful work considering particular emerging trends and lifestyle sub-segments. The research makes a largely quantitative analysis of the attitudes and behaviour of what Mintel dubs the 'iPod Generation'. The important research strategy here, which adds value to this work, is that the approach does not work too formulaically around rigid demographic designations (age, class and gender, etc.). A shared relation to technological developments can indicate commonalities between people. Such affinity groupings are potentially as valuable as those based on classic 'lifecycle' demography categories. Thus, the Mintel report:

> ... concentrates on younger people, but also takes into account the way in which this 'generation' includes older people who have fully embraced the iPod, MySpace, YouTube, and any number of formerly cutting edge technologies. (Mintel, 2008)

The research is of value to marketers across a range of product sectors and covers numerous areas of consumption and social life towards its 'attempts to understand both how new technological developments are shaping the iPod Generation and, in turn, how the iPod Generation is driving further innovation' (Mintel, 2008). Mintel produces large numbers of such reports each year covering specific product sectors, such as cars or holidays, but also looking at demographic groups and other trends. Reports are largely based on quantitative analysis of consumers' attitudes and expressed intentions. They also include economic and market data.

One common concern about large-scale data – especially when designed to capture variations in attitude rather than matter of fact – is that respondents cannot be trusted to accurately remember, predict or report actual behaviour. There may be some truth in this, as the following attests:

> When questioned about their willingness to buy environmentally-friendly products, 75 per cent of EU citizens said they were ready to buy environmentally friendly products even if they were more expensive but only 17 per cent actually did so in the month before the survey.[19]

Respondents sometimes say, however, what they *think* will please the survey researcher. Sometimes they describe their ideals and aspirations rather than saying accurately what they actually do. Sometimes respondents give answers which, they hope, will bring the telephone or street interview to a swift conclusion. Nevertheless, researchers work hard to guarantee the quality of data collection (by reducing ambiguity or vagueness in questions for example), by cross-checking and by ensuring suitable samples are questioned.

Psychographics

Marketers constantly strive to understand the key motivations, attitudes and opinions behind their customers' purchasing habits. In the 1970s the VALS system began to offer advertisers the ability to understand how consumers express their personalities through their purchase behaviours. Since then a variety of similar techniques and approaches have been developed, combining socio-economic data with attitudinal and psychological profiles and distinguishing different types of consumer motivation – idealism, achievement and self-expression.

The eight VALS consumer typologies include 'Thinkers' and 'Believers'. A Thinker has 'high resources' and is motivated by ideals. For instance, a thinker is 'mature, satisfied, comfortable and reflective' and 'tends to be well-educated'. Thinkers will 'actively seek out information in decision-making processes' and will 'favour durability, functionality and value in products'. In comparison, Believers have 'low resources', but are also motivated by ideals (rather than achievement or self-expression). Believers are conservative, traditional and slow to switch brands or try new technologies.

The basket case: transactional- and behavioural-based segmentation

Increases in computing power and the falling costs of IT hardware has enabled even the smallest brand owners and retailers to store, process and analyse large amounts of consumer transactional data gathered from EPOS (till and payment systems). Many organisations now use geodemographics and lifestyle segmentations as additional 'filters' of information in conjunction with their own bespoke customer segments. Many of the large retailers have been gathering purchasing behaviour data via their loyalty and credit cards for years, and have the ability to accurately predict a consumers 'journey' into and through their product portfolio by monitoring the contents of their shoppers typical 'basket'.

By combining historic transactional data with proprietary segmentation tools, analysts and researchers are able to develop predictive models that determine likely future product usage, preferences and behaviour.

Establishing consumer-level propensities for specific products and services enables brands to cross and up-sell existing customers by communicating with them at the right time, with the right creative message about a product that is appropriate to their lifestyle and attitudes.

Fragmentation: lifestyle rather than class as the driver

The more traditional demographic categories used in advertising and media planning tend to operate with variables based on an individual's occupational characteristics or socio-economic classifications (ABC1, for example) as key discriminators (see Table 4.4). These fundamentally fail to consider the shifts in wealth and disposable income over the last 20 years. Geodemographics, psychographics and lifestyle classifications are derived using far more diverse and regularly updateable bases of information, which are used to identify and predict likely purchasing traits, for example consumer X is a 'Striver' and therefore unlikely to prefer brand Y, but may like brand Z.

In the example in Table 4.5, the Alt middle is one of a number of 'middle class' lifestyle groups identified in a study of 'The Class of 2004'. This was aimed to address a problem facing advertisers and others trying to navigate the contemporary British class system: that, notwithstanding all the various lifestyles and consumer 'tribes' and sub-cultures, 'everyone' seemed to be a member of a different 'middle class':

> In UK 04, with the possible exceptions of a neglected sink-estate underclass and an untethered super-rich aristo elite, everyone – EVERYONE – is really, fundamentally middle class. Everyone from the retired Home Counties accountant and his bridge-club wife to the asymmetric-haircut wearing, early-adopting east London graphic designer. Everyone from the Sky+ watching, Roy Keane biography reading, self-employed Essex plumber and his OK!- flicking, South Beach dieting, tanning salon owning missus to the twenty something, text sexing, Audi-driving Manchester advertising account exec and his New Beetle-driving, Kylie listening, Seven jeans wearing PR assistant girlfriend. Everyone from the just-got-back-from-a-fortnight-in-Mauritius Notting Hillbilly to the saving-for-a-week-in the-Algarve sixty something Saga Lout. (Benson and Blimes, 2004: 9)

There is a playful element to this analysis – notwithstanding the important point about a socially excluded underclass. The intention is in part to parody rigid market research approaches of the past. Descriptions are nuanced and well-observed but they serve in part as satire – a laugh at the lifestyle clusters that conventional market research identifies. Nevertheless, the fusion of close social observation and detailed attention to trends and

Table 4.4 Key MOSAIC UK, Financial Strategy Segment and TrueTouch 'groups' of
some UK locations

Location	Group	Characteristics
Milton Keynes	Mosaic: group B Happy Families	Household income: medium Online spend: medium-high
	FSS: group E Flourishing Families	Housing – with mortgage: high Educated – to degree level: medium
	Truetouch: group B Cyber Tourists	Presence of young children: high Savings and shares: low-medium
Chiswick	Mosaic: group E Urban Intelligence	Household income: medium Online spend: very high
	FSS: group A Successful Start	Housing – with mortgage: low-medium Educated – to degree level: high
	Truetouch: group A Experienced Netizens	Presence of young children: low Savings and shares: low
Glasgow	Mosaic: group F Welfare Borderline	Household income: very low Online spend: low
	FSS: group D On the Breadline	Housing – with mortgage: low-medium Educated – to degree level: very low
	Truetouch: group D Modern Media Margins	Presence of young children: high Savings and shares: low
Carmarthan	Mosaic: group K Rural Isolation	Household income: medium Online spend: medium
	FSS: group H Mid-life Affluence	Housing – with mortgage: low-medium Educated – to degree level: low
	Truetouch: group E Traditional Approach	Presence of young children: low Savings and shares: medium

consumer brand affinities can help reveal recognisable social types – and so help in thinking about advertising appeals to complex audiences. Consumer research typifications will always raise eyebrows. There is a tendency to reject typifications. This is at the root of critical analysis of stereotyping – a continuing feature of advertising communications. It is also a feature of contemporary celebration of individualism as well as the growing experience of exclusion and dislocation prevalent across global cultures.

McCracken offers a complementary explanation. He suggests we locate fragmentation not in the ever increasing diversity of lifestyles, not in the very apparent break up of stable and stabilising media systems and not even in 'post modern' social transformations. Instead, 'dispersal' and fragmentation are characteristics of individuals' experiences – experiences no doubt amplified by the complex networks and environments, real and virtual, which at times can both divert and support personal development. McCracken (2005) suggests that:

> Each of us is a network. A messy, crowded, cloudy network. We are some rough, disorganized but not entirely unconnected composite of our experiences, relationships, interests and outlooks. We are diverse, complex and multiple. (McCracken, 2005)

Such a conception of individual experience captured perhaps via research with respondents or informally in a copywriter's investigation of contemporary life is evident in a recent advertising campaign from Orange.

Table 4.5 Quantitative versus qualitative – strengths and weaknesses of different kinds of research

Quantitative		Qualitative	
Strengths	*Weaknesses*	*Strengths*	*Weaknesses*
Rigorous reliable and trustworthy data produced	Populations are abstract categories disconnected from real human complexities	Human scale research Produces intimate 'person' centred information	Difficult to generalise in a credible way from the small-scale work sometimes done using these methods
Large scale samples easier ensuring that generalisations to the whole population might be credible	Wide ranging samples limited or mono-dimensional apprehension of products / experiences	Potential for holistic approaches to understanding consumer / product / service experiences and their contexts	Risk of responses reflecting idiosyncratic research participants or locally generated conditions – from which unhelpful generalisations might still be made
Comparative analysis possible of various groups / data segments	Rigid categories within populations elide potentially significant differences and variations	Complexity and contradiction within supposedly homogenous sample sectors readily evident	Significant variations in group interviews may be masked by a will to consensus within the group or by dominating participants / moderator
Possibility for repetition between sites and times, enabling credible longitudinal surveys and comparative data gathering	Significant novelty across population groups can remain invisible to inflexibly static measurement systems	Possibility of useful studies tailored to local and current research problems – with sufficient reach to give robust good samples	Can be overly sensitive to time, place and circumstance in ways that make repetition – and hence comparison – of some data increasingly difficult over long periods and across cultures
Clear protocols for analysis, presentation and contextualisation of data allowing correlations and connections to be made disciplines (e.g. between media data and effects data)	Seemingly objective data findings can require interpretation inviting in analysts and other research stakeholders bias	Capacity to grasp real ambiguity and contradiction in consumers' experiences and attitudes to product/ brands	Data emerges that is so flexible and 'rich' as to permit a range of contradictory and illogical interpretations – therefore inhibiting decisive conclusions

I am my mum and my sister. I am my best friend Mike who I've known since school. I am Kate who's still somewhere in Thailand. I'm all the girls I've ever kissed and the girls I will. I am the teacher that failed me and the one that spurred me on. I am my bosses and every one of my friends. I'm a bloke I'll meet travelling who'll teach me the guitar. I am the place I'll go to with mates and the jokes I share with them. I am the teacher who put me down and the one who picked me up. I am who I am because of everyone. (Orange advertisement from their 'I am' campaign)

The experience of 'fragmentation' (which means something other than 'breakdown' in any pathological, clinical sense) and the plethora of identifications available via products, persons and other relationships, have bred a further characterisation of consumer experience. A recurring and important value cutting across numerous accounts of changing consumer cultures assert the importance of authenticity (Boyle, 2003; Gilmore and Pine, 2007) and a sense of emotional connection with (branded) experiences (Pine and Gilmore, 1999; Roberts, 2004). The thirst for such 'authenticity', where it is keenly felt, is connected to consumers' paradoxical attempts, from transaction to transaction, to achieve both meaningful coherence and enervating elaboration. Dispersed experiences are mobilised to achieve moments of integration and meaning – as consumers devise, revise and project stories of themselves through goods.

Researching qualities: intimacy, empathy and insight

Notwithstanding certain caveats, large-scale survey-based quantitative research can provide solid insight into the behaviour of populations. But marketers also want to enter into a 'dialogue' with *people*, as opposed to *populations*. Qualitative research methods attempt to find ways to manage more 'dialogic' consumer research – to explore or generate new hypotheses and to learn from avidly self-reflective consumers. The research remains an indirect 'conversation'. However, it retains some flavour of real voices expressing real sentiments, ideas and opinions. For example, when the sandwich chain Subway was working to position its brand, data analysing the large-scale market situation survey research highlighting quantitative measures indicating the relative strength and penetration of other fast food competitor brands, was supplemented with some qualitative research. To find out how Subway was positioned for consumers:

> Qualitative research into consumers' eating habits on the move revealed them to be promiscuous lunchers. Spoiled for choice, their expectations were high and loyalty low. These demanding consumers knew what they wanted, when they wanted it and perhaps most importantly, how they wanted it ... Herein lay the opportunity for Subway. All elements that constitute 'the ideal' were inherent in the product and service, and it appeared to occupy some clear ground between fast-food and pre-packed sandwiches. Chameleon-like, it could be one consumer's healthy lunch option and another's Saturday morning hangover treat. It did not meet any one, fixed food mood – consumers could shape the Subway offering to suit them. (McGhee *et al.*, 2007)

Qualitative methods seemed to help to confirm two things:

1   That a flexible offering was an asset in a marketplace where variety and impulse were key motivations

2   That there is no such thing as 'a consumer'. Instead there are numerous chameleon like 'lunchers' swayed by mood and circumstance to make idiosyncratic and unpredictable choices.

There are a number of ways to manage qualitative research. Focus groups can offer a quick and relatively inexpensive way to research detailed questions. They can be adapted to capture some of the advantages of quantitative work, by sampling representative individuals from target consumer groups.

Focus groups

The focus group is often seen as the default qualitative method. It is a form of group interview typically involving a selected sample of five to eight participants chosen in line with the research aim. Groups could be recruited to reflect use and non-use of a particular product, or to compare long-term users with occasional users. Groups can be sampled to reflect traditional demographic categories (age, gender, region, etc.) or can be composed more informally – groups resemble a guided conversation focused on prompts (verbal or visual) from a 'moderator' – who runs the group. Groups typically last between 45 and 90 minutes. The moderator tries to let conversation run freely while ensuring that various voices and perspectives and internal conflicts are explored and while trying to keep respondents focused. Typically groups are recorded on tape or film. It is helpful to have an observer present to assist the moderator and to pick up on detailed ideas and interactions within groups. If facilities permit, and consent is given, the group may be watched by others sitting behind a two-way mirror. In advertising research it is common for clients to watch the group – to get a better feel for the consumers' responses to campaign ideas.

Focus groups are sometimes combined with 'projective' techniques. Projective techniques (McGrath et al.,1993) are deployed in consumer research in order to access nuanced understandings of complex subjective experiences in relation to the world of goods, services or other issues. Often visual prompts are used to provoke 'talk', which can subsequently be analysed to help explore anxieties and desires that otherwise might not be expressed in the research context.

Projective techniques were used as part of a research project conducted on behalf of London City Airport (MacRury, 2008). This was part of an investigation of different groups' relationships with and feelings about the airport. Part of the project aim was to generate discussion about the extent to which different groups (long-term residents, staff, newcomers to the area, business people) felt welcome within and disposed to use the airport facilities. Rather than ask this question directly, visual prompts were designed to generate discussion about who was and who was not at home in the airport (MacRury, 2008). For instance, during the focus groups interviews the Figure 4.2 was displayed on a large board. Respondents were invited to answer the questions: 'What is happening here?' And 'What happened next?'

The projective techniques successfully generated 'talk' about the different figures – identified by the groups as representing 'the business community' and 'local families'. Different groups suggested that there were tensions – even frustration – between the priorities of 'the international business passenger' and the 'local family'. For one group of local residents, the staff member walking away seemed 'to ignore' the potential conflict. This interpretation enabled more detailed discussion to emerge about the extent to which local people felt they belonged in the airport and the extent to which the airport 'belonged' to them.

Airport staff interpreted the image differently. They highlighted their enjoyment of different types of passenger – since 'tourists tended to be friendlier and would take time to chat'. The research – a component of a wider study involving quantitative methods and individual depth interviews – was able to feed recommendations to the airport, including the suggestion that more could be done to communicate the positive and welcoming attitude of airport staff – encouraging local people to see the airport as part of their neighbourhood rather than as a business enclave.

Figure 4.2 'What happened next?' Projective prompt used in consumer focus group.

Ethnography: engaging contexts

Ethnographic consumer research tries to focus on 'real' contexts and to avoid the contrived nature of some other methods such as focus groups or projective techniques. The focus of an 'ethnographic' study tends towards the investigative and the exploratory. There is no direct testing of explicit hypotheses and no application of highly specified categorisations. The question 'which groups of car-drivers are most susceptible to road-rage?' would not be best addressed by an ethnographic study. Instead a survey linking demographic categories (age, gender, area of residence) to self-reported responses about driving behaviour and experiences captured by a standard or online questionnaire would be the best choice. Ethnography focuses on systems and societies as holistic and 'open' to interpretation of participants and observers – as well as participant-observers (i.e. researchers engaged in activity while recording or otherwise registering events, meanings and feelings).

However, investigating how people feel about their cars and lives with them – the anxieties and quirks emerging in everyday behaviours – can readily be explored through ethnographic methods. For instance, in a component of a research programme carried out for BMW (Benson *et al.*, 2007) following up an advertising campaign based on the theme 'joy in driving' depended upon being able to watch and experience consumers' direct engagement with the product: BMW cars. An emphasis on emotion and experience in relation to the product was leant to this investigation by supplementing straightforward self-reporting and self-reflective interviews (individual depth interviews and focus groups) with in-car observational one-to-ones. The in-car interviews were consistent with the research aim: capturing drivers' feelings 'in the moment'. Individuals and couples took part in the study and were asked to drive BMWs over a controlled period. Driving is a physical and emotional activity and the immediacy of the in-car situation ensured that researchers were able to observe interaction between car and person *in situ*.

The research provided insights into the intensity and intimacy of drivers' and passengers' relationships to their cars. The research opened up thinking about the specificity of the car as a 'social' space, where couples could get relatively sustained opportunities to talk, to reflect and to argue. The 'ethnographic' observational method generated insights unavailable to straightforward interviewing and engaged participants more fully in the experience at hand.

Qualitative and quantitative: division and complementarity

Over 80 per cent of research expenditure uses quantitative methods (ESOMAR, 2006). The debate about strengths and weaknesses of different kinds of research is typically settled by a recognition of the complementarity of qualitative and quantative methods (see Table 4.5).

It is sometimes valuable to use a combination of methods to examine a particular relationship, capitalising on the strengths of different approaches (say, intimate small-scale qualitative depth interviews as a precursor to designing a wider ranging large-scale questionnaire). Typically, the thoughtful application of complementary qualitative and quantitative approaches will enrich findings – offering robust data as well as sensitive insights.

Critiquing research: constructing market relations

The question of 'description' or 'construction' of markets goes to the heart of the research relationship. Consumer research is a core contributor within the advertising process as it works to represent a general commodity (a car, a snack or a bank) reproducing it as an object of desire to fit particular contexts; particular marketplaces, particular people-specific cultural moments and local mores. Because research is part of the movement between large-scale and distant abstracting processes of manufacture and the concrete everyday world of consumers (buying, talking about, assessing, using and living with products and services), it is important that such research is planned and conducted in a manner sensitive to this latter context. The animation and flexibility of the 'fit' between producer attunement and consumers' articulations of needs and desires remains in the balance.

Consumer research is like map-making – tracing gaps and routes between production and consumption. It opens up the notional 'space' of consumer demand to thought, analysis and navigation. A significant critical analysis applied to various kinds of consumer research suggests that research processes do more than just describe the compositions and characteristics of different markets – say AB1s, 'early adopters', 'empty nesters' or 'students'. Consumer research is not, as it might seem, an act of discovery – a light shone to reveal the hitherto unseen or unacknowledged. Instead research can be understood as an operation which, in the act of 'description', functionally *constructs* its objects. Various 'groups' or segments are 'invented', these based on a limited number of observable commonalities. A superficial network of 'identities' and points of 'identification' is created.

Provision, marketing, media plans and advertising styles become loosely oriented around these constructed categories. Niches and micro-niches become instituted across the media and cultural sphere. Magazines and programmes are designed with the aim of getting the attention of this or that group. Decisions about product design, retail styles, pricing and so on come to reflect a conception of social life predicated upon these instituted categories. The research-constructed identities are translated into 'lifestyles' and products. These are framed in terms of identification of and with such constructed categories. Ritual reaffirmation of constructed (and constricted) identity categories, while generating innumerable products and varieties of provision, nevertheless seems to produce a world predicated upon market relations – at the expense of other kinds of social institution and the relations entailed to them. As Bauman argues:

> What ties individuals to society is their activity as consumers, their life organised around consumption. (Bauman, 1987: 168)

Insofar as the dialogue between producers and consumers is limited and foreclosed, either to the brute facts or price and wealth/poverty or the constricting categories of abstract demographics, the promise of an emancipatory consumer culture and society binding market solutions to real social development will be greeted with scepticism. On the other hand, insofar as production and consumer cultures becomes truly responsive to people's needs, desires and wants, then research, as a component of that change, can become a genuinely developmental resource, not just for corporations but for individuals, communities and broader social development.

Niches and networks: from consumer research to consumer researchers

Research is often understood in relation to two grand scale shifts; one economic, the other socio-cultural. In the organisation of economic life a shift permitted by and driving technological innovation has moved producers away from the mass production of standardised goods in favour, at least in theory, of more complex and flexible manufacturing process whereby goods are produced responsively. Research tries to inform such adaptive production so that goods are made in forms and functions that suit consumers' various desires and demands. Thus, marketing does not try to manufacture demand to absorb production, as in the days of Fordist mass marketing and advertising manipulation. Instead contemporary marketing and brand development, informed by research, work to try and engage consumer desire within, or even prior to, production processes. This kind of anticipatory customisation depends upon engaging consumers in various ways to inform the production process – and to find a balance between economies of scale and making products specifically attractive to significant market niches.

In some sectors some kinds of consumer research will become obsolete. It is possible in such sectors, but not others, to talk about consumers as 'co-producers', in the sense that they play a direct role in the design and specification of manufactured goods and services. One minor but indicative example is 'print on demand' books (Anderson, 2006: 94–6). Rather than selling a set inventory of pre-manufactured books stored and catalogued on shelves, e-commerce and e-storage permits publishers and book distributors to hold almost no physical books. Instead sellers wait for consumers to purchase a specific title. Only then is the book physically manufactured and sent. This simultaneous fusion of the moment of production and purchase makes some kinds of research obsolete. Where physical inventory can be kept small (e.g. with information-based goods such as books, music and other digital based products) and where goods can be produced only in response to purchase, there is no need to research markets to establish if there is sufficient demand. Even small number of purchasers can make a product viable when there are no storage costs and no risk of wasteful overproduction. Bagehot's principle does not apply in the era of what Anderson (2006) calls 'the long tail', since there is no anxiety – for a retailer or supplier – and little risk attached to holding a large inventory when storage and manufacturing costs are minimal – as is the case with goods that exist as 'bytes' and not 'atoms' (Anderson, 2006).

Consumer research was well suited to uncovering viable niches (segments, etc.) to capture enough customers to make production, storage and distribution viable. In virtual market places two things have changed:

1 Consumers become researchers – using powerful search engines and consultative networks, blogs and so on, to find new products or to assess market offerings. Consumers' research to finds products – rather than consumer research seeking to chisel out consumer niches.
2 More niches are commercially viable to online retailers. The constraints upon profitability impacting real world suppliers (the limited size of local populations and the limited proximity of interested consumers) do not apply online.

As Anderson argues:

The mass of niches has always existed, but as the cost of reaching it falls – consumers finding niche products a, and niche products finding consumers –it's suddenly becoming a force to be reckoned with. (Anderson, 2006: 6)

In the world of online marketplaces and in particular some product 'byte-based' sectors, consumers will be the 'researchers' – rather than the objects and targets of research. Producers, as the *objects* of consumers' analysis may need to adapt yet further to maintain their place in the market – for example, by pursuing more ethical policies and practices.

In socio-cultural life here has been a movement away from understanding society where social conformity and culturally normative standards were powerful guides to and constraints on behaviours and choices to one where, relatively, individual expressivities and choices are seen as significant identifiers. This has leant weight to the case for investigating consumer preferences – to feed de-massification of production and the better tailoring of goods and brand imageries. Again, the Internet and the massification of 'niches' is significant. As Anderson puts it:

Where are all those fickle consumers going? No single place. They are scattered to the winds as markets fragment into countless niches. The one big growth area is the Web, but it is an uncategorizable sea of a million destinations, each defying in its own way the conventional logic of media and marketing. (Anderson, 2006: 2)

Nevertheless, worldwide it is apparent that a good deal of time, thought and resource has been and will continue to be invested in knowing consumers – with research of various kinds developed by advertising agencies, media owners, product manufactures, social institutions (such as hospitals and universities)[20] and other service providers. However, there are challenges for consumer research as it adapts to new media and marketing environments, as marketers'abstractions will nevertheless become more or less reconnected to practical marketing issues and to the everyday lives and experiences of the mythic hero and subject of consumer research; the consumer.

Notes

1 The show is based on real and comedic opinions research data.
2 The earliest formal consumer research in the US and UK can be traced back to the second and third decades of the twentieth century (MacDonald and King, 1995: 126).
3 In some sectors, notably cosmetics, research data are relayed to audiences in support of an advertising claim, i.e. 'Consumer testing shows 83 per cent of women saw a reduction in the appearance of cellulite'. Any such detailed (falsifiable) claims are open to close regulatory scrutiny, not to mention a degree of consumer scepticism. The sources of such data are often required to be included in small print in, e.g., TV or press ads.

4   The slogan is most associated with Masterfood's Whiskas cat food brand, which has used it since the 1960s.

5   The most famous popular analysis of the research industry is Vance Packard's *The Hidden Persuaders* (1957). This was first published in 1957 in the US and focused on certain methods of supposedly subliminal communications finely tuned by depth psychologies.

6   Such as Netflix, iTunes Amazon or Google.com

7   It is also the case that a great part of advertising 'research' (insightful or otherwise) is *ad hoc*, barely reaching any kind of formal public or professional domains. Such informal research – picked up by practitioners as 'participant observers' in culture, consumption and conversation – haphazard as it may be – provides an important context for advertising intuition, decision making and practice. Arguably 'research' is the wrong word. However, cultural attunement, of various kinds, and emerging from a casual attentiveness to trends and themes in daily life, are an important component in creative and professional advertising cultures (Nixon, 2003: 35).

8   The definition of a campaign 'working' depends upon agreed measures of performance and agreed desired aims. Advertisers have been used to remembering the acronym 'DAGMAR' in this context, which stands for Defining Advertising Goals for Measured Advertising Results.

9   Claude Hopkins was an early twentieth-century American advertising guru. He worked hard to develop methods aimed at improving advertising practices and at securing the reputation of advertising as a respectable and 'scientific' activity.

10 See Powell's discussion of changing advertising industry organisation. There has been some weakening of role boundaries in contemporary advertising organisations. Nevertheless, whether in one person, or distributed across the organisation, there remains an identifiable knowledge management and planning function.

11 And, of course, as more people worked in factories and offices and specialised in this or that profession, this or that trade, the capacity of individuals, families and communities to provide for themselves within a bounded and well-known locale was rapidly reduced.

12 ESOMAR, i.e. European Society for Opinion and Marketing Research.

13 Many of the papers presented at ESOMAR conferences are available via WARC.COM, an online resource archiving research and scholarship across all fields of advertising, marketing and branding.

14 The conference was run by ESOMAR (World Association of Opinion and Marketing Research Professionals (formerly European Society for Opinion and Marketing Research)). This organisation has operated in various guises from over 60 years (White, 2007).

15 Notwithstanding the 'credit crunch' (Turner 2008) and its potential consequences for consumption-driven economic development and adjunct promotional industries.

16 Mintel describes itself as 'a leading global supplier of consumer, product and media intelligence. For more than 35 years, Mintel has provided insight into key worldwide trends, offering unique data that directly impacts client success. With offices in Chicago, London, Belfast, Shanghai, Tokyo and Sydney, Mintel has forged a unique reputation as a world-renowned business brand'. Another global research company is Taylor Nelson Sofres (TNS). TNS describes its operation as: 'The world's largest Custom Market Research company. We provide quality marketing information delivered by Global Industry Sector expert consultants, innovative Research Expertise across the entire product lifecycle, in 80 countries worldwide.'

17 Just as anthropological research became intimately linked to colonialism in earlier phases of the twentieth century (Said, 1993), consumer research will play a continuing role in opening up new markets to international direct investment driven commercial corporations, corporations in part dependent upon good knowledge of consumers and consumption.

18 'People' has an important additional connotation. In some contexts 'people' alludes to collective political action. The 'will' of the people is formally determined and expressed through the systems of democratic institutions – such as parliament, and not by 'market research'. However, there is often a cross-fertilisation between consumer research methods and political consultation as governments have begun, increasingly, to adopt some of the techniques of commercial research to inform policy development and implementation (MacDonald and King, 1995).

19 Study on the effectiveness of Directive 1999/94/EC relating to the availability of consumer information on fuel economy and CO_2 emissions in respect of the marketing of new passenger cars. Commissioned by the European Commission, Directorate-General for Environment, http://ec.europa.eu/environment/air/transport/co2/report/final_report.pdf

20 It is useful to consider the role of 'consumer' research in the management and development of such institutions – designed to provide for social needs rather than consumer desires. Some subtle but important shifts of emphasis are implicit in the re-description of students or patients as 'consumers'. See Williams (1980) for a classic critique of the elision of categories, 'citizen' and 'consumer'.

5 Advertising regulation

Jonathan Hardy

Introduction

In Britain, advertisements on television and radio have been regulated differently to advertisements in print and other 'non-broadcast' media. From the start of commercial television in 1955, broadcasting regulation was statutory, meaning it was subject to laws made in Parliament, which authorised agencies to oversee and control all broadcast output, including advertisements. By contrast, the system established for 'non-broadcast' media was principally one of self-regulation, whereby the industry regulates its own behaviour, so that, in principle at least, advertisers, agencies and media work together to agree standards and ensure that all parties comply. In 2004 self-regulation was extended to broadcast advertising and the two systems began to converge.

One of the first significant moves towards self-regulation occurred in 1890, when the United Bill-posters Association and London Bill-posters Association, sensitive to increasing public criticism of outdoor advertising, set up a Joint Censorship Committee. Bill posters decided that industry control was preferable to outside control being imposed by threatened legislation. So, under a voluntary scheme, bill posters could submit questionable posters they received to a committee who could order any they deemed objectionable to be amended or withdrawn (Miracle and Nevett, 1988; Nevett, 1982). Various business codes of practice were introduced from 1910 in both the US and the UK, but the first proper code of advertising ethics was drawn up in 1924 at an international conference in Wembley, where delegates pledged to be truthful, avoid exaggeration and misleading claims, and refrain from unfair criticism of competitors. Later that year the Advertising Association was formed to raise and promote professional standards in Britain. Against a background of mounting public criticism, the AA began with the declared aim 'to promote public confidence in advertising and advertised goods through the correction or suppression of abuses which undermine that confidence' (Miracle and Nevett, 1988: 10). In 1928 it established an Advertising Investigation Department, using industry cooperation and even encouraging prosecutions to drive out rogue advertisers. A significant factor here, as in subsequent efforts to modify self-regulation, was to stave off the threat of government imposed controls and legal restrictions. In the 1950s, controversy over advertising methods did lead to several Acts of Parliament imposing controls on such issues as poster sites and aerial advertising. Pressure to strengthen advertising regulation grew, not least once commercial TV advertising was placed on a statutory footing. In 1959 the Labour Party established an Advertising Enquiry Committee to investigate 'socially harmful ads', and supported recommendations for a statutory National Consumer Board (Brierley, 2002: 215). Responding to criticism, the AA launched the British Code of Advertising Practice in 1961, drawing on both its existing codes, such as that for medicines and treatments drawn up in 1948, and the International Code of Advertising Practice, first published in 1937 by the International Chamber of Commerce (ICC). In 1962 the Advertising Standards Authority (ASA) was created to administer the code. This new 'watchdog' of the self-regulatory system saw off the immediate threat of government legislation.

The UK self-regulatory system has three, commonly found, elements. First, there is a code-making body which represents the various parts of the industry. This is the Committee of Advertising Practice (CAP), whose membership represents advertisers, agencies, media and related marketing, trade and professional organisations. The CAP brings together 29 organisations to draw up the British Codes of Advertising, Sales Promotion and Direct Marketing. Second, there is a body that applies the codes, the ASA, whose Council meets to decide if advertisements breach them. The ASA also includes the third main element, a permanent staff that investigates complaints, carries out monitoring and research and publicises and promotes the self-regulatory system. The system was overhauled in 1974 when the Labour Government threatened to introduce a statutory code unless standards improved. Since 1974, the Chair and at least half of the ASA Council members are required to be professionally independent of advertising interests. Today, broadcast and non-broadcast matters are considered separately but the chairman and nine of the fifteen members sit on both councils. The ASA is funded by a levy of 0.1 per cent on display and broadcast advertising and 0.2 per cent on Royal Mail Mailsort contracts. These levies are collected by the Advertising Standards Board of Finance (Asbof) and the Broadcast Advertising Standards Board of Finance (Basbof). The ASA's income in 2007 was just over £8 million.

Self-regulation and the law

The framework in which advertisers, agencies and media must operate is a mixture of voluntary and statutory regulation. The ASA deals with most paid advertisements and marketing communications but it operates within a wider framework of domestic and international law and alongside various other regulatory agencies. Among the most important of these are trading standards officers who deal with in-store advertising and shop window displays. The Trades Descriptions Act (1968) makes it an offence for anyone in business to apply a false trade description to any goods offered for sale. Local trading standards services (TSSs) have a range of powers to act against false descriptions and misleading price claims and, following the 2002 Enterprise Act, have enhanced powers to tackle misleading advertisements. More than 170 Acts of Parliament directly affect advertising, with some 235 regulations and statutes affecting broadcast advertising in England and Wales alone. These include the Consumer Protection Act (1987), which sets out rules on the use of terms such as sale price, reduced price and bargain offer. The Food Labelling Regulations (1996) controls the advertising and branding of food, while the Medicines Act (1968) sets rules about claims made for medicines and the way in which health professionals can be depicted in advertising.

The CAP codes and ASA do not deal with flyposting (which is mostly illegal and is controlled by local authorities), private correspondence, telephone selling, classified ads, packaging and point of sale materials. The ASA renounced regulating political adverts in 1999, two years after M&C Saatchi's infamous 'Demon Eyes' campaign for the Conservative Party (see Chapter 14). In 2000, marketing communications, whose principal function is to influence voters, were made exempt from the CAP code, partly on the grounds that political parties had not signed up to self-regulation, nor agreed to be judged against the Code's requirement that marketers hold evidence to substantiate objectively verifiable claims. Political ads are banned in broadcasting. Complaints must now be directed to the Electoral Commission (for non-broadcast ads) or Ofcom (broadcasting).

Various CAP organisations also exercise self-regulation, with their own codes of practice and procedures to discipline members. These include the Periodical Publishers Association, the Newspaper Publishing Association and Newspaper Society (with partner organisations in Scotland), the Outdoor Advertising Association, Cinema Advertising Association, Direct Marketing Association (DMA), Institute of Sales Promotion (ISP), Mail Order Traders Association (MOTA), Direct Selling Association (DSA) and the Internet Advertising Bureau (IAB). Finally, there are other organisations with statutory or voluntary powers affecting marketing communications, such as the Financial Services Authority (FSA), the statutory regulator for investment, insurance and banking businesses.

How the system works

Responsibility lies with advertisers and agencies not to breach CAP codes. CAP provides a free resource for agencies or clients to check compliance for planned campaigns. The ASA investigates complaints and can also initiate its own investigations. The majority of complaints made are not formally investigated (77 per cent in 2007) as they refer to matters not covered by the codes (such as packaging, contractual disputes or 'editorial' content). The self-regulatory system deals with most forms of marketing communications controlled by the marketer, but not with the editorial content of publishers, which is the responsibility of other regulators such as the Press Complaints Commission. Where it investigates, the ASA favours informal resolution and, where advertisers agree to withdraw or amend their ad, complaints are not formally put before the Council for adjudication. If the Council upholds complaints, the advertiser is required to remove or amend the advertisement and is prohibited from using similar advertising approaches in any future marketing communications. According to the ASA (2008a) 'most advertisers agree to change or remove the ad' when requested, and media owners agree not to run them. The ASA thus promotes itself as highly effective; in fact, the sanctions are relatively weak and compliance levels variable. The ASA makes much of the sanctions available, which include trading restrictions, withdrawal of financial benefits or derecognition imposed by the relevant professional association. However, it has no powers to fine or take legal action itself. Advertisers risk having expensive advertising pulled, but campaigns have often finished before adverse adjudications are made. One of the ASA's principal tools is negative publicity generated by publishing rulings on its website, and subsequent media coverage. However, this has become a tool used by marketers to generate publicity for shock ads, to amplify campaigns or even promote their defiance of the regulator. French Connection's controversial fcuk advertising saw rulings from the ASA dating back to 1997 flouted by a campaign that ran until 2004.

One strength of the regulatory system is that it is underpinned by so-called 'backstop' legal powers. Advertisers who flout the rules can be referred to the Office of Fair Trading, while broadcasters can be referred to the statutory regulator Ofcom. Under the Control of Misleading Advertisements Regulations 1988, which implement a European Directive (84/450/EEC), an advertisement is deemed misleading 'if it deceives or is likely to deceive those to whom it is addressed and as a result is likely to affect their economic behaviour or is likely to injure a competitor of the advertiser' (OFT, 2004: 4). The Director General for Fair Trade can obtain a court injunction and if a civil court decides the advertising is misleading it can grant an order preventing further publication. Failure to obey such an order could result in proceedings for contempt of court, punishable by a fine or imprisonment. The ASA seldom uses its power of referral, however: only 20 times between 1988 and 2007. In 2008 the ASA referred Ryanair following a series of code breaches, seven over 2 years alone, and the company's self-promoted defiance of rulings, such as one upholding 13 complaints for an ad showing a model wearing a school uniform in a sexually provocative way, headed 'Hottest back to school fares'. According to the ASA, Ryanair's offences including making exaggerated claims about the availability of flights at the advertised price, misleading comparisons with competitors and failure to provide evidence to substantiate claims made.

The ASA system now incorporates an independent reviewer to whom complainants can appeal if they wish to challenge adjudications. The reviewer cannot overrule Council decisions but can ask for them to be reconsidered if there have been problems in the way the complaint was handled. Finally, ASA decisions may also be challenged in the courts under judicial review proceedings, but judges have tended to defer to the expertise of self-regulators where they have acted in accordance with their own rules and procedures.

Codes and complaints

There is more advertising available, and electronic communication makes it easier than ever to complain, but the increase in complaints indicates a level of criticism which decades of self-regulation have failed to mitigate. In 2007 there were 24,192 complaints about a record 14,080 advertisements, with 2,458 ads changed or withdrawn following ASA action. Complaints rose 7.6 per cent on 2006 (although 2005 had the highest recorded number of complaints at 26,236). Supporters of self-regulation highlight that only a tiny proportion of all marketing communications attract complaints, mostly from a handful of complainants, but the ASA itself acknowledges that it is code breaches, not the number of complaints, that matter. Non-broadcast advertisements receive most complaints, 13,507 in 2007 compared to 10,685 for broadcast, but 7 out of the 10 most complained of ads appeared on television. Overall, almost half of complaints concerned 'misleading' ads. Broadcast media, though, drew the most complaints about offensiveness (40 per cent in 2007).

The CAP codes set out general principles, the first being that 'all marketing communications should be legal, decent, honest and truthful', and specific rules dealing with marketing claims, content, how competitors are treated and marketers' behaviour. The self-regulatory system is in a 'constant state of revision and renegotiation' (Brierley, 2002: 218). In 2008 the ASA signalled it would address environmental claims following a sharp increase in complaints, with 561 complaints about 410 ads in 2007 compared to just 117 complaints about 83 ads in 2006. Most complaints concerned unclear, inaccurate or unsubstantiated green claims, such as 'carbon neutral' or '100 per cent recycled'.

In recent years, pressure to curb the promotion of products or services deemed to be anti-social or damaging to health has led to revisions of codes, intensive lobbying and wider public debate. Since 1975 advertisements for alcoholic products should not 'encourage excessive drinking; feature those who are, or appear to be, under the age of 25; place undue emphasis on alcoholic strength; suggest that drinking is essential to social success or acceptance; suggest that drink can contribute to sexual appeal'. New restrictions were added in 2005 to combat ads appealing to underage drinkers. A poster ad for Young's beer showing a suited man with a ram's head gazed upon by several bikini-clad women was deemed to breach the code in linking alcohol with both social success and seduction (see Figure 5.1).

Figure 5.1   'This is a ram's world'. Young and Co. Brewery's advert, banned by the ASA in 2006.

The main issues drawing complaints in 2007 were 'depictions of violence, sex and race'. Complaints about violence in advertisement almost doubled between 2006 and 2007, partly reflecting increasing concern about gun and knife crime. A poster for the game *Mortal Kombat*, press ads for the game *Hitman 2*, posters for the film *Shoot 'Em Up*, as well as a TV ad for the film *Silent Hill*, which showed a woman's throat being cut, all had complaints upheld. Yet the most complained about advert in 2007 depicted a violent image in a 'good' cause; the Department of Health's multimedia anti-smoking campaign showed adults with fish hooks pulled through their cheeks to graphically illustrate addicts being 'hooked' on tobacco (see Figure 5.3). This drew 774 complaints that it was offensive, frightening and distressing. The ASA clearly did not agree that the need to get a message through to smokers outweighed the offensiveness of the imagery and upheld the complaints against the posters (and two TV ads). A key factor, common to ASA rulings, was the media context of the advertising. Outdoor posters are a 'broadcast' medium seen by passers-by and the ASA agreed that the images were likely to be distressing to younger children.

A bus and poster ad for the *Sun* newspaper promoted a price reduction by showing two giant 10p coins superimposed over the breasts of a woman naked from the waist up (see Figure 5.2). This attracted 56 complaints but the ASA Council judged that, while distasteful to some, the advert was not overtly sexual in nature and the amount of flesh revealed was no different from other bikini ads, concluding it was not pornographic nor met the ASA's key threshold test of 'causing serious or widespread offence'. The ASA (2008b) states that '[w]e tend to be more accepting of ads that use sexy or provocative images of women to advertise products aimed at making women feel sexy or better about themselves'. Gossard's 'Hello Boys' ad in 1994 received 89 complaints but was deemed humorous and appropriate for an underwear promotion. Eighty-four complaints about Condé Naste's ad for Vogue.com, in which a woman's nipple replaced the 'dot' were rejected, and indeed the majority of complaints about sexist imagery are not upheld. The ASA has tended to tolerate sexist ads but challenged those which encourage viewers to see women solely as sex objects, such as that for a webserver in *PC Pro Magazine* of a woman kneeling in underwear, with the caption 'Bound to serve' (Amen Ltd, 2004; see ASA 2004).

Figure 5.2 The *Sun* advert made the top 10 most complained of ads for 2007. Courtesy of News International Syndication.

Broadcasting

The 1954 Television Act established ad-financed commercial broadcasting in Britain and a statutory regulator, the Independent Television Authority, was charged with drawing up a code for advertising. For this task a special Advertising Advisory Committee was formed, dominated by advertising industry interests, which drew up a permissive code. A shortlist of products or services that could not be advertised included fortune tellers, undertakers and money lenders, but also smoking cures or treatments for alcoholism. A decade later, cigarette advertising was banned on television (1965) with tobacco promotion banned altogether from 2002. Advertising regulation has grown as the regulatory body changed to the Independent Broadcasting Authority (IBA) followed in 1991 by Independent Television Commission (ITC) (when a separate Radio Authority was established) and then in December 2003 the Office of Communications (Ofcom), responsible for television, radio, telecommunications and wireless communications services.

Within a year of operation, regulation of broadcast advertising largely passed from Ofcom to the ASA. The Communications Act (2003) had required Ofcom to review whether its functions could be effectively secured by self-regulation rather than statutory oversight. Following a short consultation, Ofcom approved this approach, arguing it would provide consumers with a 'one-stop-shop' for complaints and be better able to handle convergence issues raised by the growth of digital communications. However, this was a not a straightforward transfer of powers, but rather a 'co-regulatory' arrangement, involving statutory and voluntary elements, between Ofcom, the ASA and BCAP, the broadcasting section of CAP. Ofcom has delegated its statutory powers over the content of broadcast advertisements to the ASA, which deals with all complaints, but Ofcom remains ultimately responsible for regulating advertisements on television and radio services. Ofcom also retains direct control over important matters such as the amount and scheduling of advertisements, sponsorship and teleshopping. All UK broadcasters must hold licences which include the requirement that any advertising carried must conform to the BCAP code; breaching such licence conditions risks a fine by Ofcom, or even revocation of licence. Since 2004, the Broadcast Committee of Advertising Practice (BCAP), representing broadcasters, advertisers, agencies and marketing bodies, draws up separate codes for radio, television and text services. As co-regulator, Ofcom must approve these codes, which the ASA then enforces. In a further effort to strengthen legitimacy, an Advertising Advisory Committee (AAC) provides a consumer perspective to BCAP. Significantly, there is no equivalent body advising CAP.

Broadcast advertising is subject to pre-clearance. Clearcast (formerly the Broadcast Advertising Clearance Centre) checks ads on behalf of the major TV broadcasters who fund it. Likewise, the Radio Advertising Clearance Centre (established in 1996) pre-checks national radio ads and certain categories of ads before these are aired. Teletext Ltd provides a text clearing service, while the British Television Shopping Association (BTSA) pre-vets TV infomercials. Pre-clearance has always been an economic imperative in broadcasting, where the costs for a pulled ad may be hundreds of thousands of pounds. According to CAP, the system is successful in 'eliminating almost all problems before transmission', but this ignores the high volume of complaints, many upheld, made to the ASA. These include JWT's ad for Cadbury's Trident chewing gum cleared for transmission but subsequently censured by the ASA, which upheld complaints of racial stereotyping.

Television codes and complaints

TV remains the most complained-about medium, followed by the Internet, which overtook print media in 2007. TV ads generated the vast majority of broadcasting complaints: 95 per cent, compared to radio's 5 per cent. The most complained about TV ad was for KFC's Zinger Crunch Salad in 2005, which received 1,671 complaints. Women workers in a call centre sing the praises of KFCs salad with their mouths full of food. However, the ASA rejected complaints that the ad encouraged bad manners in children, reasoning that it takes time to instil good manners and that the ads would not affect such behaviour in the long term (see ASA, 2007).

Illustrating its 'co-regulatory' role, Ofcom initiated changes to the BCAP codes, requiring that alcohol advertising 'must not be likely to appeal strongly to people under 18, in particular by reflecting or being associated with youth culture'. An underlying rationale for regulating advertising is that it influences consumption and behaviour, but it remains notoriously difficult to isolate its precise effects. Ofcom (2005a: 11) agreed with industry claims that 'alcohol advertising is only one of a multitude of factors influencing people's relationship with alcohol', but accepted the weight of academic research 'which indicated that TV advertising is likely to contribute to children's attitudes

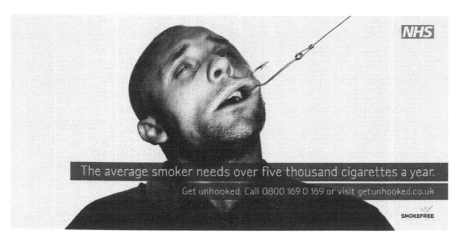

Figure 5.3 'Get Unhooked' advert. Courtesy of the Department of Health.

about drinking, albeit at a relatively minor level'. At the same time Ofcom argued that other media such as films were likely to be more significant than TV and that 'availability, price and general social mores are probably the strongest influences' on alcohol consumption. Industry argues that the effects of advertising are misunderstood and grossly exaggerated by critics; most advertising in established markets seeks to encourage consumption or brand switching by existing users rather than aggressively targeting new consumers (see Broadbent, 2007). Critics point to the vast sums devoted to marketing and argue that the economic interests of advertisers and media are too great to place faith in 'self-regulation'.

In the mid-1990s, the Labour Party began to soften its stance towards the advertising industry, shifting from its 1992 pledge to introduce a statutory code towards endorsing self-regulation, while retaining the 'big stick' threat of possible legislation to influence change. However, in Government, tensions developed between its pro-industry 'deregulatory' approach and a growing appetite for intervention. While Culture Secretary Chris Smith told the AA in 1998 he could not envisage ad prohibitions beyond tobacco, in 2006 Prime Minister Blair acknowledged that the anti-smoking ban had contributed to government rethinking, warning of 'the Government intervening directly with the food and drinks industry where, for example, you have the sale of junk food to children and the irresponsible marketing of alcohol' (*Campaign*, 2006). The industry had been divided over restrictions on tobacco advertising, with widespread concern that these undermined a principle that the industry had sought to maintain; that what was legal to sell should be legal to advertise (Brown, 2007). A common industry view is that the feared 'domino effect' has ensued, with campaigners targeting issue after issue to curtail 'freedom of commercial speech'.

Case study 1: Advertising food to children

The promotion of 'junk food' rose up the political agenda in the early 2000s amidst broader concerns about advertising to children. Increasing levels of obesity and associated health problems prompted scrutiny of the sales and promotion of foods that were high in fat, salt or sugar (HFSS). In Britain, pressure came from health professionals and groups such as Sustain, a coalition of 160 health and consumer organisations, which claimed that over 95 per cent of food ads during children's commercial TV were for HFSS foods, resulting in a 'grossly imbalanced nutritional message' (Sustain, 2001: vii).

In 2002, Labour MP Debra Shipley launched a Private Member's Bill on children's food, calling for restrictions on marketing. The following year, a Parliamentary Select Committee concluded that marketing of so-called junk food should be controlled and a Government White Paper *Choosing Health* (Department of Health, 2004) proposed that Ofcom should assess the case for strengthening restrictions on food and drink advertising to children on television. In March 2004, more than 100 health and consumer groups urged ministers to ban 'junk food' ads. Meanwhile the European Commission held discussions with the advertising industry and in July 2004 the ICC published its *Framework for Responsible Food and Beverage Communications*. Self-regulation could be trusted to work, the industry argued, in the face of mounting calls for tougher statutory regulation.

By 2006, when Ofcom launched its second consultation on HFSS advertising, it had decided that some restriction was appropriate and set out various options. A coalition of leading health charities and organisations threatened to take Ofcom to court for its failure to include the option they favoured: a total ban on HFSS advertising before the 9 pm 'watershed'. Campaigners also used Freedom of Information legislation to compel Ofcom to reveal that it held 29 meetings with food and advertising industry lobbyists during the period when it drew up the controversial proposals.

The outcome was a phased introduction of new rules on content and scheduling. From April 2007, HFSS advertisements were banned in all programmes aimed at children aged 4–9. Children's channels were required to scale back HFSS advertising to 75 per cent of 2005 levels. In January 2008, the ban was extended to programmes aimed at children aged 10–15 and HFSS advertising on children's channels was cut back to 50 per cent of 2005 levels, with a total ban imposed from January 2009.

One of the most controversial aspects concerned ads in 'adult' programmes. Children aged 4–15 watch far more 'adult' television than they do children's, on average 12 hours vs. 5 hours/week, according to Ofcom (2004a: 23). Ofcom ruled that HFSS adverts could not be shown in programmes with 'particular appeal' to children, defined as one watched by 20 per cent more children under 16 than the national average. *Which?* (2007) argued that the rules failed to prevent HFSS advertising in peak time shows watched by more children than programmes affected by the ban, but where children remained a small proportion of the total audience, such as ITV's *Pop Idol* and *Ant & Dec's Saturday Night Takeaway*.

Ofcom declared it had struck the right balance, rejecting calls for a complete pre-watershed ban which it claimed would cost broadcasters £250m per year in lost income. Instead, Ofcom estimated that the impact of its restrictions would be some £39m per year, falling to around £23m. Child-oriented satellite channels predicted a 9 per cent drop in income with dedicated children's channels fearing a 15 per cent fall (BBC, 2008). Advertisers succeeded in restricting the scope of a sectoral ban while protesting that the measures were disproportionate and misjudged in targeting advertising instead of tackling the problems of diet and exercise giving rise to obesity. Ofcom was heavily criticised by health groups, with the Children's Commissioner declaring that 'Children have been sold out in the interests of profit'. Broadcasters argued that fewer domestic children's programmes would be made, with a detrimental cultural impact. Arguably, of greatest concern is the evidence of marketers bypassing the regulations, with leading food brands such as McDonald's, Starburst, Haribo and Skittles increasingly marketing to children online via social networking sites, Internet chat services and websites (Pidd, 2007).

Case study 2: Product placement

The US Federal Trade Commission (2005) defines product placement as 'a form of promotion in which advertisers insert branded products into programming in exchange for fees or other consideration'. Such placement ranges from the visual inclusion of brands, to verbal endorsement and sophisticated 'brand integration' such as that of Federal Express in the film *Cast Away* (2000) or the Halliburton security case dominating an early episode of *Lost*, which *The Economist* (2005) described as 'product placement to die for'. Integrating advertising into programmes has been regarded as a solution to two problems: the declining reach and effectiveness of TV 'spot' advertising and the rising costs of programme production. Personal video recorders (PVRs) are only the latest in a line of innovations from the remote control and VCR onwards enabling viewers to bypass ads. Brand integration, it is claimed, offers advertising effectiveness (if done appropriately), an important source of income for programme makers and/or broadcasters and new forms of creative collaboration between advertisers and media. In the US, product placement is now a $5 billion industry, increasing annually. However, in Western Europe, a very different regulatory culture has prevailed.

The main instrument of European television regulation has been the 'Television without Frontiers' Directive, established in 1989 and revised in 1997, not least to include new provisions on advertising, teleshopping and self-promotional channels. In 2007 the European Commission unveiled the latest version, now called the Audiovisual Media Services Directive (2007/65/EC). This extends regulation of broadcast television to 'television-like' services available online and to some aspects of so-called 'nonlinear' services, such as video-on-demand. The Directive has been a key target for lobbying interests because it sets the framework for the amount and scheduling of advertising, as well as content and other rules. Under the old Television Directive, surreptitious advertising was prohibited. Many states, including Britain, took this to include product placement, but others, notably Austria and Italy, have allowed advertisers to pay for brands to appear in programmes. For the Commission this was one reason given for introducing clearer rules, but advertisers and broadcasters had also lobbied intensively for the rules to be relaxed and a fierce debate ensued with many MEPs (socialists and greens in particular), consumer, trade union and civil society groups opposed. The outcome is that the new Directive reaffirms the general prohibition, but allows individual member states to opt out and permit product placement in films, series, sports and light entertainment, although not in news or children's programmes. Anticipating the EU rule change, Ofcom consulted in 2006 on permitting PP, prohibited under section 10.5 of the Broadcasting Code (Ofcom 2005c), but concluded that there was a strong polarisation of views and made no recommendation. However, in 2008 the issues were being debated with renewed vigour as the Government consulted on implementing the new Directive.

In the US, the FTC regulates advertising and the Federal Communications Commission (FCC) regulates broadcasting. The FTC argues that product placement differs from other forms of advertising and sponsorship in that it does not make claims about products and so does not give rise to harm for consumers. Product placement is unregulated in movies. For television, FCC rules require that all commercial messages must be clearly disclosed to viewers. In practice this means that corporate sponsors are mentioned in small type during fast-moving end credits. However, recently, FCC commissioner Jonathan Adelstein has called for tighter rules and more prominent on-air disclosure. So while the practice of 'brand integration' becomes increasingly prevalent and normalised among media and marketing professionals, it has also come under increasing regulatory scrutiny. Industry groups, such as the Entertainment Resources & Marketing Resources Association (ERMA), are pitted against campaigning groups such as Commercial Alert.

In Britain, the 1954 Television Act authorised the clear separation between programmes and advertising; section 4 (6) prohibited any programme material which was or appeared to be 'supplied or suggested by any advertiser'. In fact, the early years of ITV saw the creation of 'admags', in which branded goods were promoted by characters in settings such as a public house (Murdock, 1992). However, the separation principle was reinforced after 1963 and broadcast regulation has, on the whole, been successful in maintaining it since. In 2005, Channel Four was fined £5,000 for promoting Red Bull on a daytime chat show, the *Richard and Judy Show* (serial offenders). In this context, commercial broadcasters such as ITV have moved cautiously, seeking to reassure key publics that PP will be introduced with care, and that 'editorial integrity' will not be sacrificed, while telling Ofcom it was 'imperative that advertiser-funded television companies are able to tap into new revenue streams if they are to sustain anything like current levels of investment in programming' (ITV, 2004).

Is there a problem here? Dean Ayers, President of ERMA, commenting on *Cast Away* (Abramovich, 2001) said:

> Only five years ago, people were hiding. They thought what they did was wrong and that the public was against it. They found out that the public is actually for it. The production people are for it. The companies are for it. There is really only a very small segment of people who are opposed to product placement.

In Britain, supporters highlight that viewers have long been used to product placement in movies such as James Bond or US imports such as *Sex and the City*, and point to the economic costs of maintaining tougher rules than apply to Britain's competitors. For critics, product placement breaches a fundamental requirement for transparency, that consumers should know when they are in a selling environment. Editorial integrity is another concern: 'broadcasters' editorial decisions, both in terms of programming commissioned and the content of programmes, could be skewed in order to maximise the opportunities for placing products for promotional purposes' (DCMS, 2005: 2). Writers and creative workers have led campaigns against the implications for artistic integrity and cultural diversity, while others have challenged growing commercialism. In June 2008, the UK Culture Secretary Andy Burnham, against industry expectations, declared 'I think there are some lines that we should not cross – one of which is that you can buy the space between the programmes on commercial channels, but not the space within them' (DCMS, 2008a). The following month the Government indicated it favoured prohibiting PP in all types of television programmes (DCMS, 2008b).

There is nothing new about the integration of advertising and media content. Product placement in movies can be traced back to the Lumière films of the 1890s and was well established in the Hollywood studio system by the 1920s (Newell *et al.*, 2006; Eckert, 1991). Contemporary research indicates a spectrum of views from outright opposition to acceptance, even appreciation of brand placement, with tolerance greatest among the young and those most accustomed to commercial media fare. Yet, research for Ofcom (2005b) found over 90 per cent were wary or strongly disapproved of noticeable product placement. Unlike unpaid prop placement, which meets audiences' desire for realism, product placement opens the way for programme agendas to be distorted for commercial purposes.

Convergence: regulating Internet advertising

One of the arguments for a single UK advertising regulator was the recognition that 'advertising campaigns today are often designed to run across several platforms simultaneously (press, radio, television, Internet, mobile telephony), aided by digital technology and with sophisticated links between them' (Ofcom, 2004b: 7). Since 1995 the ASA extended its remit to Internet advertising. Most CAP rules apply online as well as offline, but in advertising as in other areas of law and regulation, the Internet poses challenges of jurisdiction, reach and effectiveness. A high profile issue has been 'spam', unsolicited commercial communications. Reflecting EU legislation (from December 2003), the ASA requires that commercial e-mail should only be sent to those people who have given their explicit consent to receive it, but permits a widely drawn exception allowing unsolicited e-mail 'to existing customers about similar products without their consent – so long as customers are given an opportunity to object to receiving further e-mail' (ASA, 2008c).

Self-Regulatory Organisations (SROs) such as the ASA cannot exercise authority over non-national traders. While there is now some cross-national policing of advertising by European SROs, most 'spam' originates outside the EU and is beyond their reach. Text messaging and 'viral' advertising via mobiles have attracted increasing numbers of complaints. According to ASA research, consumers found text-based advertising from third parties most annoying but there was greater tolerance for 'clickable' banners from trusted brands on 3G and more advanced networks. The CAP set up Admark, a voluntary membership scheme for Internet advertisers, in 2000. Compliance is high, according to ASA and CAP reviews. However, it is not hard to find evidence of the regulatory challenges generated in this rapidly changing environment. In 2002 the ASA carried out its first check of Internet banner and pop-up ads and found only one of 616 ads broke the codes, while 37 were deemed 'questionable', mostly online betting adverts. However, it noted that some ads would have broken the codes if they appeared in other media, for instance ICT, telecoms and finance sector ads that contained little or no details of terms and conditions. There is no pre-clearance for Internet advertising. With the growth of 'rich' audiovisual advertising online, there are mounting temptations for some advertisers to break out of code constraints. An even greater challenge is that advertisers can easily create 'editorial' content, which is outside the ASA's remit. According to *Campaign*'s Claire Beale (2008a) 'Any advertiser that really wants to shock or surprise us can do a fine job of bypassing regulated media at the moment by going straight to a website, where they have free rein'.

Marketing communications online, as offline, must be recognisable as such. The ASA upheld its first complaint against a banner advertisement in May 2000, for an ISP advert on a financial webpage that was not clearly distinguished from the editorial content. The CAP code applies to online advertisements in 'paid for' space, such as banner, pop-up ads, ads in commercial e-mails and sales promotions wherever they appear online (including in organisation's websites or in e-mails) but not companies' 'editorial' content, for instance McDonald's *Kids Zone*. This means that regulation fails to grapple with one of the Internet's key features, the ability to seamlessly integrate editorial and advertising, telling and selling. It means too that the ASA rejects the majority of complaints it receives, which relate to claims made on companies' own websites. This failure challenges the self-regulatory system, with one government source stating bluntly: 'It cannot be right that 90 per cent of the complaints to the Advertising Standards Authority about online ads were outside its remit' (*Campaign*, 2008b).

In 2008 the Government renewed calls for the advertising industry to bring online ads fully under the remit of its voluntary code or face the threat of legislation. Online marketing

3. Look at advertising that has been put before the ASA Council for a formal adjudication (www.asa.org.uk). Go straight to the advertisement and apply the relevant CAP code to make your own adjudication, identifying whether the advertising breaches specific sections of the code and what the grounds for your adjudication would be. Then read the actual ASA adjudication. Did you reach the same conclusion? Did you identify different factors from those that informed the ASA's ruling? How successfully do you think the ASA applied the codes to its adjudications? On the basis of the material examined, do you think the regulatory system is working effectively?

4. 'Marketers, publishers and owners of other media should ensure that marketing communications are designed and presented in such a way that it is clear that they are marketing communications.' (Section 22.1 British Code of Advertising, Sales Promotion and Direct Marketing, 11th edition, 2003).

   Choosing specific media sector(s), consider the evidence and the implications of the erosion of the separation between media content and advertising? Is product placement a legitimate tool for marketers?

5. How would you wish to reform advertising regulation? Can you make a persuasive case, using evidence from advertising practice and current regulation, for the changes you propose?

6. Consider the arguments for and against HFCC food advertising to children on television. Livingstone and Helsper (2004) provide one of the best surveys of the literature on effects; their 'web of causality' model illustrates the complex, multi-directional influences acting on children's food choices within which television advertising is situated (Livingstone 2005, 2006). There is a tacit consensus that food promotion has modest 'direct' effects on children's food preferences, with the likelihood of even greater 'indirect' effects arising from its influence on cultural conventions, food perceptions, family food choices, peer culture, and so on. Are the findings sufficient to justify regulation of food advertising to children? What should the regulations be, who should regulate, and on what grounds?

Part II

Themed chapters

6 Lynx: the challenges of lad culture

Julia Dane and Hyunsun Yoon

Introduction

This chapter explores the way in which youth offers both possibilities and ongoing challenges to advertisers. Lynx, also known as Axe in some countries, will provide the narrative drive for the discussion and function as an illustration of the way in which a brand became aware of and tapped into the development of a new market sector, namely deodorants and bodysprays for young lads. Acknowledging Lynx's 20-year history, the chapter will focus on how the brand through its advertising has continually reinvented itself, keeping pace with both the rise and reconfigurations of lad culture. In view of this, the main topics considered include characteristics of the youth market, development of brand loyalty, identity construction and media/new media influences.

The youth market and Lynx

The youth market is one of the most coveted of all segments, due to youths' spending power, their ability to be trendsetters, their receptivity to new products and their tremendous potential for becoming consumers for life (Wolburg and Pokrywczynski, 2001). It is difficult to define the youth market as today's children are growing older younger (KGOY: Kids Growing Older Younger) and many older people have mindsets similar to those of the younger generation. The youth market is complex, segmented and hard to understand. Young people are vulnerable to short-lived fads, individualistic, extremely media-savvy, advertising literate and resistant to advertising efforts. The main challenge for advertisers is to understand youth and to 'reach' young people in a credible way (Saxton, 2005). Lynx's target audience is young men, primarily adolescents, aged 16 to 24.

Lynx advertising was developed around the core brand property of seduction; Lynx helps the young man to get the girl, with the brand being portrayed as a 'confidence booster' and 'an accomplice' (Fennell, 1999). According to Lynx's agency, Bartle Bogle, Hegarty, 'when the Lynx campaign was developed, the deodorant market was characterised by functional communications that focused on odour control' (Nicholls and Raillard, 2004). It was then decided that its primary benefit was actually the provision of confidence and that this was most relevant in the context of getting a girl. This is the so-called 'Lynx effect'.

Launched as Axe in France in 1983, Lynx is now available in more than 60 countries worldwide. The brand is called Lynx in the UK and Australia but Axe in other countries; Axe being considered too aggressive a brand name for English-speaking markets accompanied by other trademark issues. For simplicity, the name Lynx will be adopted throughout this chapter. Lynx started life as a deodorant and has also been expanded into other personal care niches, for example, aftershave, body sprays, shower gels, shaving gels and razors. However, despite a series of extensions into aftershave (1989) and roll-on deodorant (1991), the brand's growth had tailed off by the mid-1990s. Lynx is a youth brand and as such is subject to constant regeneration to attract younger new users (Weed, 2000), ranging from brand positioning to product packaging and effective communication. To counter the halt in growth, the Lynx marketers went clubbing and shopping in order to develop new marketing strategies for the brand that would capture the interest and imagination of their target audience. When considering new ways for Lynx to go beyond just being a male toiletries product, 'the brand had to think about everything to do with seduction and masculinity' (Weed, 2000). This theme underpins the whole of the brand's identity and therefore, in addition to television and print advertising, some rather laddish web-based activity in the form of viral marketing was also used to both reach and connect with its target audience. It was a success. In 1996 the new marketing campaign re-established the identity of Lynx, especially in the UK, as an icon in the revitalised young men's grooming products market.

Lynx in a socio-cultural context

The growth of the male grooming market is part of the sector dedicated to what the beauty industry refers to as male image maintenance. Lifestyle magazines first highlighted the importance of grooming for the modern man and Unilever took this one step further by introducing male grooming parlours. At this point the Lynx Barbershop was created, the intention being to fill a gap in the market between traditional barbershops and women's salons, by providing an environment totally dedicated to young men. Lynx salons offered Playstations and TV before and during the grooming experience with, of course, the opportunity to purchase from the range of Lynx products on the way out. The first Lynx Barbershop opened in Oxford Street, London in 2000; however, this idea was abandoned after 14 months. A company spokesman stated 'Brand extensions are not simply a sideline for us – we set aggressive targets for all our initiatives, the barber shops were successful and generated a lot of publicity, but failed to meet the targets.' (Cozens, 2002: 23). This is evidence of consistent brand innovation, a key theme of this chapter, but also shows that not all produce the outcomes expected.

However, despite the success of the regeneration of Lynx in the mid-1990s, in 2001, according to the consumer market analyst Mintel, one in five men still considered grooming products as being solely for women (Mintel, 2001). The reluctance of the male population to embrace male grooming products was a concern for both the producers of such products and for the advertising industry. Before we present two case studies of recent Lynx advertising, which demonstrate how this second wave of challenges was addressed, it is important to look at social and cultural discourses around changing masculinities, which preceded and followed the attempt to target the male consumer.

Prior to the 1980s, concerns around grooming and therefore desires to purchase grooming products were socially constructed as feminine. Campaigns for products such as Brylcreem for hair in the 1950s and Brut aftershave in the 1970s were very careful to ensure that their advertisements emphasised a traditional masculinity. The term 'traditional masculinity' refers to the dominant discourse of masculinity prior to the 1980s. Men were seen as the breadwinners, the wage-earners who supported their families. Also masculinity was defined in opposition to femininity through ideas of machismo, rationality and lack of emotion. For example, Brylcreem showed in one advertisement a man in overalls, working beneath a car and covered in grease. Later in the 1970s, Brut used the successful and well-known boxer Henry Cooper in its campaign. Such images aimed to negate the possibility of either feminization or homoeroticism in male grooming products.

The emergence of the new man

The 1980s brought economic and social changes that impacted greatly on the male grooming market and concomitantly the advertising industry. As John Beynon states, 'Masculinity was more extensively transformed by economic and commercial forces in the 1980s than at any previous time' (2002: 100). It has been argued that men emerged as a gendered group in the 1980s. What exactly does this mean? To consider changes in discourses of normative masculinity, it is important to consider the social context in which they occurred.

One of the key social discourses to emerge prior to this time is a feminist critique of female representation. The Women's Movement of the late 1960s, early 1970s, problematized gendered representation in the media. Another movement which emerged in the early 1980s to challenge dominant discourse and representation was found in the Gay Rights campaigns, which like the Women's Movement sought to achieve equality with heterosexual masculinity. Together, these movements drew attention to the images of men in the media. Prior to such critiques, masculinity was treated unproblematically. However, in the 1980s we see the rise of masculinity studies in academia, with key figures such as Bob Connell and Michael Kimmel interrogating social discourses and representations of masculinity. It is around this time that the idea of a crisis of masculinity is seen to emerge as a response to the criticisms made against it, and it is around the 1980s that we see the emergence of the 'new man'. The new man represented a dis-identification with traditional masculinity. New man participated in the domestic sphere. That is to say, domestic labour was no longer seen as an entirely female domain, with men now seen to engage in both household chores and childcare. Prior to this, the domestic arena was seen as a feminine arena and therefore any man participating in such labour was deemed to be exhibiting feminine attributes.

New man believed in gender equality, was anti-sexist and in touch with his emotions. He was sensitive, caring and happy to incorporate traits that had previously been considered feminine into his life. The reality of this shift is debatable and, of course, it is impossible to definitively separate the social reality of masculinities from media constructs. However, this shift to a discourse of the new man is relevant to consider in the context of the emergence of the male grooming market that we see today. Beynon (2002) describes the new man as both nurturer and narcissist. Sigmund Freud (1914) identified narcissism as a feature of the psyche. He drew on the Greek myth of Narcissus as a metaphor for his account of self-directed libido. Narcissus was a Greek mythological character who spurned the advances of nymphs, eventually falling in love with his own reflection in the water. Narcissism has come to describe 'a tendency to self-worship and to develop an excessive interest in one's own personal features' (Cashmore, 2006: 102). Therefore, the identification of new man as nurturer and narcissist, traits previously identified with femininity, had a specific impact on male representation and the male grooming market.

The 1980s also brought new visual representations of men. There was an increasing display and sexualisation of the male body in mainstream cinema, television and advertising (Evans and Gamman, 1995; Mort, 1996; Edwards, 1997). Accompanying this, the emergence of male style magazines such as *GQ* and *Arena* presented images of the self-confident and well-groomed man. Furthermore, as traditional industries fell, economic and social changes led to a loss of 'status, self esteem and the old moral authority, which men used to have just by being men' (Coward, 1999: 86). At the same time, an increase in 'image industries' such as advertising, media, promotions and public relations, led to what has been termed the commercialization of masculinity.

Pertinent questions have been raised as to whether a genuine development in the nature of masculinity and an advance in sexual politics occurred. Arguably, the notion of a change in masculinities simply represents a crude marketing device or a media-driven illusion (Edwards, 1997; Beynon, 2002). Certainly advertising led the way in a new erotic objectification of the male body, breaking taboos regarding display and feminization. The often cited Levi's advertisement featuring Nick Kamen stripping to his underwear in a launderette in order to wash his jeans exemplifies this. As Mort (1988) suggests, this new visual coding of masculinity produced representations of a more self-conscious sense of maleness.

The new lad

The 1990s sees the rise of what has been termed the 'new lad', with laddism as a response to the idea of new man. There was a shift in both discourse and representation that seems to revert to the promotion of traditional masculinity. Lads' magazines such as *Loaded* and *FHM* arrived on the scene, achieving considerable success with their focus on drinking, football and sex. Arguably, an antidote to new man was offered to the next generation. Also, new laddism represents a more working-class machismo in response to the anti-sexist, sensitive new man. There is a reassertion of something fundamentally masculine (Gill, 2007).

The coding of male bodies to be looked at and desired in a way traditionally associated with female bodies remains. Bordo argues that:

> Feminists might like to imagine that Madison Avenue heard our pleas for sexual equality and finally gave us 'men as sex objects'. But what's really happened is that women have been the beneficiaries of what might be described as a triumph of pure consumerism – and with it, a burgeoning male and fitness and beauty culture – over homophobia and the taboos against male vanity, male 'femininity', and erotic display of the male body that have gone along with it. (Bordo, 1999: 179)

So the 1990s sees a backlash to the new man, yet the display of idealized and eroticized male bodies in advertising increases. Contemporary advertising for male grooming products attempts to negotiate representations that combine sensitivity and machismo. For example, the recent use of Pierce Brosnan in L'Oreal adverts for their skincare range for men demonstrates how the combination of sensitive yet macho masculinity is used to persuade men that skin products are not only for women. This is the social context of masculinity within which Lynx addresses its target market, the next generation of men.

Lynx's address

In 2000, *Advertising Age* reported that there was a need for the industry to increase adspend for men's grooming products. The aim was to counter the problem of such products, even basics like shampoo, being perceived as in some way un-masculine and that a strategy was needed to persuade men that grooming was not only a feminine trait. Noting the shift to new laddism, Bartle, Bogle, Hegarty produced a series of campaigns which addressed the problem by employing a laddish approach. This approach aimed to connote social values around male status and identity through the magical promise of 'the Lynx effect'. Not only does the Lynx effect offer a transformation in terms of attraction, but also in terms of the rite of passage from boy to man through what Goffman (1979) termed 'hyper-ritualization'. These social issues are the concerns of the male youth market. Playing on young men's anxieties around status and attraction, Lynx advertising offers a resolution. The transformation produced through the Lynx effect is not that of the idealized male Adonis, but to an ordinary man who now has status and the potential to attract many women. The adverts are not solely engaged with selling the product; they are also constructing the brand image which revolves around the possibilities of the Lynx effect. To demonstrate how Lynx advertising taps into and offers to resolve the anxieties associated with male youth, this chapter will conclude with two case studies looking at the campaigns for Lynx Boost and Lynx Pulse. Lynx Boost directly addresses the issue of changing masculinities while Lynx Pulse highlights the need to draw upon popular culture to engineer effective communication.

Case study 1: Lynx Boost and Towelboy

The 20-second ad opens in a sparsely accessorised white tiled bathroom with only a three panelled mirror and a corner shower with a plain white curtain. This is a functional masculine bathroom. As the music, *Change My Mind* by The Blueskins (2006) begins, the curtain is swept to one side and a young man emerges swiftly from the shower cubicle. Chest covered in soap suds, he grabs a blue towel, wraps it around his waist and is next seen leaving the building through gated doors. As he passes a hotdog stall on the street other customers turn and stare. The vendor passes him a hot dog as he strides past and the camera focuses on a young woman who, hot dog in hand, gazes longingly at him. He enters a busy night club, dancing purposefully through the crowd. The camera cuts to a shot of an older man standing behind a young woman at the bar. The older man's tongue protrudes from his mouth as he tries to lick the young woman's shoulder, a move she rejects with a hand gesture as she turns away from him. Our hero whips the towel from his waist and the camera pans back to allow a full view of his towel flick attack on the older man. The older man turns in surprise and we see but do not hear Towelboy's verbal dismissal. The young woman turns and looks at her hero with an expression of both gratitude and seduction. Over his shoulder another woman is giving the same admiring look. In the final scene, he wraps the blue towel around the woman's shoulders and they walk down the street, his arm placed protectively around her shoulder and his nakedness displayed as they walk away from the camera. The female voiceover announces in a sultry voice, 'New Lynx Boost, stimulating shower gel' as the final scene is a return to the white bathroom and we see the product placed on a shelf in Towelboy's shower.

This advert contains many signs and referents that will appeal to young men's anxieties around attraction and status. A resolution is offered through the Lynx effect. In Goffman's terms, the advert represents a hyper-ritualization of the rite of passage from boy to man.

A symbolic entry into desired social and sexual worlds is affected through the hero's supremacy over the older man in competition for the woman. This advert is also informed by the juxtaposition between nature and civilization through the imagery of the naked man breaking free from civilized restraint. Not only is Towelboy naked in the world, his freedom from social restraint is symbolically marked as he leaves his apartment through a gated door. This advert then is about a masculinity which can escape from rules and restrictions, which is close to nature. It is about access to status, seduction and magic through power over others. The advert addresses anxieties around becoming a man in a time of shifting gender roles through control of women, via the product of course, and through a realistic image of man rather than an idealized image of an unattainable masculinity. For the target audience of boys and young men, Lynx advertising presents a powerful message through visuals, narrative, music and humour. This message taps into discourses of new laddism to present a promise of desired transformation.

Case study 2: The Lynx Pulse campaign

Key to the ongoing success of Lynx has been the strategy of launching a new fragrance variant every year, around 20 in total. Lynx has used an array of methods to develop these new variants; firstly, fragrance descriptors (Lynx Musk, Marine, Oriental); geography used to evoke feelings (Lynx Alaska, Africa, Java); abstract names (Lynx Apollo, Gravity, Dimension); and more recently, mating game insights helped to develop Lynx Pulse, Touch and Click (Millar *et al.*, 2006). Launched across Europe in 2003 (with the hugely popular 'Dancing man' commercial), the Lynx Pulse fragrance has been one of the most successful variants. We now consider the Lynx Pulse campaign in detail as an effective example of integrated, multi-channel communication. It took an insight into the mating game and leveraged it in a humorous and inspirational way, along with a recognition that 'women love a man who can dance'. Furthermore, it developed a mix that created a music track, a dance-floor craze and an award winning TV commercial.

The big idea behind the Lynx Pulse campaign was the use of the right kind of 'music' and 'dance'. A number of studies have shown that music is one of the key influences in the lives of young people (Saxton, 2005; White, 2006). Music is an intrinsic entertainment for young people and it takes up more time in their lives than sport, the cinema or going to the pub (Saxton, 2005). Dance relates to Lynx's brand territory of seduction: getting girls. The Lynx Pulse campaign featuring *Make Luv* by Room 5, proved it is possible for an unknown track to score a huge success off the back of a suitable ad and for sales of the advertised product to rise similarly. The music was simple and infectious (Nicholls and Raillard, 2004). The first phase of the campaign was to send this music track to key opinion formers such as DJs, ensuring that it was exposed to the right people in the right places (Saxton, 2005). The music track was accompanied by merchandise such as T-shirts, DJ slipmats and record bags.

The next phase was to introduce an animated online character called 'The Dotman', made of the same graphic elements as the Lynx Pulse logo, available as a screen saver, and performing the Lynx Pulse dance on the screen. The TV commercial and PR efforts followed the seeding stage of the music and dance elements. *Make Luv* was number one in the UK official charts for a month (Nicholls and Raillard, 2004) and a survey showed that 73 per cent of people identified the ad as a conversation piece while the UK average for 'word of mouth' stood at 25–39 per cent (Nicholls and Raillard, 2004). Lynx have continued to maintain a strong online presence, developing content that is both participatory and reflective of the brand's evolving identity.

New media strategies and brand loyalty

As discussed earlier, youth becomes increasingly 'wired' and it is possible to use new media to reach key movers and shakers and lead the market (White, 2006). The Lynx Pulse campaign demonstrated the success of viral marketing and word-of-mouth among young people. Youth audiences thus became one of the key targets of the developing fashion for so-called ambient media and event marketing. At the end of 2004, Lynx held a live music concert north of the Arctic Circle. An audience of 300 competition winners enjoyed a show which was filmed by *Channel 4* and aired in its youth slot, *T4*. This is an example of 'brand entertainment'. Brand entertainment is a new and growing marketing discipline. It is best defined as where a brand creates consumer entertainment that would not have existed without that brand and where consumers choose their involvement (Dawson and Hall, 2005). In October 2006, Myspace launched a branded community for Lynx Boost, allowing users to interact with the character from the Lynx Boost ad, Towel Boy, and play online computer games. As Western cultures are increasingly driven by entertainment, brands have to deliver entertainment to compete for attention (Dawson and Hall, 2005). In addition, as cynical consumers increasingly edit out brands that fail to entertain them, brands such as Coke and Nike are becoming entertainment media in their own right through activities such as My Music and Run London.

Young people are more brand 'aware' than other market segments but that does not mean automatically being brand 'loyal'. And where loyalty exists, while it may be intense, this does not mean that it is deeply rooted (Lammiman and Syrett, 2004). Brand loyalty, long a central construct in marketing, is a measure of the attachment that a customer has to a brand (Aaker, 1991: 39). Levels of brand loyalty vary ranging from the non-loyal buyer who is completely indifferent to the brand, the satisfied and habitual buyer to the committed buyer. A brand that has a substantial group of extremely involved and committed buyers might be termed a 'charismatic' brand (Aaker, 1991. 41). Although Lynx was the essential kit for the teenage seducer, once he approached 18 or 19 he started to grow out of the brand. In other words, it had become a victim of its own success; Lynx was a rite of passage for teenage guys and this placed a glass ceiling on growth (Bottomley, 2005). Lynx has subsequently developed marketing strategies aimed to hold onto their market as they grow from boy to man. This was the context in which the 'Getting Dressed' (2005) campaign was launched; its objective was to broaden Lynx's appeal without alienating the core audience. The slogan was 'You never know when'. The research has shown that Lynx was seen as part of a pre-going out, pre-pulling ritual (Bottomley, 2005) and that needed to change because it was not relevant for older guys. For older guys, the whole mating game process was less predatory and more engaging. Lynx had to reassure them that they would always be prepared. The commercial began with a young man and woman waking up in bed. In reverse, they proceed to follow their trail of clothes back to where they first met, the supermarket. Then they push the two trolleys off in different directions. The focus was not on the guy pulling a girl but on the relationship. It was a mature way to play the mating game. It demonstrated that girls want the same thing as men and the mating game is always afoot (you can pull any time, any place). The idea was that the Lynx guy could pull in the most unexpected places because he was always ready. The Lynx 'Getting Dressed' TV commercial won a Gold Lion at Cannes for international advertising quality

The advertising industry must be continually aware of and able to tap into a youth market which is subject to constant change and regeneration. In 2005, Saxton identified celebrity culture; music and fashion; technology and innovation; and family, leisure and diversity as the key influences in the lives of 15–24-year-olds in Europe. According to

White (2006), authenticity and honesty have now become important ingredients in today's brand communications to youth. Lynx achieved initial success through the awareness and ability to tap into the development of a new market sector in terms of young lads taking an interest in their appearance while also facing anxieties around changing gender roles in society. By grounding their brand identity in realistic narratives of attainable male appearance while playing to young men's anxieties and fantasies, Lynx have retained a dominant share in the youth grooming market. In 2007 global sales of Lynx reached the €1bn (£750m) mark; quite an advance on its €300m (£228m) total of 10 years ago (Jack, 2008). 2008 heralded a further brand innovation as 'Lynx 3' was launched: allowing the user to customize their fragrance on the basis of an innovative dispenser. This comes at a time when 'laddism' has potentially waned but at the same time Lynx's advertising still needs to keep a firm hold on lad culture.

Conclusion

This chapter has looked at how the advertising industry addresses the male youth market through the example of Lynx as both brand and product. Targeting this group has posed specific challenges: challenges that must be continually faced in order to maintain brand success, particularly as the era of the lads' mags appears to have peaked. As BBH UK chairman, Jim Carroll, has argued, the quest is to remain relevant (Jack, 2008). Using the example of male grooming products, we have shown how advertising must be aware of and tap into evolving discourses around gender and identity. Furthermore, how changing media environments present both problems and solutions in appealing to contemporary youth.

Questions for students

1. In the various Lynx campaigns discussed above, what are the associations that the Lynx brand has developed?

2. Who are the competitors of Lynx? How does Lynx differ from the profile of competitor brands?

3. What does the Lynx brand mean to the youth market segment?

4. Consider Lynx's use of ambient media and new media strategies. What is your experience in relation to Internet advertising and event marketing in general?

7 Celebrity

Helen Powell

Introduction

This chapter seeks to chart the history and effectiveness of a particular creative approach, namely the use of the celebrity in advertising campaigns, which is worthy of consideration for both its longevity and frequency of use across a range of market sectors. In discussing its history, of particular note is the way in which advertising has consistently turned to popular culture in the communication of meaning and celebrities have become a familiar feature in this process since the arrival of television advertising in 1955. However, the examples chosen for this chapter have been limited to the last 10 years, in order to demonstrate how advertising creatives consistently play with the form and to look in detail and make some comparisons as to why some executions are more successful than others. For the immediate transposition of fame from celebrity to brand is not guaranteed and careful consideration is required not only in terms of the appropriateness of this creative strategy for the brand in question, but further layers of judgement are required around issues of selection and synergy. However, if carefully managed, the benefits are significant: improved sales, increased market share, high levels of brand awareness and consumer loyalty. Furthermore, as the media globalises so we see celebrities demonstrating the potential to take brands global too. In 2008 Russian tennis star Maria Sharapova was signed up by mobile phone maker Sony Ericsson to be its global brand ambassador and Reebok assigned Formula 1 driver, Lewis Hamilton, the same role.

The recognition of the value of fame

Around one fifth of advertisements in the UK feature a celebrity (Pringle, 2004a: 10) and are underpinned by a belief whereby through a process of association certain images, values and successes are transferred from the celebrity onto the brand or service being promoted. Perhaps the most effective place to start in the history of this creative style is with an advertising problem that the modern agency in its infancy faced; namely to find an appropriate form of communication that somehow mediated between its creators (white, middle class and highly educated) and the intended target audience (a mass, urban population). J. Walter Thompson in the United States initially countered this problem with two particular creative approaches. The first came to be known as a 'tabloid style' (Marchand, 1986: 86), that drew upon the language of 1920s cinema and magazines for body copy. However, of particular interest to the public, and therefore to advertisers, were the stars that populated these media, prompting Stanley Resor, chairman of the agency, to begin to explore the way in which brands could attain fame by association, through 'movies stars (Lux), Countesses (Pond's) or simply famous people (US Lines)' (Mayer, 1958: 79). In 1927 a headline created by JWT for Lux Soap read '9 out of 10 screen stars care for their skin with Lux toilet soap.' The appropriation of the Hollywood close-up shot was a critical step in developing identificatory practices between the product and the potential consumer and years of success ensued for Lux with Jean Harlow, Marilyn Monroe and other female Hollywood icons. What Resor tapped into was the promotional possibilities of fame: of the star appearing in the advertisement and the product positioned as an essential aspect of the lifestyles of the famous. He recognised that the opportunity to become famous is not necessarily democratic but access to consumer goods that the stars endorsed gave greater numbers the possibility of vicarious access to their lives. The use of the celebrity in advertising today comes from an overall appeal that is generated and located within the wider arena of popular culture. It can be argued that the public feel closer to and identify more effectively with contemporary celebrities than Hollywood stars, first due to their domestication, the location of the television set within the home, and second 'as stars develop their reputation by playing someone else' (Turner, 2004: 15), while with the celebrity there is a distinctive flow between their performances on and off screen.

The range of qualitative differences between celebrities allows agencies to identify, select and manage the choice of celebrity for the brand in question. A critical concept in this selection process is that of synergy. This registers the appropriateness of the celebrity in terms of transferring the meanings and associations affiliated to them within the domain of popular culture into the world of the brand and the targeted consumer (McCracken, 2005). In this way their cultural capital has the capacity to be converted into economic capital. However, synergy is not synonymous simply with the scale of being well known; the nuances of selection are far subtler than this, as the case studies that follow will testify. Rather, we need to contextualise the role of the celebrity in relation to their 'value': which is not a use value but rather an exchange value and a symbolic value that are inextricably linked. That is to say, the value of a celebrity to an advertising campaign and the brand they are endorsing comes from what they represent: a particular image that consumers identify with and wish to buy into. This might be affiliated to their looks, their lifestyle, their personality or a particular skill set, or any combination of these. Here their image and what it represents can be transferred through advertising, which draws its full effect from all the extra-discursive material associated with them. This makes for a very economical representative strategy as the audience draws upon what they know about the celebrity within the context of popular culture and embeds that into their reading of the advertisement; thus allowing for a much richer set of connotations than either a single poster or 30 seconds on TV can allow. This fusion of recognition plus existing emotional attachments towards certain celebrities provides the advertisement with a greater chance of cutting through the clutter and getting noticed. Hence in the lead up to Christmas 2007, the most intensive promotional period for retailers, Tesco ensured that with the help of The Spice Girls, their supermarket would remain at the forefront of consumers' minds, albeit at a cost of £1 million per Spice Girl (*Campaign*, 2007a). This provides a further example of advertising's capacity to tap into a particular moment within popular culture as the buzz generated by the reunion of the girl group, who originally formed in the mid-1990s, extended across all media platforms. Therefore, within the context of marketing and advertising a celebrity is 'anyone who is familiar enough to the people a brand wishes to communicate with to add values to that communication by association with their image and reputation' (Pringle, 2004a: xiv).

Choosing a celebrity for your campaign

The next point to address is how this concept of 'synergy' is put into practice creatively. It has been established that one of the principal features of this advertising strategy is that the celebrity functions as a vehicle to get both the advertisement and therefore the brand being promoted noticed due to the increased public interest in celebrities. Concomitantly, the celebrity also acts as a marker of differentiation, allowing the brand in question to have a highly recognisable point of promotional difference from its competitors within the market sector in question. In the UK there is no equivalent either to the USA's 'Q ratings' or 'Q score', an index developed in 1963 as a means to measure both the familiarity and appeal of celebrities or to the more recent and scientific 'Davie-Brown index' of 2006. Instead, it is up to the advertising agency to make judgements as to the appropriateness of the qualities of the celebrity and how they can be integrated into the brand message: while recognising that simply using a celebrity for celebrity's sake will only bring the celebrity acknowledgment. Therefore, as Pringle succinctly states:

> the process of casting the right star is absolutely crucial . . . creative people, and their clients, need to ask themselves the following questions before deciding on a star: How well does this particular celebrity fit in with the brand?; How famous is the star?; Which facets of this high-profile person can best work for the brand profile?; How much of this can the brand finance? (Pringle, 2004b: 58)

The players and processes involved in celebrity selection were documented in a rare study conducted by Erdogan and Baker (2000), based on semi-structured interviews with 30 managers across the UK's largest agencies whereby most interviewees reported 'a process for selecting celebrities, though it was neither written nor off the top of their heads'. Overall, across the agencies, a structured course of action was identified that seemed to 'flow' through approximately six key stages: 'initiators' (creatives), 'deciders' (account team), 'influencers' (research and legal), 'buyer' (the client), 'providers' (celebrities) and 'gatekeepers' (those who keep the process 'alive', such as agents). Finally, in November 2007, the Advertising Standards Authority, which regulates the content of advertisements, sales promotions and direct marketing in the UK, launched specific guidelines for advertisers who use celebrities to endorse products. These stated that advertisers should always hold substantiation for claims in the advertisement; make certain the featured person has granted permission; and ensure the advertisement is socially responsible (www.asa.org.uk).

The role of the celebrity in the campaign

Once the celebrity has been chosen, it is necessary to consider the role that they will play within a particular campaign. In view of this, and ahead of some specific examples, it is possible to group together different creative approaches in terms of how the celebrity is managed for best effect:

* *Testimonial*: The celebrity acts as a spokesperson for the brand.

   Examples: Gordon Ramsay's skills as a chef were effectively highlighted in an understated manner as he disastrously tried to repair his own PC in his restaurant kitchen. The tagline told him to 'Get back to what you do best with 24/7 Business IT Support' as he became in 2007 the face of BT's new services for businesses (Rainey Kelly Campbell Roalfe/Y&R). The testimonial can also have significant impact in charity campaigns, such as DLKW's long running campaign for the National Blood Service, which features celebrities telling us to 'do something amazing' and give blood, following short narratives of their own personal experiences.

* *Creation of a character*: Unique to the brand

   Example: The actress Prunella Scales featured as Dottie, the frustrating senior shopper at Tesco, for over a decade (Lowe) and was dropped in 2004 for a campaign that focused more specifically on the supermarket's low price policy.

* *Use of a character*: that builds upon the personality of a known celebrity or challenges it

   Examples: While the comedian Peter Kay plays to type for John Smith's Extra Smooth Bitter (TBWA), hard man Vinnie Jones shares his sweets while a car park prang is resolved using RAC insurance (AMV BBDO).

* *Aspirational*: Where the star's known credentials are placed in association with the brand

   Example: After parting company with David Beckham, the start of 2008 saw Gillette unveil its first TV campaign with Tiger Woods, Thierry Henry and Roger Federer for the Fusion Power razor. The 30-second spot, created by Abbott Mead Vickers, BBDO, features a montage of great moments from each of their careers with the tagline: 'Prepare to be your best today'.

* *Brands create their own stars from their employees*

   Example: Back in 2000 Howard Brown, a Halifax Bank employee, was the first star of the longstanding campaign whereby staff members sang along to reworded versions of popular songs in order to promote services and offers (DLKW).

From the general to the specific: Beckham, Moss and Oliver

There are three celebrities who, over the last decade, have perhaps made the greatest impact as brand representatives. Kate Moss and David Beckham demonstrate the potential for a successful celebrity to endorse multiple brands, allowing questions to be asked around issues of consumer identification and recall. In contrast, Jamie Oliver has remained constant in terms of his brand affiliations and his contribution to Sainsbury's supermarket profitability.

In late 2006, Kate Moss was voted number one in a *Sunday Times* survey of the most powerful celebrities in Britain (Spicer, 2006). At that point Moss was involved in 14 campaigns that were earning her around £30 million per annum (ibid.: 24). In this context Moss provides an interesting case study concerning the effectiveness of multiple brand endorsements and the difficulties this might pose for the agencies involved. In particular, it raises issues of how certain qualities of the named celebrity might be both isolated and emphasised over others in order to ensure the effective transmission of the appropriate meanings an agency wishes to engender around their brand. This strategy is not without its risks. First, each brand's individuality has the potential to become diluted and second, multiple endorsements 'negatively influence a consumer's perspective of endorser credibility and likeability' (Souza and Quintanilha, 2006). However, Moss seems to challenge this whereby clearly defined sides of her image and personality allow her powers of representation to become amplified. Even when questioned over whether associated scandals would tarnish her promotional capacity David Golding, the Planning Director at Rainey Kelly Campbell Roalfe/Y&R, argued: 'The bigger story was how many companies dropped her and then took her back. To me this is proof that she is a great brand icon' (Bussey, 2006: 25).

In a similar vein, David Beckham has capitalised upon his celebrity status positioning himself as footballer, father, fashion icon and fundraiser to maximum impact in relation to the brands that he has endorsed, often globally. In this context his success in endorsing so many brands comes from the fact, Cashmore argues (2002: 157), that 'there are many, many different Beckhams'. Furthermore, Milligan (2004: 88) believes that the reason why Beckham has remained successful as a celebrity endorser across so many different brands is due to his composition: the essential and unchanging elements (Beckham, the footballer) and the ephemeral and adaptable parts (changes to style and image). This also allows him to communicate with different target audiences. Thus, in relation to the Police sunglasses deal, Milligan (2004: 105) states 'It demonstrated that Beckham didn't need football to appeal commercially to audiences.' Taking the year 2002 as an example, Beckham endorsed products for Adidas and Pepsi, which featured his footballing skills, Brylcreem, for his sense of style, while Vodafone drew upon a deep-seated sense of ordinariness as he chatted on his mobile promoting their new Vodafone Live! Camera phone and data offering service. Following this campaign, Charles Dunstone, chief executive of Carphone Warehouse, reported that customers were specifically asking for a 'David Beckham phone' (Budden, 2003: 8). As a family man, Beckham also launched his, albeit short-lived, DB07 youth clothing range with High Street giants M&S in September 2002. More recently, despite playing out his twilight years in the footballing 'Galaxies', his advertisement for the Motorola RAZR (2007) once again draws upon his iconic style as a promotional vehicle for the handset accessory, illustrating that Beckham's image is, as the tagline states, 'sharper than ever'. However, it does seem that his ability to attract endorsers is primarily linked to the exposure he receives in relation to his primary trade: with football's ability to attract global audiences, his exodus from the back pages has seen his earnings from endorsements fall heavily (Bokaie, 2007).

Finally, in juxtaposition to the above examples, Jamie Oliver has remained loyal to the supermarket chain Sainsbury's, whose agency, AMV BBDO, recruited the celebrity chef in an attempt to halt a five-year decline in sales by bringing in new consumers to the stores while simultaneously holding onto its existing customer base. It intended to do this through the promotion of brand values based not on price, unlike its major competitor, but on quality: good food that can be trusted but that also should be tried. A recognised chef could personify both of these objectives. In view of this, 'Oliver had a brand print that was an almost perfect fit with where Sainsbury's wished to be' (Angear and Moody, 2002). The impact of the long-running campaign can be evaluated at both a micro- and macro-level. AMV BBDO won an Institute of Practitioners in Advertising award (silver) for its finding that the campaign generated an incremental £1.12bn in sales during its initial 21-month lifespan (Angear and Moody, 2002). However, sales of individual ingredients featured in recipes, such as asparagus, would also sell out quickly from store to store (Smith, 2008). But to what factors can we attribute Oliver's success in this campaign? Silverman (2006) argues it is attributable to the way Oliver blurs the lines between what constitutes advertising and entertainment. Oliver's success spans a number of media platforms, including his cookery books and more factual, politically driven television programmes that also give him high press and PR coverage. Therefore, when appearing in ads for Sainsbury's, this extra-diegetic material all feeds into the communication. The fundamental elision between Oliver as endorser and entertainer has certainly seen Sainsbury's benefit from these pluralised and yet highly connected roles.

Expect the unexpected: Flat Eric and Monkey

Some of the most engaging and indeed successful campaigns over the last few decades in generating awareness for the brand have centred not on a recognised celebrity, as explored above, but rather around a character that has either been appropriated or created for a campaign and which cultivates celebrity status. The Smash Martians, Tony the Frosties Tiger and the Tetley Tea Folk all come under this heading. However, two more recent examples are worthy of closer attention for their ability to generate interest in the brand beyond the 30 seconds of the advertisement through news and PR coverage. These are Levi's Flat Eric and Monkey, with his partner Al (comedian, Johnny Vegas), who first appeared in commercials for the rebranding of ITV Digital and more recently have made an advertising comeback to promote PG Tips. Such examples demonstrate how a campaign can turn itself into a talking point beyond the initial paid for media as stories circulate by word of mouth, the net or column inches in newspapers and magazines.

Flat Eric
Based on a short film by a Parisian director, Bartle, Bogle Hegarty's campaign featuring Flat Eric, aimed to shed jeans of the 'Jeremy Clarkson effect': that is to say, to make denim 'cool' again rather than the property of middle-aged men. There were no formal introductions to this character: he appeared in a car with his friend, Angel, and the commercials that ensued were devoid of any narrative structure, any trajectory and seemed to have no specific message to communicate. Along with the music, Flat Beat, which sold 2.5 million copies across Europe, the advertisements quickly became a cult phenomenon. The success of the campaign, which initially featured just three ads ('Dancing', 'ID' and 'Fly'), derived from the successful alignment of the creatives' vision of the brand's target audience and the composition of the final execution. They were not advertisements that everyone was meant to 'get'; rather their appeal and the interest they generated emanated from their fusion of the surreal and the 'cool'. The campaign furthermore was significant in heralding a new turn in advertising culture, namely the embedding of advertising within the entertainment economy: whereby the ad is viewed repeatedly on the basis of the blurring of the boundaries between entertainment and promotion. The Internet sites that sprang up in response are further testament to this. Due to public appeal Flat Eric returned for a second and final burst in August and September 1999 and, while like much of celebrity culture his fame was short-lived, his creative legacy has endured.

Monkey
Voted *Campaign*'s 'Campaign of the Year' (2002) 'for sheer impact, creative and strategic insight and what it has done for sales of grey wool' (*Campaign*, 2002), the introduction of the Monkey and Al soap opera was an attempt to rebrand and re-inform consumers

Figure 7.1   Flat Eric. Courtesy of Bartle Bogle Hegarty.

about ITV Digital (formerly ONdigital) in the face of sliding market share in a highly competitive sector including Telewest, ntl and BskyB. The campaign is driven by education and humour: each spot informing consumers about a particular aspect of the service through the comedic interaction of the main protagonists. What is particularly interesting about Mother's campaign, however, is the way in which they capitalised upon the ability of the characterisation of Monkey to steal the public's heart through a series of strategies to keep the brand current. These included:

- Postcards of Monkey re-enacting famous movie scenes are sent out as part of a direct marketing initiative.
- A free Monkey is given out on subscribing to ITV Digital in the winter of 2001. Security guards are placed on doors of stores to prevent theft, not of the set top boxes, but of the stuffed toy.
- Guest appearance at the 2002 *Brit Awards*.
- Mother team-up with the agency Naked to add a guerrilla marketing strand to the campaign.

Despite the initial success of these saturation tactics, with sales increased by 15 per cent within a month of the launch of the rebranding campaign (*Campaign*, 2002), the company went into receivership and unexpectedly brought into play a three-way legal battle for the knitted star between the administrators, the digital station and his creators. But Monkey was to rise from the ashes again in 2007 in another Mother campaign, this time for PG Tips, winning *Campaign*'s 'Best Celebrity Advertisement' for that year (*Campaign*, 2007b). His popularity among a new generation was confirmed by his online presence whereby he gained 4,400 MySpace friends within a few weeks and with the advertisements becoming a YouTube favourite, highlighting a new register of creative popularity.

When things can and do go wrong

The chapter has sought thus far to explore the rationale behind the execution of a celebrity campaign, with particular consideration given to the issue of synergy between the brand and the person chosen to represent it. However, following these steps in a meticulous manner does not necessarily produce success as the precariousness of this creative strategy in relation to the uncontrollability of many of its facets now comes under consideration.

Legal considerations: the issue of permission

A number of legal cases have arisen whereby permission has not been granted by the celebrity for their image, in whatever form, to appear in an advertising campaign and issues around misrepresentation have ensued. In March 2002, a landmark High Court ruling stated that advertisements should not feature celebrities without their explicit permission after Formula 1 driver, Eddie Irvine, brought a case against radio station, *Talksport*, for a brochure that featured his unsolicited image (Harvey, 2002: 3). In that same year, German goalkeeper, Oliver Khan, sued EA Games for using his image in its *FIFA World Cup 2002* without consultation. The case of the 118 118 twin runners and the close proximity of their image to the middle distance runner from the 1970s, David Bedford, also attracted much media attention. In January 2004, Ofcom ruled that while the WCRS' runners did caricature the British athlete, it did not go as far as banning the ads. Despite such previous cases, early in 2008 a French court ordered Ryanair to pay damages to French president, Nicolas Sarkozy, and his new wife, Carla Bruni, for using an unsolicited image of them promoting the airline (Sandison, 2008).

Celebrities misbehaving badly

On adopting this strategy, it must be recognised that the agency does not control the representation of the celebrity outside of how they appear in the advertisement. As a consequence, a persistent media gaze can often shed light on an aspect of celebrity behaviour that can be deemed damaging to the associated brand. For example, Bacardi dropped Vinnie Jones from its 2003 campaign after a drunken incident on an aeroplane and similarly Churchill insurance dropped the comedian Vic Reeves in 2005 after five years as the voice of the Churchill insurance dog following charges for drink driving (Bowery, 2007).

Unforeseen circumstances

When employing sports stars in campaigns, problems can arise when a performance fails to live up to expectations or injury rules them out of both media exposure and the public eye. The issue of expectations and performance can be a difficult gamble for brands. In 2000, after the Sydney Olympics, Nike dropped the athlete Kelly Holmes and signed a lucrative sponsorship deal with Paula Radcliffe. In 2001, Nike rivals Reebok signed Holmes to their stable of stars. Ironically, at the next Athens games, Radcliffe was unsuccessful in both the 10,000m and the marathon, while Holmes picked up two gold medals for her country and much coveted publicity. Another example of where sponsorship deals and performances don't quite go to plan involved the early departure of England striker Michael Owen from the World Cup qualifiers for 2006 with a damaged knee. This was a blow to Asda and Domino's Pizza. However, due to the footballer's already famous persona, both companies decided to go ahead and air their campaigns.

The issue of recall

Advertisers believe that by using a celebrity in a campaign, recall is enhanced. However, one of the critical questions needing to be asked therefore is does this actually work? In their own research Costanzo and Goodnight (2005: 55) reached the conclusion that overall 'the use of celebrities *did not significantly* result in higher brand recall' (their emphasis). That is to say, it is the celebrity *per se* that is remembered rather than the brand being endorsed. Furthermore, when the celebrity is seen out of context of the advertisement, the consumer does not necessarily make a reflexive link in their mind to the celebrity's brand associations. How B&Q bucked this trend was by using their own staff as the face of the brand. The long-running 'staffer' strategy, as it was known, ran on the basis of countering the number of advertisements featuring celebrities. That is to say, the campaign was based on the premise that if it was to make DIY realisable then it had to be grounded in reality. Thus, the next step creatively was to make the staff the spokespeople for the brand. The 'staffer' campaign achieved high levels of advertising awareness featuring in the annual *'Marketing* Adwatch' survey as the most strongly recalled campaign in the UK from 2000 to 2003 (Bethel, 2004). This was replicated by a campaign for PC World (M&C Saatchi) that again in the same survey for 2007 (Kemp, 2007) reached number one in terms of 'highest recall across the year' based on its approach whereby staff, this time played by actors, introduced the product range and latest offers.

Public sensibilities and the role of the ASA

As discussed in Chapter 5, the UK advertising industry is self-regulated. The industry is governed by codes of practice designed to protect consumers and provide guidance to agencies in terms of what is acceptable creative practice. The codes are the responsibility of two industry Committees of Advertising Practice: CAP (broadcast) and CAP (non-broadcast) and are independently administered by the ASA (Advertising Standards Authority). In May 2005, the ASA responded to 57 complaints to a TV commercial for Reebok featuring US rap star 50 Cent. The ASA described the ad as follows:

> He was shown sitting in a large darkened room while various sounds were heard including rap music, sirens, and different voices saying he had been 'gunned down' and 'taken to Jamaica hospital' and later that he was the 'best male hip hop artist' . . . The voiceover said 'shot nine times' and 50 Cent slowly counted from one to nine . . . Towards the end of the commercial another voice asks 50 Cent 'who do you plan to massacre next?' He laughs briefly then stares towards the camera (www.asa.org.uk)

The ASA upheld complaints that the ads irresponsibly glorified or glamorised gun culture and could encourage violence, especially among youths. In its ruling, the ASA considered the subject matter unsuitable, especially in the light of high profile gun-related crime in some areas of Britain at the time. In summary, the ASA stated that the advertiser 'had a particular responsibility regarding the celebrities it chose to appear in its advertising . . . the overall effect was to suggest that 50 Cent's life was inspirational for the wrong reasons' (www. asa.org.uk). The advertiser responded by withdrawing the advertisements from broadcast.

Conclusion

The consistent use of celebrities in advertising can be located within the broader context of what is termed the entertainment economy. Indeed, Wolf (2000) has argued that it is the quest to entertain that justifies their use, giving the commercial what he terms the 'E-Factor' (Wolf, 2000: 27). This term recognises the way in which consumers demand increasing value from all media content located within a context of exponential media growth. However, 'all the evidence suggests that campaigns featuring celebrities are no more likely than those featuring any other sort of creative idea to be successful' (Pringle, 2004a: 95) and 'as budgets have tightened, the added cost of using a celebrity needs to be factored in' (Warren, 2007). Yet where executed, agencies justify this expense on the basis that celebrity endorsement benefits the brand, the celebrity and the consumer. For example, Marks and Spencer is an established brand that has relied in the twenty-first century on 'showmanship' to get its customers returning to its stores (Binet and Field, 2007: 60) and through the generated 'Twiggy effect' have simultaneously demonstrated that celebrity appeal is not necessarily applicable only to the youth market. However, it must be noted that the inclusion of a celebrity alone is not enough to engage attention: celebrities must support a creative idea, not be the idea. Therefore, when considering this creative strategy, agencies must ask themselves two things: first, will the returns justify the additional costs and risks of using a celebrity and second, how good is the creative strategy? In addition, an agency always needs to be aware of the fundamental paradox and concomitant risks that underpin this strategy: brands need to develop a stable brand personality but celebrities are fragile human beings who are consistently re-inventing themselves within the public arena. This is something the agency cannot control.

Questions for students

1. Are there particular market sectors to which celebrity endorsement is more applicable? If so, which sectors and why?

2. Compile a list of questions that any agency would need to ask in considering the appropriateness of using a celebrity for an advertising campaign and in the choice of a particular celebrity, i.e. (a) Why a celebrity? (b) Which celebrity?

3. With specific reference to the youth market, what do you see as the advantages and disadvantages of using this particular strategy?

4. How might you envisage the future of the celebrity as a marketing tool?

8 Gender and ethnicity in the advertising industry

Andrew Blake

The industry

At first sight the advertising industry of the early twenty-first century seems a playground for the talented. Advertising employees think of themselves as members of a profession, chosen without fear or favour as the people best able to perform as the vanguard of consumer capitalism. They were encouraged in this view by an intellectual apparatus that put them among the leaders of the 'creative class' (Florida, 2003). In this context the key advertising workers were not salespeople, account managers or client relations developers, but the people who wrote copy, designed layouts or directed and cut television and film promos. These 'creatives' were among the key manipulators of symbols in a world in which the manipulation of information was the key to the creation of new business.

This position of cultural authority brought with it certain social and political obligations. In Britain, the industry's supporters included a government which went to considerable lengths to support the 'creative industries' or the 'knowledge economy', in each of which, when asked, advertising placed itself. Yet government, while unblinkingly supportive of industry, requires of all public and private employers that they do not discriminate on grounds of age, sexuality, religious belief, gender or ethnicity, and encourages them to promote cultural diversity in all their employment policies and practices.

Advertising, then, has to respond to the demands of a changing society. It is the purpose of this chapter to enquire how far the advertising industry has responded to this key legal, political and cultural task, and whether its attempts to do so may have impacted on the nature of advertising itself.

UK employers have to promote equality and diversity through a number of laws that apply to all their staffing, recruitment and promotion policies. These UK laws include the Equal Pay Act 1970; the Sex Discrimination Act 1975; the Race Relations Act 1976; the Disability Discrimination Act 1995; the Human Rights Act 1998; the Race Relations (Amendment) Act 2000; the Civil Partnership Act 2004; the Disability Discrimination Act 2005 and the Equality Act 2006. There are a whole host of supplementary regulations (which also have the force of law) dealing with aspects of the operation of these legal requirements.

In other words, employers must not discriminate against any individual from any group in respect of pay, benefits or workplace conditions. They should, for example, treat those employees who are pregnant, and/or their partners, fairly and offer new parents maternity and paternity leave without reference to those employees' sexuality or marital status, and without prejudice to their future employment. They should make reasonable adjustments to working conditions for the benefit of disabled employees; they should respond fairly when any employee requests the right to work flexibly. Employers are liable for the behaviour of their employees in the workplace and so they have to take reasonable steps to prevent the occurrence of sexual harassment, for example.

These laws were not made in a cultural vacuum; they were passed in response to changes in social composition and values which happened in the wider world. Since the 1950s, the US and Europe have been socially and culturally transformed in several ways. Advertising is now a graduate profession, and women have been entering higher education in ever larger numbers; as graduates they demand equal opportunities for employment, in advertising as well as the other areas of work; and as earners of disposable income, women expect to be addressed by advertisers as an important part of the market. At the same time, immigration has altered the structure of the population; significant groups of people with shared but very different geographic, cultural and ethnic backgrounds now live alongside each other. They too have entered higher education and have demanded equal opportunities to work in the advertising industry. They are also an increasingly important part of the market, and expected to be addressed as such – as do gay and lesbian, disabled and older people, who have demanded acknowledgement of their presence in society.

A brief look at the industry at play in the early twenty-first century might seem to indicate that it had responded to these legal requirements and cultural changes to produce an arena of equal opportunity. OgilvyOne's campaign for Cancer Research UK, 'Ashtray to Vase' won a prize, a Bronze Lion in the Direct category at the 2008 Cannes Advertising festival. The company's website proudly identified the team responsible for this triumph – seven men and three women. Back at Ogilvy Group's London headquarters, at the same time, a women's netball team was about to enter a charity contest in aid of the National Advertising Benevolent Society. 'The Ogilvy lovelies', we were told, 'will be competing in Group A, up against AMV, DDB, i-level, Lowe and Titan Outdoor. They will be supported by a trio of pom-pom waving cheerleaders – three downtrodden male specimens from the Ogilvy rugby team' (www.ogilvy.co.uk).

However playfully 'downtrodden' the men might be in this particular instance, it seems that the advertising industry is still at this point structured around gender difference, in which men are more likely to be found in creative work and client relations and women are more likely to be planners or account managers. This is the world of advertising as represented in Sean Nixon's book *Advertising Cultures* (Nixon, 2003; Broyles and Grow, 2008). In his ethnographic study of the profession during the decade up to the mid-1990s, Nixon represents the creative side of advertising as increasingly powerful and influential, not just within advertising but within the whole of the British (and European and American) business world. These economies were coming to value 'creativity' as the potential future of work, as the old forms of manufacture and highly-regulated commerce were replaced by the under-regulated manipulation of information as the principal means of adding value. The 'creative' side of advertising was dominated by playful boy-men, Nixon found, who existed in a Neverland of creative excess in which women were seen not just as irrelevant but – since their presence at work will, it is assumed, alter the 'boys' behaviour – a potentially dangerous block to free male creativity. Women who attempted to operate as creatives were therefore, Nixon reported, given a hard time by male colleagues, in fact bullied in several ways: frozen out of networks, often sexually harassed and routinely denied opportunities for advancement.

Claire Beale, the editor of *Campaign* (the most important British journal of the advertising trade), echoed this view of gender relations in the industry. In one of her regular columns for the *Guardian*, Beale pointed out almost gleefully that 'if you brave the creative department, among the stubble, Ts and jeans, women are rarer than a black pencil' (Beale, 2008b). The purpose of this particular article was to lionise one of the exceptions, Christine Walker, and her successful career since the 1970s; but the only way Beale could do so was by underlining her exceptionality: Walker had succeeded as a woman in a man's world. While employment in the UK industry was almost equally balanced between men and women, men still held most of the key jobs, both in creative work and in client relations. By and large, Beale explained, male clients prefer dealing with male account executives because they feel more comfortable with them; in Beale's own reductive example, it means they are more likely to be taken out to Spearmint Rhino (lapdancing club).

This somewhat gloomy picture of contemporary masculinity was reinforced culturally, legally and politically in the first decade of the twenty-first century. In 2007 the first series of the television drama *Mad Men* was broadcast in the US, produced by the cable channel American Movie Classics (AMC). Ostensibly, a representation of the Madison Avenue advertising industry of the early 1960s (and in essence a clever, if repetitive, re-narration of the biblical story of the Fall), everywhere it was shown, this series led to anguished press debate about gender roles and representations within contemporary advertising and broadcasting. The show's arrival in the UK in 2008 (where it was shown on BBC4) led to a predictable debate in the online version of the *Guardian* newspaper, whose readers were asked to agree that *Mad Men* was not merely a representation of its sexist early-1960s times, but was actually a deliberately misogynist text for our own. By and large, the online respondents agreed that it was racist, anti-Semitic and homophobic to boot. Several respondents who claimed to work in the contemporary advertising industry said that the show was not historical at all but an accurate reflection of existing attitudes among white men working in the industry, whose views on gender and ethnicity had not changed since the 1960s. One respondent wrote that *Mad Men* is:

> Exactly what ad agencies were like when I was there in the eighties: Except we were paid pretty well and could afford to buy our own vices. Nasty? Yes. But as training for how to read people/clients and deal with chauvinistic men in a clever, subtle way it couldn't be bettered. (MacLean, 2008)

All too often, even such occasional success as Christine Walker's is rendered impossible by deeply structured misogynist beliefs and practices. In October 2005, Neil French, the WPP worldwide creative director (and, relevantly, sometime road manager of heavy metal band Judas Priest), had been asked to explain the absence of female creative directors within the industry as a whole. He responded that this was due to women's priorities: they chose not just to be biological mothers but to be active child-rearers. This lifestyle choice meant, he is alleged to have said 'that 'women don't get to the top because they don't deserve to. They're crap.' (Creamer, 2005). After a brief but vigorous debate within the industry (and the media more generally), French was forced to resign. In 2000, Clarinda D'Souza, then a VP – Creative with McCann-Erickson in Mumbai, resigned and filed suit against the company, citing in particular its head in Mumbai, Sorab Mistry, and alleging sexual harassment, and that she had been victimised and publicly humiliated by a proposed transfer out of Mumbai (the head office and the nerve centre of advertising in India) to Hyderabad. At the time of writing, Sorab Mistry was still McCann-Erickson's principal executive for the whole of South Asia, Clarinda D'Souza was nowhere to be seen, and the court case had not been resolved (Thackeray and Pinto, 2005).

These aspects of dominant, patriarchal, masculinity are tested – whether debated in cultural production or in the courts – partly because the industry itself is fully aware of them, and has been trying to correct them for some time. The UK's Institute of Practitioners in Advertising (IPA) commissioned a major 1990 report by Saatchi and Saatchi Vice-President Marilyn Baxter. This document, *Women in Advertising*, argued that women were under-represented in the industry, which was therefore deprived of a great deal of talent. To remedy this, Baxter argued, special care was needed in recruitment, promotion, and especially in early-career support and promotion to senior positions. One of the industry's responses was to set up Women in Advertising and Communications London (WACL), a mutual support and mentoring group which meets regularly. In New York, a similar organisation, Advertising Women of New York, did more than just provide mutual support. Arguing that a profession dominated by men often produced advertising which was offensive to women, they founded 'The Good, the Bad, and the Ugly Awards' in the late 1990s, in order to reward 'intelligent, respectful, insightful images of women in advertising' – and to expose and criticise work which is demeaning to women.

Marilyn Baxter's report was brought up to date a decade later by Debbie Klein. This report argued that women and men now entered the UK industry in roughly equal numbers, but women continued to leave disproportionately early. Inflexible employment practices, employer expectations of long working hours and routine after-hours business-entertainment meetings with clients were the principal reason for this discontent; though Klein also noted that more men were complaining along similar lines about their industry's unreasonable demands on their time (Klein, 2000).

It would seem, then, that while it may appear to follow the letter of anti-discrimination legislation (in that approximately half the industry's young employees in the UK, and over 60 per cent in the US, are female), the advertising industry remains structurally patriarchal. A quick glance at the makeup of senior management at some of the key worldwide agencies supports this view. Whatever the merits of Ogilvy's netball team and its downtrodden male cheerleaders in producing a feeling of equality among the company's younger workers, as of August 2008 Ogilvy's senior body, the Group Board, consisted of 23 men and 4 women. All were white. This was the rule rather than the exception. Table 8.1 illustrates the composition of the governing boards of the four holding companies which dominate global advertising.

It's worth noting that this percentage of female membership is above the average for FTSE 100 companies and their European equivalents (European Professional Women's Network *et al.*, 2008)

Just below this strategic level the picture is less uniform. While the board of DDB London, for example, has ten men and two women, all of whom are white (and all drawn from roughly the same class and educational background), the Creative Council of Lowe Lintas includes Indian, Chinese and Thai men, while Young and Rubicam's leadership group includes Latin American and African men and women and there are many more

Table 8.1 Gender and ethnicity at group boardroom level, the very top of the advertising profession, August 2008

Company	Men	Women	Apparent ethnic diversity
Publicis	10	5	2 Japanese men
WPP	12	3	None
Omnicom	9	2	None
Interpublic	7	3	None

in national and regional management positions. During the next decade, many of these people would be available for promotion to the board level of the group or holding company; it will be interesting to see what actually happens.

The advertising industry, like many aspects of contemporary capitalism, subscribes to an ethical code: DDB, for example, proudly announce that they have:

> Respect for Our World: As communicators DDB is in a position to use our creativity as a force for good. As [co-founder] Bill Bernbach so eloquently put it, 'All of us who professionally use the mass media are the shapers of society. We can vulgarize that society. We can brutalize it. Or we can help lift it onto a higher level'. (www.DDB.com)

Many advertising companies do *pro bono* work (i.e. they work, for free, for a cause recognised to be for the public good and in the public domain), and they often choose to support environmental, medical or human rights charities. Beacon Communications KK Tokyo, part of Publicis Groupe, works on behalf of the Wild Bird Society of Japan; Ogilvy's prize-winning work for charity Cancer Research UK has already been mentioned; and the same company's aggressive work on behalf the Free Burma campaign is another excellent example, pulling no punches in its depiction of the evils of that country's leadership.

This hard-hitting symbolic production in favour of freedom from oppression, which was produced in London by an ethnically mixed team, does not of itself mean that the advertising industry is a successful equal opportunities employer. The employment of people from ethnic minorities in UK advertising, at least, would seem to indicate that the industry has a structural problem. A 2005 report by Mehboob Umarji for the IPA indicated that only about 8.5 per cent of the UK industry's employees were from ethnic minority backgrounds (Umarji, 2005: 4).

This was despite the IPA's own efforts, which included a late-1990s project to increase the employment of people from ethnic minorities within advertising. The IPA had set up an ethnic diversity committee; it had sent letters to all advertising companies asking them to ensure that they address the question of representation of ethnic minorities; it had followed this up with a pointed guide to the recruitment and treatment of people from the ethnic minorities in the profession. The industry had, the report argued, failed to learn from similar professions such as broadcasting, which had made a more vigorous effort to recruit and deploy people from the ethnic minorities. Meanwhile, the net effect was a vicious circle in which the young and talented from the ethnic minorities did not consider that advertising was for them. The report recommended that the industry should make a more concerted effort to recruit people from wider backgrounds, for example by looking to a wider group of universities for its graduate recruits, or by instituting a modern apprenticeship scheme aimed at ethnic minority school-leavers.

It's worth noting that an unemphasised, but important, finding from Umarji's report was that advertising, like management consultancy and finance, recruits almost exclusively from among middle-class people who have enjoyed a conventional 'good' education at school and at one of a dozen or so universities – strategies aiming to recruit from a wider range of universities might also address this deficiency.

Gender and ethnicity in the practice of advertising

Of course, whatever its employment structure, advertising no longer deals in the crudest stereotypes: advertising can and does deal, fairly in some ways, with the multicultural nation.

Figure 8.1   Howard Brown advertises the Halifax Bank, in happier times before the 2007–8
'credit crunch'. © Louis Quail/Corbis.

In 2000, DLKW Creative Directors Malcolm Green and Gary Betts thought up the first
of what proved to be a long-running series of television adverts for the Halifax Bank, in
which the bank's own staff starred in a new series of adverts. Employees sang in praise
of the bank and its services, with new lyrics to tunes by well-known pop acts such
as Shaggy, Barry White and Aretha Franklin. The films were made by directors with
experience in pop promotional videos. Howard Brown, a clerk from a branch in Sheldon,
near Birmingham, was the first and most popular of these singing and dancing Halifax
employees, and he 'starred' in a number of these 'pop videos'; as the above photograph
indicates, he became not just the bank's advertising figurehead, but something of a star.
When in April 2008 it was announced that Brown would not be taking part in any more
Halifax commercials, though remaining an employee, there was widespread public
comment (Knapton, 2008).

    From this chapter's point of view, the important thing about Howard Brown was not
his pleasant singing voice or his obvious enthusiasm for his new role as a minor celebrity,

but that throughout it all he looked like the bank clerk he was, a man in a suit who just happens to be black. In early twenty-first century Britain this was not a risky symbolic experiment but an *ordinary image*. Indeed, as it turned out, Howard Brown's ordinariness was itself a piece of symbolic manipulation, providing continuity and communicating a sense of security, while the bank was itself treading on dangerous ground. Part of the HBOS group, the Halifax was among the victims of the 2007–8 credit crunch, its over-ambitious lending among the factors leading to the takeover of HBOS by another bank, Lloyds TSB, in September 2008.

The global city and its wide range of middle-class consumers from all backgrounds, is perhaps harder to target inclusively, though the purveyors of aspirational goods have made strong efforts to do so. The 2006 promotional brochure for the Arcam DV79 DVD player provides a good example of the ways in which advertising and promotion have addressed this new world. Arcam is a medium-sized company based in Cambridge, UK, which designs and manufactures hi-fi audio and video products for the relatively affluent consumer and exports its products worldwide. The centrefold of this particular brochure was not designed around the usual hard-focus photograph of the unit itself – though there was one – but instead was dominated by a much more interesting image, a carefully soft-focused black and white photograph of two men and two women. All are slim, apparently in their late twenties or early thirties and black, Asian or 'mixed-race'. The photograph signals very clearly the connection the manufacturers and advertisers wish to make between their high-technology leisure products and the vibrant new information economy of the contemporary multicultural city such as London or Paris, New York or Los Angeles, or indeed Delhi, Shanghai or Sao Paolo, and of which they themselves are a part. The youngish people are pictured sitting on a sofa, glasses of red wine in hand, and smiling delightedly at each other. There is no obvious connection between this image and the particular piece of technology on offer; or with film or music as such; or with watching DVD video or listening to music through Arcam products, for that matter. Instead, the metropolitan arena is represented as a world of limitless possibilities for personal adventure, whether auditory or otherwise. It's an arena open for everyone, whether male or female, and from any ethnic background.

And yet the industry also remains complicit, at least, in the production of advertisements which could be called racist, sexist or both. The Ogilvy group company website in mid-2008 boasted of a successful campaign for a new model of the Ford Fiesta – a car aimed directly at the female buyer. The campaign had been led by creatives Serge Pennings and Steve Clarke, whose 'blipvert' film was to be seen during the advertisements shown before the movie *Sex and the City* – a film, again, aimed directly at the female consumer. The blipvert film employed the frankly pornographic trick of trying to show the new Fiesta to advantage by revealing a few of its 'sexy' curves without ever showing the whole car. The film was shot by John Selby from Wanted Films; the producers were Leila Bartlam and Charlotte Lawrence; and Mark Gretton and Isabel Read were responsible for planning and accounts (www.Ogilvy.com). Three men, in other words, had created an advert for women, which represented the car as if it were an objectified and eroticised female body, while a man and three women made sure the creative men were paid on time.

This may be an extreme example of sexist advertising aimed at women created within what seems to be a patriarchal structure; certainly (white) women of all ages are routinely represented in advertising. Ethnic diversity has been harder to achieve. Though there have been significant changes during the past 20 years of the type exemplified by Halifax and Arcam, it is still the case that relatively few black and brown faces are seen on television or posters, even in European countries such as France and the UK in which there are sizeable non-white communities; though, as I have argued elsewhere (Blake, 1997), these

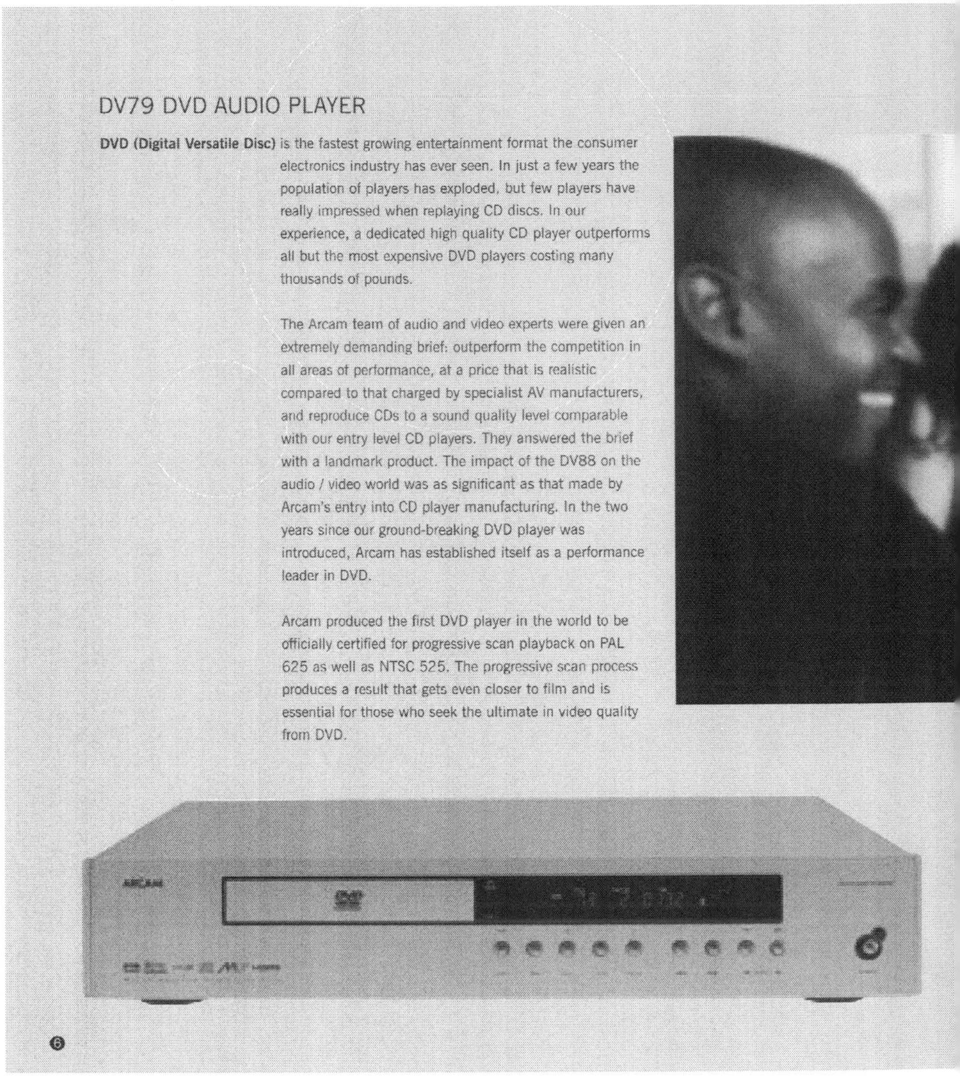

DV79 DVD AUDIO PLAYER

DVD (Digital Versatile Disc) is the fastest growing entertainment format the consumer electronics industry has ever seen. In just a few years the population of players has exploded, but few players have really impressed when replaying CD discs. In our experience, a dedicated high quality CD player outperforms all but the most expensive DVD players costing many thousands of pounds.

The Arcam team of audio and video experts were given an extremely demanding brief: outperform the competition in all areas of performance, at a price that is realistic compared to that charged by specialist AV manufacturers, and reproduce CDs to a sound quality level comparable with our entry level CD players. They answered the brief with a landmark product. The impact of the DV88 on the audio / video world was as significant as that made by Arcam's entry into CD player manufacturing. In the two years since our ground-breaking DVD player was introduced, Arcam has established itself as a performance leader in DVD.

Arcam produced the first DVD player in the world to be officially certified for progressive scan playback on PAL 625 as well as NTSC 525. The progressive scan process produces a result that gets even closer to film and is essential for those who seek the ultimate in video quality from DVD.

Figure 8.2   DV79 brochure. www.arcam.co.uk.

communities and their histories are often accessible to the careful decoder through the television and film adverts' soundtrack music. In a sense, advertising which *sounds* black, though the people represented are white, could be seen to be promoting, if with too much subtlety, a form of multiculturalism. But advertising can also work in an equally subtle way to produce or reinforce racist positions.

In the mid-2008, two prominent examples of this tendency came to light, advertisements which were both racist and sexist. In India, a television mini-series portrayed the Bollywood star Priyanka Chopra using a product called 'White Beauty' to regain the attention of a former lover who had gone off with a whiter woman – though to most eyes Chopra was already fair-skinned. A similar campaign, a single-slot television advert in which an almost-white shop assistant advises a client that she is too brown to get a husband, then reacts with astonished admiration when the newly-whitened client returns to the store, pointed

out the advantages of the Ayurvedic skin whitener 'Fair and Lovely'. Indian social commentators were not impressed by these latest manifestations of an existing prejudice within India against dark skin, and the subsequent debate spread round the world (Bedi, 2008).

At the same time as this debate was making its way into the newspapers of Europe and the United States, the *New York Post* carried an article describing a L'Oréal Paris feature for *Vogue* magazine. In a full-page head and shoulders shot promoting a hair highlighting product, it was alleged that the African-American singer Beyoncé Knowles's skin had been whitened along with her now cherry-blonde locks. L'Oréal spokespersons categorically denied that the photograph had been altered in order to make Ms Knowles's skin appear lighter, but commentators on both sides of the Atlantic refused to believe them; again, newspapers round the world picked up the story (Glaister, 2008).

Figure 8.3   Beyoncé Knowles, 'before' and 'after'. Glaister (2008).

While it would be far too crude to argue that an advertising industry, worldwide, which took more care to recruit, retain and promote people from a wide variety of backgrounds would make such work less likely, the advertising industry's failure to recruit from as widely as possible deprives it of one obvious defence against such charges; the continuing domination at board level by white men deprives it of another. The advertising industry is not in any simple sense the sexist, racist, white man's world represented in *Mad Men*; much of its work, as well as its personnel, have moved with the times. But it isn't yet an equal-opportunity utopia, and anyone thinking of entering the industry should bear that in mind.

Questions for students

Let's assume that, as argued above, both the creative side of advertising, and the boardrooms of the top companies, are dominated by white men. With that in mind, discuss the following questions:

1. Should this situation be changed? If so, how would you go about changing it? If not, how would you ensure that these men hold on to their privileged positions?

2. Do you think that this situation tends to produce a certain sort of advertising?

3. Would advertisements themselves be different:

    a. if women were more empowered within the advertising industry?

    b. if people from ethnic minorities were more empowered within the advertising industry?

9 Viral advertising: Internet entertainment and virtual sociality

Eleni Kasapi

Advertising as a mode of marketing communication, as well as a marketing service industry, has been immensely affected by technological advances that have been accelerating in the last decade. This chapter focuses on a new form of advertising, which appeared in the 1990s as the result of the industry's response to the expansion, development and new uses of the Internet: 'Viral advertising'.

There are different terms that refer to the types of viral communications, such as ' viral marketing', 'buzz marketing', 'word of mouth marketing', 'e-word of mouth' and 'viral advertising' and all of them have attracted the interest of popular and trade press. The knowledge on this new and rapidly developed mode of commercials is limited and informal. A close look at this emergent marketing trend is essential as part of any assessment of current advertising and the promotional industries working to develop and disseminate contemporary brand communications.

A timely response and constant adaptation to the ever-changing economic, social and technological conditions is imperative for the success of any kind of business. For the advertising industry in particular, the need to consider and adapt to trends in social-technologies and network communication is a pressing one. The rate of change is such that it would benefit communications professionals to be able to predict future trends well before they happen. Viral advertising is part of the changing communications environment and a part of the advertising industry's response to recent technological and social changes. But what exactly is viral advertising, when and how did virals start and what are the conditions that have given viral advertising its growing momentum?

The history of virals starts in the mid-1990s when the number of Internet users started to increase significantly and at a faster pace across the world, and when Hotmail, the most popular free email server, became widely available, notably after its acquisition by Microsoft in 1997. Hotmail, one of the first free web mail services, attracted its users by deploying a viral marketing tactic itself. The term 'viral marketing' was coined in 1996 by Steve Jurvetson and Tim Draper, from the venture capital firm Draper Fisher Jurvetson (DFJ), when they described the DFJ marketing strategy of the free email service Hotmail. Their tactic was based on the idea of appending messages originating from Hotmail accounts with the tag line 'Get your free private, free email from Hotmail at http://hotmail.com' (Jurvetson, 2000, in Porter and Golan, 2006). Hotmail was never advertised by any conventional advertising mode but achieved global domination within months.

The success of Hotmail's marketing strategy can be seen in the fact that in seven months it gained ten million users and that happened at a time when there were not as many Internet users as now. However, the success of Hotmail viral marketing was based on the offer of a free email service. Typically with virals there is no obvious gain for the sender – who nevertheless spreads the message across his or her social networks.

'The concept of a viral – as generally understood in commercial terms – is an email with a full video attachment or a link to a clip hosted on a website.' (Reid, 2005: 14). Viral marketing, as currently perceived, involves online promotional messages that are novel, intriguing or entertaining enough to drive consumers to pass them to their social networks via the Internet. That results in spreading viral messages across the World Wide Web like a virus passing rapidly to a large number of people and equally importantly at no cost to the advertisers. The new idea that virals bring into communications today is that the Internet user who receives a message will forward it to his/her social network and a similar dissemination wave will follow, initiated this time by the receivers. In that way these messages are spreading throughout the web at an exponential rate.

Some virals in the past, for example, Budweiser: Wassup, John West: The Bear, Cadbury: The Gorilla, took the form of a 'communicational epidemic'. It is said that a social epidemic begins when a successful idea passes a threshold that epidemiologists call 'the tipping point' and this is when growth of that social epidemic shifts from linear to exponential (Gladwell, 2002). In virals, in contrast to other social epidemics, the potential to develop the characteristics of an epidemic is embedded into their communicational form; there is something to be gained by anyone who passes along a viral message. By the time virals are seeded by an advertising agency, usually in promotional microsites, or by the time a few members of the audience start passing it along, they start spreading exponentially. In the case of Hotmail there was the benefit of getting a free service but what is there for an advertisement to offer that makes consumers forward the email that carries an advert as an attachment or the actual link to a website where this advert can be seen?

In order to answer that, one should look at the social uses of advertising and the attitudes of today's audiences towards ads. As has frequently been pointed out, in order to understand advertising as a form of social and cultural communications, it can be helpful to draw attention not to 'what advertising does to people' but, instead, 'what people do with advertising'. To understand how virals develop in the first place and how and why they are spread, some of them at a remarkable pace and to a great extent, it is important to start by understanding the social uses of advertising and how different audiences relate to ads.

Ritson and Elliot (1999) argue persuasively that 'because the solitary subject receives, processes, and acts on advertising messages with no interpersonal interaction with other audience members, advertising research has generally ignored the social uses that emerge from advertising reception' (Ritson and Elliot, 1999: 262 cited in Mitchell *et al.*, 2007). The existence and growth in popularity of viral advertising invites continued consideration of the limited conception of the 'solitary subject' and his or her ways of viewing/consuming ads. The viral process deconstructs the formal opposition between individual and mass reception in conceptions of audiences. Interpersonal interaction is the *condition* of viral reception.

In the past, research has shown that ads are elements of culture commonly shared within and across different segments of society (Wright and Snow, 1980 in Mitchell *et al.*, 2007). They become what the public wants to talk and laugh about. Advertising provides people, in any social context, with a common and familiar subject to discuss. As Ritson and Elliot note, talking about an advert among a group of friends 'serves to strengthen the group's shared interpretation of the ad and extends its members sense of shared identity' (Ritson and Elliot, 1999: 268). Adverts are used in people's everyday lives as a 'social glue' or as 'social capital'. For many years, TV or other forms of ads have been used as tokens of social exchange (O'Donohoe, 1994, 1997; Ritson and Elliot, 1999; Kasapi, 2007). In the era of Facebook, MySpace and Bebo these tokens, ads in the form of virals, are suitable to be used as a 'social currency' in web mediated social communication.

Social networking websites are vital for the circulation of viral advertising and viral advertising is important to them because it is a 'social currency' that usually is 'invested' in online contexts to pay good dividends for members of groups, clubs and communities in terms of self esteem and social status (Mitchell *et al.*, 2007).

People want to be liked and using humour in social interactions is very likely to increase someone's likeability (Martin, 2007). Moreover, the use of humour among groups has an impact on bonding. Sharing and enjoying the same joke is like sharing the same 'secret code'. It can evoke a feeling of belonging and builds stronger bonds among the members of the group, the virtual community, or within a circle of friend who can laugh together (Mulkay, 1988; Shiota *et al.*, 2004). Even if that joke is within the context of an ad, when it is sent as a viral by friends, it seems to shed its marketing purposes in the eyes of the sender and receiver and becomes a material for bonding and building their relationship.

In the process of this communication, although the message sent is an advert or a link to it, the fact that the sender has already judged the content as worthwhile to be forwarded and shared allows the viewers to feel that they are in control themselves as consumers of the message and not an advertising agency that has created the viral campaign. Hence the social use of ads is once again reinforced.

Humorous ads, until recently mainly TV commercials, have been used to lubricate social relations, as other forms of humour, for instance jokes, usually do. It has been shown that ads play this role successfully and rather regularly in the national culture (O'Donohoe, 1997; Ritson and Elliot, 1999) and even among people with different cultural and national backgrounds (Kasapi, 2007). What these studies have concluded is that ads are often used for purposes and within environments beyond the ones where they were designed to be consumed. Advertisements are consumed by viewers for social purposes that have very little or nothing to do with the ad's marketing goals.

The studies that examined how consumers incorporate advertisements in their everyday lives' social interactions share one common finding. Humorous advertisements in social communications create humorous situations in very similar ways to the social uses of joking. This is the point where virals, humour, advertising and audiences converge.

Humour is a common advertising 'tactic'. However, despite the fact that the use of humour in advertising is frequent and valued, its specific effectiveness is still debated. This uncertainty is due to the complex nature of humour and advertising, as forms of communication, and to the complexity of both of them working in conjunction – as happens in humorous advertisements.

According to advertising practitioners, humour is deployed in advertising because it attracts viewer's attention, enhances sources credibility, decreases counter argumentation and increases likeability for the product or service advertised. It creates a positive mood (Sternthal and Craig, 1973; Madden and Weinberger, 1984). Despite humour's popularity among advertisers as a communication device, there are still contradictory views regarding the effectiveness of humour in relation to successfully supporting advertising's main marketing goals. Humour has often been considered by practitioners not to be a very safe tactic, especially in international campaigns. It is considered as a 'high risk – high reward' technique (Kasapi, 2007). But it seems that there is one type of advertising in which the use of humour is imperative and that is virals. There is an abundance of anecdotal evidence that humour makes the virals go around and in many cases even go around the world. The *Guardian*'s article 'infectious humour' noted that:

Bored office workers have always known that email's main use is for passing on jokes. Now the advertising industry has woken up to the power of viral marketing. . . . Once it would be nothing more than a text-only joke but with broadband nearly everywhere and editing software ever more sophisticated, so virals have upped the stakes. . . . 'It used to be "did you see that TV ad?" that was a hot office conversation topic but now with the immediacy of email it's viral that people are talking about' says Dan Brooks, one half of Lee and Dan (leeanddan.com) (Burt, 2006)

In a recent study in the UK, the Millward Brown research company tested 32 different ads among more than 3,000 people in order to understand the properties of a successful viral ad. According to their findings there was a strong relationship between the degree to which an ad was enjoyable and the likelihood that it would be forwarded. But enjoyment alone was not sufficient to inspire viewers to share. The ad had to offer some additional dimensions beyond being merely nice or pleasant, and most often that dimension was humour. Ads that were really funny – 'laugh out loud' funny – were most likely to be passed along (Hollis, 2007).

Another study by Phelps *et al.* (2004), focusing on electronic word of mouth, examined consumers' responses and motivations to pass along email. Through focus groups, content analysis and intensive interviews, these researchers found out that advertisers focus on 'desire for fun, entertainment and social connections' (Phelps *et al.*, 2004: 345). In a more recent study that examined the social uses of advertising among young male adults, regarding viral advertising, the prevalence of humour in ads that were used by them was overwhelming. '. . . ads with humour appeals may have an increased likelihood of being used within a social context and stimulating word of mouth' (Mitchell *et al.*, 2007).

The results of these studies can be explained by some of the main humour characteristics. Humour connects people; 'getting the joke' has always been a signal that people can form a relationship, in this line, liking the same funny commercial, enjoying the same punch line of an ad or the same witticism in the tag line, creates the same connection among the ones who are sharing a laugh. Humour has the ability to create a unique sense of bonding among those who laugh together at the same joke. 'However spontaneous it seems, laughter always implies a kind of a secret freemasonry or even complicity with other laughers, real or imaginary' (Bergson, 1911: 7). Humour provides strong affective connectivity among and between people. Those who share the same humorous experiences tend to have a sense of general community, a sense of belonging.

'Having a common sense of humour is like sharing a secret code' (Critchley, 2002: 68). Sharing a secret code builds bonds. Audience members who appreciate the same joke or laugh at the same humorous commercial create a bond between them. When humour is used in e-marketing, it intensifies the value of such connectivity. It destabilises the established polarity between traditional advertising and its individual addressee within the mass audience. In the era of advertising virals, of 'e-word of mouth' and technological advances that have introduced new forms of a global social networking (YouTube, MySpace, Bebo, Facebook), humour appears to be a catalytic source of global connectivity among communities of viewers and consumers across the globe.

A crucial factor that enables and facilitates this role of humour in advertising is advertising literacy (Kasapi, 2007). By advertising literacy is meant 'the ability of consumers, to understand many advertising conventions, to have a flavour for what the advertising is trying to do and to be able to use the jargon of the advertising industry' (O'Donohoe and Tynan, 1998: 468). The levels of media/advertising literacy are high and audiences, in particular young audiences, in many countries, are media and advertising savvy (Leiss *et al.*, 2005). If that is the reality in the developed world, with the expansion of the Internet the levels of audiences' advertising literacy will rapidly increase throughout the developing world as well.

The ability of viewers to decipher advertising codes and create common meanings from the messages allows advertisers a wider scope for creative experimentations and also underpins viral potentiality to travel across cultures. As it has been observed, advertising messages, in particular humorous ones, are welcome within particular segments of societies across the globe (Kasapi, 2007). That is the case for a clearly defined group that Leiss *et al.* (2005: 573) call the 'urban cultural elite' that can be found in any country. There are several other groups that comprise subcultures within countries' cultures and constitute significant market segments; these groups usually share common levels of advertising literacy and the circulation of virals becomes easy among them. Thus it can be said that virals are shared and circulated among groups that are located globally because they have attained similar levels of understanding and appreciating ad messages, but at the same time as that happens and a viral is spread, that also contributes to increased levels of ad literacy globally. So every viral, in a way, creates a better environment for circulation of the next one.

Some of the landmark viral campaigns confirm the association between humour and the success of virals internationally. Although viral ads had been circulated through the web earlier than 2000, one of the outstanding campaigns was produced at the end of 2000. The London agency Leo Burnett posted a preview of a TV ad for its client John West on the US website adcritic.com in December 2000. The ad, showing a kick-boxing scene between a bear and a fisherman, was forwarded to other Internet users by those who initially saw the advertisement. This film for John West, 'the bear', was a milestone campaign for viral advertising. Although it was never sent to a customer database it achieved one of the biggest viral marketing successes worldwide (Howell, 2003). The humorous content of the ad seems likely to be considered as the key factor that motivated millions of people to circulate the short film through their social networks. It seems that the moments of entertainment this advertisement offered to viewers were well appreciated by culturally different audiences. This viral's humour seems to have generated a wish within its viewers to share its 'visual joke' with someone else and that led to the worldwide distribution of that particular ad.

Another very successful campaign, in terms of how many times the clip was downloaded across different countries, is one for Trojan condoms titled '2004 sex Olympics'; downloaded more than 40 million times (Reid, 2005). This campaign comprises various clips that parody the Olympic Games. Its humorous content has achieved great popularity among viewers across the world. The universally recognisable element of sex in the advertisement in combination with the universally recognisable Olympic Games factor produced a campaign in which humour could be understood and appreciated globally.

An extraordinary and more recent example of successful viral advertising is for Blendtec. The entitled 'Will it blend?' virals have been an Internet phenomenon with more than 20 million views for the various executions (WARC, 2008) and generating more than 2.7 million views on YouTube alone (*Campaign*, 2007d).

The power of viral ads to be distributed exponentially has also been demonstrated by the VW Polo suicide bomber viral that attracted global media coverage (Brook, 2005). This ad shows a VW Polo driver pulling over his car near a crowded café while he straps explosives onto himself. He pushes the detonator and an explosion happens. Not even a window breaks. Then the tag line appears: 'Polo small but tough'. This short film was produced by two creatives, Lee Ford and Dan Brooks, without the consent of Volkswagen and was only for their own use for a show reel, a film to be shown to clients of their advertising agency. However, once this piece of 'black humour' was posted on the web it was forwarded extensively. The media coverage and the number of people who saw the ad made it one of the recent cases best illustrating the power of virals to spread, especially when they contain an intriguing, controversial or humorous moment.

'Word of mouse' (Kirby, 2004) is the way advertisers always wanted to reach audiences, at a minimal cost. Yet this new type of marketing message does not come without disadvantages. This last example evidently illustrates how one of the main strengths and advantages of viral for advertisers, wide distribution at minimal cost, can also be one of the weaknesses of virals when things go wrong. The more widely the viral is circulated the higher the degree of negative publicity. As with any other electronic virus, the moment a viral ad reaches the World Wide Web it is almost impossible to eradicate.

Virals are not subject to regulations because their environment, the World Wide Web, is still relatively unregulated and certainly far less regulated than the TV or press or any other conventional types of advertising. That allows advertisers a space of endless possibilities in terms of creativity where they can push the boundaries far beyond what is considered acceptable in advertising in other media and be able to create shocking but still humorous advertisements. Advertising companies can go to extremes and produce outrageous or humorous commercials that could not pass the test of the Advertising Standards Authority (ASA) for a TV commercial but they can become successful viral campaigns. This again is a double edged sword, because if a campaign passes the wrong message across for any reason, then from the moment it is available on the Internet the agencies are unable to stop the viral circulation. The agencies in these unfortunate cases are at the mercy of the audience/ Internet users. As Gibbon and Hawkes (2006) put it, if a viral campaign is popular, there is no way that the genie can be put back in the bottle. If a campaign was generated via email and was passed on, there is virtually no way it could be retracted.

The degree of control over virals that digitally-empowered consumers have is demonstrated by the circulation of spoof commercials via emails and web2.0 sharing platforms such as YouTube or Facebook or other social networking websites. The popularity of this category of viral ads, which are funny videos that parody well-known adverts, lead advertising companies to create a new form, the 'subviral'. Subvirals are adverts made by advertising companies that are mainly humorous and are produced in such a way as to look like they were made by an amateur, a member of the public and not by an advertising company:

> Subviral marketing is said to be being pioneered by brands including Budweiser, Ford, Levi's and MasterCard. While traditional viral attachments feature short, slapstick video clips stamped with the brand's logo and web address, subviral campaigns are carefully shot to seem like they were produced by an Internet prankster. "They're designed to look amateurish, to leave recipients with the impression that the advert has a cult following," says Matthew Smith, director of viral marketing agency the Viral Factory, which masterminds subviral campaigns for clients ranging from large drinks brands to government departments. With firms reluctant to own up to subviral campaigns, spotting fake spoofs has become a popular pastime among those in the know. (Harris, 2002)

Subvirals show that viral advertising has already started to evolve in new modes. Now with Internet facilities offered on mobile phones, the already increased possibilities given to advertisers to reach vast audiences at minimal cost have extended immensely. That means before the phenomenon of viral advertising has the chance to be studied and understood thoroughly, it moves to new communicational territories and develops even further.

The major revolution in marketing communications in recent years has been the introduction of online modes of marketing. This has produced a new interface between advertisements and their audiences, which have been transformed from passive or reactive to proactive audiences. In a sense, at the forefront of these changes are various kinds of e-marketing. E-marketing is a hybrid of advertising modes and direct marketing methods. On the one hand is the individual and on the other is the mass audience, and this is peculiar. Viral advertising is a perfect content for the articulation of that marketing relationship, because it is enjoyable on the individual basis but it is also social, in the sense that it is circulated across social networks. An advert is consumed individually but also it is consumed by a group, it is shared. That mode of sharing is a new way of constituting audiences. In that way audiences constitute themselves and each other, rather than being there in front of a TV set without any interactive power over or relation to the message.

The phenomenon of viral advertising appeared unexpectedly. It may seem astonishing now but an ARF/AMA industry survey in 1997 showed that no advertising and marketing practitioners thought that the Internet was important for their companies at that time. A significant percentage of them did not even think that the Internet would be important, even by the year 2000 (Parsons, 1997).

The technology that allowed virals to exist came at the moment when audiences had become so advertising savvy that they were often bored with conventional advertising (Leiss et al., 2005). The timing was perfect to allow consumers to take a pivotal role in how ads should look and what purposes they can facilitate, apart from the marketing ones, in order to attract consumers' attention. The media audiences have now dictated advertising agencies to consider carefully the trends that consumers created in their relationship to adverts.

The growing interest and attention that viral advertising draws is shown by the number of agencies now specialising in viral advertising and the establishment of prestigious advertising competitions solely for this genre of ads. The fast pace at which virals are becoming popular and spreading around the globe may provide some reliable suggestions about the future of advertising. It seems that the evolution of advertising is driven by advertising savvy, media literate and proactive consumers who use advertising beyond its marketing purposes.

Questions for students

1. What advantages and disadvantages can you identify in the use of viral advertising for advertising agencies?

2. Name at least five prerequisite conditions for a successful global viral campaign.

3. In what ways does viral advertising differ from conventional advertising and how do these differences affect the future of the advertising industry in financial terms?

4. Why are popular viral campaigns mostly humorous?

5. Describe and analyse the relationship of social networking websites and viral advertising.

Part III

Case studies

10 Sponsorship, advertising and the Olympic Games

Iain MacRury

This chapter examines sponsorship and its relationship to advertising. It includes a detailed account of Olympic sponsorship in order to illustrate some of the practical issues facing brands using sponsorship as part of a promotional strategy.

Competition and complementarity

Advertising is intimately linked to other promotional activities and other modes of promotional communication. Advertising has a complementary relationship to sponsorship expressed in successful integrated marketing campaigns. As one example from among many; it is by a combination of sponsorship and advertising (often in connection with the Olympics), as well as via numerous other promotional activities, that we have come to accept Visa – an abstract system for the management of credit payments – as a highly familiar global brand. To sponsor the Olympics as an official worldwide partner costs in the region of £50 million for a four-year global Olympic partnership. However, brands will typically spend three times that amount on media-based advertising around the Olympic event and in broadcast media (Davis, 2008). Visa is one of about a dozen such brands. Such activity is on a grand scale but by no means exceptional – with the Olympics just one of a number of events, large and small, serving to provide a structure and a rhythm in the promotional cycles of major global brands seeking to add value, increase recognition and enhance consumer engagement.

Advertising amplifies brand communications and sponsorships, for instance featuring sponsored celebrities in traditional ads. Sponsors of events typically also pay for advertising in media and around event sites. This ensures the sponsorship is fully registered, to link the sponsored event to main brand themes and imageries and to offset the risk that competitor advertising might diminish public recognition of the sponsorship relationship.

Advertising also operates in competition with sponsorship. Advertising is sometimes used by advertisers in order to jam or ambush competitor brands' sponsorship messages, with non-sponsoring brands trying to steal major official sponsors' thunder by advertising alongside live and broadcast events. Mega-events such as the Olympics, FIFA World Cups and European Football Championships produce high levels of media coverage, large sponsorship expenditures and big increases in advertising expenditure. This has knock-on effects for the advertising industry – with extra staffing required in advance of large mega-events to support increased levels of global and local promotional activity. At the industry level, advertising and sponsorship compete for a share of clients' marketing expenditure, even while the overall levels of expenditure increase around mega-events.

Sponsorship: definitions and key features

Sports, music, comedy and charities; individual players, artists, bands and teams; stadia, leagues, concert halls and hospitals – sponsorship arrangements of various kinds allow brands to build associations to events and activities. Sponsors pay event organisers fees, or goods in kind, in return for packages of rights in relation to the sponsored event (Poon and Prendergast, 2006). Sponsors' brand imagery and sounds are used to secure the association. These are then also featured across the event space and in broadcast and other media dissemination. Events such as the Olympics, large football tournaments and Formula 1 motor racing involve a number of event sponsors. Sometimes, also, teams and individual participants are sponsored, further increasing the number of logos circulating across the event space.

Sponsoring brands seek cultural and emotional connection with consumers by combining a wide range of associations – to engage different market segments and to convey different aspects of the brand 'story'. Vodaphone's recent brand communications have included sponsor relationships with the Ferrari motor racing team, the Vodaphone Live Music Awards, The England Cricket team, the UEFA Champions League, Cirque du Soleil, The Epsom Derby, Manchester United Football club and also a charity called Action for Children. Sponsorship works across marketing agendas, from building brand awareness, to corporative responsibility and Cause Related Marketing[1] (Pringle and Thompson, 1999). Sponsorship provides a mechanism for commercial corporations, such as Vodaphone, to assert and re-assert brand presence in the public imagination. It is now unusual to see popular public cultural events operating without some form of brand sponsorship in place. Sports events claim the lion's share of sponsors' investments, partly because sport is typically covered in close detail and in predictable media outputs on TV, radio and in high circulation media – providing PR-type coverage to maximise exposure – before, during and after the event.

Sponsorship: the marketing rationale

Major marketing, cultural and advertising trends identified since the 1980s point to an emerging media culture where the role of traditional main media advertising in brands' promotional work is under continual review. As a number of chapters in this book make clear, standard advertising approaches have been under pressure from other kinds of promotional communications.[2] Sponsorship is one such alternative branding approach and has benefited when brand owners and marketers have sought to diversify promotional expenditure. Marketing expenditure on sponsorship in the UK increased by 11 per cent in 2007 against decline and slowed growth in other traditional marketing and communication media.

High-quality audience 'attention' is an increasingly elusive, and increasingly sought after media commodity (Davenport and Beck, 2001). Television audiences are fragmenting or going online and national press readerships are declining. Nevertheless, sports and cultural events continue to provide foci for attentive fans; locally, nationally and internationally; live, in the press, and on-screen. Sponsorship depends on media too. However, the intimate link between sponsor and event means the sponsoring brand potentially maintains an open channel to the event audience across media platforms – without having to negotiate the uncertainties and approximation of pre-bought advertising space and switched off/switched-over fans.

In addition, when sponsorship and advertising are used as complementary elements of a promotional strategy sponsoring advertisers will typically have better access to advertising and promotional space in and around the venue. The special relationship afforded to sponsors of such mega-events provides a further marketing rationale for selecting sponsorship as part of large-scale integrated media and marketing activity.

The last big show in town?

The cultural and media patterns surrounding 'big hit' blockbuster films, TV shows and celebrities (Anderson, 2006) is receding in favour of niche channels and specialist markets for cultural goods. The water cooler is giving way to the globally distributed special-interest chatroom. 'Did you see?' and 'must see' television events are becoming rarer. The remaining 'big hit' and wide audience events – such as the Olympics opening ceremony and other international and national level sporting events, offer the rare advantage of being able to access and deliver otherwise harder to reach national and global 'mass' audiences. On the other hand, the number of such events covered across media is increasing. Advertising clutter is at risk of being replaced by sponsorship clutter.

Branding entertainment and editorial

Wolf's (1999) analysis of the 'Entertainment economy' highlights the centrality of spectacle and event-based activities in contemporary marketing; an argument developed further by Donaton (2004), who highlights the convergence of advertising and other types of media entertainment. This convergence is an emergent and ongoing phenomenon. It is a response to technically empowered audiences' tendencies to cut out traditional main media advertising. Some new models of media entertainment delivery, for example, pay per view and download services, make sponsorship a more convincing marketing option.

Marketing messages in sponsored events are continuous and parallel with the event-space/time. This convergence of the branded message or event activity differentiates sponsorship from main media advertising. Advertising runs in discrete blocks before and after events. By definition it is sectioned off from the main broadcast – a characteristic underscored by regulatory agreements governing advertising. Advertising is contiguous to rather than continuous with the main focus of attention. As Hall puts it: 'Sponsorship is part of editorial space, not advertising space' (Hall, 2004).

This makes advertising more susceptible to filtering than sponsorship. Audiences filter ads by means of technologies (Tivo or Sky+). Media providers can offer 'ad free' content in return for pay per view relationships. In some cases, event mangers regulate advertising – either banishing it altogether from venues – as at the Olympics, or by tying advertising billboards and hoardings into a sponsorship package.

As well as the changes in the marketing environment discussed above, a further stimulus to the sponsorship industry has come from changes in the way public events and popular entertainments have been managed and conceived in recent decades. Klein offers an account of this shift with reference to changing economic and cultural policy in the 1980s when:

corporate taxes were dramatically lowered, a move that eroded the tax base and gradually starved the public sector. As government spending dwindled, schools, museums and broadcasters were desperate to make up their budget shortfalls and thus ripe for partnerships with private corporations. It also didn't hurt that the political climate during this time ensured that there was almost no vocabulary to speak passionately about the non-commercialized public sphere. (Klein N., 2000: 30)

One of the first events to develop a more assertively commercial approach in this period was the Olympics. Alongside the FIFA World Cups in 1986 and 1990 were the Olympic Games in 1984 (Los Angeles) and 1988 (Seoul).

Sponsoring TV programmes

As well as event-based sponsorship there is a now established trend towards sponsoring individual television and radio programmes. For instance, mobile brand, O2 used its sponsorship association with reality show *Big Brother* to support its various marketing activities:

> What better vehicle than Big Brother for establishing much-needed credibility for O2 with young adults, 78 per cent of whom made the brand connection? Additionally, Big Brother provided a fantastic showcase and trial generator for non-voice services via the programme's text chatroom. This was a hugely valuable sponsorship that has been evaluated in isolation by econometric modelling: no fewer than 646,000 new connections were credited to the sponsorship, as well as higher average revenue per user. (Field, 2008)

Sponsorship is also frequently used to build brand awareness because it conveys complexes of feelings and values that connect to consumers at a different level of cognition than, say, a marketing communication promoting new product features. However, the O2 case illustrates the contribution an imaginative sponsorship can make to further and more detailed marketing objectives (Field, 2008). O2's sponsorship of London's Millennium Dome as a music venue has provided further success for the brand.

Sponsorship: experience and authenticity

Pine and Gilmore (1999) and Gilmore and Pine (2007) highlight two further marketing trends. These again support particular rationales for marketers' investments in sponsorship. The 'experience' economy (Pine and Gilmore, 1999) focuses on the premium consumers give to memorable and affective activities. Sports, arts and other live events tune into the contemporary hunger for experientially rich activities – even when consumed vicariously. Sponsors aim to build associative links to their brand. They trade on just those exciting, touching, thrilling and controversial moments produced by sports and the arts, but also on the aura and tradition surrounding events such as the Olympics or the major football competitions.

Gilmore and Pine (2007) develop this idea further by pointing to contemporary consumers' quest for 'authenticity' (Boyle, 2003; Lewis and Bridger, 2001). Sponsorship offers brands an opportunity to connect with the feeling of authenticity emerging from 'live', 'unique' events and athletes or artists marked as 'the real thing'. The Olympic Games is an event that works hard to convey the feeling of authenticity as part of its own 'brand'. The 'authenticity' of the Games is kept in delicate balance with the commercialising tendencies of sponsorship. Commitment to the heritage and traditions of events, for example, in the range of sports included at the Olympics, remains a priority in order to protect the Olympic brand from the incremental diminutions that can arise from pragmatism and commercial compromises. The Olympic movement depends upon the integrity of its brand for its sustainability.

In an era of marketing globalisation, branding sponsorship offers a degree of global media reach that is unavailable to other forms of marketing communications. Yet sponsorship can also tune into local sentiment and local activities. Sponsors can utilise small-scale events to reassert commitments to local agendas and to convey brand messages to local markets. For instance, Coca Cola's sponsorship of the Football League worked to tie in with local fans' partisan engagements:

> Coca-Cola . . . wanted to boost sales by engaging community passions, and successfully avoided cynicism as a global brand sponsoring the Football League by realising that football fans support individual clubs rather than leagues. Therefore, all activation of the sponsorship has focused on helping fans support their local clubs in new ways. Not only did Coca-Cola change its corporate colours – the first time in the brand's history – to each of the 72 club colours, but it also gave fans the chance to win a player for their team. This promotion alone led to 210 million extra cans sold in one season. (Wareman, 2008)

Sponsorship depends upon a tripartite relationship between the event, the sponsors and the fans, including the media audience conceived as potential consumers. Successful sponsorship occurs to the extent to which the interests of each party are adequately satisfied. This must happen without any infringement of the priorities and commitments of any of the other constituent parties. Sponsors' activities must not damage the reputation of the event: the event must operate in such a way as to deliver the exposure and associations desired by the sponsor. The fans are invited to give their attention 'live' or via media, and to assess the extent to which they assent to the credibility, relevance and appropriateness of sponsors' associations with that event.

When fans respond positively, there are possible knock-on effects in relation to consumer attitudes and behaviour. The value or otherwise of sponsorship depends on some perceptual or behavioural shift, leading to a good marketing outcome for the sponsor. While there are ways of assessing the effects of sponsorships, precise calculations of return on sponsorship investment can be elusive (Wareman, 2008).

Events are also brands. In some respects they are like traditional media channels. Like brands and like channels it is important that they maintain integrity and a style in the content they provide and the values they transmit. To overexploit the commercial potential of one edition of an event, for example as happened at the Atlanta Olympics in 1996, is to risk diminishing the long-term value of the event-brand. The 1996 Olympics were dubbed the 'Hamburger Games' because many fans felt that the event was overly dominated by marketers – to the detriment of the sporting spectacle (Barney et al., 2004)

Sponsorship and controversial products

Sponsorship has developed partly as a consequence of the differences between the regulatory regimes for advertising and other types of promotion. In the UK, for instance, restrictions and bans on tobacco advertising and alcohol enforced since the 1970s lead many brands to use sponsorship as an alternative way to promote cigarettes and alcoholic drinks. Subsequent EU regulation of sponsorship has outlawed long-established links between cigarettes and sports – notably snooker and Formula One racing. The whisky brand *Johnnie Walker* maintains a prominent association with golf through its international tournaments. Alcohol remains a key sponsorship category accounting for 10 per cent of all sponsorship deals in 2005. During the FIFA World Cup 2006, an estimated 12m people attended fan parks sponsored by Budweiser (EAA, 2005: 2). The Institute of Alcohol Studies points to World Health Organisation research suggesting that in the US, 'spending on indirect promotional activities such as sponsorship, product tie-ins, contests and special promotions is around three times higher than spending on direct advertising' (IAS, 2007: 3) and that UK figures are proportionately comparable.

Controversies surround associations between certain food brands and sporting events. Tobacco brands cannot have any association with the Olympic Games – notwithstanding the Japanese launch of Olympic cigarettes coinciding with the Tokyo games in 1964. Yet, alcohol, fast foods and confectionery brands have developed links with the Olympics. McDonald's is an international partner. Budweiser describes its sponsorship arrangement with the Olympics as follows:

> Budweiser is the official international beer sponsor of the 2008 Olympic Games in Beijing, China, as well as the official beer sponsor of the National Olympic Teams in 25 countries. During the Olympic Games in Beijing, Budweiser will host eight exclusive parties for athletes and consumers at Club Bud, building on the success of Club Bud at the 2006 Winter Olympic Games in Torino, Italy.

The recent partnership agreement between LOCOG and Cadbury's has provoked controversy from commentators and lobby groups, highlighting the potential discrepancy between the sponsor and the London Games' commitments to youth and healthy eating.

Sponsorship and Olympic mega-event-brand

> Without the support of the business community, without its Technology, expertise, people, services, products, Telecommunications, its financing – the Olympic Games could not and cannot happen. Without this support, the athletes cannot compete and achieve their very best.
> Dr Jacques Rogge, President, International Olympic Committee

Olympic sponsorship and the advertising and other promotional activities attaching to this 'mega-event' (Roche, 2000) highlights some of the themes related to event-branding, marketing, sponsorship and advertising so far discussed. The remainder of this chapter outlines the particular characteristics of Olympic sponsorship and advertising and treats the Olympic Games as both exemplar and major case.

The Olympics generates income from corporate promotional activity in two major ways: one direct, the other indirect. The majority of income generated by the IOC to support Olympic activities, including primarily the Games, comes from selling television rights. Within the IOC, the TV Rights and New Media Commission manages negotiations selling rights for TV as well as increasingly important mobile and Internet rights. Typically broadcasters from continental and national TV bodies purchase these rights in the expectation that they will be able to sell to national TV companies who will sell advertising alongside Olympic programming. In the UK, the BBC broadcasts the Olympics – without

Table 10.1   Olympic income from broadcasters

	1993–6	1997–2000	2001–4	2005–8
Income from broadcasters (US$)	1,251,000,000	1,845,000,000	2,232,000,000	2,570,000,000

advertising. It pays for this using the licence fee. This absence of advertising on the BBC, when combined with the IOC clean venues policy, makes it difficult for sponsors to confidently assert presence. However press and TV ads continue in other channels and media to try to establish links.

The second way that the Olympic movement gains income is via its partnership schemes. Sponsors can buy into different kinds of relationship with the 'Olympic family' in return for their financial input – but also goods and services. The TOP Programme generated US $866 million in 2005–8. A further element of the Olympic promotion comes via the mascots. Mascots are useful for merchandising souvenirs – hats, T-shirts and so on – as well as producing a distinctive 'face' for the city. As with other events, the Olympic Games also makes income from ticket sales.

The TOP programme is a scheme developed in the 1980s to manage the commercialisation of the Games in such a way as to maximise revenues while respecting the Olympic movement's traditions and priorities. It aims:

- To contribute to the independent financial stability of the Olympic Movement
- To generate continual and substantial support through sustained, long-term partnerships
- To provide equitable revenue distribution throughout the Olympic Family
- To ensure the financial and operational viability of the Olympic Games
- To prohibit the uncontrolled commercialisation of the Olympic Games.

A distinctive feature of the Olympic sponsorship arrangement is the 'clean venues' policy. This operates in the spirit of the Olympic brand, in the sense that it operates as a baulk against blatant commercialism. However, it is also a form of protection pursued in the service of official commercial sponsors. Thus, in the case of London, LOCOG (2006) states:

> . . . there can be no advertising on or around the field of play or seen by TV cameras covering the Olympic Games. They will also enable London 2012 to offer its sponsors an exclusive opportunity to advertise outside these areas but in close vicinity to venues, so that their exclusive association with the 2012 Games can be maintained and spectators are not bombarded by commercial messages from other companies who have not invested in the 2012 Games. The Advertising Regulations are likely to apply to any form of advertising (e.g. billboards, fly posting, the handing out of leaflets/ products, etc.), but will only prevent unauthorised advertising in a clearly defined vicinity around 2012 Games' venues and only for a maximum period of two weeks before and during the 2012 Games. (LOCOG, 2006)

The TOP sponsors gain a number of benefits in return for the investment. These include promotional media-based benefits and high-level access to venues and the event space for promotional activities. The Olympic Movement promises 'unparalleled returns on an investment' for sponsors (Table 10.2).

Table 10.2   IOC offers the following benefits for Olympic sponsors

Sponsors gain:

An association with the rings – one of the most widely recognised symbols in the world.

A global marketing platform, based on ideals and values, providing excellent opportunities for a company's sales, showcasing, internal rewards and community outreach programmes.

Sponsors are also able to develop marketing programmes with various members of the Olympic Movement, including the IOC, the NOCs and the Organising Committees.

In addition to exclusive worldwide marketing opportunities, partners receive:
*   Use of all Olympic imagery, as well as appropriate Olympic designations on products
*   Hospitality opportunities at the Olympic Games
*   Direct advertising and promotional opportunities, including preferential access to Olympic broadcast advertising
*   On-site concessions/franchise and product sale/showcase opportunities
*   Ambush marketing protection
*   Acknowledgement of their support though a broad Olympic sponsorship recognition programme

Table 10.3   Summary and analysis of TOP sponsorship branding themes

Sponsor	Industry category	Message theme
McDonald's	Retail food services	*Bringing the games to life*
Lenovo	Computing equipment	*Celebrate and live*
Manulife	Life insurance/ annuities	*Bring their dreams to life*
Coca Cola	Non-alcoholic beverages	*Bringing unique Olympic experiences*
Panasonic	Audio/TV/video equipment	*Sharing the passion*
Kodak	Imaging	*Message not known*
Atos origin	IT services	*For the spirit*
Visa	Consumer payment systems	*Celebrating human achievement*
Johnson & Johnson	Healthcare products	*Caring for others*
Samsung	Wireless communications	*Everyone's an Olympic Games champion*
GE	Diverse offerings	*Leaving a legacy*
Omega	Time pieces/ timing systems	*Official time keeper*

Source: Davis, 2008: 283.

The TOP scheme restricts sponsors to one per product category. Thus there can only be one computing firm, one life insurance provider and so on. Table 10.3 shows a brief summary and analysis of TOP sponsorship branding themes (Davis, 2008: 283) from the TOP sponsors in Beijing/Torino.

Official Olympic sponsors' advertising

The Johnson & Johnson ad (Figure 10.1) from a billboard in Beijing is indicative of the ways that advertising is used to bolster both the sponsorship theme – 'caring' – and the fact of the sponsor relationship in the public imagination. Only an official sponsor would be permitted to use the imagery of a gold medal in this way during Olympic time –

especially on a billboard in the host city. The presence of the Beijing Olympic logo and the Olympic rings ensures that Johnson & Johnson is clearly identified as official Olympic sponsors. During the 2008 Games, it was almost impossible to find a billboard which was not carrying a TOP sponsor's ad, or an official Beijing partner sponsor. Likewise, other main media were ad slots dominated by Olympic sponsors. This was for four main reasons:

1. Sponsors use advertising – at considerable further cost – to secure public recognition of their official status.

Figure 10.1   Beijing billboard 2008 – Johnson and Johnson: Caring for others.

Figure 10.2   As well as TOP sponsors there are host city partners and host city sponsors exclusive suppliers. These packages cost varying amounts reflecting the levels of promotional entitlement and exclusivity.

2. The Beijing audience during the Games included numerous international tourists and business people. Advertising and other official games-related VIP events contributed to the sponsors' aim of securing a strong position in the rapidly growing Chinese market – by visually 'owning' the promotional spaces of the city[3].

3. Having invested in the partnership used a blanket coverage approach in the centre of Beijing to reduce the possibility for 'ambush' marketing. See below.

4. Sponsoring games was typically part of a wider strategy in which brands were challenging dominant competitors in China, trying to establish the brand in China or reasserting dominance in this new and important market.

London 2012 Sponsors

In London 2012, the sponsors' line up so far is as follows. There are two main types of sponsor. As with Beijing there are also official suppliers.

As well as the TOP sponsors and the partners to the host city, there are partnerships operating at national level and arranged between the IOC and NOCs. In the Czech Republic, Pilsner Urquell sponsored the Czech Olympic team.

There may have been good reasons, including cost and brand strategy considerations, for Pilsner Urquell not to invest in becoming a TOP sponsor. Budweiser, Tsingdao and

Table 10.4 The two main types of sponsor

The Olympic partners for the London 2012 games *(as at October 2008)*
Worldwide partners – i.e. members of the TOP scheme
Coca Cola
Atos Origin
GE (General Electric)
McDonald's
Omega
Visa
Panasonic
Samsung
Official partners – i.e. partners linked with LOCOG (The London Organising Committee of the Olympic Games)
Adidas
BP (British Petroleum)
British Airways
BT (British Telecom)
EDF Energy
Lloyds TSB
Nortel
Official supporters
Deloitte
Cadbury

Figure 10.3 As well as TOP sponsors, there are various arrangements made between NOCs (National Olympic Committees) and 'local' sponsors.

Yanjing Beers were all prominent sponsors for Beijing. There was clearly a good case to be made for national level sponsorship however, related to the Prague bid to host the 2016 Games and the opportunity to assert identification with national cultural pride.

Brands can also sponsor individual athletes. This can be a good way to bypass the exclusivity rights of the main sponsors. Thus, Nike sponsored a number of individual Olympians, including Chinese hurdler Liu Xiang. Speedo's sponsorship of record breaking medallist Michael Phelps resulted in excellent coverage for its brand.

The Olympic brand

Olympism is a philosophy of life, exalting and combining in a balanced whole the qualities of body, will and mind. Blending sport with culture and education, Olympism seeks to create a way of life based on the joy found in effort, the educational value of good example and respect for universal fundamental ethical principles. The goal of

Olympism is to place everywhere sport at the service of the harmonious development of man, with a view to encouraging the establishment of a peaceful society concerned with the preservation of human dignity ... Its symbol is five interlaced rings. (IOC, 2008a: Appendix)

No major multi-national will want to miss the platform offered by the Olympics'. (CEO of WPP, Sorrell, 2007)

The Olympic five-ring symbol 'is said to be the best-known logo in the world, above that of Shell, the McDonald's golden arches, and the Mercedes star, and well ahead of the Red Cross or the United Nations' (Chappelet and Kubler-Mabbott, 2008: 37). In return for the rights gained through the various kinds of partnership, the Olympic movement benefits in the following ways:

- Sponsors provide support for the staging of the Olympic Games and the operations of the Olympic Movement in the form of products, services, technology, expertise and staff deployment.

- Sponsors provide direct support for the training and development of Olympic athletes and hopefuls around the world, as well as essential services for athletes participating in the Games.

- Sponsors provide essential products and services for broadcasters, journalists, photographers and other media.

- Sponsorship activation enhances the Olympic Games experience for spectators and provides the youth of the world with opportunities to experience the Olympic ideals at the global and local levels.

- Sponsorship support contributes to the success of the educational, environmental, cultural and youth-oriented initiatives of the Olympic Movement.

- Sponsors develop advertising and promotional activities that help to promote the Olympic ideals, heighten public awareness of the Olympic Games and increase support for the Olympic athletes (IOC, 2008b).

The Olympic brand is protected and maintained in order that it sustains values and affective impact. The IOC works hard to ensure that sponsors take the duty to build and defend the Olympic brand values seriously within their ads. The IOC has also done some advertising of its own, producing a campaign called 'celebrate humanity' to highlight and disseminate Olympic values in an advertising / branding friendly format. The major way that the IOC and the host city organising committee protects the Olympic brand is by asserting a strict defence of the trademark and IP rights connected to Olympic imagery and words. The Olympic insignia are protected closely and suspected infringements are actively sought out and assessed. For London 2012, the IOC, sponsors' and LOCOG's Olympic Marketing Rights are protected by the London Olympic Games and Paralympic Games Act 2006 and the Olympic Symbol, etc. (Protection) Act 1995 (OSPA).

In Beijing there was a publicity campaign reminding visitors to the city to respect Olympic copyrights. Some have argued persuasively (NEF, 2008: 4) that the stringent rules applied to commercial, but also non-commercial bodies seeking to boost activities by means of associations with the Olympic movement, prevent a degree of local engagement and participation in favour of the image rights protected for the benefit, primarily, of large corporate sponsors. LOCOG have published guidelines to discourage any kind of infringement of the Olympic brand. These refer to commercial and non-

Figure 10.4   Poster in a Beijing underground station: 'Observe Olympic marketing norms, enhance corporate brand image.'

commercial enterprises and activities (LOCOG, 2007a; LOCOG, 2007b). Guidelines include a key list of protected words and symbols:

> . . . for 2012 the following visual and verbal signs are regulated. The Olympic symbol, The Paralympic symbol, The London 2012 Olympic and Paralympic emblems, The words 'London 2012' and '2012', 'Olympic', 'Olympiad', 'Olympian' (and their plurals and things very similar to them – e.g. 'Olympix', The words 'Paralympic', 'Paralympiad', 'Paralympian' and their plurals and things very similar to them – e.g. 'Paralympix' The Olympic motto: 'Citius Altius Fortius' / 'Faster Higher Stronger', The Paralympic motto: 'Spirit in Motion', The Team GB logo, The Paralympics GB logo.
>
> The British Olympic Association logo, The British Paralympic Association logo, London2012.com (and various derivatives). (LOCOG, 2007a)

LOCOG have also prepared guidelines outlining ways in which advertisements might infringe image rights (Table 10.5).

These guidelines are aimed in part to prevent 'ambush marketing'. Ambush marketing describes the attempt by non-sponsors to use advertising or other promotional material and activities in order to create the impression of an association between the ambushing brand and the sponsored event. As LOCOG describes it:

> ambush marketing describes a business' attempts to attach itself to a major sports event without paying sponsorship fees. As a result, the business gains the benefits of being associated with the goodwill and public excitement around the event for free.

Table 10.5   LOCOG's (2006) guideline recommendations regarding image rights
infringements for advertisers

Unlikely to infringe	Will infringe
An advert for running spikes showing runners in a non-descript setting and claiming: 'Helping athletes run faster'	An advert for running spikes showing runners in a stadium, carrying Olympic type torches and claiming: 'Helping athletes win gold at the London Games'
An advert for hair gel featuring a famous Paralympian and showing some of their inspirational career performances with the tag-line: 'Some people create magic which can make your hair stand on end. We've bottled it'	An advert for hair gel which shows athletic images and an athlete being presented with a gold medal outside one of the iconic London 2012 venues, with a voiceover: 'Is the excitement of the 2012 Games making the hairs on your neck stand on end? Use X Brand Super Gel to make sure your head matches.'

This damages the investment of genuine sponsors, and risks the organiser's ability to
fund the event. (LOCOG, 2007b)

There have been numerous instances of such activity in previous Games. For instance,
as Davis (2008:251) reports, Kodak sponsored TV broadcasts during the Games, despite
Fuji being the Olympics sponsor. Fuji did the same to Kodak in the Seoul 1988 Games.
Famously, Nike bought out the billboards around many of the Atlanta 1996 Olympic sites,
leading to conflict with Adidas – the official sponsor. Ambush marketing remains part of
the competitive marketing strategy of contemporary brands. Thus Nike continued its 'war'
with official partner Adidas, buying up advertising space and gaining significant coverage
by sponsoring teams and individuals (Birchall, 2008). This included the Chinese Olympian
Liu Xiang, perhaps China's most famous athlete. Unfortunately for Nike, the hurdler pulled
out of 110m race.

Celebrity, authenticity and the Olympic athlete

There is a certain degree of scepticism about the sponsorship of mega-events. Consumers
are conscious of the commercial intentions of sponsors, even while grasping the dependence
of the event upon sponsorship and other commercially derived income. However, the
Olympics offer a particular opportunity to sponsors as it fulfils the thirst for authenticity
discussed above, in a way that other aspects of celebrity commercial culture fails to do.
Sunderland (2008) draws a distinction between 'class one' celebrities, whose fame is based
on a real talent or achievement, and 'class two' celebrities, whose fame has less admirable
provenance and who are connected to gossip columns and tabloid magazines, in the
following terms:

Confusion over values seems to have migrated into all sorts of other arenas, not least
the public figures we choose to admire. Take two women, both young, both attractive,

Figure 10.5   Olympics sponsorship and the 'authentic celebrity'.

both named Nicole. The first, Nicole Cooke, won a cycling gold medal for Team GB in Beijing this summer, yet she is much less of a celebrity than Nicole Richie, whose accomplishments are to be a clotheshorse and the on-off best friend of Paris Hilton. Nicole Cooke has 'class one' fame: her gold medal will shine whether the public looks at it or not; Nicole Richie is 'class two', and is only famous if we think she is.

Olympic 'celebrities' offer advertisers some of the advantages of 'reality' TV celebrities – but without many of the disadvantages. They are unknown, fresh and likely to receive a good deal of intensive coverage. However, Olympic athletes differ in one important respect. Their fame and the values that they can embody depend upon genuine commitments and achievements. These athletes/celebrities are distinguished as 'gifted' athletes and high level performers. They operate, nevertheless, only at the seeming periphery of sports-promotional-commercialism. This lends their presence an authentic and authenticating quality. This is useful to advertisers seeking to communicate a sense of their sponsorship as 'philanthropic' and seeking to convey a sense of their engagement (with Olympics team members) as authentic, deep- seated and connected to practical benefits or athlete and team.

Sponsorship and advertising: gifts, marketing and simulation

What advertising attempts to do, is to simulate the gift relationship in the market economy. A 'gift' is an exchange in which a transfer is not mediated by price, but is rather reciprocated at the discretion of the receiver. It is driven by the pursuit of 'regard', i.e. the intrinsic benefits of social and personal interaction. Gifts are used to personalize the exchange, and to authenticate regard. (Offer, 1996: 225–6)

Offer makes an illuminating analysis of the cultural and marketing function of advertising. He proposes it as a genre designed to humanise market relations; to make the product and its exchange more personal so that 'buying' a particular good (a new computer or a *Mars Bar*) might seem like receiving a gift – notwithstanding the fact that the consumer will pay the price in a contractual transaction. By doing so – where successful – advertising serves the advertiser by distinguishing its 'humanised' products and brands – given regard via a personalised affective relationship – against the array of competitors' commodities. These seem relatively inert in comparison with its advertised products – and the ad expenditure becomes justified. This conception of advertising has some validity, even while it disregards the highly mercantile discourse of many price-based and product focused advertisements.

Offer's analysis of advertising is yet more pertinent in thinking about sponsorship, for two broad reasons. One of the arguments made in favour of sponsorship expenditure as part of a broad strategic branding and marketing push, is that advertising alone suffers from a diminishing return on investment (RoI) in current cultural and media contexts. This is because sceptical, 'savvy', etc. consumers see even elliptical and subtle advertising as necessarily and primarily a *marketing* genre. Its capacity to simulate gift relations and to humanise market relations is therefore hampered.

Offer's conception is helpful here in that while advertisers seek the de-commodifying power of advertisement as 'gift', understanding its value in promoting the quality of a desirable brand-consumer relationship, they have at times come to see sponsorship (rather than traditional advertising) as a yet more suitable means to convey the gift element of brands. Sponsorship more closely resembles a gift than does an advertisement, since, as it is understood by, and as it perhaps appears or *feels* to consumers, the act of financial sponsoring is a donation; one, when compared with and relative to advertising, is somehow less directly associated with discredited marketing functions – selling goods and so on. Regarding sponsorship in contrast with advertising, an older and more widespread commercial communications strategy, consumers intuit or attribute a relatively more indirect relation between marketers' commercial agendas and the promotional act – sponsoring the event.

Summary: planning and assessing sponsorship

In practical terms, it is important that a balance is struck between fulfilling the imperatives of marketing the brand – getting it noticed, affirming associations, etc. – and respecting the specificity of the sponsors' relationship to the fans and to the event. If the marketing presence of the brand is felt to disturb the character of the event and the experience of the fans, then it is likely that positive associations to the sponsoring brand will be

Table 10.6 Sponsorship questions

Does the brand fit with the culture and values of the event?	A high street bank may think twice about the extent to which it could credibly sponsor an alternative music festival. Cadbury's sponsorship of the Olympics has provoked some scepticism which has potentially damaging effects both for Cadburys (seen as exploiting the event) and for the Olympic brand (seen as compromising values). Similar anxieties have been voiced in regard to McDonald's and Coca Cola's Olympic links. These are countered by sponsors' commitments to health messages and in the provision of coaching and other active-youth events.
What kinds of brand imagery and adjunct creative work need to be developed for the event and subsequent broadcast?	Sponsoring an event requires that links between brand and event are made readily and credibly. Brand imagery needs to integrate with the event space – via clothing, temporary structures (tents, etc.). For large-scale events highly elaborate 'experience' venues might be used. Flyers, ads and other promotional materials should be in keeping with the event style, whether it is an Olympic event or a rock music festival.
How can the sponsor capitalise on the investment in the event? Who will get to know about it, and how?	The 'live' crowd forms an import audience for the sponsor, especially as by being there they experience the full range of the branded experience *live*. However, the rationale for much sponsorship lies in gaining wider media attention. The TOP sponsors work very hard to ensure that the investment in the Olympic partnership is fully recognised. In Beijing 2008, it was very difficult to find any poster sites in the city which had not been taken up by a TOP sponsor or by a sponsor of the Beijing Games. Sponsors developed branded web sites to enable fans to follow the sporting and other events surrounding the Olympic festival.
What balance should be struck between positive prominence and obtrusive commercialism?	This is important, as a brand should not be seen to take over the event unless, of course, the brand is the event. Over-interference may well lead to rejection of the brand and is likely to damage the brand values. Sometimes less is more. In the Olympics there is no direct advertising within Olympic venues. However, because of the special status of the Games as a highly prized cultural asset, the commercialisation of the Games experience receives close scrutiny.
What benefits will accrue to the brand? And how can the effectiveness of the sponsorship be measured?	There are various ways that a sponsorship can be evaluated. The extent of media exposure, reach, impacts can be quantified and it is possible to measure the impact of the sponsorship on attitudes to the brand. The extent to which consumer recall the association between sponsor and event is another helpful measure. Crimmins and Horn (1996) suggest that measures should reflect on the strength of the associative link between the sponsor and the event, on the gratitude felt due to the link and any resultant change in fans' perception of the sponsoring brand.

diminished. The sponsored 'donation' will be seen as a simulation rather than as a supportive contribution to the experience. Likewise, the dissemination and broadcast of sponsored events should strike a balance between overt commercial imperatives and a respect for the fans' rightful sense of ownership of the event-experience. Where this is implemented creatively there is a likelihood of demonstrable gains in the standing of the sponsors' brands.

Sponsorship is an attractive option for marketers. But it has weaknesses too, and is not always the most suitable choice. Brand owners' best decisions about which events to sponsor are now made in an informed way, weighing up strengths and weaknesses of

Table 10.7   Sponsorship strengths and weaknesses

Strengths	*Weaknesses*
Sponsorship can bring longstanding associations with high profile, highly energising events.	Impacts and effects of sponsor relationship are hard to assess.
Can deliver up, offer large 'mass' audiences (e.g. Olympics opening ceremonies) also highly targeted, specialist and special interest audiences – e.g. via local golf events or local literary festivals.	Clutter has come to affect the sponsorship arena as much as the advertising media. Association can be lost or misattributed to competitors – due to 'ambush marketing'.
Events have credibility and authenticity – e.g. Olympics or Edinburgh comedy festival (e.g. Perrier Awards). Association with authentic cultural activities is at a premium and enhances the brand. The Olympics offers an association to immediate thrills and excitement as well as to a historical tradition of sporting and cultural excellence.	Audiences put off by commercialisation of well loved cultural 'assets' or consider the 'fit' between sponsor and event/individual to be inappropriate. The political significance of sporting events such as the Olympics – as evident in relation to the torch relay and the 'Dream for Darfur' campaign – might also cause some concerns for sponsors anxious about controversy.
Offers an opportunity to provide VIPs and other corporate guests with high-quality entertainment. Good internal branding and staff development opportunities within the sponsoring organisation.	Provokes criticisms of the de-authentication of the live event and 'real fan' experience and undermines events – seen as 'commercial'. Undermines admiration for sponsors' contribution if the guests' event access provokes negative press.
Events can get high levels of good coverage over a sustained period. Individuals can work across platforms to enhance advertising and other promotional activities.	The sponsored team, or athlete might fail, cause a scandal or become injured – diminishing positive associations. The event might not be successful or attract bad press – e.g. Nike's sponsorship of Chinese hurdler Liu Xiang.
High profile global events offer opportunities for high level lobbying, as national governments are often large stakeholders in events such as the Olympics.	Events such as the Olympics demand and depend upon high levels of probity and corporate responsibility on the part of stakeholders. There is close media scrutiny of sponsors who might fail to live up to the established high standards of the Games.

promotional modes, as well as considering what an event may or may not offer the brand. Sponsorship selection has moved from 'management ego trip' towards 'marketing success' (Crimmins and Horn, 1996).

There have been strong increases in the quantities of sponsorship funds coming to the IOC for the Olympics. However, a number of sponsors have reviewed their relationship with this mega-event. There are various reasons for this. Partly it is a matter of cost. Also sponsors are concerned that consumers do not register that sponsors have contributed. Some long-standing sponsors, for example, Kodak, have recently ended their association to the Games in favour of new promotional strategies.

Notes

1   This type of sponsorship binds brands to charitable causes and promotes the work of charitable organisations.
2   Numerous challenges face traditional national advertising approaches. The 30-second prime time TV slot or the double page spread in main media outlets, i.e. the standard and dominant advertising formats of the twentieth century have been conceding share of clients' marketing spend in the face of various interrelated pressures including: the distractions and flexibilities of new media; audience fragmentation and the multiplication of media channels and platforms; increasing 'clutter'; increasing main media costs; audience cynicism and scepticism; elusive youth audiences (who are migrating online and playing computer games); clients' renewed commitments to demonstrable ROI and effectiveness measures; attenuation in the stability and predictability of class-based identities and the aspirational scripts guiding the modern consumerist habitus.
3   As the International Herald tribune reported in the run up the Games, this end was readily supported by the games organising committee: 'The Beijing Organizing Committee for the Olympic Games, which is known as Bocog, has asked advertising agencies to avoid using Olympic symbols without authorization and is asking media companies to carry ads of Olympic sponsors on their channels featuring Olympic content . . . Starting on Friday, "all prominent advertising space in Beijing, including at the airport and on subway lines, will be controlled, giving official sponsors priority," said Chen Fong, deputy director of marketing for Bocog, according to a report in Xinhua, the Chinese state-run news agency . . . According to a report in Advertising Age, the government has removed more than 30,000 outdoor ads in Beijing in the last year (Clifford, 2008).'

11 Advertising universities: re-presenting complex products in a difficult marketplace

Iain MacRury and Sarah Hawkin

An emergent market sector

This chapter looks at advertising in a specialist product sector: university institutions. This area of advertising is significant because of the nature of the 'product' being advertised. In the UK, the complexity of the sector is partly a consequence of government-driven shifts in the management and provision of higher education and related changes in its consumption. Since the 1990s, universities have begun to advertise far more frequently. Simultaneously various changes in the composition of the higher education 'market' and significant changes in the ways university education is funded have made marketing and advertising appear to be more compatible with 'The Idea of a University'[1] than was the case in former times. Advertising made no sense when demand for higher education places typically outstripped supply and when universities and polytechnics were entirely publicly funded – as a limited public resource – by local authorities and central government.

Today, UK higher education operates as a hybrid public/private sector activity. Universities belong wholly to neither the public nor the private sector. This reflects the policy shifts begun in the 1980s, which have increasingly passed the costs of university education on to the growing population of students, who pay fees and who are increasingly referred to and understood as 'consumers' or 'customers'.

Universities are still in receipt of public funding, via HEFCE[2] in particular. This reflects the continuing and important public service role of universities. Such funding connects the management and operation of universities to government polices and priorities such as widening access, employability and increasing student numbers. On the one hand, as a consequence, universities work in the manner of a state provided public service. In this mode, government and other stakeholders guide and regulate university institutions' development and activities, while also trying to respect the principle of institutional autonomy. On the other hand, universities sometimes behave like individual corporations in a competitive marketplace. It is this shift, broadly from public service to commercial-style provision, that has opened up the 'space' for advertising communications. Advertising has begun to take on a role – in an area of social, educational and cultural life where, in the UK at least, and until these 1980s policy changes[3], it had almost no part to play (Wernick, 1991: 154–80).

Advertising, as a prominent element of universities' total marketing activities, is most obviously associated with this second commerce-like behaviour.

In marketing terms, the university is typically a very 'high involvement' product. This means students – and other stakeholders in the decision process – are likely to invest heavily in seeking information and other search activities, as a prelude to decision-making. In addition, the costs of fees, lost earnings and living costs mean that there is a significant incentive to make a good decision. This is especially the case where students consider options across international boundaries.

Advertising takes on various functions in this emerging space, alongside other more traditional communications but also and especially alongside a range of web-based communications – from Facebook to blogs and to numerous guidebooks. There are a number of official and semi-official information sources available nationally and internationally. In the UK, *The Times* publishes annual league tables and its *Good University Guide*. There are further such guides, some modelled on travel and tourism guidebooks. These rank universities and different university courses and record detailed accounts of student experiences. They are an important source for students. Universities often highlight successful league table performances, picking out variables where they have achieved a top ranking for inclusion in marketing communications.

A complex 'market' and a contested 'product'

'Master your future . . .', 'Become what you want . . .', 'Bring your dreams . . .' Each of these slogans comes from a different university advertising campaign. Higher education is the 'product'. University managers[4] are increasingly turning to advertising agencies to promote what institutions have to offer (Fearn, 2008). The ensuing advertisements reflect many of the same techniques – visual and verbal – that are used to promote the kinds of product on sale in supermarkets, in a travel agent or the local bank branch. Mary Evans, an academic who is largely critical of the ways the modern university sector is developing (Evans, 2004) writes, 'the high street has entered the academy' bringing 'its own motivational language for consumption', for example with the promise that 'this degree will make you employable and slightly richer' (Evans, 2007).

Such analyses, and the significant unease that they represent within the university profession, brings further complexities for those seeking to advertise university courses as a 'product'. There is a considerable degree of scepticism about the value of advertising in this area, precisely because 'learning' is difficult to productise credibly. Critique comes from academic staff, but also from 'risk averse' institutional marketing managers. As universities commission advertising they are often conscious of the danger of cheapening or undermining universities' reputations in a market where promotional communications often need to convey elite-style aspirations in a media savvy marketplace attuned to popular sensibilities and the complex and conflicting ambitions of young people.

For example, Dundee University recently successfully negotiated such contradiction producing a campaign based on the oxymoronic underlying concept: 'Serious Fun'. Just as in mainstream advertising, the youth market presents a particular further challenge to universities. The pressure to find credible media and to convey credible messages to the latest 'media-aware' generation – and often on a relatively small budget – means universities need to be creative among the clutter. Cumming (2005a) describes students as part of the 'media-savvy, computer games-reared, generation', pointing out that prospective students are 'the ABC1 consumers of the future' who 'do not tolerate corporate-style advertising, finding it patronising and stale' (Cumming, 2005a).

Universities *can* credibly be said to be 'selling' a 'product' and communicating its benefits to consumers. Policy makers have worked to ensure that this description of university activity is practically in force and is structuring aspects of promotion but also, and more controversially, other institutional activities, such as programme structures (MacRury, 2007). Alongside the consumer-marketing conception of education, it is also important to be alert to the specificity of education, as something to be understood not as a product to be chosen, bought and sold, but as a transformative experience linked to the generation of insight and innovation and to personal and social development. When the specificity and value of educational provision is underplayed, in favour of cautious advertising linked to limited and limiting benefits, the credibility of the advertising and of institutional promotional efforts become diminished. This can reduce the value of institutions' investment in advertising; or even make it irrelevant.

Unlike most consumer marketplaces, access to different parts of the HE 'market' for undergraduate and most post graduate higher education places is not mediated by money alone. Universities seek to admit students on the basis of previous qualifications as well as willingness to pay fees. While most marketing seeks to increase the quantity of 'customers', for universities, and to varying degrees, the priority is to increase the numbers of higher quality applicants. For universities and applicants there is a market mediated by 'grades', which differs from consumer-product markets. Universities in the UK currently charge similar fees for similar courses, except in Scotland, where no fees are payable. Government legislation prevents differential pricing. This means that competition is for high-quality students as much as it is for raw numbers. In addition, universities often have conflicting priorities. An institutional and educational commitment to widening access can sit uncomfortably with a campaign focusing directly on attracting applicants with high grades.

The functions of university advertising

Broadly speaking, universities invest in advertising to:

- increase the numbers of students studying at the university or on selected programmes within the university
- increase the number and quality of applications to university places
- draw attention to specific promotional activities, such as open days and other events
- build or update the university 'brand' and improve the reputation of the university in the minds of various local, global and national stakeholders
- internal branding and motivational exercises aimed at the current staff and student population and at local communities and stakeholders

Universities communicate with a number of potential 'audiences'. This reflects the various socio-economic roles fulfilled by higher educational institutions in a sector of the economy that serves students and parents, but also employers and government bodies. Current and future students understood as 'consumers' are a major preoccupation for universities engaging in advertising. Potential applicants are the main target and focus of most university advertising. It is important to note that teachers and parents, as well as peers and friends, play a significant role in decisions affecting university choices – and so serve as important intermediaries in the decision-making process. Alumni typically also retain an interest in the university 'brand', even if they are not accustomed to thinking about their former university in precisely such terms. For some institutions, there is often an important international dimension in any advertising strategy, as a large proportion of fee-paying students are recruited from abroad. Here, also, alumni can pass on positive evaluations to further potential students, spurred by advertising's capacity to serve as a 'reminder'. Employers' opinions of different universities and their graduates are also important. 'Employability' is a policy-driven buzzword that marks a significant concern for parents and students. In fact, it is at the heart of many current advertising campaigns.

University staff members have a central stake in the way the university is represented. Broadly speaking, advertising is developed to reflect the ideas and priorities of universities' corporate managers. Academics tend to see advertising, at best, as an entertaining sideshow; an expensive distraction entered into the *real* work of teaching and research pursued to fulfil a mission defined as 'education'-focused rather than as marketing-focused.

Potential benefactors, research partners and various government and development agencies at local and national, and sometimes international level, form further significant secondary audiences for universities' communications, if not always necessarily for their advertising in particular. Advertising is the most prominent way for universities to assert a presence in the public domain. As such, advertising is ideally developed to support branding managed with an attentive eye on this wide range of agendas and priorities. The most successful campaigns manage to generate support across all these groups, but retain a primary focus on improving the quantity and quality of applications. It is notable that this positive assessment of a recent campaign works hard to contextualise the advertising in the broader work of the institution and its stakeholders:

As Vice Chancellor in 2000, I was extremely concerned that I was about to inherit serious problems. I have been very impressed by the impact and results delivered by the Serious Fun campaign. It resonates with students and prospective students. The university's reputation ultimately depends on excellent staff and students, and advertising communications also play an important part in our ongoing progress. (Sir Alan Langlands, Principal, University of Dundee)

University advertising is aimed primarily at a 'consumer market' consisting of parents, schools advisors and school leavers. Some attention is given to mature students in some campaigns. George Cumming (2005b) offers this useful model for thinking about the

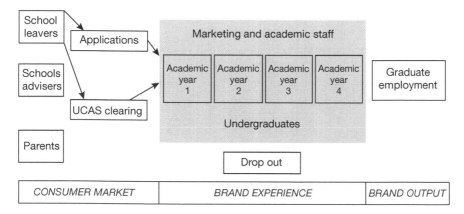

Figure 11.1 A marketing-orientated conception of the university.

higher education market. It posits an input – output model beginning with students accessing the university 'brand experience' either via the application system or via clearing. Undergraduates pass through the system over four years – following the Scottish convention – and, if they stay the course they can expect to move into graduate employment. This is a limited model of the university 'narrative' but accurately reflects general marketing approaches to higher education.

This recruitment conception of university advertising is central. However, advertising expertise has an increasing role in more generalised brand building and in specific communications tasks focusing on specific institutional issues.

Figure 11.2   University of Leicester diversity campaign.

A recent campaign focused on diversity at Leicester. The University of Leicester is a highly ranked Midlands university which consistently performs well in the National Student Satisfaction Survey. It is situated in one of the most ethnically and socially diverse cities in England and its student body similarly has a very broad composition.

As is the case with many universities, the composition of the staff at Leicester, both academic and non-academic, was felt to be very traditional – it was believed to be predominantly, white, middle class and conventional. The University commissioned a series of advertisements from JWT Education, linked to specific events in the city, which attempted to alter those perceptions.

The advertisement shown above appeared in local media and was timed to coincide with a Gay Pride event. Its appeal lies in its simplicity, its use of the colours of the Gay Pride flag, to precisely address its target market and a very straightforward message – a good example of the old maxim, that less is more.

The branded university

University advertising campaigns have been developed – increasingly since the 1990s – alongside an emerging commitment to the view that universities can be helpfully thought about as 'brands'. Recently, Goldsmiths University and the Open University have been listed alongside, for example, Kangol, Volkswagen and Lambretta as 'Superbrands' and singled out as distinctive and even 'cool'. Cumming (2005a) proposes that university brands have existed for 'centuries' and further suggests that, for institutions with shorter histories and less established identities in particular, it can be difficult to create a credible brand. Nor is it easy to change a university brand reputation once fixed.

There is certainly some formal similarity between the notion of universities as brands and the more traditional idea of universities as institutions with reputations established in the public domain over an extended period of time – based on inadvertent, informal but wide ranging 'promotional' efforts. After all, long before the word 'branding' had ever been used in its modern sense, universities and colleges strove to maintain a particular standing in the public imagination.

Universities even had crests as a way to embellish buildings and for validating documents. Such crests resemble brand 'logos' in a cursory way. But the two types of emblem are also different in that such crests symbolise and affirm relations between the university, the state and the crown. And, because university crests would appear on degree certificates – as they continue to do – they also marked the achievements of graduates. The 'logo' refers, instead, and increasingly, to relations between the university and the marketplace. It refers, at least in part, to marketing management practices and relationships. Branding is a practice most fully realised in a commercial marketing setting. In this sense, university brands have existed only for as long as and to the extent that universities have operated within markets and the reputation systems attached to a market system. Mary Evans (2007) compares university brands to the fashion labels of *haute couture*, arguing that a complex marketplace has emerged, in which 'most universities are like shops, borrowing the imprimatur of elite labels to sell copies of the real thing' (Evans, 2007).

There is a sense that overt marketing de-authenticates certain brands. This can be true of certain elite brands in the commercial sector. This elite sensibility pervades discussion of higher education. In the higher education sector, where traditionally universities have not advertised, advertising, however well crafted, can become a sign of inauthenticity and a lowering of the value of the brand.

Whether university brands have existed for a long time or whether the branded university is a recent invention, *advertising* university education is certainly a relatively new practice in the UK. The routine inclusion of advertising as a concerted part of university communications works, in any case, to *constitute* the university as a brand – even when such a conception is limited or contested in relation to the full range of a university relationships, activities and functions.[5]

Universities: public service and private corporate advertising

University advertising is a small but growing sector. Universities are sometimes grouped with charities in discussions of marketing and advertising. This is partly because a proportion of university advertising has traditionally been linked to fundraising.[6] The 'Universities and Charities' grouping works to denote a distinction between these kinds of institutions and other types of uncomplicatedly commercial corporate bodies, notably those selling products or services; for instance, car manufacturers or banks. In different ways, universities and charities are understood to be engaged in the marketing and provision of socially valuable services; orders of activity where, in intent at least, the relation to market imperatives and the motive towards profit (as an end in itself) are attenuated and, if they are not absent, they are nevertheless subordinated (to a degree) to working notions of the public good. It is useful to think about advertising when mobilised in the service of such sectors of activity, since there are some particular characteristics of the non-commercial sector 'marketing relationship' and particular difficulties facing advertisers – and advocates for advertising – using advertising communications genres to 'sell' or 'brand' institutions and activities where there remains a residual mistrust of marketisation and commercialism.

The government's 'Aim Higher' campaign aims to make potential students aware of university education as a national resource and an opportunity. It aims to attract students who have had little or no engagement with the reality or idea of university education, also working to focus the attention of more engaged potential students to better ensure they are equipped to make fully informed choices. The campaigns also seek to communicate to parents so that they can assist in decision making and planning. Aim Higher also seeks to engage older people who might imagine that university had 'passed them by', and to provide information to parents.

Aimhigher ran a radio advertisement for three weeks, the transcript of which is given in Figure 11.4. The media plan was designed to reach 60 per cent of 25–34 year olds (C1C2Ds) in full- or part-time employment via youth-oriented radio stations. The advertising campaign was supported 'by media relations activity featuring case studies

Figure 11.3   The Aim Higher can be used by universities and other organisations promoting the idea of university education. The logo operates as a public service 'brand' to coordinate and identify activity undertaken in the name of the Aim Higher agenda.

Radio script:

Client: DfES

Date: 14/10/2008

Product: Foundation Degrees

Length: 30"

Title: Cheerleader

FX: The sound of a busy factory floor.

MV1: [North London, cockney] Right team, how we getting on?

SFX: Murmurs of yes, good, okay's are cut short by a very excited woman responding as a cheerleader . . .

FV2: [replying as a cheerleader] G-R-E-A-T, GREAT! Yehhhhhhh!!!!

SFX: Pom Poms shaking

MV1: Err . . . who was that?

FV2: [still replying as a cheerleader] I-T-S-M-E, IT'S MEEEEEEE!!!!! Yehhhhhhhh!!!

SFX: Pom Poms shaking

MV1: Err . . . you alright?

FV2: [joyfully] Noooooooooooooo!

FVO: There's a better way of getting noticed at work. Foundation Degrees are designed with the help of employers, so you can become better qualified in your chosen career. And you can do one working. For more information, visit foundationdegree.org.uk.

Figure 11.4   Radio script from a Department for Education and Skills advertisement. The ad aims to engage students to the idea of higher education, as part of the Aim Higher initiative.

of employers, students and the courses themselves'. It is of interest that further work to build on this campaign was intended to link local institutions and the British Chambers of Commerce. The campaign operates on the basis that students accessing higher education will be motivated by improved work prospects. The media targeting and the creative content of the ad reflect a widening participation brief. The aim is to prompt mature students to consider reconnecting with the education system and to do an access course.

University advertising is often taken on by small specialist agencies or by sub-offices of larger agencies. While advertising agencies conventionally have not managed accounts from competitor clients, so that holding the account for Motorola would mean that an agency could not hold the account for Nokia in the mobile phone sector, specialist university advertising offices will service a number of institutions concurrently. This is a function of the specialist nature of the HE advertising marketplace and, in particular, of economies related to universities' typically small-scale advertising expenditure. Most universities' advertising budgets are insufficient to warrant an agency's building expertise in the area for the sake of just one client.

Universities and advertising media

Main media advertising is typically a small portion of universities' promotional effort, which can include prospectuses, directory inserts, PR, e-marketing, institutional websites, 'outreach' work and open days. Advertising supplements, supports and amplifies such efforts. If done well, it can provide an integrative focus for such work – in the manner of and as a contribution to a developing 'brand'.

The small advertising budgets of universities, in particular, as opposed to many other types of advertiser, mean that this sector does not immediately come to mind when considering 'advertising' taken as a unitary practice. Universities are relatively less prominent across the mediascape than holidays or insurance products. Most advertisements appear in print or outdoors, often adorning transport-related sites. The cheaper broadcast media, radio and cinema are often part of university advertising campaigns. However, some television advertising is broadcast, a development emerging from the multiplication of local and special interest channels, as well as from universities' increasing preoccupation with and expenditure on marketing and advertising.

Social networking sites, such as Facebook, are becoming popular with university marketing departments operating with the logic that – since teens and students are heavy users of such websites – it might be easier and cheaper to reach potential students online than via relatively expensive and cluttered main media ads: this, especially given the received wisdom that the youth audience is typically more indifferent to traditional advertising formats and appeals. University advertising expenditure is linked to seasonal focus, with bursts coming at key times of the year, notably to coincide (in October and November) with the application cycle and, for many institutions, during the summer months to coincide with 'clearing'.[7]

Universities 'recruit' students in a number of ways. As with traditional types of commercial brands – selling products and services on the high street – electronic media has become a central part of university promotions. Given the relatively youthful character of prospective students, even in relation to the 'mature' sector of the market and the likely aptitude of university students in utilising Internet-based communications, it is important to recognise that traditional 'above the line' advertising, on TV/cinema, outdoors, on radio and in the press, must take its place in a complementary way alongside other integrated marketing efforts – with the quality, accessibility and attractiveness of a university website of central importance. Web-based 'touch points' must be of the highest quality – most especially in an era when students are looking for universities across the globe, and when increasing amounts of university-based education is, in fact, based 'online', via 'virtual learning environments'. Tahir (2008) reports a senior branding and communications consultant's suggestion that 'the web would be "the principal battlefield" in the competition for students' and that 'Information on consumer and social networking sites, such as Facebook, could become as influential as that on universities' own websites' (Tahir, 2008).

However, traditional media have continued to have an important role to play. Here is an example from a recent successful campaign from Salford University. The link between campaign objectives and media choice is clear in their approach to a region-based re-branding campaign:

> The media plan focused only on the North/North West because Salford's intake 'was coming from a decreasing radius and to reposition Salford on a national basis would be to try and impress students who had more reasons than just our poor image to reject us. TV was the lead medium for all the obvious reasons. We needed to reach everyone at once, we needed 30 seconds of sound and image to fully explain ourselves and we needed the right kind of environment. This was a message from a university that knew how to find you outside of careers guides, directories and the 6th form common room. C4 North delivered best and we deduced the minimum weight we could get away with without compromising OTS. Minimum weight, because we had decided it was also

key for our message be seen in more than one medium. Leicester De Montfort and Central Lancs had both been on TV the year before and got talked about just for being on TV. We were going on TV with a new and distinct message. Maximum recall would be gained by secondary hits of that message off the screen. (Cheetham-Bell-JWT: 2001)

Scripting the higher education commodity: products, services, experiences and transformations

The constitution of universities as brands and the opening up of a 'marketplace' in university courses contributes to the constitution of higher education as a commodity. This process of commodification is stimulated by internal management and regulatory processes working to assure the quality, accountability and transparency of the courses offered by universities. This process is yet further underscored by league tables grading institutions and programmes with reference to various indices designed to mark the total quality of provision and student experiences. This has lead to criticisms, frequently levelled at a *McDonaldisation* of education – where institutions have begun to conform to a management and service model comparable with the hamburger chain and as described by sociologist George Ritzer.

Once commodification is acknowledged, the question becomes: 'what kind of "commodity" is higher education?' There are certainly formal similarities between university provision and the provision of other services – be it fast food or financial services. It is important to grasp the specificity of the education 'product'. Advertisers need to present a sense of the institutional offer that authentically reflects demand and enhances the brand. It could be that for some institutions and for some consumers the very act of advertising is seen to compromise the brand, regardless of the quality of the advertising message. However, in an increasingly promotion oriented sector, advertising is becoming accepted within the wider array of promotional tools. Good advertising can play a decisive role as a number of case studies demonstrate (Cheetham-Bell-JWT, 2001; Cumming, 2005a; Cumming, 2005b; Griffith, 2004). In a high involvement sector, such as university education, a good deal of thought is likely to go into the final decision to select this or that institution. Consumers seek to gauge institutions' statements about themselves against internal conceptions – life and education-related desires and aspirations. The working conception of the educational commodity is at the heart of any university brand – and traceable across numerous institutional discourses. Advertising is one of these; prominent but typically not definitive. Ideally advertising and other promotional materials will affirm a positive, informative and imaginative conception of what the university is and what it offers – one that feels authentic and credible to the full range of institutional stakeholders; from staff to prospective and current students and from parents to benefactors.

Pine and Gilmore (1999) offer a useful and relevant typification distinguishing various types of provision ranging from material goods to intangible human experiences. In Table 11.1 they describe five types of business.

The constitution of the educational commodity takes place across a number of transactions, from marketing, to pedagogy, to the everyday life on campus. The university's branding and advertising script points out, if not the real character of the university, then at least a leading institutional statement pointing to a significant conception of what the university is offering. Pine and Gilmore (Table 11.2) give a clear picture of the different relations implicit in institutions and settings, where either products, service, experiences or transformations predominate the script.

Table 11.1   Five types of business

A *commodity* business charges for	undifferentiated products, such as rice or oil
A *goods* business charges for	tangible things – processed and manufactured goods, such as ready meals
A *service* business charges for	the activities you perform.
	for the benefit customers (or charge for 'guests')
An *experience* business charges for	the feeling customers get by engaging in it
A *transformation* business charges	received by spending time there

Pine and Gilmore (1999).

Table 11.2   Conceiving the commodity and the organisational relationships emerging around various types/conceptions of commodity

Economy	Agrarian/ mineral	Industrial	Service	Experience	Transformation
Economic function	Extract	Make	Deliver	Stage	Guide
Nature of offering	Fungible	Tangible	Intangible	Memorable	Effectual
Key attribute	Natural	Standardised	Customised	Personal	Individual
Method of supply	Stored in bulk	Inventoried after production	Delivered on demand	Revealed over a duration	Sustained through time
Seller	Trader	Manufacturer	Provider	Stager	Elicitor
Buyer	Market	User	Client	Guest	Aspirant
Factors of demand	Characteristics	Features	Benefits	Sensations	Traits

Pine and Gilmore (1999).

Pine and Gilmore's *The Experience Economy* (1999) also sets out a useful way of distinguishing the parameters of the service economy and of setting it against other, more developed, economic activity – which they see as taking place in 'the experience economy' (Table 11.2). The experience economy supercedes the service economy. Its product is more valuable to consumers. It is a more profitable mode of production (in commercial terms), and a richer contribution to the social and cultural environment (in public service terms). 'Experience' is not accounted so readily among the benefits of an HE 'service' in the way that, say, employability benefits are. The experience economy is itself exceeded in the progression along the scale of economic value by what Pine and Gilmore call the 'transformation' economy. Higher education institutions are really operating in that space. These different conceptions of what is on offer in the institution are a useful prelude to thinking about how the university 'commodity' is scripted and constructed in advertising. The following advertising copy, a voiceover from a TV ad for Napier University, focuses on the education *product* in an informal but also informative way. It balances this focus on named degree programmes with a more generalising commitment to university as a 'preparation for life'. It uses a basic ad appeal structure and aims to 'sell' the prospectus as much as the university experience and embeds the information in a chatty voiceover:

> If it's time to get prepared for the future, read this, Napier University prospectus. It'll open up the whole world from film and design to nursing, midwifery and social science, hospitality, tourism or even festival management.

Rather than focus on the courses as 'products', the following ad, from Teesside University, concentrates on the campus as a kind of destination-product, affordable and with good SU facilities. However, overall, the ad offers a primarily *service* oriented conception of the higher education commodity:

We have some of the most affordable university accommodation in the UK. We've been awarded students union of the year twice. We've invested nearly a hundred million pounds in new facilities. The quality of our careers advice has won national recognition, which means our students leave with great career and salary prospects, and you thought we were just another university. You're on your way with the University of Teesside.

The ad voiceover gives emphasis to higher education as a careers-based education *service*. The emphasis is on desirable service outcomes such as enhanced earning potential. In a similar way, another ad voiceover text, from Huddersfield University, picks up on services, with a tagline underlining a commitment to employability:

Looking back the University of Huddersfield transformed my life. I gained so much more than a degree, like great friends and practical skills. With over 500 courses and superb facilities, it's no wonder so many of us choose to come here. The first time I saw the place I knew this was the place for me. The University of Huddersfield, educating tomorrow's professionals.

But the ad also touches on the *experience* sector outlined in Pine and Gilmore's schema (Table 11.2). It does this by lending emphasis to the importance of extra, unanticipated benefits and experiences such as friendship and belonging. The ad also explicitly offers university education as a 'transformative' experience. This conception of the university commodity is structured into the copy with the use of a narrative, memory-based account of how the university 'transformed my life'.

13th of September 04: I didn't understand micro molecules: then I understood. 20th of the second 2002: that was I realized I can do this. Mine was the 6th of June 03. Which day will change your life? Study at a first choice university with an award winning campus [. . .] University of Sunderland, life changing. Which journey will change your life? (University of Sunderland)

The ad from Sunderland is more subtle and elliptical in its approach. It focuses on educational 'epiphanies'; 'eureka!' moments of transformational learning. This approach does a good job of affirming the potential of university education as a *transformative* commodity and locates that transformation at a more personal and intimate level than those ads emphasising career-related outcomes or specific product and service benefits. The ad invites a conception of the university which is not about turning 'students' into 'professionals' through the achievement of staged outcomes. Instead the advertising highlights the sporadic, organic and developmental aspects of university education. The ad supports a view of education as open-ended; as a 'journey' and as life changing. Concrete service outcomes are barely given emphasis, a 'journey' is evoked to invite students as aspirants.

Scepticism: consumers and providers

It is useful to think about the impact advertising has on the target consumers. A detailed study looking at students' accounts of their university decision-making processes found that advertising actually provoked negative views from some students. One respondent suggested:

I mean, to me, it is like, that university must be really desperate to be advertising on the Northern Line underground and stuff like that, so I wouldn't go, no way. Female applicant, school leaver. (Ball *et al.*, 2004: 130)

A mature student offered a similarly unenthused response to universities who advertised:

to be honest if I've noticed adverts at all it has been to put me off. I think I don't want to go somewhere that's pleading for me to go there'. Female, mature student

As observed, advertising can have a negative impact on the reputation of the institution because

advertising conveys the idea that entry to the universities in question is too easy, they are 'desperate' or 'pleading' and, by implication, are undiscriminating. In effect, the students place and classify themselves in relation to the status and reputation of these universities as indicated by the students who are able to attend and the degree of selectivity involved in access. (Ball *et al.*, 2004: 30)

Thus for some potential 'consumers' the act of advertising can undermine the advertising intention, that is, it can risk depleting the institutional reputation rather than boosting it. The increased use of credible alternative media and imaginative creativity nevertheless works to offset scepticism, especially in those sectors of the market where commitments to a traditional conception of education are not so firmly rooted.

Advertising in this specialist market requires alertness to the complexities of a high involvement 'product'. As such, university advertising offers a useful object of analysis. It is a reminder of the importance of understanding the specific character of a product sector as a prelude to developing advertising communications. It is useful to think about relatively 'new' product sectors, such as those where advertising has not formally or formerly been part of traditional consumer or provider habits, as with universities, and where advertising has therefore not been, necessarily, a part of 'audience' expectations. Universities are not alone in being relatively 'new' to using promotional advertising. Indeed, the university sector is illustrative of a notable trend in the economy, which has had significant, largely beneficial consequences for the advertising industry. The range of product sectors using advertising today in the UK is far larger than in the earlier decades of the twentieth century because of a significant shift in ideas about economic management. In the 1970s, in the UK, as in a number of other economies, it was decided that it would be a good idea to manage a number of public services and national industries (e.g. railways, car makers, electricity providers and so on) as if they were private commercial businesses such as ICI or Sainsbury's. This political philosophy, based in the view that private industries were more efficient, offered 'consumers' more choice and were better 'lead' by 'market forces' than by governmental policies, lead quickly, in many cases (e.g. the telephone service and the railways) to the actual transfer of public sector organisations and industries into the private sector.

Once changed – or 'marketised' – these service industries turned to advertising; advertising serves not just to boost demand, but as an alternative way of achieving consumers' trust in the absence of the formal relationships which were characteristic of earlier times. Providers of all types of public services, from politicians and government departments, to universities and charities, are now routinely communicating in forms developed by the advertising industry in the early decades of the twentieth century. The post-war era has seen the authority structures, which formally underpinned communication in the public sphere, continually challenged by the demands for modes of openness, entertainment and accessibility for which advertising provides powerful models. Advertising becomes one of the modes of information most congenial to that particular spirit of 'democracy' spawned in the post-modern marketplace. There is much understandable ambivalence about the role of advertising in these areas. Finally there is the recognition of universities as significant sites for advertising and other kinds of promotion and the identification of 'students' as an important market for advertisers.

It is useful to think about how education is conceived within a marketing and advertising context – especially if 'living' the advertised 'product', i.e. as a part of a university education. Given the multi-dimensional nature of 'higher education' and the relative simplicity of advertising claims about universities, examining HE advertising serves as a kind of case study in the product transformations brought about by advertising re-presentations. A background question for students reading this chapter might run as follows: 'To what extent is what advertising "makes of" higher education related to what you, as students seek, find and, in turn, hope to "make of" higher education – and of yourself?'

Questions for students

1. Why do universities represent a specialist area for advertising?

2. What type of 'commodity' is higher education? Compare a selection of advertisements and consider what is represented as being 'on offer'.

3. How should universities select advertising media?

4. In what other ways, apart from advertising, can universities promote recruitment and widen access?

Notes

1   This is the title of an important book on the philosophy of university education published by Cardinal John Henry Newman in 1852. A flavour of Newman's influential thinking lies in this brief excerpt: 'If then a practical end must be assigned to a University course, I say it is that of training good members of society. Its art is the art of social life, and its end is fitness for the world. It neither confines its views to particular professions on one hand, nor creates heroes or inspires genius on the other.' (Newman 1852)

2   HEFCE, i.e. the Higher Education Funding Council. It is relevant to point out that Scotland has a different funding structure which means that students don't pay fees directly, as is the case, e.g., in England and Wales.

3   When De Monfort University launched its advertising campaign in 1994 on national TV – Channel 4 – it received a good deal of coverage as the first university television campaign of that scale.

4   Baty (2005) cites a report by advertising agency Euro RSCG Riley suggesting that university managers were increasingly preoccupied with a need to 'move towards the "corporate adoption" of a marketing mentality, to think targets, revenue, tuition fees and branding' (Baty 2005). Thus, as the report claims: 'Asked to identify important topics, 84 per cent of managers cited the competitive nature of the higher education market, 81 per cent highlighted the impact of tuition fees and 75 per cent singled out "branding".'

5   Universities produce a certain amount of academic research. The meaning and value of this research is not formally connected to any 'brand' considerations – although there is sometimes to attribute value to research on such bases. Other areas of work, such as the content of courses and the development and communication of teaching materials, are not connected to the university 'brand'.

6   Alternatively, it university advertising can be distinguished from other much bigger areas, such as cars or FMCG, by linking it to recruitment advertising – i.e. finding staff for companies – on the grounds that universities *recruit* students.

7   As the UK University and Colleges Admissions Service describes it: 'Clearing is used by applicants who have not managed to secure a place at university or college for the current year. It begins in August and it can help people to find suitable vacancies on higher education courses: more than 30,000 people gain a place during Clearing every year' (http://www.ucas.ac.uk/clearing/).

12 FMCG advertising: the home of branding

Tim Broadbent

Introduction

It is rare to find a senior advertising executive who has not worked in FMCG. It schools the brightest and best. What makes FMCG special is the depth of brand understanding it offers. This is because branding has a longer history in FMCG and there is more brand research available than in other fields. Advertisers in all categories have built on the understanding of brands first developed in FMCG.

What FMCG advertising is

Textbooks say FMCG is an acronym of '*Fast Moving Consumer Goods*'. 'Fast moving' means goods that households buy frequently, that is every week or every few weeks. Two important consequences follow from this definition:

1. FMCG goods are cheap. They must be, to be bought so often. Many are 'single coin' purchases, that is they cost less than a pound. The manufacturer's profit from each unit is therefore measured in pence. In order to afford the millions of pounds an advertising campaign might cost, manufacturers must sell tens or hundreds of millions of extra units. The business model in FMCG is always high volume/low margin.

   Sales volume is a function of two factors: the number of buyers multiplied by the quantity bought per buyer. FMCG manufacturers cannot survive in business unless many category buyers choose the advertised brand regularly (Ehrenberg, 1972). In this way, brand loyalty is built into the FMCG business model.

   Profit is also a function of two factors: the margin per unit multiplied by the sales volume. Margin improvements of even a fraction of a penny increase profit significantly because of high volumes. Branding creates consumer preference over products that perform as well or better in blind tests: one measure of a brand's strength is the price premium it commands over close substitutes. In this way, brand equity is also built into the FMCG business model (Feldwick, 2002).

   On the other hand, the cheapness of FMCG goods means that trying a new one is low risk. FMCG marketing is characterised by high levels of new product development. But whether advertising is used to launch new products or support old ones, it has a central role. FMCG brands have high advertising/sales ratios, and the two biggest advertisers in the world, Procter & Gamble and Unilever, are FMCG.

2. From the consumer perspective, buying an FMCG brand for the first time can be like making the first of many regular journeys, say to a new place of work. The first trip involves conscious decision-making: one consults a map, researches bus and train routes, counts street numbers, etc. However, after a while the journey becomes automatic. It is hard to remember afterwards what happened on a routine journey because the conscious part of the mind was not engaged.

We can see unconscious choice in operation by observing buying behaviour in supermarkets. Shoppers pick familiar brands and drop them into their trolleys without breaking step. Brands help make shopping quicker and easier: a decent sized supermarket today might carry 40,000 product lines, a fourfold increase over 20 years ago, and it would be appalling to have to study every product in a category before deciding which one to buy (Schwartz, 2004). For instance, Robert Heath tried to buy a tin of tuna and nearly gave up:

> In my local Sainsbury's store the tinned tuna section is over 20 feet long: in it you have big tins, small tins, multi-pack tins, tuna steaks, tuna chunks, ordinary tuna, skipjack tuna, South Seas tuna, tuna in brine, tuna in sunflower oil, tuna in olive oil, tuna in tomato sauce, tuna in mayonnaise, tuna in mustard sauce, tuna in mustard mayonnaise, and more besides . . . all priced at very similar levels. (Heath, 2001: 32)

As Walter Dill Scott wrote in the first academic book about the psychology of advertising:

> In the first instance the purchaser may be seen induced to act only after much hesitation, but after a few repetitions the act becomes almost automatic and requires little or no deliberation . . . (This) gives great value to advertising by making the effect of the advertisement to be not merely transient but permanent. (Dill Scott, 1908/1998: 132).

In other words, FMCG advertising has two roles: not only to get a brand into a shopper's repertoire in the first place, but also to keep it there in the face of competition.

There is a difference between the textbook definition of FMCG and how the term is used. For instance, newspapers would count as FMCG products under the definition but newspaper marketing departments do not consider themselves FMCG marketers: they would say they do news, media or entertainment marketing. In practice, FMCG refers to packaged groceries. This is for historical reasons. Brand advertising began with packaged groceries and there is a continuous tradition stretching back further in time than many realise.

FMCG and the development of brand advertising

'Brand' is a Saxon word that probably entered the English language in the fifth century, after the Romans left Britain. It meant a burning piece of wood. From hot wood to heated metal is just a step. Scarring the skin with a shaped piece of hot metal was used to identify the owner of mobile property such as livestock or slaves. Branding began as a means of protecting the rich against theft, and it still is.

The very first nationally advertised brand was probably Warren's Shoe Blacking, a shoe polish. It was advertised from the 1820s throughout the nineteenth century.

Ad agencies had nothing to do with the content of Warren's ads. Although ad agencies have existed since 1611, they were still space salesmen in his day; what we would call media agencies rather than creative agencies. Ad agencies were so insignificant that a monumental history of advertising published in 1874, over 600 pages, did not mention a single one (Sampson, 1874/1974). The advertisement's content was the manufacturer's responsibility. Either he wrote the copy himself or he hired freelance creatives. Warren's ads featured a charming drawing of a cat spitting and bristling in challenge at its reflection in a highly polished black boot. It was by Cruikshank, the great cartoonist. There followed some humorous verses about the mirror-like shine of the boots which, Warren liked to hint, might have been written by Byron or Thackeray. One sign-off line was 'Ask for WARREN'S Blacking', but another was more assertive: 'ALL OTHERS ARE COUNTERFEITS'. These four words are significant. They show why Warren spent money on advertising, what specific problem he needed to solve. He needed to protect his brand.

Counterfeiting or passing off has a long history. Today fakes are associated with Chinese manufacturers but the problem dates back at least to the sixteenth century. In 1590, an English cloth maker took a rival to court. He charged:

> Whereas he had gained great reputation for his making of cloth by reason of which he had great utterance to his great benefit and profit, and that he used to set his mark to his cloth whereby it should be known to be his cloth; and another clothier, perceiving it, used the same mark to his ill-made cloth on purpose to deceive. (Upton, 1860)

So the story is this: our man was famous for the excellence of his cloth and put his (trade) mark on it. A villain copied the mark and put it on inferior cloth. It was theft, plain and simple, and happily our man won in court. Twelve years after the case, Shakespeare wrote in *Othello*: 'Who steals my purse steals trash . . . but he that filches from me my good name . . . makes me poor indeed.'

But going to law is uncertain and expensive. Advertising offered a solution. *The Art of Advertising Made Easy* is probably the first professional analysis of what advertising is for. It was published in 1825, at the same time as Warren's campaign. The author, an experienced copywriter, gave this advice to advertisers: 'The public must be cautioned against everything on earth but the identical article advertised', and urged them, to dwell mainly on Counterfeits – to caution – to entreat – to challenge – to bully – to rave against Counterfeits'.

Brand manufacturers face competition from two sources: from rival firms (horizontal) and also from retailers (vertical). Retailers make more profit selling a cheaper product at the price of an expensive one. An early example of retail copying comes from Rowland, a manufacturer of macassar oil, a sort of hair gel. His brand, Rowland's Macassar Oil, was hugely popular and retailers copied both product and packaging. Rowland ran an ad in 1843 that explained his business problem:

> Numerous Pernicious Compounds are now offered for sale such as 'Macassar' . . . by shopkeepers of apparent respectability, who copy the Bills and Labels of the Original Articles, and substitute either a fictitious name or the word 'GENUINE' in place of 'ROWLAND'S. (From an 1843 advertisement for Rowland's branded product)

Helpfully the ad goes on to explain how the real thing may be identified in store by close inspection of the packaging: 'To further insure the real Article, the words 'Rowland's Macassar Oil' are engraven on the back of the Label 1,500 times, containing 29,028 letters'. So we should shun the retail counterfeit with only 29,027 letters on the back of its label.

Advertisements for other FMCG brands continued this theme throughout the nineteenth century and beyond. Procter & Gamble's Ivory Soap in the USA was also plagued by copies. P&G made a mass mailing about Ivory Soap in April 1885, an early example of a direct mail campaign; it gave the now familiar warning against 'counterfeits', and urged 'patronesses' to demand the authentic Ivory when shopping for soap. Similarly, an 1893 press ad contained A WORD OF WARNING:

> There are many white soaps, each represented to be just as good as 'the Ivory'; they ARE NOT, but like all counterfeits, lack the peculiar and remarkable qualities of the genuine. Ask for 'Ivory Soap' and insist on getting it.

The essay on advertising in the *Encyclopaedia Britannica* of 1911 confirmed:

> The average man or woman who goes into a shop to buy soap is more or less affected by a vague sense of antagonism towards the seller. There is a rudimentary feeling that even the most ordinary transaction of purchase brings into contact two minds actuated by diametrically opposed interests. The purchaser . . . has some hazy suspicion that the shopkeeper will try to sell, not the article best worth the price, but the article which leaves him the largest margin of profit; and the purchaser imagines that he in some measure secures himself against a bad bargain when he exercises his authority by asking for some specific brand or make of the commodity he seeks. (Encyclopaedia Britannica, 1911)

In this view, advertising is effective when it protects and increases consumer demand for 'a specific brand or make'. That is what FMCG advertising is for. Rather surprisingly, the apparently obvious idea that advertising is for selling more products did not arise until some years later, with the growth of direct response (reason-why) advertisements. But direct response is seldom practical in FMCG, because the margins per unit are so small. FMCG is the home of brand campaigns.

The rise of brands

Today, manufacturers call retail copying the own label problem. In many FMCG product sectors, the chief rival to a manufacturer brand is own label. It is said that Gillette took three years and spent a billion dollars developing its Mach 3 razor but a retailer copy was on the market a month after it was launched. Grocery own labels increasingly resemble manufacturer brands and are heavily advertised, albeit with distribution restricted to a single chain of stores.

The underlying question is, who 'owns' the end consumer, the source of all cash flow? Is it the retailer, who takes the money? Or is it the manufacturer, who first creates the goods? Before manufacturers got into branding, the answer was simple: the retailer owned the consumer. One adman wrote in 1915, looking back to a time before brands dominated FMCG markets, 'The merchant was then the King of Commerce, with the manufacturer grovelling at his feet.' FMCG manufacturers today may think they grovel to the big retail chains, but their grovelling is as nothing, simply nothing, to the grovelling they had to do when they made commodities.

Brands overtook commodities by offering three main consumer benefits which are still relevant today, as we shall see:

1. *Guaranteed size and weight.* In 1826 'Honest John' Horniman first measured tea leaves into sealed paper packets, each with a guaranteed weight. Commodities were weighed out of bins or barrels, and a shopkeeper might rest his thumb on the scales. It was less easy to cheat with sealed packages. Cheating is still an issue with things bought in street markets such as fresh produce.

2. *Product quality.* In 1851, *The Lancet* asked a doctor to examine 30 commonly bought food groups. The results were shocking: of 100 samples of sweets, 59 contained lead and 78 had poisonous colourings. Legal protection for consumers began with the Food Adulteration Act of 1860, but people could already protect themselves to some extent by buying brands. For instance, Crosse & Blackwell changed its pickle recipe and started using non-poisonous colourings in 1855, before the law required. Sales slumped at first, people didn't like the look of brown-coloured pickles, but picked up again after an advertising campaign explained the benefits of the change. Consumers still trust brands to live up to higher quality standards than most own labels, particularly in categories where manufacturer expertise is considered important.

3. *Convenience.* Until 1872, sugar was sold in large, conical loaves which had to be chopped up – a rough, heavy job for a man. The chopped-up sugar would then be cut into smaller, useable pieces by the housewife, using a special tool called 'sugar nippers'. Sir Henry Tate, of Tate & Lyle and the Tate Gallery, made his fortune by patenting an invention for cutting up sugar loaves mechanically to make 'sugar cubes', a new and more convenient way of using the product. Some brands offered convenience in products that average housewives found difficult to make themselves: in 1861, even Mrs Beeton recommended making curries from bought curry powder. Other brands made it possible to eat exotic or out-of-season foods: tinned foods were first used to supply Napoleonic armies but were prone to explode; the tin opener was finally invented in 1858 and the explosion problem was solved in the 1860s. Convenience is still a major driver of new product development in FMCG.

However, these explanations, guaranteed quantity, quality, convenience and the lack of explosions in the kitchen, only explain why brands are useful. They do not explain how brands have an emotional life to people, what are called brand personalities. Consumers find it easy to talk about brands as though they were people. Stephen King has described how consumers say 'Mrs Ariel' is the sort of person 'to always have a baby sitter at the ready' so she can go out in the evening, while 'Mrs Fair Snow' would 'just sit by the fire and watch television' (King, 2007). Brands have come to embody attributes not inherent in the physical product that exist in people's perceptions. They are amazingly durable and form a strong defence against the appeal of own labels: people like themselves for liking certain brands. The question is how Victorian consumers benefited from the first imaginative acts of perceiving personalities in inanimate objects. What was in it for them?

The full answer is beyond the scope of this chapter but probably lies in the need for people to define their social relationships in the melting pots of the new mega cities of the industrialised age. For one thing, people used brands as indicators of social status. Brands were and are more expensive than commodities so buying them showed the buyer to be socially successful. It is still the case that FMCG brands are most often bought by the lower social groups, that is by the people least able to afford them, while the more socially confident middle classes are disproportionately heavy buyers of own labels.

The anthropologist Kate Fox studied contemporary English life as one might study mud-hut tribal societies and observed the same phenomenon:

Along with the lists of ingredients and calorie-counts, almost every item of English food comes with an invisible class label. (Warning: this product may contain traces of lower-middle-class substances. Warning: this product has *petit-bourgeois* associations and may not be suitable for upper-middle-class dinner parties.) Socially, you are what you eat . (Fox, 2004: 305)

Brands perform a function beyond that intended by manufacturers. Brands help people play a better game of social chess.

Advertising theory driven by FMCG

The need to protect demand for FMCG brands in the face of increasingly acute trade and retail competition fuelled the three major developments in advertising theory from the simple announcements of the early days: brand image advertising, then reason-why, and then Unique Selling Proposition (USP) advertising.

1. *Brand image advertising* first appeared in the closing decades of the nineteenth century and is a dominant school again today. For years, Ivory Soap used artistic images of beautiful, elegant, well-dressed women in its ads. As a result of the association of ideas, Walter Dill Scott wrote that he did not think of Ivory:

   > merely as a prosaic chunk of fat and alkali . . . I actually enjoy using it more than I would if the soap had not been thus advertised. The advertising of this soap not only induces me to buy it, but it influences my judgement of the soap after I have bought it. (Dill Scott, 1908/1998: 193–4)

   It is the association of ideas that creates the 'habit' of buying the brand.

2. *Reason-why advertising* appeared in the early years of the twentieth century. Messrs Tipper, Hollingworth, Hotchkiss and Parsons, the team that coined the term 'consumer demand' a few years earlier, published an advertising textbook in 1920 and almost exactly 100 years after *The Art of Advertising Made Easy*, the goal was the same:

   > Competitive conditions are such that it is often not enough for the advertiser to create a desire for his type of product. The response he needs is a deliberate choice of his particular product . . . The important part of the work of reason-why is to make the reader choose the advertised article. (The Art of Advertising Made Easy 1920: 142)

   Reason-why works better for immediate sales than brand image because it does not rely on repetition to create an association of ideas. However, there is a cost, often overlooked: it requires the manufacturer to pay for a continuous stream of new product benefits or promotions or price cuts, so that its advertising can always convey 'new news'. Promotions and price cuts have the advantage of being the easiest things to measure in marketing, which makes them attractive to brand managers of limited horizons. However, they have little or no effect on consumer preference for the brand and often reduce overall profitability (Ehrenberg and Hammond, 2001).

3. *USP advertising* is the synthesis of these two schools. It is designed for the contemporary situation in which lasting product advantages are rare or impossible. Rosser Reeves, the inventor of USP theory, described the problem he needed to solve: 'A client comes

into my office and throws two newly minted half-dollars onto my desk and says, "Mine is the one on the left. You prove it's better!"' (Mayer, 1958: 58). USP advertising involves creating a differentiated brand positioning: that is, making a benefit claim not made by other brands in the market, and associating it with the brand through repetition (Trout and Rivkin, 2000; Ries and Trout, 2001). The benefit might be emotional or rational but must always be unique. USP theory underlies current thinking about brands. Agencies and their clients search for a unique Big Idea to unify the brand's communications in the increasingly complex media world. For instance, the number of channels cited in IPA Effectiveness Award winners has more than doubled in the last 20 years, from 2 to 5. Examples of global Big Ideas from my own agency, Ogilvy & Mather, would include those for Dove (the campaign for real beauty), American Express (membership has its privileges) and IBM (e-business). These Big Ideas are organising principles which inform all communication channels so the brand is presented coherently at all consumer touch points.

Learning from experience

The best way to learn about FMCG advertising is by doing it, but next best is to learn what others have done. The IPA Effectiveness Awards, a case history competition, have been running since 1980. There are more than 1,200 cases in the IPA DataBANK, many if not most for FMCG campaigns. All are in the public domain and can be accessed online (www.warc.com) or in hard copy (see Green, 2005 and Binet and Field, 2007 for important summaries of the learning they contain). The following classic cases show how the consumer benefits of branding described above sell hard.

Case study 1: Protecting the brand against own label: Colgate

This case (Wood and Broadbent, 1999) shows how perceived product quality protected and grew the brand despite intense competition. Colgate has been selling toothpaste since 1877. It competes horizontally with major FMCG firms such as Unilever and Procter & Gamble, and vertically with supermarket own labels. In the mid-1990s, Colgate learned that Sainsbury's planned to launch a new oral care range.

J Sainsbury plc was the biggest grocery chain and had the best reputation for product quality. Sainbury's management exploited this by attacking leading manufacturer brands head on: JS Classic Cola took on Coca-Cola and increased JS's share of the cola sector from 20 to 65 per cent within JS stores, and JS Novon detergent took 12 percentage points of market share away from P&G/Lever, losing them £45 million of sales. As the best selling toothpaste, Colgate had the most to lose from the launch. Worse, if consumer demand for Colgate was seen to be 'soft', other retailers might follow suit and market their own oral care ranges more aggressively. It was a big problem.

The first step was to understand the consumer issues thoroughly. Extensive qualitative research, mainly group discussions among housewives, showed that Colgate's brand personality was that of a 'trusted family friend', but also that many didn't particularly care which brand of toothpaste they bought. They didn't believe it made much if any difference to the health of their children's teeth. Colgate's consumer franchise was therefore vulnerable to Sainsbury's launch.

However, even loyal Sainsbury's shoppers were less likely to buy JS own label in categories where manufacturer expertise was believed to be vital, such as medicines. Colgate and its ad agency Young & Rubicam decided on a strategy of repositioning Colgate as a brand with medical-like benefits. The marketing plan to achieve this involved a

'THROUGH THE YEARS' TV AD

Old woman: Well carrying on like that, just look!
(MVO) We've been making toothpaste for a long time. But we're still not bored, because we've never stopped improving it to help make your teeth healthier, your breath fresher . . .
Dancing man: Lucky man, she's a honey!

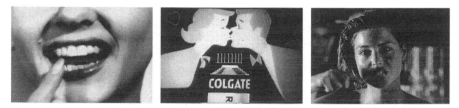

(MVO) . . . and your mouth go, well sort of ping. And over the last few years, we've really pulled out the stops, with dual fluoride with calcium, tartar control, bicarbonate of soda, strawberry cheesecake flavour . . .
Man: I like that Colgate flavour!
(MVO) Okay, not strawberry cheesecake flavour, but we do have a formula so advanced that is actually works between brushings.

TV announcer: Yes, everyone in the family loves Colgate.
(MVO) And we'll carry on improving because we reckon as long as we keep changing our toothpaste, it means you won't have to.

Song: Brush your teeth with Colgate, Colgate Dental Cream, it cleans your breath (what a toothpaste) while it cleans your teeth.

Figure 12.1   Colgate storyboard reproduced from the IPA case study 'Colgate: the science behind the smile', published in *Advertising Works* 10 (Kendall, 1999) and available at www.WARC.com. Courtesy of WARC.

coordinated suite of operations. First came a PR campaign which challenged mum's complacency about the fight against cavities. The articles in magazines and newspapers did not appear to be sponsored by Colgate, which clearly has a vested interest. They raised the general issue of the role of toothpaste in dental health.

Then came a major communications push involving a new TV commercial and a heavyweight poster campaign: the TV commercial described Colgate's history of innovations, such as inventing the first toothpaste to work between brushings, and the posters were based on dentist endorsements, such as the fact that more dentists use Colgate at home than any other brand. This brand campaign ran as well as Colgate's normal product ads. The advertising used USP strategy. No major toothpaste brand was claiming the benefit of dental health. Colgate did not improve its products for the campaign; the benefit became attached to the brand through repetition. Finally, just before Sainsbury's own label launch, a tactical price cut incentive (3 for 2) took many toothpaste buyers out of the market, so that the initial sales figures would disappoint Sainsbury's management and reduce future marketing support for the range.

The combined effect of these activities was extraordinary. Own label's share of the toothpaste market grew by a third after the JS launch (from 9 per cent to 12 per cent), but Colgate's share grew too, from the mid-20s to over 30 per cent: its highest-ever level. Sales of Colgate even grew in Sainsbury's stores too, exceeding £1 million a month for the first time. What happened was that the share loss caused by the inevitable growth of own label had been diverted to smaller brands. At the same time, Colgate's margins improved significantly, more than the same products sold in other countries. Higher volumes at higher margins meant bumper profits: what could have been a disaster became a triumph.

Case study 2: Meeting an unmet need: Batchelor's SuperNoodles

This case (Kent and Calcroft, 1999) shows how offering convenience created a dynamic and hugely profitable new market sector which the brand then owned, without any significant changes to the product or its packaging. Batchelor's is another brand founded in the Victorian era. In 1895, William Batchelor first saw a market opportunity for packaging foods in convenient cartons.

Batchelor's SuperNoodles was launched in 1979 as a mainstream, everyday, side-of-plate alternative to chips for children. At first it did not face much competition because other noodles were adult oriented, but its success inevitably attracted rivals. Own labels and me-too products competed on price. The result was reduced profitability and slower growth for SuperNoodles (sales grew at only half the market rate). Batchelor's and its agency Mother started looking for a big new market opportunity.

First came large-scale quantitative research (a Usage & Attitudes study, which measures both usage of the products, how often they are bought, how they are used, who uses them, etc., with brand imagery research questions). While confirming that SuperNoodles was mainly used by children at teatime, it also showed an unexpected and intriguing 'spike' in consumption among young adults. Detailed qualitative research among this segment showed what they were doing.

These people led lifestyles where time for 'filling up' was at a premium. The food had to be quick and substantial. Throwing together whatever happened to be in the kitchen was the norm: they were in 'troughing' mode. They would dig into doorstep sandwiches, munch bowls of cereal or rip chicken meat off a carcass, all while standing by the kitchen worktop. Sometimes they would even scoff a plate of SuperNoodles. Consumers called this 'foody nosh', while to Batchelor's marketing department it was the 'substantial snacking sector'.

POSTER ADS

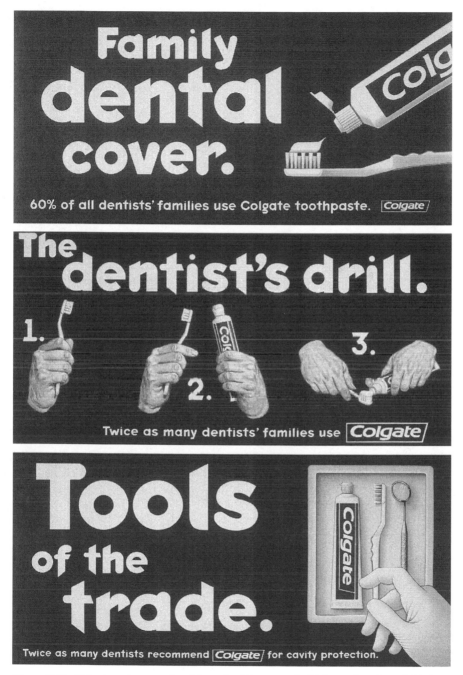

Figure 12.2   Colgate poster reproduced from the IPA case study 'Colgate: the science behind the smile', published in *Advertising Works* 10 (Kendall, 1999) and available at www.WARC.com. Courtesy of WARC.

'SELFISH'

Julie: So how are your sweet and sour
SuperNoodles then?
David: Mmm.

Julie: . . . just a taste.
David: Look, I hate it when you do this, I
offered to make you some.

David: Look, you can finish them off if you
like.

Julie: You really love me, don't you?

(VO) Batchelor's SuperNoodles, because
noodles can be super, can't they?

Figure 12.3   Batchelor's Supernoodles: leading from the front. Courtesy of WARC.

Showing great boldness, Batchelor's decided to reposition SuperNoodles away from its heartland as a nutritious children's meal accompaniment after school, towards a target of 25 years olds who wanted a meal at 11 o'clock at night after the pubs had closed. The product was a convenient alternative to homemade sandwiches or chicken meat torn off a carcass. But could an established kid's brand ever be cool?

A staggeringly successful TV campaign made it so. The creative strategy was to own 'foody nosh'. It was USP advertising because no brand had claimed this territory before. The ads were modern, distinctive and above all funny. SuperNoodles became an 'event' campaign, with up to 80 per cent of the target audience recognising stills from the ads in research, and it reached the top 5 per cent of the most enjoyed campaigns ever tracked.

The number of meals involving SuperNoodles almost doubled in a few months, rising by 95 per cent; interestingly, consumption rose among both young adults and children. Sales rocketed from 65,000 kilos/week before the campaign to 112,500 kilos/week during it, an increase of nearly 75 per cent. Every single pack of SuperNoodles on the shelves was sold. Supply to retailers was restricted. A new factory had to be built to meet the demand. SuperNoodles' market share, which had been falling, rose to an unprecedented 84 per cent, while own label share, which had been rising, fell from 17 per cent to 10 per cent.

Conclusion

Learning about FMCG is learning about branding. FMCG branding has a longer history than many may realise. Its purpose is and has always been to reduce theft. Branding identifies a product as coming from a certain supplier. It encourages end consumers, the source of all cash flow, to buy that particular make instead of buying a similar, often cheaper product. Advertising is central to FMCG marketing. As we are social creatures, it matters what other people think of us, and the brands we choose send social signals. Mass advertising makes sure other people understand the signals in the same way we do. In this sense, brands offer more benefits than manufacturers intend: we use them to play a better game of social chess.

Questions for students

1. Audiences are fragmenting. New media channels are emerging. How will FMCG manufacturers, who need mass sales, reach mass audiences in future?

2. If Tesco own label products are so good and sell so well, will Sainsbury's ever stock them?

3. The Chief Executive of United Biscuits once wrote, 'Buildings age and become dilapidated. Machines wear out. People die. But what live on are the brands.' Is that true? Are brands really immortal?

13 Advertising and new media

Joseph Bassary

Introduction

This chapter will chart the development of the Internet, detailing the range of communication possibilities the Internet offers to advertising such as email, e-commerce, search, banner adverts, viral marketing and user generated content. The chapter will combine detailed case study examples with a broader analysis of business and market trends to assess both the characteristics and impact of the Internet and interactive advertising. In terms of relevance, it is an exciting time for online advertising, with a growing proportion of ad spend being invested into digital campaigns. Marketers are increasingly devoting more of their time and budget into connecting with an audience which is on the go and wants access to information at its fingertips.

Since its inception, there has been much confusion as to what exactly the web is and its shifting terminology has seen it evolve from '*the web*', to '*the Internet*' and now '*digital*'. Originally the web was first conceptualised by the United States Department of Defence, Advanced Research Projects Agency (ARPA), intended as a military defence mechanism against possible nuclear attacks. It wasn't until 1969, and the first version of ARPANET, that this breakthrough marked the beginning of the Internet. The first public face of the Internet was launched in 1990, and this coincided with the development of personal computers that were available in this period. Over time it was adapted for other purposes. What has made the web we know today has been its effective use and growth in assisting commerce. The commercialisation of the web really began in 1995 with the emergence of e-commerce websites such as Amazon, eBay, MSN, Yahoo! and later Google. All this ahead of the infamous dot.com crash of 2000.

Prior to the crash, the early success of the web alerted companies to its business potential, and companies soon began investing in it. However, by 1999 there weren't enough people online and the slow experience of using the web inevitably caused the crash to occur, with not enough return on investment to support the unsustainable business models in place at the time. At this point there were 300 million users on the network; now there are 1.1 billion. In addition, due to advances in technology and changes in infrastructure (broadband), the Internet is a much more viable option for businesses today. Unlike the previous model, it now offers both speed and simplicity. Due to the significant amount of change to the infrastructure of the web, terms such as 1.0 and 2.0 have made it simpler for people to define periods within its evolution.

Figure 13.1 The Google homepage in 1998.

Web 1.0

The term Web 1.0 refers to the introduction of the interconnected network of content that was available to users. In this early period, the Internet was only a 'push' medium, meaning that websites published the content and users simply looked at it. The experience of using the Internet at this point was flat with no interaction or interconnection for users and content was largely disorganised. In many cases people accessed the web using 56k dial up connections and the experience of using the Internet was markedly slow. While there was some video content, it too took time to load and tended to be low-quality footage. However, it is important to recognise that everything available today has its roots in this early period but just in a very basic iteration. For example, Six Degrees was launched in 1996 as a very basic social networking site that allowed users to share their contact details and information with friends, but it didn't have any of the advanced features that Facebook offers, such as uploading and tagging photos of yourself.

Email

The first application of the Internet was email and similar to traditional direct marketing, email can be used as a personalised approach to contacting consumers with product offers or information. The advantage of using email is that it can distribute information to a wide range of specific, potential customers at a relatively low cost. However, email is becoming more obsolete with the rise of RSS feeds (a point discussed later in this chapter) but it is still a low cost communication tool. From a marketing perspective, this method of communication isn't the best for reaching target audiences, as users are becoming sceptical and bombarded with spam, the electronic equivalent of junk mail. When using advertising messages in email, the key to effectiveness is relevance. Email, when used correctly, can still deliver personalised, tailored messages. Currently, most email marketing doesn't understand the user's behaviour on the Internet. A good example of this would be to imagine shopping on Amazon and purchasing a present for a friend, only to receive consecutive follow-up emails that suggest similar products that we might be interested in buying for ourselves.

Online retail

Online retail or electronic commerce (e-commerce) describes the process of purchasing products or services over the Internet. The increase of e-commerce has caused a surge in the creation of more dynamic and intelligent web pages. Websites can store high degrees of information about an individual and the Internet offers a personalised approach that would be humanly impossible in relation to more traditional retail spaces.

Case study: Amazon and eBay

Amazon.co.uk is an example of how the consumer has control in the digital environment. As an Amazon customer you have a password to make you feel part of the network. You can also get recommended purchases based on your past orders and the chance to give reviews and share your views with other customers. This allows users to interact on the site and it personalises the experience for every customer. Amazon has also demonstrated the capacity to manage the facilitation of customer choice via the addition of reviews and recommendations, offering simultaneously a specific brand experience. The contribution Amazon customers make to the brand experience amounts to more than simply adding authenticity to the brand. These users have become, in effect, extensions of the Amazon marketing department. Their endorsement of a product can help change sales far more effectively than a promotional campaign, although for this endorsement to be legitimate it must be an authentic user review (Figure 13.2).

In addition, if we look at eBay, we can see how users have been empowered to manage the content of what is sold. From selling cars to vintage record collections, the users of eBay have effectively made everything available for sale. Unlike traditional auctioneers,

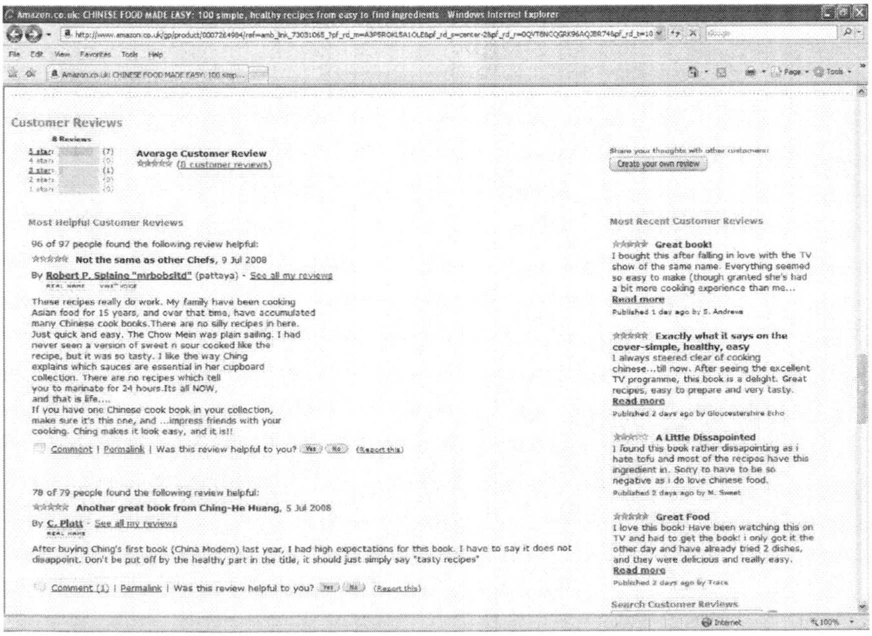

Figure 13.2   Amazon.co.uk customer reviews.

eBay are not the arbiters of what's desirable but as 'the people's marketplace' the contribution eBay's users make directly informs the success of the brand. eBay effectively acts as a facilitator for the transactions, leaving the rest to the consumer. Quite often, peer to peer recommendations online are more useful than brand advertising.

However, this is nothing new. Word of mouth and personal recommendation have always informed consumer choice. The Internet has allowed for participation by a global audience, whereby a single voice can be heard by millions. Since its introduction in 1995, the process of online retail hasn't fundamentally changed and it isn't likely to. And yet although the way we transactionally buy products online may remain the same, the experience that surrounds it will not. Through technological advances it is now possible to recreate the experiences we have in store. At the moment most people will probably claim that they choose online shopping due to cost and convenience, but over time we will see this change, with people choosing the online option for the experience as well as the ease.

Search

By searching the web, portals such as MSN and Yahoo!, perform an important function in organising and indexing information, helping select the most suitable products for the user's needs, with the minimum amount of effort. Search engines are usually the first port of call on the web. Due to the number of websites and vast amounts of information on the Internet, this service allows users to find the content they want easier and faster. Advertising is the main source of revenue for search engines as they sell advertising space at a premium to allow companies to have their listings ranked higher in the search results. Fundamentally, the model operates on the same basis as traditional print advertising but applied to the web with space sold to advertisers. Originally, search started as a transactional based platform used for driving online traffic, but later it also developed into a brand based platform as the Internet changed into a user focused platform. One of the most significant changes in recent years has been the move from cost per thousand click throughs to the current cost per click system, meaning that the ability for advertising online changed from purely large corporations to individuals with small businesses.

Given the amount of information on the Internet, using search is an important retrieval tool and the search terms used also help form a core source of customer insight and activity. In terms of revenue, search is dominant, making up 57.1 per cent of online ad spend and growing at 44 per cent year over year (http://www.marketingcharts.com/interactive/us-online-advertising-market-to-reach-50b-in-2011-3128/). Recent advances in web programming have allowed more interesting additions to traditional features. For example, a search box can now second-guess what you are searching for as you type, or you can view a large version of an image within the same window as an alternative to clicking on a new page.

Pop ups

Pop up advertising was originally used as a way of prompting an action from the user and was later used by advertisers to display messages that interrupt and divert the user away from what is being viewed on the web browser. The pop up occurs when a web page opens up a new web browser window to display the advertisement. This can be seen as quite intrusive and to a majority of users pop ups and even pop unders, which display ads behind your browser, can seem quite annoying. Most modern web browsers now come with pop-up blocking or ad filtering tools that can block out advertisements, so action has already been taken on the issue.

Banners

Web banners represent one of the oldest uses of advertising on the Internet and have been around since 1993. Banner adverts are embedded into web pages around editorial content similar to conventional press advertising. Their purpose is to drive online traffic to a website by linking to the website of the advertiser. Banners come in all different sizes, although the main sizes are leader boards, skyscrapers and mid-page units. Web banners are bought in packages, and these vary depending upon the total number of times the banner will be displayed and measured by the amount of times that people click through. When clicked on, a small amount of money goes to the website as a payback. This is made possible through the sale of the web space in which the ad appears, which is brokered through media agencies. Display advertising makes up 22 per cent of online ad spend and grew some 33 per cent in 2007 (based on the previous year)

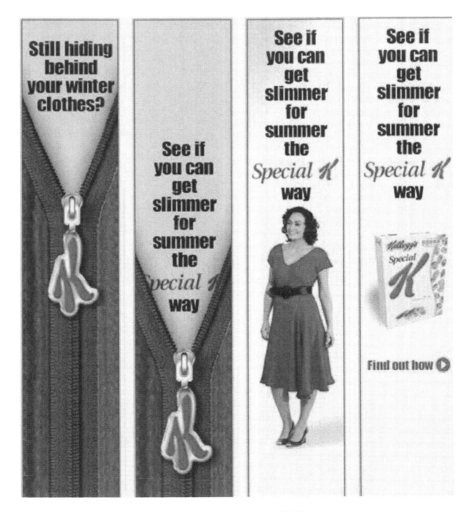

Figure 13.3   Kellogg's Special K 'Zip'. Agency: RMG Connect.

(http://www.marketingcharts.com/interactive/us-online-advertising-market-to-reach-50b-in-2011–3128/). Banners have gradually evolved into rich media executions. On sites such as the MSN homepage there have been mid-page unit rich media executions, which allow the use of interactive video and sound in the banner as well as an expandable display that takes over the homepage to grab the user's attention. In Figure 13.3, we can see how an interactive skyscraper banner was used to encourage user participation.

In this example, the client wanted to create a digital campaign to drive spring sales of Special K among new and existing customers. In the brief, the agency was told that seasonal triggers play a big part in Special K's strategy, for example, in spring and summer people want to wear lighter, more revealing clothes. The agency's solution was to create a rich media banner concept that dramatised how Special K can help women 'stop hiding behind their winter clothes'. In 'zip', the agency made the medium the message and enticed consumers to interact and unzip skyscrapers and leader boards. Based on Mindshare (a media agency) statistics, the campaign has performed well to date, with a click through rate of 22.28 per cent on MSN alone. The click through rates are collected by various media companies who measure the effectiveness of the money spent on media and the quality of the creative execution. When a user sees a banner, they usually know that it's trying to sell something, and ignore it. As a result, advertisers are now trying to engage customers in a conversation or interaction instead of this flat communication involving simply clicking 'on' something.

Between the dot.com crash of 2000 and the slow rise of the web, there have been many changes to the world. Some of these have been the growth of broadband, advances in technology and personal PCs, and most importantly the growth of a digital audience who have grown up alongside these changes. All of these have worked hand in hand expanding and assisting the growth of the Internet we know today. In recent times these changes and the impact they have had on the web and the audience using has come to classify the web, 'Web 2.0' – the evolution and re-birth of the web.

Web 2.0

Web 2.0 refers to the creation of a participatory web environment as opposed to its former use of only gathering information. The term was coined by Tim O' Reilly (founder of American media company O'Reilly Media) to describe the second coming of the Internet, and more importantly the emergence of the connected empowered web. In this web environment, users are encouraged to be active and contribute to the site, and websites such as eBay, Wikipedia and Facebook are benefiting from such user participation. This highlights a shift from the previous passive viewing of web pages into a new interactive environment that encourages collaboration among users, putting the user in control of their environment and letting them shape their own unique web experiences. A significant highlight is that this platform allows non-tech savvy users to contribute to the medium.

Contextualising the emergence of Web 2.0 in relation to the advertising industry, when compared with the use of traditional advertising media, online ad spend is still lagging behind more traditional advertising media such as TV, particularly in larger more traditional industries such as the fast moving consumer goods (FMCG) sector (Chapter 12). In the US, growth of above the line advertising revenue is expected to be slow through 2009 at around 3 per cent growth per year. However, online advertising spend in its various forms is expected to grow by around 17 per cent a year through to 2012. It is predicted that online advertising, when both search and display are combined, will experience double-digit growth every year through 2012 (http://www.screendigest.com/press/releases/press_releases_03_03_2008/view.html).

With other media channels such as TV providing mainstream exposure, some advertising agencies have struggled to communicate and translate the advertising benefits of digital to more traditional clients. However, times are starting to change, with brands gradually increasing their online advertising spend while publishers improve targeting, inventory and yield management. Currently the Internet accounts for 20 per cent of media consumption, but only 7.5 per cent of ad spend. By 2011, these numbers should increase to 25 per cent of consumption and 15 per cent of ad spend (http://www.marketingcharts. com/interactive/us-online-advertising-market-to-reach-50b-in-2011–3128/).

Viral

Viral is an illustration of how advertisers are currently using Web 2.0 to reach their audience. Viral advertising refers to a video clip or similar media that is propelled socially over networks to drive brand awareness and experience. When seeded, hosted onto different websites and platforms, through viral processes, messages have a high potential of being seen, shared and passed on to peers, thus creating a ripple effect. Users can embed viral clips into their personal blogs, social networking pages and websites or upload them to video stations such as YouTube, commenting and rating on what they see; 77.6 million viewers watched 3.2 billion videos on YouTube.com in 2007 (41.6 videos per viewer) (http://www.marketingcharts.com/interactive/us-online-advertising-market-to-reach-50b-in-2011–3128/).

Example: Dove 'Evolution'   Ogilvy & Mather, Toronto, used time-lapse photography to show the transformation of a normal woman into a glamorous billboard model using beauty stylists and Photoshop enhancements, as part of the Dove 'Real beauty campaign'. The clip was released under the slogan 'No wonder our perception of real beauty is distorted'. Dove Evolution took top honours in both the Cyber and Film categories at the Cannes Advertising Festival (2006). It was the first time in the festival's history that the same execution won in both categories, an even more impressive achievement considering that its success was almost single-handedly attained using online seeding. Only on very few occasions has the commercial been aired on television, but it is fast becoming one of the most watched videos on the Internet. In the two years since Dove began it's 'real beauty' campaign, this strategy has rewarded the company with double digit sales increases.

Blogging

A blog (web log) is a personal website usually maintained by a user and updated regularly, with commentary, descriptions of events, pictures, audio or video. Strong opinions are formed and cultivated quickly in the blog community with posts having an impact on search engines' page order. Blogs are extremely self-referential and some blogs even endorse brands or discuss services and products they might have used thus spreading a viral message, as discussed above. Every time bloggers write a post, they also invite user comments on blog postings, to allow other users to share their own views and join in. In addition, users can decide whether or not they want web banners to feature in their blogs and normally receive a small fee for hosting a banner.

RSS

RSS (Really simple syndication) feeds pull in information from different websites into one page so that users can aggregate news that is relevant to them. A typical news feed will contain a link to the site in which the news feed has been published, last published information (time, author, etc.), a title relating to the news item, a summary of the news item and a link directly pointing to the item in question. By composing a news feed on

Figure 13.4   A typical blog layout, with different post topics being displayed on the front page.

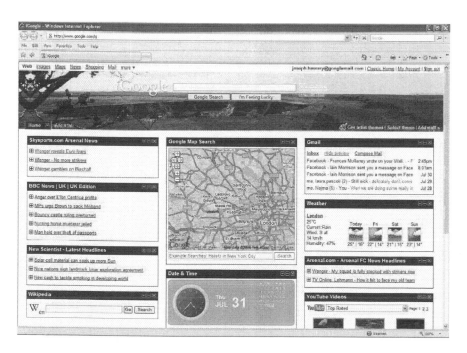

Figure 13.5   My Google homepage, www.google.com/ig.

a website, users can 'subscribe' to the feed and add it to their news 'aggregator', a piece of software that informs the user whenever a new item has been published. A typical example being the My Google Homepage found at: http://www.google.com/ig. This example shows a mixture of software agents, searching and finding content relevant to the user.

RSS feeds are becoming a core part of the new ways of communicating on the web. Email used to be the primary means by which content was received; however, RSS is the new form of email, bringing the Internet to us. Most importantly with RSS feeds, the users control the information that they receive, which means that advertisers cannot enter this stream unless they are allowed by the user.

User generated content

At an even more sophisticated level MySpace is the quintessential customer-driven brand. People communicate on MySpace by leaving private or public messages on their peers' pages. Users can customize their pages with music by their favourite artists, design their own background wallpapers and build a representation of their personality online for others to interact with. Users can also upload their own music, photos and video content to share with others as a form of self-promotion. This is known as user generated content, a form of media that is produced by the end user and made freely available. As a result of the increase in user-generated content, brands are trying to encourage more interaction with users by setting up their own product pages on sites such as these.

To individualise your page, you can add songs, clips and personal information. By adopting this user controlled platform, MySpace is breeding innovation among users.

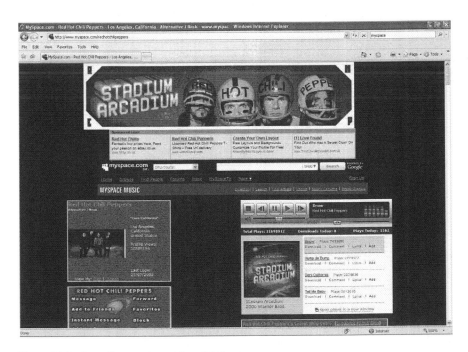

Figure 13.6   A profile page layout from MySpace.

From an advertising perspective, user generated content is all about getting people to talk about the brand in their own environment: the user becoming the media. People have replaced traditional advertising as a selling mechanism. That is to say, the industry is becoming more reliant on the user carrying messages. However, the challenge for advertisers is 'how do you do it?' In this context, advertising is used to actively engage the consumer into a branded experience with the product. From an advertising perspective, user-generated content provides a platform for users to interact with brands in an expressive manner, although any interaction relies heavily on the contribution and creativity of users. The capabilities of digital media offer a new sphere in which to construct an identity, hence the essence and arguably the success of networking sites such as MySpace, Bebo and Facebook. The significance of this for advertisers is that this represents an opportunity to build relations with a group of social content distributors and have direct connections with the audience. To have the ability to start a dialogue and conduct unique customer relations is invaluable in today's crowded marketplace.

Web 3.0

Web 3.0 is the organisation of the web via every user. Web 3.0 signifies how the Internet itself is learning a logical rationale of how to collect information and present it to us based on our habits. StumbleUpon, an Internet community that allows its users to discover and rate web pages, photos and videos, is a perfect example of Web 3.0 as people who use it simply rate what's good and bad and connect with each other by sharing their opinions.

Figure 13.7   StumbleUpon.

Web 3.0 is also a defining moment for digital media. Digital (as opposed to analogue) media refers to electronic media that works by the exchange of digital codes. This allows information to be created and distributed via other digital processing machines. The Internet is the best example of this, as content can be created from one machine, uploaded to a server and then accessed by different users, wherever and whenever they want. Multiple devices are becoming better connected to the web with mobiles, games consoles, interactive TV, PCs and outdoor becoming linked in real time dynamics. Via wireless capabilities, information can be accessed anytime and anywhere.

Previously it was possible to watch videos on our phones, but because of the cost involved and the experience of viewing content on small screens, it never fully took off. However, when the Apple i-phone was launched, the amount of people looking at video or surfing the web from handheld devices changed as contextually it's evolved into a more fulfilling experience. The increase in popularity of software applications such as games and media players has allowed users to download what they want, personalise their experiences and 'make the web their own'. For applications to be useful, their success is largely dependant on the interaction between consumers and the object. This presents a difficult challenge to advertisers, to be able to engage with users via the establishment of social networks that encourages users to participate and generate their own content. Instead of being told what to do, the user now chooses to personalize their experience how they want. This signals an important shift in the way that advertising is changing under the influence of the digital climate. Brands have realized that their greatest challenge is to be more useful to their customers than their competitors and are creating more value, engendering deeper loyalty and encouraging greater advocacy among their customers. RMG Connect's Head of Digital, Nima Yassini, states that: 'Brands have been stripped of their power and must listen to their consumers. Consumers can communicate their opinions easily and we must listen to what they have to say'.

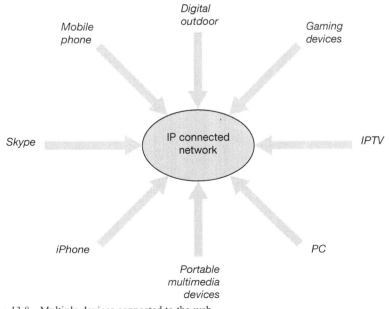

Figure 13.8   Multiple devices connected to the web.

Targeting the consumer

Through the insight that online interaction provides, users can now be targeted on a personal basis, through what is known as behavioural targeting. Through targeting the ideal consumer set, we are aiming towards one-on-one messaging and relevant content delivery. In an environment where data can be recorded and saved, it is now possible for advertising and media agencies to gain an understanding of their consumers and start to build profiles every time content is accessed. Through behavioural targeting, every time the user logs on, content or advertisements based on their previous transactions and interaction on the site will appear. Using a dynamic system like this allows a greater understanding of the consumer in the digital world and a chance for advertisers to build individual profiles and deliver relevant content to users.

Furthermore, messages in adverts are being tailor-made with the words and images becoming easily interchangeable. For example, if a banner ad is served with two different images with 200,000 impressions each, through analytics we can understand which is performing better and then run the more successful ad. We can also test the components inside the advertisement to create a winning formula. This is called multivariate testing, and it works by finding out how numerous different versions of content (or layout) perform in combination with one another in real time. The content that we can test includes headlines, body copy and any imagery. This level of testing is extremely cost efficient in online advertising because it is relatively easy to track and alter campaigns. This means that campaigns can be adapted in live time. This level of dynamic optimization and user customization should prove to have a greater return on investment for marketers. In principle, this system is allowing marketers to get closer to their customers through hard quantitative data (such as click throughs, time spent interacting, etc.), which is allowing greater insight about customers and products but also multivariate testing allows the customer to have a greater voice to shape their environment how they want.

Summary

The Internet is increasingly becoming part of our lives and as the technology speeds up the more people will want to use it. With the fragmentation of media channels and the reflexivity involved between them, audiences will be harder to target and reach on an 'en masse' basis. Brands will have to work harder to inspire loyalty among consumers and they will only become engaged if the consumer has the opportunity to interact with the brand. It's a subtle and complex task to reach the consumer with the right idea, and importantly, to make the idea appropriate for the medium through which it is being delivered. Used in the right way, branding through digital channels allows for new and exciting creative executions to engage, interact with and entertain consumers.

Digital advertising will be largely a product of its users and the influence of the consumer on the medium cannot be underestimated. Through user generated content, the consumer has virtual control of various different touch points – using it, shaping it, creating it and customizing it to suit a variety of purposes. Where the world wide web was once a singular entity, it now resembles much more of a collection of meta-webs; each linked but organized according to individual user preference. Functionally, Web 3.0 is basically user-centralization; where the user is allowed to mould the web to suit their preferences. The personalization of Web 3.0 has started to leave advertising trailing in its wake. Many brands, however, have realized that traditional advertising methods are, alone, no longer enough to deliver a sufficient impact on campaigns.

Conclusion

The Internet has changed into an involvement platform and while many past activities remain alive, the step up from Web 1.0 to Web 3.0, which centres primarily on developments in infrastructure (broadband), has resulted in much richer engagement between brands and users. The concept of 'user centralization' (listening to the consumer) is nothing new, but the way in which digital media is able to listen to the consumer is changing rapidly. With the fluid movement of information and file exchanges in live time from wireless devices now available, the possibilities for users are endless. Content will always be king but perhaps user engagement is becoming equally important in an online atmosphere. The importance of planning online and understanding usage habits, patterns and frequencies will play a significant role in understanding and creating platforms of engagement. Agencies will learn more about usage habits over time, and this will help ensure that we are making content that is relevant and where possible, localized to ensure that messaging is tailored or if possible, personalized. Digital requires active participation from the user as they decide what they see and it is they who customize that experience. Consequently, the way marketers need to re-think their brands and the broader communication strategies they use have largely been influenced by possibilities created by digital. The last five years has witnessed an explosion of brands on the Internet whose power and appeal is as much a result of their consumers' contribution as it is about the creativity of the advertising. Digital media is about enabling the idea of a user-based environment where anyone can create, share or purchase goods and services.

As we move towards a new system based on connectivity with multiple touch points, fulfilling seamless journeys across a variety of devices, brands must market themselves more fluidly, being seen as easily adaptable and accessible to consumers with busy lifestyles and not much time. It is now becoming normal practice for businesses to offer their customers a choice in either physical or digital consumption. We are becoming used to the idea of always being connected to the Internet, with the ability to 'switch off' when required. This range of digital communications can bring us into contact with more people than any other society that preceded us. The Internet's main advantage over traditional media is that it enables users to socialize and consume a diverse and varied knowledge base that can be personalized and tailored to suit the users' own needs. When online, we choose which brand experiences we want to pursue and therefore we have total control of our interaction in that space.

Seminar exercise for students

Your digital agency is considering pitching for the online account of a leading brand of bottled water, with the specific aim of targeting the student market. In small groups work as a project team which will feed back preliminary ideas as to how this campaign might shape up. Think about the different digital touch points discussed in this chapter, selecting which you feel would be the most appropriate in the development of your campaign. Be able to explain the rationale for both your creative ideas and digital media plan.

14 Political advertising

Darren Lilleker and Richard Scullion

Introduction

Advertising has long been an established feature of competitive electoral politics. Throughout the history of its strategic employment, political advertising has adapted to a range of media: print, radio and television (Scammell, 1999) and is now in the process of locating itself across various electronic media platforms from static websites to social media (Jackson and Lilleker, 2008). As with commercial advertising, the purpose of political advertising has increasingly become part of an attempt to build and maintain brand (party or candidate) awareness, gain attention and recall for messages and brand attributes (party or candidate values and personalities) and gain interest in the brand's products (policy and personality) (Fill, 2002). While few scholars of corporate communication unquestionably accept linear or processual models that lead advertisement's audiences from offering attention, gaining interest, desire and then acting upon that desire [AIDA]; perhaps in political communication such notions remain central to strategic thinking (Bartle and Griffiths, 2001). Election campaigns, when advertising is most frequently employed, build to a crescendo of activity culminating on the day when voting takes place; hence models such as AIDA are employed and expected to work by party strategists.

The latter comment may suggest a lack of sophistication in strategy underpinning political campaign strategy; the reverse is the case. Campaign strategy, and hence the design and placement of advertisements, is driven by an electoral cycle and the need to ensure that resources are targeted for maximum return on investment. While parties and candidates may desire office in order to positively affect the society they stand to represent, the unavoidable consequence is to campaign to win an election. Therefore, almost any advertising message that is considered to make a contribution to this hoped for victory will be considered – hence many over the years have been very controversial (for example, the Conservative Party's 1997 Demon Eyes advertisement won *Campaign*'s campaign poster of the year award but was accused of being too negative as well as likening then UK Labour party leader, Tony Blair, to Satan) (Figure 14.1). Elections are usually intensively competitive, require all possible resources to be invested and targeted to ensure minimum wastage. In practice this means that donations are solicited, depending on national regulations, and election communication is targeted at voter groups whose support is identified as being crucial for the party or candidate to meet their objectives (Savigny,

Figure 14.1   New Labour New Danger poster. Courtesy of the Conservative Party.

2005). Electoral objectives can be short of outright victory but may include gaining a greater share of representation of inclusion into a coalition government; whichever the case, the general rules and norms of political advertising apply.

Political advertising, as hinted at earlier, takes many formats. At the turn of the twentieth century, political advertisements would consist largely of posters that would be placed on streets and public buildings and replicated in newspapers and magazines. However, first radio and then television revolutionised design and reach moving political communication from the street to a mediated model. Television quickly established itself as the easiest media politicians could use for rapidly reaching a critical mass audience, with the benefit of offering emotionally powerful points of connection with the electorate. Television advertising is a key feature of most election campaigns and has also driven the increasingly 'design and style' led campaigns. The genres of news programming, documentary, the quiz show, chat show, comedy sketch, drama and horror, as well as commercial advertising, have all been borrowed from in the creation of political advertisements. While commercial advertisements also have strong links to popular culture and televisual content, political advertising tends more towards developing a narrative, particularly within nations where advertising is within free slots of several minutes. That said, political advertising is also more likely to attempt to have an emotional and psychological impact upon the viewer in order to shape perceptions of a party or candidate, as opposed to simply offering factual information to aid the electorate's decision making. Political advertisements often feature negative messages about an opponent rather than a positive message about the sponsor. A range of different styles is often used in a single campaign, but all are designed to build a meta-narrative that drives voting behaviour. The desired impact of any single advertisement within a campaign depends upon the purpose of the advertisement and so it is useful to develop a typology of political advertisements in order to understand the differing style and content and how this links to their strategic purpose.

Categorising political advertising: typology development

One way to 'make sense' of advertising is by treating each story being told – each discreet scene within each ad – as a separate entity and then applying a coding system to each of these units (Riffe *et al.*, 1998). In effect this generates a series of political advertising typologies. Previous work that has followed this method includes the research of Hodess *et al.* (2000), Kaid and Johnston (2001), Dermody and Scullion (2001; see also Price *et al.*, 2002) and Scullion and Demody (2005). Thus each political advertisement can be viewed in terms of a series of analytical categories including: main message, stance adopted, focal point on issue or image and source of the message. To offer the necessary depth for this case study, our primary focus is on the stance and tone adopted, since the notion of negative advertising has a scholarly history stretching back over 25 years and many commentators argue it is the key differentiator as a communication method (Ansolabehere *et al.*, 1999; Hartman, 2000; Kaid, 2004). Hence we present here a typology by which political advertisements can be classified: this helps us to understand the underlying strategy of the campaign.

Political advertising is frequently placed on a scale running from positive to negative. Positive classifications refer to 'self-praising and optimistic' messages. Negative classifications refer to 'overt criticism of opponent's personality and/or policy areas'. Midway between these polar opposites we find comparative classifications; these refer to messages that 'deliberately encourage viewers to compare the information in the advertisement against the position(s) of competing parties'. Indirect comparative advertising has been positioned as the weakest strain of negative political advertising, because inherent within it is a two-sided argument inviting the electorate to evaluate and choose. Generally, comparative ads are more cognitively rooted, thereby encouraging the electorate to judge alternatives and/or consider the implications of rejecting the argument presented to them. However, the tone of advocacy used within these arguments can increase the negative intensity of the message, thereby pushing direct comparison messages higher up the negativity spectrum. Attack advertising, that focuses on the personal image of political opponents, has been positioned as the most malicious strain of this genre of advertising because it is personal and emotive, rather than argument (cognitive) based. To complete the list of typologies, we have added what Benoit *et al.* (1997) call acclaiming

NEGATIVE   **POSITIVE**

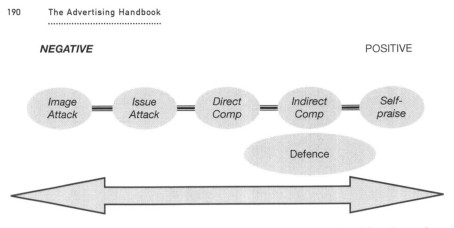

Figure 14.2   A continuum of stances adopted by political advertising. Adapted from Dermody
                and Scullion, 2003.

and defending ads. Here the focus is on the sponsoring candidate or party talking about
themselves. Figure 14.2 illustrates this categorisation in a simple continuum which, of
course, in reality is more complex because each ad is made up of many layers as outlined
earlier.

One of the more interesting dimensions to consider when looking at political ads using
this continuum is how both self-praise and attack ads tend to employ an emotive style of
message, tone, music and imagery; while comparative and defensive ads have a stronger
cognitive element. Advertisements that require an audience to consider an argument must
provide evidence; hence these ads will contain facts, reinforcements and endorsements
in order to give credibility to the case being made.

The use of 'negative and positive' political ad spots

A brief review of what academics, practitioners and commentators have said about the
use of negative, and positive, political advertising reveals four core themes. First, the
classification of political ads in this way is widespread and often used as a basis for
comparative studies. Second, claimed effects of negative ads fall into very contrasting
camps. The demobilization hypothesis suggests such ads engender cynicism in politics
as a whole and so depresses turnout at elections, while others point to high recall and
salience of ads that carry a negative tone and message. Third, a growing body of work
looks at how the media cover and report the political advertising activity of the candidates
and parties and how the 'spin' commentators place on their reportage can shape the
electorate's perceptions. Finally, from a more practical angle, there has been an interest
in the strategic merits of when to use negative and when to use positive political ads for
maximum impact. Advertising agencies and campaign managers tend to concentrate on
the apparent virtues of going negative. These are:

• gaining voter attention
• increases ad memorability
• cognitively and emotionally engaging

- simplify messages for the many low involvement voters
- increasing chances of pro-sponsor attitudes and voter intention
- aiding party loyalty

Empirical findings offer, perhaps not surprisingly, a more blurred picture than the standard good – bad scale. Research by advertising agency DMP DDB found that the electorate accepted and welcomed attack ads that highlighted 'new facts'. These 'legitimate attack ads' are countered by the rejection of ads that 'slag off' the opposition with no underpinning argument (Powell, 1998, 43). This later type of ad sustains the doubt, fear, anxiety, violation and viciousness discussed by Ansolabehere *et al.* (1994) and James and Hensel (1991). The electorate's desire for 'facts' finds support in a UK-based study exploring the attitudes of young voters towards the advertising in the 2001 British General Election: policy (issue) attacks were tolerated, while personality (image) attacks were not (Dermody and Scullion, 2001). What this plethora of previous work tells us, when considered collectively, is that the stance adopted in a political ad is likely to be noticed and commented on. Due to the high investment and widespread usage, political advertising is seen as a very important and effective tool within any election contest. Therefore academic and journalistic attention is paid to strategy and potential effects, attempting to draw inferences that can aid future campaign strategy.

Case study: the campaign within a campaign

American elections enjoy the highest spend, employ the most sophisticated and persuasive techniques and thus offer the most expansive and most extreme examples of political advertising use across the globe. The highly competitive, two-party system means all types of advertising are used, each with their own function within the campaign, in order to deliver victory for the sponsor. In the interests of being most up-to-date, so incorporating the harnessing of new and interactive technologies and tools, the case study chosen is the most recent example at the time of writing – the battle for the Democrat Party candidature in 2008. The contest very quickly developed into a two candidate race between Barack Obama and Hillary Clinton, directly fighting one another for the Democratic nomination. The fact that it had been a very close and hard fought race, one that has used every technique we would expect from the main Presidential contest despite the candidates representing the same party, makes this an ideal case study, and one that has undoubtedly informed the strategy of the Presidential campaign proper. Hence this campaign within a campaign, apart from its focus on a state-by-state basis in sync with the calendar of primary contests, is an appropriate lens through which to observe political advertising in practice.

As Figure 14.3 shows, Hillary Clinton's ad campaign was consistently her talking about herself, though about a sixth of the ads featured others endorsing her; these others being a mix of high profile politicians and 'celebrities'. These 'self-praise' ads, making up over 70 per cent of the total, were stylistically very similar to each other, indeed they were often constructed from a pool of clips showing her meeting voters with a slightly different voice over. The use of this type of ad meant her campaign often lacked drama and excitement, focusing on more mundane 'everyday' subjects so designed to give the impression that Clinton understood the electorate's concerns. The ads were mostly versions of the 'talking head' style, with the candidate talking directly at the camera, so attempting to build a pseudo-interpersonal relationship with her audience. In effect, the tone, style and genre is Clinton asking the viewer to believe what she was saying about herself; a style of ad that includes commercial ads where the owner of a car salesroom urges you

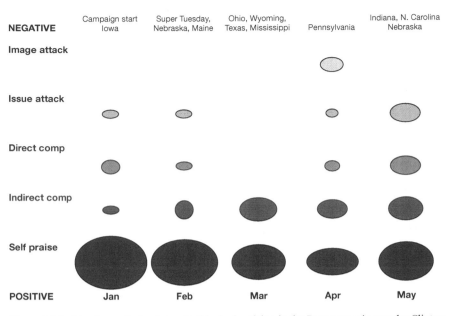

Figure 14.3   Typology of advertising. Political advertising in the Democrat primary: the Clinton campaign, January–May 2008.

to buy from his dealership but, in a political context, also draws on techniques used for crisis communication where trust in the speaker is a required objective. Content was limited in range with a clear dominant theme emerging that can be summarized as 'in difficult times you need somebody with experience who is prepared for the top job'. In about 20 per cent of her self-praise ads, there is an indirect, implicit comparison being made; early in the campaign she was comparing herself to President Bush and only later in the campaign did the focus switch to her Democratic opponent, Obama. Strategically, the Clinton ad campaign was trying to strike a balance between appearing 'presidential' and appearing like a potential candidate for President. Perhaps in hindsight, not focusing on her opponent earlier was a mistake?

A relatively small number of her ads attacked her opponent; they appear to be blips in each of the five months of data analysed, within an otherwise positive ad campaign (in terms of sheer numbers). Most of these attack ads focused on a small number of issues – health care being prominent – rather than on Obama's personality. These attack ads used a well established advertising communications method of presenting a problem (her opponents approach to tackling the issue of health care) and briefly ending the message with the solution (her alternative plan) or contrasting her record with Obama's lack of experience.

These attack ads almost universally feature a third-party endorsement of Clinton's position on the issue, usually in the form of a headline from a newspaper article that suggests support for her stance. Designed to satisfy the audience's desire for fact and evidence, this classic persuasive message technique tells the viewer: 'You don't have to take just my word for it'. Rather than believing that the candidate would say that and rejecting the message, Clinton borrows her credibility from other sources. This type of attack ad also allowed Clinton to argue she was *not* going negative but doing her duty by making the electorate aware of the flaws that others had already noted in her opponent. As the campaign drew to a close, Clinton introduced personal attack ads that began to question the integrity of Obama. Stylistically, these ads stand out because they use more powerful imagery and mood cues such as music, attempting to generate a sense of menace or threat. These gained much publicity within the US media and across a range of websites and weblogs; a common theme asked whether these more personal attacks would resonate with the audience. This highlights a new set of considerations that face the twentieth-first century political strategist; ads can now be the raw material for others to manipulate to their own ends and thus could introduce new dangers as well as potential when considering how to develop a negative message.

Political advertising in the Democrat primary: the Obama campaign

At least superficially, as Figure 14.4 shows, the Obama advertising campaign looks very similar to Clinton's. The majority of ads used were self-praise with an increased use of attack ads in the latter stages. In addition, these self-praise ads were almost entirely fronted by Obama himself and, as with Clinton's campaign, many of the attack ads use the same persuasive method; highlighting a problem (Clinton), ending by offering a solution (Obama). However, there are a number of important differences between the two candidates' use of advertising. Obama rarely used third-party endorsement spokespeople in his ads – this is perhaps surprising given the importance the news attached to him being supported by people such as Oprah Winfrey. Although it is Obama giving self-praise, the technique used relies far less on him talking to camera, instead the strategy was to show

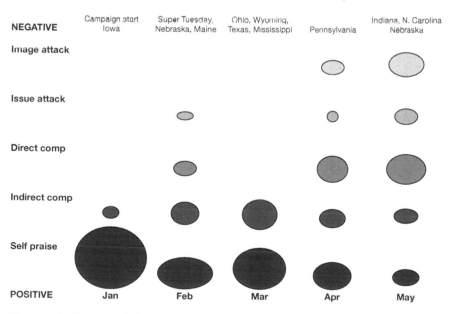

Figure 14.4 Typology of advertising: the Obama campaign, January–May 2008.

clips of him speaking at rallies, this technique being his way of building an emotional connection while also positioning himself as close to the people conversing directly with the masses. Not only might this have increased the integration of his message across all his communication, it also played on his acknowledged strength of oratory. Other media, notably his website and posts on *You Tube*, do, however, play up his celebrity and other third-party endorsements; in particular his website offered a series of videos posted by ordinary people endorsing his candidature. This strengthens his unique selling point as the 'people's' candidate.

However, a more substantive difference is that Obama introduced an indirect comparison background tone to most of his ads and aired more direct comparison ads than Clinton. In keeping with his projected brand attributes, a large proportion of his advertising consistently portrayed him in contrast to 'the political elite'. He was positioned as an 'outsider', being funded by 'the people' and so the only candidate representing only the American electorate and not corporate interests. In contrast, the establishment, and this included Clinton, is portrayed as the cause of political disconnection between those who govern and those who are governed. This persuasive method, that might be characterized as creating the perception of 'them' and 'us', has often been used by the candidate/party adopting a challenger strategy. In this case, what is most interesting is that when Obama became the favourite to win, and so no longer the challenger, this message strategy did not change. A final significant difference between the two ad campaigns is that almost all of Obama's attack ads are positioned as a defensive response to something that Clinton or her campaign team have said or done. The most obvious example of this strategy can be seen when he aired an ad (Ringing) that was visually a copy of an earlier Clinton ad (Children) with a different script and voice over. Both videos offer a narrative that asks the audience to consider, if the phone is ringing at 3 am in the White House, and an emergency is taking place in the world, who they would want to answer that phone; the conclusion of both is the candidate appearing presidential.

The strategy of refutation was designed to give the appearance that Obama was not using negative ads, but was being forced to refute Clinton's dirty tricks campaign.

Issues arising from the analysis of the ad campaigns

How closely did the ad campaigns adhere to the models of how advertising works, such as AIDA referred to earlier? Our overview suggests only to a limited degree. The self-praise ads, essentially trying to generate awareness and interest, continued throughout, but, of course, the nature of the contest meant the candidates were moving into new geographic areas all the time. It may be that the nature of the primary elections, fragmented as they are, convinced the candidates to focus much of their effort in these early stages on a persuasive process, and so we see little attention in the ads focusing on the raising desire or hardening convictions stages, while the call to action appears only briefly as a visual cue in the ads (i.e. a message reading 'Vote for Obama in next week's primary in Texas'). Again, it is obvious that both campaigns mostly used forms of media other than TV advertising in an effort to get their supporters to act (actually go and vote). In this way the political advertising was employed in a similar manner to much commercial advertising, with its focus on trying to establish an impression about what the offering is rather than directly urging you to buy it. The similarities of the ads used by each candidate may in part reflect an attempt to keep production costs low, and hence production and aesthetic values were low too! But is more likely to be based on an assumption being made that most of the viewers held moderate or low cognitive involvement in the campaign and therefore, as per communication theory, repetition and reminders were considered necessary for a message to gain recall. An unintended consequence of this is that the ads seem rather dull in comparison with the many commercial brand ads that constitute the normal viewer's advertising break.

The unique context of political advertising

The case study in this chapter has been written for a handbook of advertising where the overriding context is commercial brands operating in a liberal market. It is worth us concluding by at least briefly pointing to some of the contextual aspects that shape this form of advertising.

Political advertising is considered to be a key unmediated way for politicians to reach the electorate and is thus afforded a crucial role in legitimizing plural democratic societies. However, there are a number of caveats to this claim that are made apparent when analysing the Clinton–Obama contest to become the democratic candidate in the Presidential election of 2008. Considerable indirect mediation takes place in two ways. Many of both Clinton and Obama's ads made reference to news coverage of either themselves or their opponent and, in addition, the ad campaigns generated a lot of commentary in the media with regular comments about the advertising being aired. This offers an amplification effect to the paid-for advertising and so may serve to better connect politicians to the electorate. However, this amplification is delivered at a price. Despite the US media itself reporting that the self-praising ads of both Clinton and Obama have had the most paid-for airtime across key states and when run nationally; conversely free air time on news programming was awarded to the two identical attack ads run by both candidates featuring a telephone ringing in the White House at 3 am asking the audience what kind of President they wanted to answer that phone. And despite both campaign teams being keen not to be seen as running a negative ad campaign and our own analysis which shows that over 70 per cent of Clinton's and nearly 70 per cent of Obama's ads were positive (see figures 14.3 and 14.4), the media coverage of the advertising campaigns gave massively disproportionate focus to the attack ads aired – perhaps because these types of ads fulfil the media's own agenda better and perhaps also they offer more dramatic and interesting copy than self-praise ads and so they gain greater amplification.

Political advertising in this campaign, and more generally, makes little attempt to encourage direct engagement and political participation *per se* – focusing instead on offering a simple 'autobiographical' opportunity for each candidate to make people aware of who they are. Very limited areas of policy are covered in the ads, with the candidates staying in the same terrain; in this case policy was restricted to security, health and the macro economy. Linked to this idea of a restricted agenda, it is very apparent that both candidates made efforts to develop and then stick to a central theme, in commercial terms a brand positioning. For Clinton this can be summarized as 'My experience means I have a plan ready to implement'. For Obama it was 'They have had their chance, now it's time for us to change the way politics is done'. From an advertising perspective the emergence of a single proposition from a communication campaign is considered positively – perhaps in the world of politics multi-faceted messages fit the reality better? Of course, in this chapter we have limited our attention to paid-for TV advertising, while recognizing that both Clinton and Obama used many other forms of communication with a special mention of their web presence being pertinent here. Both candidates own websites and their use of YouTube extended the life of many of their TV ads, perhaps most significantly the original intention of the ads were often subject to reinterpretation in their online form, a case of the campaign teams losing control of the message but gaining greater interest.

Conclusion

Political advertising is perhaps a unique sub-field of advertising. It is only within a political context one finds overtly negative messages communicated about a rival; hence we find typologies useful in order to detect the overall strategic aims of the campaign. However, while useful, typologies can also be constraints upon our understanding. While many advertisements neatly adhere to one classification, ad creatives are increasingly mixing messages in order to present the audience with a number of reference points regarding both the sponsor and their opponent. Hence, it is perhaps more useful, as we found, to refer to some advertisements as crossing boundaries and having multiple objectives.

However, due to the nature of a political campaign, there is less consistency in message content as the campaign reaches a conclusion. This was found to be more fragmented in this case due to the nature of the primary calendar; however, it would be expected to see more negativity towards the end of the campaign running alongside the self-praising messages. Factual information is provided, but often in a simplistic way and using endorsements from the media, political experts, celebrities, family members or ordinary people to increase the credibility of the candidate's argument. Thus, while it is most common to find personal messages being delivered using emotive devices, often comparative ads that contain facts will also work at an emotional level: thus there are messages requiring cognition as well as some acting as emotionally charged peripheral cues. Overall, however, a campaign will begin by introducing the candidate through self-praise videos, positioning them and advertising their brand attributes, prior to considering comparisons or making attacks on the opposition; the strategic choices will also be made in line with shifts in public opinion and analyses of the strengths and weaknesses of the candidates and what opportunities are open to them and what threats exist from pursuing one or another strategy.

Both Obama and Clinton followed this strategy. The attacks came as the contest became a close, two-candidate run off with little to separate them. With the unique propositions of both having resonance among the audience, and comparisons giving little advantage, the audience began to be increasingly asked whether they should trust either candidate. Before Obama's victory was announced it was impossible to speculate confidently as to who would win and what role, if any, advertising had in that victory. The one effect we could detect, given the similarity in strategy and timing, is that advertising perhaps maintained the close proximity in support for both contenders. However, the problem is that, in itself, advertising does seek to engage with voters, just to deliver simple messages. Engagement is achieved more through using a range of Internet tools that borrow from advertising but are more related to direct marketing and public relations. This was a key feature of the Obama campaign to raise money. Thus perhaps while advertising remains a crucial feature during any campaign, its importance, and the spend involved may be reduced should any single route of communication become more important. As the use of Internet tools increases, could this be at the detriment of traditional advertising remains a question for students and practitioners of political communication.

Obama's historic victory election to become the 44th President of the United States cannot be attributed to his advertising campaign anymore than his victory over Hilary Clinton to become the Democratic Party nominee. However, these ads allowed him to introduce himself to a wider public and so become a relatively familiar brand – few unfamiliar brands succeed especially in the short term. The content of his advertisements collectively helped create a persona for the Obama brand, a set of peripheral cues to aid those not that interested in the election to understand what he stood for. This had at least two positive long-term effects. First, it meant that he did not have to spend a lot of time and resources introducing himself nationally when the race for the White House began; and second, the brand personality the ads created for him suited the environment he was operating in. Obama portrayed himself as the careful and considered candidate, an ideal image for a Presidential candidate running for election in the midst of a major economic crisis. It was also apparent that his campaign switched from being negative/comparative when challenging Clinton to being positive/comparative to meet the challenge of his Republican rival John McCain, a subtle but important change of strategy. This is important because the audience was looking for somebody with the qualities and values to be President: statesmanlike and above petty squabbles. Equally, Obama enforced his outsider credentials and compared himself not to specific opponents (Clinton or McCain) but to a system that had earned public dissatisfaction; while this could be seen as placing him as a diametric opposite to McCain, the insider, it meant he did not have to make personal attacks but led on criticisms of a system that the audience would already be likely to possess. Furthermore, Obama outspent McCain $207,410,911 to $119,906,703; while also forcing McCain into a more attacking strategy that may have made him appear desperate and petty. Perhaps more importantly though, was the continued multi-platform approach that made Obama ubiquitous across social networking sites. This gave his advertising a far wider reach than the televised slots alone and also afforded him the advantage of expanding the range of messages communicated. Obama not only placed his televised advertisements onto YouTube and other social networks, but produced mobilisation appeals, intimate behind the scenes insights, and quick video responses to news stories. This strategy encouraged a wider support network to promote him, such as videos produced by Will-I-am and Obama Girl, or attack McCain, Paris Hilton's message to 'old white guy' for example; this, along with his use of endorsements by ordinary Americans, gave the campaign a sense of joint ownership based on the co-production of campaign materials between him, his team and his movement. The advertising strategy was a function of wider campaign values and objectives that promoted notions of social inclusion and being 'of the people'; while in part it mirrored traditions of political advertising, it quickly also offered new departures utilizing new technologies and platforms and perhaps gives an insight into the political campaign of the future and the role of advertising within political communication.

Questions for students

1. What factors make a political campaign distinct to the marketing campaigns of commercial organizations?

2. What ethical issues are raised by the widespread use of negative advertising by electoral candidates?

3. Which of the two candidates, Obama or Clinton, do you think had the most strategic advertising campaign? Justify your answer with specific examples from the case study.

4. When Hillary Clinton's advertising team decided to employ advertisements attacking her opponent's personal integrity and judgment, which particular part of the AIDA model which explains how ads are processed do you think they were trying to generate and why?

5. To what extent, in your informed opinion, does political advertising have a future; and what do you see as its key function?

15 Using a history of Ivory to explore changing advertising design

Jacqueline Botterill

Introduction

A consumer-created advertising revolution, supported by image literate pro-sumers, personal computers, homespun creativity, and a YouTube distribution channel, is creating a buzz in contemporary advertising circles (Yohn, 2006; Klaassen, 2007; Walker, 2006). Running shoe brand, Converse, created a popular website housing video clips created by brand devotees documenting, in creative and heartfelt ways, their relationships to their 'Chucks'. Doritos, a taco chipmaker, aired the winner of their consumer-created promotional contest during the expensive 2007 Super Bowl time slot. Global brands, General Motors, and Master Card, use consumers' grass roots creative content. McCraken (2006) argues that these 'co-creations' are part of a branding reformation. Advertising agency creatives, once the cardinals of promotion, he argues, now must share power with a generation of consumers who have the technology and interest to play a role in the brands that surround them.

In 1892, before the 'pro-sumer' and 'consumer-created advertisements'; before Apple computers and Photoshop; before YouTube, or any Tube for that matter, Ivory soap invited consumers to compose promotional verses. Proctor and Gamble (P&G), the parent company, received over 27,388 contributions. Ivory published a long-running campaign of the winning verses. Ivory's brand history suggests today's consumer-led advertising, and other contemporary brand techniques, are not particularly new. However, the quest for novelty surrounding the advertising industry, according to historians, often stems from creatives who, rewarded for projecting cutting edge designs, are quick to pronounce their techniques as 'new', 'genre', or 'ground breaking' (Nixon, 2003).

So, too, because audiences are critical and clients need reassurance, have advertisers been keen to professionalize their practices (Lears, 1995). Particularly in America, home of more top brands than anywhere else in the world, advertisers referenced experts, science, and research, to position themselves as more than barrow boys. But, while their brand philosophies frequently contain important insight, market communication is shaped as much by intuition, craft knowledge, and trial and error as a rational plan. In the clubby world of advertising, where agencies are prone to following the leader to avoid risk, brand philosophies can become self-fulfilling prophecies. Furthermore, messages sent are not necessarily messages received. Audiences understand messages in light of prevailing interpretive schemata, values, uses, interests, and other commodities on offer. People cut their own paths through the barrage of messages that make up a brand. In this sense, it is correct to suggest that popular brands belong as much to the audience's interpretive authorship, as creatives' copyright (Davis, 2000).

Whether understood as attracting 'butterfly consumers' (O'Dell and Pajunen, 2000), imprinting 'love marks' (Roberts, 2004), forging 'interfaces' (Lury, 2004), providing fabric for common culture (Arvidsson, 2006), destroying public space (Klein, 2002), or creating iconic myths (Holt, 2004), brands mediate the relationship between producers and consumers. Brands unfold in a complex set of negotiations between clients' interests, changing media technologies and conventions, historically shifting cultural sentiments, altering audience illiteracies. This chapter sketches some of the design techniques advertisers have used over the nineteenth, twentieth, and twenty-first centuries to negotiate the making of the Ivory soap brand.

Ivory soap: using consumer insight

One of Ivory's core attributes originated from a consumer/producer negotiation. P&G developed a pure white soap to compete with the dominant yellow soap market. Ivory was named after Psalms 45:8: 'All thy garments smell of myrrh, and aloes, and cassia, out of the Ivory palaces, whereby they have made thee glad'. In 1879, shortly after its initial distribution, customers wrote to P&G requesting more floating soap. Unaware, Ivory investigated and found that a batch stirred too long contained extra air and thus floated. Acting on the popularity and novelty of this consumer-introduced feature, P&G made all Ivory soap float (Swasy, 1993). Ivory went on to corner the soap market until the 1960s.

P&G further encouraged consumer interaction. A mail order business, designed to ensure Ivory's national distribution, became an exploited promotional and consumer research tool and young children were encouraged to collect and mail in soap wrappings in exchange for colouring books and writing pads. Advertisers invited adult consumers to interact with the brand through a variety of contests and coupons. P&G parlayed its Ivory branding knowledge into a profitable corporate empire of over 80 brands, including Pantene shampoo, Gillette razor blades, Pringles chips, Tide laundry soap, and Tampax.

Looking at the 1,260 Ivory soap advertisements, which circulated in the press between 1883 and 1998, housed on the Ivory project website along with more contemporary campaigns (http://americanhistory.si.edu/archives/Ivory/index.asp), it is possible to note several changes in advertising design typical of promotion more generally. These changes include a shift from a product to a consumer focus and a mass market to a more refined consumer focus. Once associated with a progressive belief in the power of Ivory to civilize, by the twenty-first century Ivory concentrated on the everyday brand values of purity, family hygiene, and female beauty. New media technologies changed designs. Advertisers' initial formal literary devices became more informal, vernacular, and imagistic.

Nineteenth-century advertising: what is it, what does it do, why buy?

Ivory brand pioneers linked the trademark name to messages by including a representation of the bar of soap, with Ivory chiselled on its surface, on the bottom of advertisements, or in the image. Nineteenth-century designers showed Ivory as it would appear in shops, to allow consumers to find and ask for it. Advertising gave P&G a tool to control retailers. Early ads warn people about retailers trying to sell them soap 'like Ivory'. Ads like

'Catchpenny Soaps' explain how 'counterfeits lack the peculiar and remarkable qualities of the genuine', as noted in the chapter on FMCGs. An 1898 ad depicts a maid holding an Ivory wrapper telling consumers to purchase only authentic Ivory. Whether retailers behaved as Ivory claimed is debatable. What is clear is that these techniques sought to present Ivory as an honest, genuine, quality soap, and competitors and retailers as greedy, cheaters peddling inferior products.

To make messages intelligible and engaging, designers mixed visual art, theatrical, and literary conventions. Frames, white space, lined rectangles, and art deco vines focused attention and isolated messages. A picture book format, image stacked above text, was endlessly employed. Images, typically covering two-thirds of the page, began as thinly drawn black and white sketches, gradually becoming more lifelike over time. Coloured images appear, although sporadically, in 1887. Compared to the text-heavy press content that surrounded them, promotional messages stood out. Advertisers wrote full, elaborate, carefully punctuated prose, using poetic devices such as rhetorical questions, rhyming couplets, and elision. Some ads invited readers to sing along to songs that encouraged them to wash their faces with Ivory (1887). Text was typically presented in two columns or a single block. Designers adhered to a standard 12-point serif font, due to type-setting limitations, although the first letter of the first word was frequently enlarged and embellished. This practice, typical of religious or storybooks, drew attention to the text. Unlike contemporary advertising, where copy tends to serve to anchor the meaning of images, images illustrated written meanings. Advertisers used text and image to create Ivory short stories imparting lessons about what the soap was, what it did and why one should buy it. Advertisers seemed to view consumers as sensible individuals looking for honest reasons to buy.

Concerned that audiences might not believe them, advertisers employed techniques which allowed others to proclaim the brand's benefits. Medical and scientific testimony was particularly popular. An early Ivory ad explains why audiences should believe in science:

> Advertising can never, perhaps, be as single-hearted as science, which has nothing to sell. But we have always believed that there need be no clash between the scientific attitude and the advertising of an honest product ... and in that belief the Ivory advertisements have been designed.

Medical and scientific spokespeople helped to make Ivory messages appear credible, because they appealed to a higher order: fact rather than simply promotion.

Build credibility

Ivory distinguished itself in the market on a claim of purity and science was used to validate that claim. Purity mined a deep cultural nerve. Douglas (2002) demonstrated how notions of dirt, pollution, and contamination are deep taboos in many cultures. Many religious texts link purity to the divine. In romantic art and literature, purity represents the innocence unscathed by industrialization. Since epidemiology and the Broad Street pump, impurity has been associated with disease and death. In a culture endlessly irritated about contamination, dirt, and corruption, Ivory purity had much attraction, but it had to be proven. P&G hired a chemist who documented a 0.56 per cent impurity level and Ivory ran campaigns claiming scientists confirmed Ivory was 99.44 per cent pure. Ivory was pure, said the ads, because it was made with vegetable oil instead of animal fat. Advertisers asked readers if they were aware they were washing their dishes with soap made from the fat of diseased cows. Other ads suggest 'Infections lurk in many cheap soaps' (1890). In 1891, attacking the popular foreign Castile soaps made of olive oil, advertisers suggest yellow soaps go rancid and harm innocent babies' skins. Designers also used science to confirm Ivory's superior cleaning capacity, for example an 1892 ad depicted a female chemistry graduate attesting that Ivory outperformed eight other soaps tested in her class. Ivory cleaned hospitals and asylums full of germs and the nurses testified to the superior germ killing ability of the soap.

Another technique used to create credibility was to place characters in dialogue. Using playwriting conventions and personal names for intimacy, advertisers shaped a fly-on-the-wall perspective that placed audiences in the centre of gossip rituals. This cloak of eavesdropping made the message appear happenstance, instead of contrived. Designers also aped honesty by acknowledging that people do not believe advertising. An 1896 ad confessed that few bought Ivory solely because it is suggested in an advertisement. The copy encourages readers to ask a friend about the soap instead of believing the ad. Another 1900 ad noted: 'Don't you try to believe in the ad just try the soap . . . It will tell the story'. These are a few of the ways early brand designers sought to construct a sense of sincerity.

Initially positioned as an all-purpose soap, early advertisements document Ivory's many uses. Ivory cleaned dishes, fabrics, floors, woodwork, horses' sore backs, harnesses, and buggies. It lubricated bike chains (1895) and killed insects on plants. But Ivory was unique, said the ads, because it was 'pure', thus gentle to fabrics and skin. It cleaned precious objects such as artwork, needlepoint canvasses, fine lace, and babies. Ads told consumers why they should pay the substantial cost of $1 per cake for Ivory in 1886: 'A cake of Ivory Soap will do more work than a cake of the ordinary, poorly made, highly chemical soaps, and it will save five times the difference in price'. Another ad notes a hotel purchased fewer sheets and table linens since using Ivory. An 1891 ad encourages the poor to purchase the 'true soap' because 'Cheap soaps are notoriously expensive' because they 'have no value'. Advertisers told married women that their husbands want allowances spent on high-quality Ivory and an 1896 ad depicts a wife justifying the extra household expense of Ivory as well worth it.

Elite lifestyles are referenced, not because of a targeting strategy, but rather because early managers and advertisers had difficulty seeing beyond their own privilege. Using drawing room drama techniques, advertisers spoke through small circles of genteel characters; lone characters rarely appeared. The eye was invited to wander through ornately decorated rooms with luxurious draperies, fine wood furniture, and chandeliers. Characters sit swaddled in layers of clothing, a not so subtle reminder of the need to wash fabric. An 1892 ad depicts the lady of the manor explaining she let the last laundress go because she did not use Ivory and thus ruined the linen. Social judgement of home, staff, and family looms large.

Modern values: efficiency, economy, populism

In the 1920s, efficiency, convenience, and the rights of everyday citizens to the goods of the good life became dominant themes in the advertisements. Fredrick Taylor's application of scientific management techniques to labour processes broke production into carefully planned tasks carried out by individual workers overseen by management. Using scientific management techniques, an automated assembly line, and increased pay, Henry Ford produced more cars more cheaply than any manufacturer in the world. Scientific management became the darling of US corporations which used it to produce a vast pile of modestly priced goods which entered the homes of everyday consumers and contributed to new expectations towards standards of living. Scientific management went beyond the shop floor as efficiency and marketplace populism became powerful cultural values, which Ivory advertisers exploited in several ways.

Ivory followed scientific management and celebrated it within their ads. Production was not a matter of 'luck nor chance' but rather 'science, the labs testing, and analysing'. Ads introduced the bucolic Ivorydale factory, where making Ivory appeared more of a calling than a career. An ad titled 'Inspiration', had a regal worker suggesting: 'It is the certainty that the soap which he helps to produce is the purest and most economical, the soap that is doing the greatest good in the world, which enables him to look beyond the drudgery of the moment and see his labor glorified'. Ivory production appeared to be a divine union of spirit and science.

In this mass-market moment, advertisers reached out to everyday consumers previously ignored. Class hierarchies were given in nineteenth-century advertising. By 1916 Ivory 'knows no class distinction'. Advertisers fashion Ivory as a class neutralizer. In a 1920s campaign a baby orphan, born in poverty, has 'baths as kind and gentle as any silver-spoon baby in the world' because of Ivory. In another ad, a nurse, who recommends Ivory, saves foreign baby 'Olaf Jensen', born on a steamship, from his wretched fate of rough, cruel foreign soaps. Ivory also celebrates industrious workmen. Ads called out to the 'men who work in the great out-doors: the men who fish, who farm, who build' and appreciated the 'widely different qualities combined in Ivory Soap'. Brave men, who risk life and limb to building urban cathedral skyscrapers, use Ivory. Advertisers shifted their focus from the elite to the masses.

Brand designers celebrated the mass sale of Ivory to sell more soap. The massive numbers of bars sold were visualized in pyramids, trains, icebergs made of Ivory. A 1906 ad pronounces that 'nearly everybody uses Ivory Soap nearly all the time for nearly everything'. In 1907 advertisers celebrate globalization stressing the 'ring of cleanliness' created by Ivory use that stretches beyond America to Japan, China, the Philippines, the Hawaiian Islands, East Indies, Alaska, South America, and Europe. Designers tell Ivory's customers that 'continuous advertising is proof of the public's confidence in it'.

Mass production and consumption supported economies of scale and lower costs. Advertisers destabilized the belief (that they had helped to establish) that expensive goods were superior. Cheapness became virtue. 'Grocery Shelf Gossip' depicted two women discussing the 5-cent bar of guest Ivory: 'Yes, they certainly are attractive. But you can't expect much from a soap that costs only 5c a cake . . . Oh, so you're one of those who think you've got to pay 25c or 50c for a cake of delicately perfumed, imported toilet soap, are you? I'm surprised at you. Mary, honestly. Don't you know that there's no soap made that is as pure and safe for the face and hands as Ivory?' Advertisers show modern women rejecting expensive, perfumed, foreign soaps, to establish Ivory's purity and honesty. In a 1925 promotional story, 'the Marquis' (fancy foreigner) brings gifts of oil and perfume to win a young woman's affections. She marries 'the nice young man who offered her a cottage by the sea and unlimited supplies of honest Ivory'. Anne, in a 1927 ad, bypasses the 20 expensive soaps, 'each with its rosy promises and foreign accent', for Ivory because she was 'brought up to recognize and choose the fine, the exquisite, the genuine, whatever the price may be'. Elsie spends a fortune on her hats and skin care, but Joan looks just as good by using Ivory Soap. Another ad stresses that money cannot buy good taste.

Advertising design techniques reflected the new sense of populism and movement. As twentieth-century typesetting became more flexible, advertisers used more varied font sizes and styles. Text, instead of appearing below the picture, now appeared behind, beside, or within the image to dramatic effect. In a post telegraph industrial age, where time was increasingly money, advertisers radically reduced their copy. The Ivory Soap became simply Ivory in 1944. Trusting audiences' knowledge, advertisers began to play with conventions, unshackling themselves from formal English. Nineteenth-century advertisers produced serious and earnest messages to relay a sense of honesty. Twentieth-century designs embraced more humour, whimsy, and word play. By the 1930s, as advertisers sought to get down to the level of people on the street, vernacular speech entered advertising copy: 'Dy Ya mean t'tell me ya ain't through bathin' yet, willyum? We won't get to freddy's party in time for tha ice cream!'

Public relations: from product to consumer

Procter and Gamble began to worry about sustaining its Ivory success. In 1923, the corporation hired Edward Bernays, believing he had fresh insight about consumers. Bernays had quite a reputation. Using the ideas of his uncle, Sigmund Freud, Bernays helped organize the propaganda during the First World War for the US government. After the war, Bernays began to discuss Freud's theory of the unconscious mind with US businessmen, changing the name of his profession from propaganda to public relations to make it more palatable. Bernays argued against the dominant business model of the consumer. The consumer, he said, was not a rational agent who could be convinced to purchase a product if provided with clear reasons to buy. Rather, consumer behaviour was governed by complex inner desires that defied rational logic. He argued that to shape consumer behaviour, appeals should be made to people's deeply seated emotional needs, not their objective needs. Goods could become a palliative for the many anxieties, wants, and yearnings that plagued the modern subject. Bernays' ideas played a significant role in turning advertisers' attention from the product to the consumer, from reason why advertising to more emotively directed advertising.

Ivory faced competition from the numerous new beauty treatments that arrived on the market and, positioned as an all-purpose cleaner, was not prepared for either this rivalry, or the growing accent on beauty. Bernays addressed this problem assuaging consumer anxieties about their looks by establishing clean, pure beauty as a scientific fact. He commissioned a study of doctors, asking whether they preferred white, pure, non-scented soap or coloured, perfumed soap. Ivory published that doctors chose Ivory and proclaimed that 'the physician, the dermatologist, who has nothing to sell' assert 'so-called "beauty-treatments" are usually worse than useless, and often harmful'. Emphasizing the idea of clean beauty, a 1927 ad asks: 'Cosmetics? If you like . . . but don't substitute them for this simple care'. Another ad suggested 'Daily cleansing with Ivory and lukewarm water will do more for your skin than all the costly beauty treatments in the world' (Bernays for Ivory Soap, 1928).

Advertisers mocked the young who fall for 'any kind of beauty treatment, preparation, or method that anyone is ingenious enough to devise . . . The scientific fact that a girlish complexion ordinarily needs nothing but pure soap and water to keep it glowing with health is too simple an idea for youth—there's not fun in it ' (Bernaysfor Ivory Soap, 1925).

Public relations also taught Ivory to establish a voice for the cause and enter the communication channel of trusted others who had access to Ivory consumers, such as doctors, teachers, and retailers. Ivory voiced its concern about beauty product advertising in an open letter to medical men:

Dear Doctor: It is our belief that soap advertising to the lay public should make only those claims that could honestly be approved by the medical profession. The tremendous sale of Ivory has been built on straightforward, friendly advertising of a fine product . . . advertising that avoids exaggerated claims and promises. (Bernays for Ivory Soap, 1939)

Ivory offered doctors handouts for patients:

It takes a lot of a doctor's time to explain supplementary home treatment for many common ailments—time which often can be saved. That's why Ivory Soap developed for you this series of Handy Pads. They provide printed answers to many routine questions which patients ask . . . They're short, to the point and contain nothing controversial or intended to take the place of diagnosis. (Bernays for Ivory, 1947)

Ivory also offered guidebooks to teachers and retailers. A guide titled 'The cleanliness crusade' was offered to schoolteachers to help them educate students about health and hygiene. Ivory also provided written pamphlets to home economics teachers to teach students how to correctly wash fine fabrics with Ivory (Bernays for Ivory Soap, 1931).

Babies: innocent messages
....

Bernays also helped Ivory expand its association with babies. Advertisers had depicted babies and Ivory together since 1881. Early ads inserted the brand between mothers and babies, reminding women to keep infants clean. Ivory was endlessly associated with women, sometimes nannies, and, later fathers, bent over the tub washing a baby. The importance of swaddling the baby in the best of fabrics, and free of skin irritation, is also stressed (1895). A 1915 ad stated: 'Babies and Ivory Soap seem to belong to each other'. It is natural to think of Ivory Soap in connection with the baby's tender skin and it is almost impossible not to think of the baby's bath when recalling the many particular things which Ivory does so well. But early advertisers treated babies as little more than an object to be cleaned. Bernays' great insight was that the child was a subjective creature with feelings, interests, and anxieties.

One childhood anxiety was soap. Children, according to Bernays, resented the authoritarian intrusion of bathing rituals. He recommended Ivory host a soap art sculpture contest, professionally judged by artists. By turning Ivory into a medium of art, Bernays believed soap was transformed into a tool for inner self-expression, personal enjoyment instead of authoritarian restriction. Bernays said of the campaign:

Children, the enemies of soap, would be conditioned to enjoy using Ivory. And nothing would be wasted—soap shavings could be used for washing. The coincidence of public and private interest in the mingling of soap and art was so incongruous that it was bound to be newsworthy.

The idea that babies were sentient beings with personalities influenced 1930s advertisers and informed their designs. In the Ivory ads of this period the baby needs protection from their mother who does not know how to care for skin. A young mother asks a medical professional: 'Is she sick? Why does she cry so much?' The professional responds: 'She's a fine strong baby, but her skin is chafed and sore. Never use any but the purest soap on a baby's skin. Bathe her everyday with Ivory Soap. And wash all her little clothes with

Ivory, too' (Bernays for Ivory Soap, 1931). Advertisers take on the voice of the baby. Mothers are told by their babies to buy Ivory to avoid causing them pain, and discomfort, and ruining their skin. Ivory continued its old trick of accusing other brands of harming babies. A 1934 ad titled, 'Does mother always know best?' notes: 'Often these "special" baby soaps have a good reputation which is not justified. In fact, laboratory tests made on 20 such soaps (many of them imported) showed that a considerable number contained free alkali and free fatty acids. Wouldn't mothers be surprised to know this?' Babies show concern for their appearance and awareness of its value. 'A girl can't be too careful', a baby girl says 'Now that I'm ten months old, I've decided that a girl can't start too young with the right beauty treatment. Why, some gentlemen of my acquaintance have barked like dogs and walked like bears for the privilege of kissing my cheek. And grown-up ladies are really envious of my complexion' (Bernays, 1930). Babies also encourage women to use Ivory: 'If you want a baby's clear, smooth skin use a baby's beauty treatment' (Bernays, 1932). Using the baby's soap, claims one ad, helps a woman win her husband back from another woman and look '10 times prettier' (Bernays, 1935).

Advertisers adopted a different structure of feeling. The genteel exchanges between refined, polite, and elegant individuals grew coarser, louder, more direct. No longer just instructed, readers were warned, chastized, yelled at like children. The exclamation mark became the favourite tool of advertisers. For example, a 1932 ad insists 'No odours cling after a bath with Ivory. That fact pleases a man! And he relishes the comforting bath where Ivory floats!' Another ad instructs women: 'Don't coarsen your skin! Only a soap that's pure enough for a baby should touch your face!' (Bernays, 1934). Characters engaged in heated exchanges. Advertisers focused on characters' faces to allow audiences to glean thoughts and feelings. The growing prominence of cinema likely supported the turn to more emotive conventions. Advertisers turned away from the earlier emphasis on duty, deference, and class respectability towards representations of an inner world of anxiety. In the new populist frame of advertising, people were not resigned to their fate but encouraged to use products to improve it.

Building self-reflexive consumers: horrid hands and knotty nerves

Armed with their consumer surveys and psychological insight, advertisers grew confident, assuming a particularly judgmental position towards consumers. For example, in the 1930s world of Ivory soap advertising, the value of women was measured by the state of their hands. It was as if all the anxieties of the war and economic depression zeroed down onto hands. The hand became the principle obstacle preventing social acceptance. A 1931 ad asked women to scrutinize their hands by placing them in an outlined hand on the ad and examine for faults. Women cry over the state of their hands: 'When rich Mr Manson said, "I always judge people by their hands", I got sensitive about my own—they looked so coarse' (Bernays, 1938). Jane, a brand new bride, tells readers: 'My woodwork's spotless . . . but look at my poor red hands! I feel like sitting on them to keep them out of sight' (Bernays, 1930). The goal was to have 'lady of leisure hands' (Bernays, 1935), or as another ad suggested 'ornamental hands'. In short, the cultural valuable hand displayed no evidence of labour or use. To help women achieve charm, 'of which dainty hands are essential', Ivory offered women a charm booklet. Women, who in the nineteenth century feared judgements towards the cleanliness of their homes, now appeared to fear judgement of their hands.

The ads also suggest men were anxious. A 1937 ad claims thousands of scientists have identified a new disease called 'knotted nerves'. Advertisers asked consumers to reflect:

'Do you chew your pencil . . . jump at noise . . . twitch your eyes? Do you rush around crazily . . . smoke endlessly . . . lie awake nights . . . If you do any of these, you have knotted nerves' (Bernays for Ivory Soap, 1937). Ivory soap cured this affliction, absent in earlier advertising. A 1940s campaign suggests Ivory baths defuse angry husbands, thus preventing family strife. Advertisers use before and after cartoons: Men scream at their wives in one frame and look lovingly towards them after their baths. Supporting text suggests: 'After his IVORY bath, dad is a calm and contented man'. Another ad notes: 'Blues disappear! The secret: a bath with pure Ivory Soap soothes your skin, soothes your nerves' (Bernays for Ivory Soap, 1934). The soap which once lubricated bicycle chains, now lubricates social relationships.

Let me entertain you

Advancements in photography changed advertising design. Images became more abstract, stylized, and experimental. Showing their new command over light, designers made artistic use of shadows. Instead of whole bodies, advertisers began to focus on parts, inviting audiences to use their imagination to fill in the rest. Using multiple pictures arranged around the page, descriptive titles and text, new ways of telling stories with images emerged. A new sense of movement was created because the eye, unburdened by the logical progression of text, could jump around rapidly assimilating information as it went. Frames became more varied. The popular circle created a sense of keyhole voyeurism. Advertisers, the great recyclers, continued to use the line-drawn black and white sketches of the past, but now these designs invoked a sense of authentic simplicity or ironic humour.

To retain their audience's attention, advertising and media content was blended in new ways. Ivory began to publish serialized stories and promotional soap operas, such as 'Life and Letters of Ivory Soap', the authorized biography of America's best known soap (Bernays for Ivory Soap, 1925). The formats invited readers to look for the next instalment. In the 1930s, Ivory sponsored a variety radio programme to retailers: 'It's here! Radio's first million dollar programme; a completely new full hour Broadway show every Saturday night to help you sell more Ivory soap . . .' (Bernays for Ivory Soap, 1934). An Ivory soap opera, built around the exploits of the Gibson family, appeared in 1935. Through the 1940s a cartoon serial titled 'The young married set' sold Ivory. Ivory was the first soap to advertise on television and entertaining the audience was becoming as important to branding as building credibility.

War, nationalism, women, and pure beauty

Two world wars contributed to changes in advertising content. Ships and soldiers began to appear in 1918 ads and the brand became more blatantly nationalistic. One ad suggests that 'Ivory Soap follows the flag'. Wherever America goes, it is 'among those present'. A soldier writes in a 1919 advertisement (after the war ended) that Ivory in the battlefield was like getting a letter from home. Soldiers abroad washing in community troughs bring fascination into the faces of those in war torn countries with the American floating soap. By 1930 the nation and Ivory are eclipsed: 'American soap. Ivory Soap'. The two are synonymous: an American spirit of cleanliness, efficiency, and economy.

During the Second World War, with increased numbers of women home alone with their families, taking on jobs to support the war effort, Ivory is sold upon its convenience and washing speed. A 1942 ad stresses how Ivory can help with 'speed dishwashing' yet not result in dishpan hands. Advertisers acknowledge women's labour, their need to 'baby their men, oversee a tight budget and mind the children'. Yet, advertisers retained that looking good was a woman's most important duty. For example, advertisers introduced readers to 'Mrs Ralph E. Bakers, of 268 Institute Street', who does part-time secretarial work, is also an efficient housekeeper and knows a lot about cars. She says, 'These days we women want to do our part in every way . . . and one of them is looking our best no matter how busy we are'.

After the war, Ivory solidified its focus on purity, beauty, and family, the core values of Ivory today. In 1947 it ran the 'cutest baby contest', followed by the highly successful 'Miss Ivory' in 1948. A series of wholesome women advertised 'Young America's look is that Ivory look!' Advertisers added a lifecycle dimension to the 1950s ads, advertising biographies of beautiful women who used Ivory throughout their lives. Mothers and children were brought back together in a new sense of intimacy during the 1960s, frequently depicted cheek-to-cheek, naked in warm embrace. Ad designers no longer chastized the consumer as they did in the 1930s; rather they charmed and complimented their readers. Ivory mothers appeared so young audiences were asked whether they could tell the difference between mother and daughter. A later successful campaign showed generations of Ivory users; grandmother, mother, daughter. Teenagers make an appearance in the ads in the 1960s and Ivory women were celebrated through the 1970s as wholesome beauties, loved by their children and husbands, enjoying a fresh and full lifestyle. 'Come into Ivory's young world . . . your complexion can look younger for it' (1976).

Conclusion

By the 1980s, Ivory's grand narratives about progress and racism embarrassed the brand. Advertisers' innocent reliance on science in a world that had witnessed nuclear disaster, genetically modified foods, and the environmental horrors wrought by technology simply looked silly. Ivory had contributed to a culture in which self-transformation, eternal youth, and beauty were central activities, but the Ivory girl with her golden locks and shiny face could no longer proclaim universalism in a world of diversity. The Ivory girl was a pop culture caricature, favourite victim in B-slasher movies. Dove challenged this vulnerable aspect of Ivory in its highly successful Real Beauty campaign that attacked the beauty myth and sought to sell firming cream with the novel beauty of real models who were old, fat, and black. Ivory has fallen to eighth in the most purchased bar soap brands in a highly competitive sector of shower gel and organic goat milk soap.

In the twenty-first century, Ivory, like many other advertisers, play with brands as pop culture caricature but also heritage. From one angle, contemporary advertisers can now joke about the God-fearing, pure American white soap but on the other hand the powerful associative links between Ivory purity and youthful beauty have become resources of common culture which competitors cannot hope to claim and which Ivory would have difficulty escaping. In their most recent national campaign, advertisers have used the popular retro theme. While Ivory had long leveraged its brand heritage, celebrating in 1919, 1926, 1938, 1941, 1944, and 1979 the amount of time the soap has been on the market, the latest campaign is uniquely late modern because it is more of a knowing wink to the brand's past. The campaign included a return to old packaging and a series of old style ads. Twisting its unique selling proposition, 1,051 bars of Ivory were produced to sink. Like a Willy Wonka chocolate contest, those with the sinking soap were eligible to enter a contest to win $250,000. Contemporary advertisers hope that in a world of anxieties and hyper change, audiences will be receptive to the simple appeal of brand endurance.

Questions for students

1. In what ways are advertisers similar or dissimilar to artists?

2. Considering contemporary advertising, which is more important; entertaining audiences or constructing credible messages? What are the implications?

3. Discuss the different ways in which Ivory advertisers thought about their audience. How did this shape their designs?

4. How and why did Ivory soap shape the Ivory girl? The Ivory girl took on a life as audiences, other media producers, and changing cultural attitudes brought new meanings to her. Discuss the Ivory girl and other advertising caricatures in relation to brand control.

5. Consider how advertisers used anxiety in their designs. What are some of the social and personal consequences of advertisers' use of anxiety formats?

16 Conclusion: the future of advertising and advertising agencies

Janet Hull

....

Introduction
....

The advertising and marketing communications industry is going through a period of unprecedented change. Not since the introduction of commercial television more than 50 years ago has there been such disruption in the marketplace. The digital revolution is rewriting the rulebook for commercial brand communications and the principles, processes and practices of advertising and marketing communications development and measurement are being reinvigorated to keep abreast of the trends.

The Institute of Practitioners in Advertising (IPA) is the UK's professional institute and trade body for over 270 advertising and marketing communications agencies; from creative to media, digital to sponsorship, search to healthcare. The IPA membership comprises 19,000 individuals who, between them, allocate 85 per cent of media expenditure in traditional media, 65 per cent of direct marketing expenditure by agencies, 55 per cent of sponsorship advertising expenditure, and 45 per cent of digital advertising expenditure The IPA is also at the forefront of training and development for UK practitioners and is a thought-leader in promoting new ways of working.

In the spring of 2006, during the presidency of media agency head David Pattison, co-founder of Pattison Horswell Durden (PHD), the IPA decided to embark upon a significant programme of research and development on behalf of, and in consultation with, its members. In partnership with futures consultancy, the Future Foundation, the industry body set itself the brief of addressing the following questions:

1. What will advertising mean in 2016?
2. How big will the UK advertising market be?
3. Who will be the competitors to advertising agencies?
4. What will agencies look like?
5. How will agencies get paid?

The object of the exercise was to answer these questions in order to prepare the IPA membership for the challenges of the next decade and prepare them for change.

This chapter summarises the main findings of this investigation, which took place over an 18 month period, and its main implications for the future of the business.

What are the key drivers of change for advertising?

In workshops led by the Future Foundation, IPA member agency representatives were asked to analyse and prioritise the impact of over 50 different trends already evident in the marketplace including social, political, economic, technological, global and local. The four most significant were identified as:

1. The networked society and new bandwiths galore

These two drivers were combined because they were interdependent; 'new bandwidths galore' provided the impetus for 'the networked society'. The key characteristics of the networked society were defined as:

- Peer-to-peer communication
- Word of mouth, accelerated though Internet-enabled networks
- Free to market, not paid-for space
- No agency intermediary necessary

The overall impact of these drivers on the size of the market for commercial communications in the UK, going forward, was likely to be negative.

2. Navigating choice and complexity

The workshops provided relevant data to illustrate this driver:

- An increase in TV channels from 5 to 200 in the last 10 years
- UK citizens are exposed, each day, on average, to 3,000 different commercial communications messages and 300,000 product and service messages

It was agreed that there was more of a need than ever, in the midst of this potential confusion, for 'branding' and 'agencies' to help decipher consumer choice. On this basis, the impact of this driver on market size was likely to be positive.

3. Legislation creep

The workshops referenced historical UK bans on tobacco advertising and current controls on alcohol advertising. The workshops also explored the financial impact of the most recent changes in regulation around food advertising (high fat/sugar/salt per 100 mg) to programmes with a majority audience of under 16-year-olds; £39 million had been knocked off broadcast advertising revenues in the UK at a stroke. It was obvious that, if legislation creep continued, its impact on market size would be negative.

4. Overall impact on market size, 2006–16

From a base figure of £31.4bn in 2006, research demonstrated that the most likely forecast for future expenditure on commercial communications in the UK was modest growth, averaging 4.6 per cent per annum, slightly above the rate of inflation at the time.

So how is advertising changing?

Having developed a projection of total expenditure over the next 10 years, it was important to understand the potential relative fortunes of different communications channels

(Figure 16.1). The Future Foundation forecasting model predicted the inexorable rise of the Internet, to a point where it exceeded both television and press in advertising revenues. It also suggested that direct response, commercial messaging via mobile, database marketing, experiential marketing and promotions would grow faster than traditional display advertising. High growth in Internet advertising and commercial communications was, of course, partly explained by growth in the role played by the Internet. Already, in its short history, Internet communications have expanded exponentially; from information exchange, through distribution and commerce, into communication exchange and social networking. Looking into the future, broadband Internet would provide the digital platform for all other media channels; from mobile, to outdoor, to television. In this way there would be a blurring of boundaries between all the different media channels, as media convergence became a reality.

In this new world, it was likely that the traditional channel-led segmentation of the media market would lose currency and relevance, and new definitions would emerge, which were less focused on individual channels than on the manner and style of the communication opportunity; 'display' versus 'classified', 'two-way' versus 'one-way', 'named' versus 'not named', 'screen' versus 'non screen'. These, in their turn, would lead to new models of communication and new ways of campaign planning and execution. The future of classified, in particular, raised interesting debate. It was Jeremy Bullmore, industry guru and former creative giant of agency JWT, who had first introduced the industry, at an IPA seminar, to the notion that paid-for search was 'classified' advertising in another guise. Classified advertising had led the charge in embracing the new interactive opportunities provided by the Internet. When classified advertising went on-line, in the form of paid-for search, it opened up a lucrative new business stream for mainstream agencies, who up until that time, had been mainly focused on display. Increasingly, whole agencies, or divisions of agencies in the IPA membership, were dedicated to optimising search opportunities. However, there was growing recognition that search, on its own,

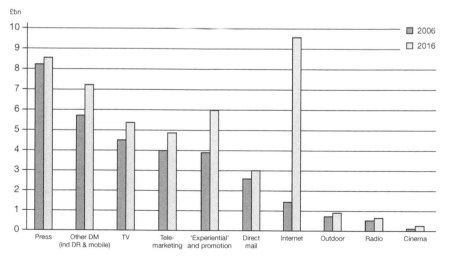

Figure 16.1   Channel impact chart. Courtesy of the IPA/Future Foundation.

was less powerful than search integrated into a mainstream campaign. The need for help in 'navigating choice and complexity' was as pertinent to Internet search as it was to supermarket shopping. In addition, case material was beginning to appear which demonstrated that the most potent campaign media mix was one which combined emotional and rational communications; strong audio-visual content, to create engagement, underpinned by strong classified content, to provide supporting information and explanation and the opportunity for instant transaction.

New communication models

Looking ahead to 2016, the Future Foundation model predicted declines in traditional 'display' advertising and growth in 'two-way' and 'screen-based' advertising. The 'interruption' model of advertising would be supplemented with the 'engagement' and 'participation' models of advertising. Two existing campaigns illustrated this direction of flow rather convincingly: Ogilvy's 'Campaign for real beauty' for Lever Faberge Dove, and Fallon's 'Balls' campaign for Sony Bravia. The former had successfully combined the two models of interruption and engagement (Figure 16.2). It leads with traditional media and follows through on-line. On-line consumer comments fed back into campaign development and on-line polls provided inspiration for mainstream PR and advertising messages. Fallon's 'Balls' campaign was one of the first to experience the brand communication potential of the participation model. Getting consumers to transmit images from the television shoot, around their networks, in advance of the first film edit, had certainly not been in the media plan. However, the visual power of 250,000 coloured balls being thrown down the hilly streets of San Francisco captured the imagination of tech-savvy San Francisco residents and they could not wait to show their friends. The volume of 'buzz' and 'word of mouth' generated ensured currency for the campaign when it eventually hit cinema, television and web screens. There were 500,000 downloads of the advertising at the time of launch and, perhaps not surprisingly, Sony 'Bravia' sold out in the UK.

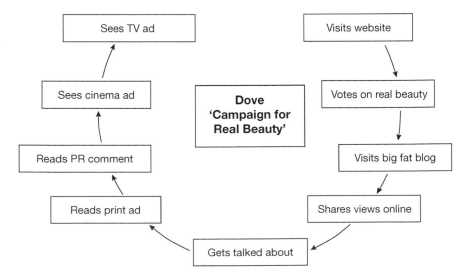

Figure 16.2   Interruption–engagement. Dove 'Campaign for Real Beauty'.

Re-inventing 'television'

One of the other big messages to come out of this particular case example was the dynamic power of quality content in the Internet age . . . and TV (audio-visual) content at that! Consumers of commercial communication choose whether to participate in disseminating brand messages or not. Their choice of message says something about them, so they are going to apply judgement to what they send on. The participation model of communications places a premium on the entertainment value and likeability of commercial communications. In an environment where word-of-mouth has the potential to multiply the impact of paid-for media exponentially, creative differentiation and innovation are key.

With less control over media channel strategy going forward, the prediction is that there will be a renewed focus on creative content. Far from broadband Internet killing television advertising, it will reinvent it; allowing scope for more elaborate forms of audio-visual branded entertainment, at the push of a button, or via on-line streaming and video-on-demand. In addition, as rules around sponsorship, product placement, advertiser-funded programming and advertising minutage evolve, new media opportunities will emerge. Agencies will need to get to grips with new commercial formats and learn new techniques for dealing with them.

New advertising formats

While traditional advertising, as it has been understood over past decades, may contract, the opposite is expected for the new formats. Growth is predicted in consumer-influenced content and brand-influenced editorial. In addition, every brand has the potential, through its website, to become a media company, content creator and distributor in its own right. One measure of campaign and brand success, going forward, may well be the degree to which other brands, advertisers and consumers are attracted to collaborate.

How agencies are changing

As the marketplace for commercial brand communications is changing, so agencies are changing with it. The pace of change varies, but the majority of IPA member agencies now recognise that digital will be central rather than peripheral to their service offer in the next decade and are restructuring to facilitate the digital revolution in relation to content creation, channel understanding and data capture:

* *Content creation*: Creative agencies are being challenged to deliver coherent multi-platform and interactive, solutions. More than ever, clients expect agencies to deliver short-term tactical results, while still nurturing and developing a long-term brand idea.
* *Channel understanding*: Media agencies are now required to be experts in total channel planning from a consumer perspective. In addition, they are expected to provide negotiating and buying skills across new platforms.
* *Data capture*: All agencies with an interactive component to their campaigns are now expected to demonstrate capability in data capture and manipulation. Better data, and better understanding of data, allows for more effective and efficient targeting and provides valuable learning for campaign improvement and development.

However, agencies are not the only players in this new world of content creation, channel understanding and data capture. Agencies are surrounded on all sides by individuals and commercial operators keen to take a slice of the action.

New content can come from anywhere

In the area of content, Internet channels such as YouTube and Facebook have created the opportunity for consumers to become broadcasters and editors in their own right by getting involved in content development. Many case examples of consumer-generated brand content now exist, among the best of them the Coca-Cola Mentos campaign experiment. Consumer-generated content can be attractive to clients when it is 'on brand', that is, in keeping with the essence of what the brand stands for. It not only takes the participation model of advertising to a new level but also has the potential to offer savings from the client's production budget.

New channel opportunities bring new ways of working

With the relaxation of legislation around media ownership, commercial operators in one channel category have taken the opportunity to become multi-platform. The Murdoch family now owns television, radio, print and Internet channels. ITV owns Friends Reunited. So individual media owners can now offer clients multi-platform solutions, which are often negotiated in multi-package deals, directly with the client. The role play between agencies and media owners is increasingly complex. Media owners now interface with agencies on a number of different levels; they can be, at one and the same time, *clients* of agencies, in search of marketing communications campaigns for their media brand, *suppliers* to agencies, in their provision of space or airtime to meet the requirements of their clients' media schedules, and *competitors* to agencies, when and if they by-pass agencies and deal with brand owners directly.

Channel opportunities are changing the game plan. Even supermarkets are now becoming media owners (e.g. Tesco's in-store shopping channel) and setting up in-house planning and buying shops to exploit this discrete advertising opportunity.

Google is taking back control of its advertising sales. Programme formats rather than channels, for example Big Brother, are now becoming the focus of media planning and buying strategy. As programme formats become less channel dependent, more multi-platform and independent, the opportunity exists for the commercial relationship to be with the production company rather than with the channel distributor.

Single source data becomes a reality

New interactive communications opportunities have created new opportunities for more sophisticated data capture. Most brand and channel owners of any size now control substantial marketing databases, at least for their existing and past users or customers. In some cases single source data sets are now being created, which track the consumer journey from first contact to the point of purchase. Ten years ago, agencies were able to add value to clients' businesses because they had access to more consumer, market and media data than their clients and were able to aggregate this data to offer superior consumer insights.

Nowadays, many client companies employ their own data analysts and consumer insight specialists, or have in-house data management systems that can manipulate the data for them at the touch of a button.

Thus, in this new era of multi-channel, multi-platform commercial communications, the traditional linear model of 'client' to 'agency' to 'media' to 'consumer' relationship is breaking down and the opportunity for 'disintermediation' (i.e. by-pass the agency in contracting media services between client companies and channel owners) is increasing. At the same time, creative services can come from a variety of different sources, including direct from consumer.

The agency of the future

In order to focus thinking about what the agency of the future might look like, the Future Foundation recommended to the IPA membership that they develop three different scenarios: a middle way and two extremes. The three scenarios selected were: a central scenario, a media-lead scenario and a consumer-led scenario. Workshops for each scenario were then conducted to brainstorm what the agency of the future might look like.

Central scenario: 'The Core'

The agency in the central scenario was described in outline as 'more of the same but better'. It assumed that agencies would be successful in moving up the value chain and communications chain in companies, 'where brands and corporate reputation meet' and 'brand assets were championed in the boardroom'. This agency of the future would help clients understand the relationship between brand and reputation, the relationship between brand investment and profitability and help clients develop brand management systems, which allowed them to track key performance indicators for their marketing activities. Perhaps not surprisingly, this agency of the future had fewer clients, but more in-depth, longer-term relationships. New disciplines created within this style of agency included that of 'threat analyst'; a futures specialist and assessor of market and brand risk, and 'mood changer'; an in-house resource manager charged with developing environments, which enhanced the ability of both client and agency teams on any piece of business to immerse themselves in the brand.

Media-led scenario: 'The News Room'

The agency in the media-led scenario was described in outline as 'pushing the boundaries' in order to capitalise on the opportunities provided by 'the fusion of advertising and editorial' and the convergence of all media forms. Central service roles for this agency of the future were: 'network provider and innovator'; bringing brand owners and channel owners together in new and appropriate ways, 'deal maker'; bringing deals to the table that suited all parties, and 'media environmentalist'; and helping brand owners stay abreast of media trends and media opportunities, which would identify new opportunities for differentiated brand communications. This agency of the future also added value through the quality and breadth of its exchange network. Brand owners and channel owners would pay a retainer fee to belong to the agency's network, whether they had a specific brief in mind or not. In order to represent their point of difference, this agency subdivided its office environment into 'the news room', 'the brain' (a members only space) and 'production'. In the words of David Pattison, IPA President at the time, and Chief Executive of PHD Worldwide:

> One of the things that is going to be important in the future if not just how you promote a brand, but the company that brand keeps. This concept provides a way of matching the right brands with the right brand owners. If somebody wants something, and it's a rarity, you can charge more for it. We have to prove to media owners that the ideas that we have are not the ideas they have. They are producers of media product. You might argue that, in 10 years time, media product and brand product may become one and the same thing. I think we have to prove to them that we are much better at brand product than them.

Consumer-led scenario: 'Leverage'

The agency in the consumer-led scenario was described in outline as 'breaking down the boundaries between companies and consumers' in order to capitalise on new opportunities in word-of-mouth and social networks. In this scenario, consumers have become so powerful that they are effectively treated as an outsourced element of the marketing and creative departments. Key skill sets required by this agency of the future, in terms of insight, would be: understanding how networks work; how to identify the opinion formers or 'mavens' in networks who provide the 'nodes' to other networks; and how to develop messages which fit with the conventions of the networks. In addition, this agency of the future would employ 'strokers' with responsibility for recruiting and retaining high-value networked consumers. This agency of the future adds value by delivering 'the media that money can't buy'. It also makes its money by charging for access to consumer data and consumer networks. Performance incentives are linked to 'return on maven investment' and 'brand share of network voice'. The office and staff reflect the purpose of the business: essentially it operates as a network itself, bringing experts together through remote access, meeting face to face when necessary, in a club-like environment. Underpinning the whole operation is an investment in the rational analysis of network operations – mathematicians are welcome members of the team.

Summary and conclusions

The overall trends in advertising and marketing communications over the last 10 years, have important consequences for the way agencies of all descriptions remodel their business for the next decade. In overall terms, the patterns produced from an historic 10-year analysis confirm the need for the business to focus its thinking in three critical areas: content, channels and data. Looking ahead to the next 10 years, the business is challenged to:

- invent new roles for commercial advertising to match social and consumer dynamics;
- develop news channels for commercial advertising to win permission to engage with consumers;
- create new commercial advertising formats to attract and entertain consumers.

Over and above all of these dynamics, the business needs to take a position on the role and importance of brands and branding to corporations, products and services and argue the case for the business being included in the brand development and brand management process.

In the emerging battle ground, the blurring of lines between advertising and editorial and between commercial and consumer communications intensifies as new relationships are forged and innovation creates ingenious new ways to get the message through. Over-supply may well worsen in the future, producing a more cut-throat competitive environment. The marketing communications environment is likely to become 'high risk, high reward', with greater polarisation between winners and losers. As the commercial advertising sector gets relatively smaller, it is incumbent on agencies to invade the new advertising space. By 2016, the hypothesis is that media owners of all kinds – including on-line search (Google), all networks, gaming environments and interactive digital TV – are integrating brands directly into content and editorial. Savvy consumers are taking increasing control of content and the directional flow of interactions. Client emphasis is on gathering data and knowledge about consumers and interacting with them on a 'permission only basis'. Matching messages to modes becomes one of the key tenets of good planning. So, it is not only about targeting people (right time, right place), but also being more conscious than ever of their receptivity. Moreover, quite different types of communication are required, and technology makes it possible. While in work mode, short, sharp messages are required that people can ignore or engage with on their two-way, small-screen devices. While in leisure mode, more elaborate forms of branded entertainment (subtle or overt) are more suitable, which people can passively receive on big home/cinema screens/third-space stages. Traditional display advertising, typified by a 30-second television commercial, is increasingly anachronistic. Increasingly, creativity will move away from a selling proposition to a big-brand idea, executed through a multi-channel/experiential environment.

Whichever way you look at it, re-invention is key to the agency of the future. Agencies, like advertising, need to mutate to take on multiple roles and relationships: at one and the same time servicing and maintaining existing traditional business, while preparing the ground for new forms of business relationships. New freedoms in the delivery of content, data and channels will provide new business opportunities while still maintaining the overriding focus on brand creation and development: agency as media brand owner, joint venture partner, content collaborator, programme producer, network creator, data provider, and data aggregator. Inevitably, the nomenclature 'agency' will be questioned. All of these opportunities provide agencies with new ways to assert their value-add, to retain the high ground in their relationships and renegotiate their remunerations packages. The change is more likely to be gradual than overnight. New business entities within existing corporate structures will be created to test out new business relationships and models.

Glossary

....

Above-the-line media   All media that remunerate agencies on the basis of commission, e.g. TV, radio, newspapers, magazines and posters. This term, like below-the-line and through-the line (see below), refers to a system of ad agency remuneration that is now largely defunct.

***Ad hoc* survey**   One-off research of a particular topic during a particular time.

Advertisement   Paid-for dedicated space or time sequence in which only the advertiser is represented (can be in newspapers, magazines, TV, radio, posters, or in direct mail, retail, etc.).

Advertisement appreciation   Measures the likeability and interest in advertising. Respondents rank likeability from one to five.

Advertiser   The manufacturer, government body or organisation which wishes to have advertisements created and placed.

Advertising   Any form of paid-for media used by a marketer to communicate with their target audience.

Advertising Association (AA)   Information and lobbying organisation for the advertising industry, jointly funded by agencies, advertisers and media owners (UK).

Advertising industry   Advertisers, advertising agencies, the media and trade organisations representing their interests, whether at national or supra-national level.

Advertising Standards Authority (ASA)   The semi-independent watchdog of the UK advertising industry set up in 1961 by the Advertising Association.

Advertorial   An advertisement that has the appearance of a news article or editorial, in a print publication; it usually includes 'Advertisement feature' at the top.

Affinity marketing   Selling products or services to customers, based on their established buying patterns.

Air date   The date of broadcast for a radio or TV commercial.

Ambient media   Out-of-home promotional messages inserted into traditionally non-promotional spaces, such as bus tickets, luggage racks, in public toilets, on vehicles, shopping trolleys, images projected onto buildings, human heads, golf course holes, among many other things.

American Association of Advertising Agencies (AAAA)   An association of advertising agencies in the US.

Animatic   Moving picture illustrations developed from a storyboard used in pre-testing commercials, to give clients an idea of what the finished commercial will look like.

Audience appreciation   Measure of how much audiences were interested in and enjoyed or were entertained by TV programmes. Conducted by BARB and gives an Appreciation Index score for programmes.

Audit Bureau of Circulations (ABC)   Audits the number of copies sold for magazines and newspapers and verifies media performance across events and digital media platforms.

Average Issue Readership (AIR)   The average number of people who are estimated to have looked at an issue of a publication for three minutes or more in a specified time period.

Average weekly reach   The number of persons (aged 4+) who watch at least 15 consecutive minutes of a specified TV channel or genre in a specific week (or in an average week over a longer period).

Banner ad   A graphic image used as an advertisement that is placed on a web page and is usually hyperlinked to an advertiser's website.

Barbara   Electronic system for measuring audience appreciation for programmes administered by BARB.

Bar code   A small block of vertical lines on products containing information about the product, which can be scanned by retailers, manufacturers and consumer panels.

Below-the-line media   All media that do not remunerate on the basis of commission, e.g. sales promotion, direct marketing, public relations and sponsorship.

Brand attitude   Commonly a campaign communication objective which reflects the link between the brand and its benefits to a customer.

Brand awareness   The extent to which consumers have heard of, or seen and recall a brand. This is often monitored through surveys such as *Marketing*'s Adwatch.

Brand filling   Involves filling a gap in an existing market, e.g. Coke launching Tab to fill the clear soft-drink segment, or Colgate launching Bicarbonate of Soda toothpaste.

Brand image   Term used by David Ogilvy, which indicates a unique emotional personality for a given brand.

Brand positioning   Term used to describe the unique added values and appeal of the brand in relation to other brands in the same market; often describes how it is positioned to consumers.

Brand stretching   New models, versions and sizes of a brand, e.g. Coke, Diet Coke and Caffeine-free Coke.

Break ratings   The audience rating during a commercial break.

British Direct Marketing Association   The trade body of direct marketing companies.

British Rate and Data (BRAD)   Provides monthly information on costs and specifications in advertising media.

Broadband   A service or connection that is capable of supporting always-on services, which provide the end-user with high data transfer speeds.

Broadcasters' Audience Research Board (BARB)   A pan-industry body that measures television viewing and produces TV ratings and audience appreciation data.

Brown goods   Electrical goods, such as hi-fis, TVs, CDs, video recorders. So named because the first generation had brown wooden casings.

Burst   An intensive period of heavyweight advertising activity, usually repeated during the year.

Cable TV   A system of direct-to-home cables (some copper, some fibre-optic), which relay TV signals; some also carry satellite channels, and since the late 1980s also telephony.

Campaign   Weekly advertising trade magazine; takes its name from the industry term for period of advertising publicity.

Cinema Advertising Association   Trade body representing UK cinema advertising companies.

Circulars   Also known as direct mail, sent direct to people's home or place of work via the post.

Classified advertising   Advertisements that do not usually use illustration, including recruitment, business-to-business, family notices, etc. Usually arranged under subheadings that describe the class of goods or service being advertised.

Clearcast   A self-regulatory body that pre-vets TV advertisements.

Demographics   Classificatory system of research based upon shared characteristics of people, such as age, sex, class and ethnicity. Systems include ACORN, MOSAIC and Superprofiles.

Demonstration ads   Advertisements that include a demonstration of the product in use and/or a comparison of the product with others on the market.

Depth interview   An informal interview, usually between an interviewer and one respondent (sometimes more), meant to explore the hidden motivations of why consumers buy and consume goods.

Desk research   This involves using publicly available data and previous data to examine markets; the cheapest form of research.

Diary method   Method of research used in a number of media research activities, such as RAJAR; involves respondents filling in a diary of their media and consuming habits.

Direct mail   Marketing communications delivered directly to a prospective purchaser via a postal service or delivery company.

Direct response   Promotions that permit or request consumers to directly respond to an advertiser, by mail, telephone, email, or some other means of communication.

Discount   Percentage awarded to an agency by a media owner, either for booking large sums of money or booking early, or trying to attract them because of low circulation revenue.

Display advertisement   Advertising that usually involves an illustration, photograph or image and usually takes up large amounts of space in newspapers and magazines. Its aim is to attract immediate attention, rather than rely on people searching through (as with classified).

Double-page spread (DPS)   An advertisement occupying two facing pages (usually in a magazine).

Drip   Long period of lightweight advertising activity.

Drop   Door-to-door advertising material dropped in designated areas.

Early payment discount   Given when an agency agrees to pay the invoice earlier than usual.

Econometrics   The application of mathematical and statistical techniques to economic problems. It is concerned with testing the validity of economic theories and providing the means of making qualitative predictions.

Establishment survey   Establishes the demographic profile of homes in ITV regions to gain a representative sample for the BARB panel.

European Advertising Standards Alliance (EASA)   Organisation promoting self-regulation for the advertising industry in Europe.

Execution   A new execution is a new treatment of a consistent theme, e.g. the Andrex puppy in a new situation.

Facing matter   The advertisements face editorial pages in magazines and newspapers.

Fast-moving consumer goods (FMCG)   Also packaged goods; frequently purchased goods such as confectionery, toiletries, cereals, etc.

Fee payment   A flat fee paid by the client to the agency for all work done.

Fibre optics   Cable system that allows interactive programming via fibre optic cables, multiple channels and quick two-way communication between sender and receiver.

Focus groups   Groups of usually around eight respondents who are invited to talk about the brand and product sector for qualitative research purposes.

Forty-eight-sheet   A standard poster size of 7 x 3 metres (20 x 10 ft); a 96-sheet poster is double this size.

Frequency   The average number of times the target audience will have an opportunity to see the advertisement.

Full-service agency   While still active in the USA, whereby an agency offers a full range of communication services, their function has been replaced to a large degree by holding companies that offer a range of services to a client via subsidiary agencies.

Geodemographics   A method of classifying consumers via segmentation according to their shared characteristics in the areas of income, property ownership, neighbourhood type, age and family status.

Guaranteed Home Impressions (GHI)   The number of home impacts guaranteed by the TV contractor for the given TVRs in a specified period of time at a fixed cost.

General Sales List (GSL)   Medicines available in any retail outlet.

Guerrilla marketing   The use of unconventional marketing approaches that promote brands without full disclosure of the marketer's interests or organising activity.

Head-on site   An outdoor poster site that faces traffic.

High in fat, salt and sugar (HFSS)   Food or drink containing a high level of fat, salt or sugar content.

Impressions   Used in web advertising to refer to an ad view. Advertising is often measured in terms of impressions.

Incorporated Society of British Advertisers (ISBA)   The trade organisation representing clients.

Infomercial   A commercial that is very similar in appearance to a news programme or other non-advertising programme content. The broadcast equivalent of an advertorial (see above).

Institute of Practitioners in Advertising (IPA)   The trade organisation that traditionally represented full-service agencies but began admitting direct marketing companies in 1991 and admitted media independent TMD Carat in 1993.

Integrated Marketing Communication (IMC)   A management concept that is designed to make all aspects of marketing communication (e.g. advertising, sales promotion, public relations and direct marketing) work together as a unified force, rather than permitting each to operate and communicate in isolation.

Interactive media   Digital media such as text, graphics, video and sound, which users can interact with, typically delivered via the Internet.

Interstitial   A type of advertising that loads between web pages without having been requested by the visitor.

Involvement advertising   A type of advertising that attempts to involve consumers by either humour or emotions in the advertising, to help them warm towards the brand.

Lifestyle   A method of classifying consumers via segmentation according to their shared characteristics in the areas of hobbies, interests, behaviour and purchasing preferences.

Line-by-line   Buying individual sites of posters that are not part of packages.

List broker   Someone who trades lists of names of consumers who may be compatible for direct marketing purposes (e.g. insurance companies and mortgage companies).

Luxury goods   Goods consumed for their symbolic value over their use value.

Market segmentation   The means by which the shared characteristics of a group of consumers can be determined.

Marketing   The management process responsible for identifying, anticipating and satisfying consumers, profitably.

Market segmentation   The means by a market can be subdivided based on the shared characteristics and needs of different consumers groupings.

Media dependent   A media department hived-off from a full-service agency.

Media independent   A media planning and buying agency that has no link to a full service agency.

Media plan   Recommendation for a media schedule, including dates, publications, TV regions.

Media research   Research conducted into the relationships between different media and audiences, quantity of media audiences and the quality of viewing, listening or reading.

Media schedule   Record of bookings made for a campaign, or a proposal for a campaign with dates, times, sizes and costs.

Merchandising   Traditional term for sales promotion, use of in-store leaflets and materials.

Multi-media   Use of space- and time-based media via computers and fibre-optic cables, allowing the consumer to control the order, timing and selection of programmes and advertising.

National Readership Survey (NRS)   Produces a monthly survey of readers for national and regional newspapers and consumer magazines, run and funded by a joint industry committee. Provides an Average Issue Readership.

Near Video on Demand (NVoD)   A service based on a linear schedule that is regularly repeated on multiple channels, usually at 15-minute intervals, so that viewers are never more than 15 minutes away from the start of the next transmission.

Net advertising revenue (NAR)   Revenue received by a television channel for the sale of airtime (usually spot advertising) to advertisers.

Newspaper Publishers' Association (NPA)   Trade body representing national newspapers.

Newspaper Society   Trade body representing regional newspaper groups.

Next matter   An advertisement appearing on the same page as editorial copy.

Office of Communications (Ofcom)   Regulator for the UK communications industries, with responsibilities across television, radio, telecommunications and wireless communications services.

On-the-run colour   Colour can be put on to the paper in a single run through the printing machine(s). Before, the paper would have gone through four times to have the yellow, black, red and blue inks printed. This was extremely expensive, time-consuming and prone to breakdowns. Now, the four separate inks are applied on one run of the paper through the machine, quickly and at much lower cost.

Opportunities to see (OTS)   The number of possibilities an individual has of being exposed to an advertising message on billboards, on TV and in the press.

OSCAR   Outdoor site classification system run by the Joint Industry Committee for Poster Audience Research.

Outdoor Advertising Association (OAA)   Trade body representing outdoor contractors.

Outside back cover   The very last page of the publication.

Over-the-counter (OTC)   Drugs which are available without a prescription in chemists' shops and newsagents.

Pay-TV   A system whereby consumers can pay directly for programmes viewed, usually in an advertising-free environment.

Payment by results   Usually an agreed sum (fee) between the agency and the client, plus a percentage increase for achieving the advertising goals.

Peak time   The time of day when usually the highest numbers of the TV audience are watching; the rest is called off-peak.

Penetration   The percentage of homes or people reached by a brand in purchase or usage.

Peoplemeters   Electronic method of collating research information for BARB on numbers and profile of people in a room while the TV set is switched on.

Periodical Publishers' Association (PPA)   UK Trade body representing magazine publishers.

Personal video recorder (PVR)   A device, usually built into a set-top box or TV set, which records content digitally onto a hard disk.

Persuasion shift   A type of advertising research popular in the USA, which suggests that the consumer has been directly persuaded by the advertising message contained in the advertisement to buy the product.

Platform   The mechanism through which content or services are delivered to the home, e.g. digital terrestrial television, satellite, cable, IPTV and broadband.

P medicines   Pharmacy-only medicines.

Point of sale   The place in which the goods are bought or sold, usually a place in which other display material is used to reach the consumer before the decision is finally made.

POM   Prescription-only medicines.

Poster specialists   Intermediary media buyers who specialise in outdoor advertising.

Pre-empt   To buy commercial advertising time at the last minute at a higher rate, thus displacing ads already booked.

Premium offer   Offering another product or service free, or at a reduced price with purchase of a product, e.g. Hoover offering two free flight tickets for Europe or the US with every purchase of a Hoover product over £100.

Presenter   A style of advertisement that either includes a testimonial from a famous person or authority figure, or features an actor or personality talking directly to the consumer.

Press date   The date a publication is finally printed.

Pre-test   A test of advertising before it is transmitted among target consumers.

Product placement   A form of promotion in which advertisers insert branded products into TV programming, radio, films, games or other audiovisual media in exchange for payment or other valuable consideration.

Product tests   Tests carried out to measure the strength of brand values, often disguising the brand name of the product. Other tests include observing the usage of the product for incorporation in advertising and marketing.

Profile   The breakdown of an audience by a specific set of characteristics e.g. age, income, readership preferences. Often used to compare one target audiences preferences against another to enable improved media planning.

Programme schedule   Usually issued four times a year to media buyers in TV, from which the buyer estimates the size and profile of the audience.

PR shops   Consultancies that deal in public relations, public affairs and corporate promotions.

Psychographics   A method of classifying consumers via segmentation according to their shared characteristics in the areas of values, beliefs, opinions, personality traits and attitudes.

Public relations   Covers non-paid-for publicity, such as press or media relations, sponsoring events, lobbying government, donations to charity by which the company promotes its image to the public, government and other businesses.

Quota sample   Interviewers collect information from a set number of people with specific demographic characteristics to gain a cross-section.

Radio Advertising Clearance Centre (RACC)   Self-regulatory body set up by the Radio Authority to pre-vet radio commercials.

Radio Authority   The regulatory body covering commercial and public service broadcasting.

RAJAR   Research body jointly funded and run by BBC and commercial radio.

Random sample   Sample in which each member has an equal chance of being selected from a pre-given list.

Rate card   Issued by media owners to give an indication of the structure and levels of prices for advertisements. These are hardly ever adhered to by advertising agencies, who usually manage to obtain substantial discounts.

Reach   The percentage of a total audience that will be exposed to a specific promotional communication during a defined period of time. In TV, reach is the proportion of total TV households viewing a particular channel over a specified time, expressed as a percentage of total available TV households.

Ready-to-Eat (RTE)   Ready-to-eat cereals, which do not need preparation, such as corn flakes, Shredded Wheat.

Recall   Used in research to find out how memorable an advertisement was, i.e. after an ad has been broadcast or shown in newspapers (day-after recall); also 'spontaneous recall', where the interviewer simply asks respondents to list ads recalled, and 'promoted recall', where the interviewer suggests ads and asks the respondent to give details.

Release form   Signed by anyone photographed or filmed, allowing advertisers to use their image in advertisements.

Retail audit   A measurement of brands from a sample of retail distributors, which indicates the sales performance of brands during promotions.

Run-of-month and run-of-week Ads that appear whenever and wherever the media owner decides within the time period given, for cheaper rates.

Run-of-paper The media owner decides where the ad appears, for a standard rate.

Sales houses Representatives of media owners who sell space or time to agencies; these are sometimes owned by media owners or act for independents on their behalf.

Sales promotion Also known as merchandising; form of promotion used at the point of sale that includes posters, stickers and stands; also the use of money-off coupons, competitions and other promotions to stimulate trial.

Salience A style of advertising that tries to stand out from the rest of the advertising and media messages, to grab the attention of the viewer and break down resistance.

Sample A scaled-down version of a research universe, used to estimate patterns in the total universe; supposedly, the larger the sample size, the more accurate the estimate.

Sanpro Sanitary protection products: tampons and sanitary towels.

Sans serif Typefaces without curls or strokes at the end of letters.

Segmentation A technique used to identify groupings of customers that possess similar characteristics, preferences or purchasing behaviours.

Self-regulation Regulation carried out by the industry, profession or sector regulated.

Self-regulatory organisation (SRO) A body set up and funded by the advertising industry to apply a code or rules regulating advertising content.

Semiotics A method of analysis sometimes applied in advertising and market research to assist in capturing and articulating meanings associated with brand communications. Its focus is on communications understood as constituted in *signs* on socio-cultural processes of *signification* and *interpretation*.

Series discount A discount offered for advertisers who book a series of advertisements over a number of issues.

Serif Typefaces with curls and strokes at the end of letters.

SFX Sound effects used in TV, cinema and radio commercials; can include music or background noise.

Share (TV) The proportion of total TV viewing to a particular channel over a specified time, expressed as a percentage of total hours of viewing.

Shopping goods Goods in which a comparison is made by the consumer before it is bought, often on price/value for money.

Single-column centimetre Unit of measurement for advertising in newspapers: a centimetre high and a column wide.

Slice-of-life A style of advertising that can be in either print, TV or radio form, which invites the viewer to eavesdrop on a situation, usually one in which the product is being discussed, used or consumed.

SMS Text message sent on a mobile phone.

Social networking Takes place on sites such as MySpace, Facebook and Bebo, which allows for online communication that is highly personalised and particularly favourable among youth.

Solus position An advertisement which is placed where no other ads appear; can be in print media or billboards, or in broadcasting breaks.

Speciality goods Goods that consumers will travel distances to buy; usually expensive or highly desirable goods, such as cars and luxury furniture.

Split run test Test made by placing different ads in the same publication, either split by area (north/south) or in alternate copies over the same area.

Split transmission Simultaneous transmission of separate advertisements offered by TV contractors for test purposes within one region.

Sponsorship A form of promotion that involves payment by the advertiser for an editorial product (in the media) or for an event in which the company are often allowed to have the brand credited and promoted, and can use the product/event in their own promotions.

Spot advertising   Short advertisements on television and radio, most often of 30/20/10 second duration.

Spot colour   A single colour in an advertisement.

Spot rating   A rating for a single commercial.

Staggered campaign   A mixture of burst and drip advertising campaigns.

Statutory regulation   The function of any regulator whose powers are provided by legislation.

Subscription   Method of payment for media (publications and TV) that involves a payment of money in advance by the advertiser for media consumption over a period of time, often at a discount.

Supers   Use of words over a picture.

Superstitial   An advertisement that downloads in the background while a visitor is reading a web page and which appears in a browser window only when it has completely downloaded.

Target audience   The section of a market or consumer base which is deemed to be the appropriate recipients of a communication or promotion. They will prossess similar characteristics relating to demographics, lifestyles or needs.

Target Group Index (TGI)   A survey of product and brand usage and media usage conducted by BMRB over a year, including demographic and lifestyle categories (www.bmrb-tgi.co.uk).

Target Group Ratings (TGRs)   The combination of brand and product users in the Target Group Index achieved by TV programmes matched to the BARB figures.

Telemarketing   Use of phones to contact and receive calls from potential customers.

Teleshopping   A form of advertising enabling viewers to buy goods directly from home, which usually consists of longer advertisements or advertising features.

Television Consumer Audit (TCA)   A consumer panel of grocery purchases by TV viewers.

Television Ratings (TVRs)   This measures the popularity of a programme, daypart, commercial break or advertisement, by comparing its audience to the population as a whole. One TVR is numerically equivalent to 1 per cent of a target audience. For example, if *Coronation Street* achieved a Housewives TVR of 20 in the ITV region Yorkshire, this means that 20 per cent of all housewives in that region watched an average minute of *Coronation Street*.

Through-the-line   A mixture of above- and below-the-line promotion, generally using a combination of mass media advertising, public relations, sales promotion and direct marketing.

Tracking study   A continuous survey of recall, usage, attitude and awareness of brands that advertisers use to gauge the effectiveness of advertising and promotion.

Transmission certificate   Sent to agencies by television companies to confirm that a commercial has been aired.

Universe   The total number of a target group from which researchers take a sample.

Unique Selling Proposition (USP)   Term coined by Rosser Reeves in *Reality in Advertising*, to indicate a brand characteristic that separates it from competitors.

Usage and attitude   *Ad hoc* research conducted into the use of products and brands and attitudes towards them by consumers.

Vignette   A short description or character sketch to give a portrait of somebody or something, or a summary of a story in a few lines.

Viral marketing   This technique is often used on the web or via email and induces users or websites to pass on a marketing message to other sites or users, creating an enormous growth in the message's visibility.

Video-on-Demand (VOD)   A service or technology that enables TV viewers to watch programmes or films whenever they choose, not restricted by a linear schedule.

Voice-over   Spoken words used in relation to pictures on TV and cinema.

Voucher   A copy of a publication given to an agency to prove that its advertisement ran.

White goods   Electrical goods, often kitchen equipment such as washing machines, fridges, cookers.

Word-of-mouth (WOM)   Communications about products or services conveyed from one individual to others.

References

Aaker, D.A. (1991) 'Brand loyalty' in *Making Brand Equity: Capitalizing on the Value of a Brand Name*. New York: The Free Press.

Advertising Association/WARC (2007) *World Advertising Statistics Yearbook, 2007*. Henley-on-Thames: Advertising Association/WARC.

Abramovich, A. (2001) 'Company man', *Feed*. (Online article, no longer available.)

Advertising Association (2007) *World Advertising Statistics Yearbook*. London: WARC/Advertising Association.

Alford, N., Burrows, L., Pahl, J. and Fordham, K. (2004) 'Weetabix: how Weetabix profited from energetic brand advertising', *Advertising Works*, 13. London: IPA, bronze award winner at the IPA Effectiveness Awards.

Anderson, C. (2006) *The Long Tail: How Endless Choice is Creating Unlimited Demand*. London: Random House.

Angear, B. and Moody, R. (2002) 'Sainsbury's: a recipe for success', *Advertising Works*, 12, presented at the IPA Effectiveness Awards. (Accessed at: www.warc.com.)

Ansolabehere, S.D., Iyenger, S. and Smith, A. (1999) 'Replicating experiments using aggregate and survey data: the case of negative advertising and turnout', *American Political Science Review*, 93(4): 901–9.

——, ——, Simon, A. and Valentino, N. (1994) 'Does attack advertising demobilize the electorate?', *American Political Science Review*, 88 (December): 829–38.

—— (2006) *Brands: Meaning and Value in Media Culture*. London: Routledge.

Arvidsson, A. (2004) 'On the "pre-history of the panoptic sort": mobility in market research', *Surveillance and Society*, 1(4). (Available at: www.surveillance-and-society.org/journalv1i4.htm, accessed January 2009.)

ASA (2004) 'Amen Ltd adjudication'. (Available at: www.asa.org.uk/asa/adjudications/non_broadcast/Adjudication+Details. htm?Adjudication_id=38413, accessed 28 March 2008.)

—— (2007) Advertising Standards Authority annual report. (Available at: www.asa.org.uk/ASA_2004_Rebuild/ASAAppBase/AnnualReport2007/asa/lordborrie.asp.)

—— (2008a) 'A short guide to what we do'. (Available at: www.asa.org.uk/asa/about/short_guide/.)

—— (2008b) 'Taste and decency: the depiction of women'. (Available at: www.asa.org.uk/asa/focus/background_briefings/Taste+and+Decency+-+the+depiction+of+women.htm.)

—— (2008c) 'Factsheet on Reducing Unwanted Commercial e-Mail (Spam)'. (Available at: www.asa.org.uk/asa/focus/background_briefings.)

Auletta, K. (2005) 'The New Pitch', *The New Yorker*, 28 March.

Ball, S., Davies, J., David, M. and Reay, D. (2004) 'Classification and judgement' in M. Tight (ed.) *The Routledge Reader in Higher Education*. New York: Routledge Falmer.

Banerjee, A. (2000) 'International advertising developments' in J. Philip Jones (ed.) *International Advertising: Realities and Myths*. London: Sage.

Bannister, L. (2006) 'How clients are abusing the pitching process', *Campaign*, 26 August, p. 17.

Barney, R.K., Wenn, S.R. and Martyn, S.G. (2004) *Selling the Five Rings: The International Olympic Committee and the Rise of Olympic Commercialism*. Utah: University of Utah Press.

Bartle, J. and Griffiths, D. (2001) *Political Communications Transformed*. Basingstoke: Palgrave.

Baty, P. (2005) 'Managers put branding before staff', *Times Higher Education Supplement*, 16 December.

Bauman, Z. (1987) *Legislators and Interpreters: On Modernity, Postmodernity and Intellectuals*. Cambridge: Polity Press.

Baxter, M. (1990) *Women in Advertising*. London: IPA.

BBC (1997) 'Victory for McDonald's – at a cost', 19 June. (Accessed at: http://news.bbc.co.uk/onthisday/hi/dates/stories/june/19/newsid_2516000/2516301.stm.)

BBC (2008) 'Ban on junk food ads introduced', BBC News, 1 January. (Available at: http://news.bbc.co.uk/go/pr/fr/-/1/hi/health/7166510.stm, accessed 1 January 2008.)

Beale, C. (2005) 'Love 'em or loathe 'em, matchmakers are crucial', *Campaign*, 16 September, p. 23.

—— (2008a) 'Will web content undermine ASA's effectiveness?', *Campaign*, 2 May.

—— (2008b) 'Boys, you will just have to accept that she's the best man for the job', *The Guardian*, 8 September.

Bedi, R. (2008) 'Criticism in India over skin-whitening trend', *Daily Telegraph*, 10 July.

Benoit, W., Pier, P. and Blaney, J. (1997) 'A functional approach to television political spots: acclaiming, attacking, defending', *Communication Quarterly*, 45(1): 1–20.

Benson, R. and Blimes, A. (eds) (2004) *Class of 2004*. London: The Fish Can Sing.

——, MacRury, I. and Marsh, P. (2007) *The Secret Life of Cars, BMW*. (Available at: www.bmweducation.co.uk/publications.)

Bergson, H. (1911) *Laughter: An Essay on the Meaning of the Comic*. London: Macmillan.

Bethel, F. (2004) 'B&Q – "You can do it"', Presented at the IPA Effectiveness Awards. (Accessed at: www.warc.com.)

Beynon, J. (2002) *Masculinities and Culture*. Buckingham: Open University Press.

Binet, L. and Field, P. (2007) *Marketing in the Era of Accountability*. Henley-on-Thames: World Advertising Research Centre/IPA.

Birchall, J. (2008) 'Nike plans Olympic ad blitz', *Financial Times*, 1 July.

Blake, A. (1997) 'Music and the advertising message' in M. Nava, A. Blake, I. MacRury and B. Richards (eds) *Buy This Book*. London: Routledge.

Bogart, L. (2005) *Over the Edge: How the Pursuit of Youth by Marketers and the Media has Changed American Culture*. Chicago: Ivan R. Dee.

Boje, D. (2001) 'Carnivalesque resistance to global spectacle: a critical postmodern theory of public administration', *Administrative Theory & Praxis*, 23(3): 431–58.

——, Driver, M. and Cai, Y. (2005) 'Fiction and humor in transforming McDonald's narrative strategies', *Culture and Organization*, 11(3): 195–208.

Bokaie, J. (2007) 'Armani signs Beckham to front underwear range', *Marketing*, 14 November. (Accessed at: www.brandrepublic.com.)

Bordo, S. (1999) *The Male Body: A Look at Men in Public and in Private*. New York: Farrar, Straus and Giroux.

Botterill, J. and Kline, S. (2007) 'From McLibel to McLettuce', *Society and Business Review*, 2(1).

Bottomley, J. (2005) 'Lynx: a game for adults', *Account Planning Group (UK)*, bronze award winner at the Creative Planning Awards.

Bowery, J. (2007) 'When should brands dump badly behaved celebrities?', *Marketing*, 27 March. (Accessed at: www. brandrepublic.com.)

Boyce, S. (2008) 'Summary findings of the ESOMAR Global Market Research 2007', *WARC Report*, January.

Boyle, D. (2003) *Authenticity: Brands, Fakes, Spin and the Lust for Real Life*. London: Flamingo.

Bradley, S.P. and Bartlett, N. (2007) 'How media choices are changing online advertising', Teaching note, *Harvard Business School*, 13 February.

BrandZ (2008) 'The top 100 most powerful brands 2008', New York: Millward Brown Optimor. (Accessed at: www.brandz.com/upload/BrandZ-2008-RankingReport.pdf.)

Brierley, S. (1995) *The Advertising Handbook*, London: Routledge.

—— (2002) *The Advertising Handbook* (2nd edn). London: Routledge.

Briggs, R. and Stuart, G. (2006) *What Sticks: Why Most Advertising Fails and How To Guarantee Yours Succeeds*. Chicago: Kaplan Publishing.

Broadbent, T. (2007) 'Does advertising create demand?', *WARC Reports*.

Broadbent, T. and Best, J. (2006) 'The "Big John" campaign: advertising in the beer market (1982)' in L. Green *Advertising Works and How*. London: WARC/IPA.

Brook, S. (2005) 'Spoof suicide bomber ad sparks global row'. (Available at: www.guardian.co.uk/technology/2005/jan/20/media.newmedia, accessed 20 January 2005.)

Brown, A. (2007) 'Advertising, ethics and the environment: a personal view', *Market Leader*, Spring (36).

Broyles, S.J. and Grow, J.M. (2008) 'Creative women in advertising agencies: why so few "babes in boyland"?', *Journal of Consumer Marketing*, 25(1): 4–6.

Budden, R. (2003) 'Could I have one of those Beckham phones, please?', *Financial Times: Creative Business*, 10 June, pp. 8–9.

Buford, H. (2005) 'The gay market goes mainstream', *Gay & Lesbian Review Worldwide*, 12(1): 22–4.

Burt, K. (2006) 'Infectious humour', *The Guardian*, 29 April. (Available at: www.guardian.co.uk/media/2006/apr/29/advertising.news.)

Bush, V.D., Martin, C.A. and Bush, A.J. (2004) 'Sports celebrity influence on the behavioural intentions of generation Y', *Journal of Advertising Research*, 44(1): 108–18.

Business Week (2005) '2005 Best Global Brands,' Special Report, 1 August.

Business Week (2007) 'Skinner's winning McDonald's recipe', 5 February. (Accessed at: www. businessweek.com/magazine/content/07_06/b4020007.htm.)

Bussey, N. (2006) 'Is Kate Moss still a good brand icon?', *Campaign*, 13 January, p. 25.

Byron Review (2008) 'Safer children in digital world', London: The Stationery Office.

Campaign (2002) 'Campaign of the year: ITV Digital', 11 January, pp. 31–2.

—— (2006) 'Adland lashes out as Blair wades into junk-food row', 28 July.

—— (2007a) 'Advertising news: Spice Girls feature for Tesco', 2 November, p. 5.

—— (2007b) *The Annual 2007*, 14 December, p. 48.

—— (2007c) 'Why it's time to fight for advertising', 6 April.

—— (2008a) 'The top agencies 2008', 22 February.

—— (2008b) 'Government threatens to regulate online advertising',4 April.

Campaign (2007d) 'Top 10 virals: Blendtec "will it blend?"', 14 December, p. 38.

Campbell, J., Fauth, S., Silsbee, P. and Geraci, J. (2000) 'Understanding youth,' ESOMAR, pp. 141–53. Also presented at the Reinventing Advertising Conference, Rio de Janeiro, Brazil, November. (Available at: www.warc.com, accessed 24 April 2008.)

Cappo, J. (2003) *The Future of Advertising: New Media, New Clients, New Consumers in the Post-Television Age*. New York: McGraw-Hill.

Cashmore, E. (2002) *Beckham*. Cambridge: Polity Press.

—— (2006) *Celebrity/Culture*. London: Routledge.

Cassidy, A. (2008) 'AMV tops new-business league', *Campaign*, 1 February. (Available at: www.brandrepublic.com, accessed 19 June 2008.)

Chappelet, J. and Kubler-Mabbott, B. (2008) *The International Olympic Committee and the Olympic System*. London: Routledge.

Charles, G. (2008) 'The buddy system', *Marketing*, 6 February.

Cheetham-Bell-JWT (2001) 'The university of real life: how Salford University successfully repositioned itself', presented at the Institute of Practitioners in Advertising Effectiveness Awards. (Available at: www.warc.com.)

Chester, J. (2007) *Digital Destiny: New Media and the Future of Democracy*. New York: The New Press.

Christensen, L.T., Morsing, M. and Cheney, G. (2008) *Corporate Communications: Convention, Complexity and Critique*. London: Sage.

Clemons, E.K. (2007) 'Harnessing social networks'. (Available at: www.forbes.com, accessed 23 August 2008.)

Clifford, S. (2008) 'Olympic sponsors to benefit under a tougher stance in China', *International Herald Tribune*, 11 July. (Available at: www.nytimes.com/2008/07/11/business/media/11adco.html?_r=1&scp=2&sq=clifford%20beijing%20sponsor&st=cse, accessed September 2008.)

Cohen, L. (2003) *A Consumer's Republic: The Politics of Mass Consumption in Post-war America*. New York: Knopf.

Cornelissen, J. (2004) *Corporate Communications: Theory and Practice*. London: Sage.

Costanzo, P.J. and Goodnight, J.E. (2005) 'Celebrity endorsements: matching celebrity and endorsed brand in magazine advertisements', *Journal of Promotion Management*, 11(4): 49–62.

Coward, R. (1999) *Sacred Cows*. London: Harper Collins.

Cox, D. (1997) 'Strategic use of trends in the youth market', ESOMAR, presented at the Youth Marketing Conference, Copenhagen. (Available at: www.warc.com, accessed 22 April 2008.)

Cozens, C. (2002) 'Brand new world', *The Guardian*, 11 March, p. 23.

Creamer, M. (2005) 'The gender gap: ad industry still talking French', *Advertising Age*, 76(44): 5.

Crimmins, J. and Horn, M. (1996) 'Sponsorship: from management ego trip to marketing success', *Journal of Advertising Research*, 36 (4): 11–21.

Critchley, S. (2002) *On Humour*. London: Routledge.

Critser, G. (2003) *Fat Land: How Americans Became the Fattest People in the World*. Houghton: Mifflin.

Cronin, A. (2004) 'Currencies of commercial exchange: advertising agencies and the promotional imperative,' *Journal of Consumer Culture*, 4(3): 339–60.

Crossley, N. (2002) *Making Sense of Social Movements*. Buckingham: Open University Press.

Cumming, G. (2005a) 'University of Dundee: academic brand creation', *Institute of Practitioners in Advertising*. (Available at: www.warc.com.).

—— (2005b) 'University of Dundee: university challenge. Serious fun', *Institute of Practitioners in Advertising*.

Davenport, T. and Beck, J. (2001) *The Attention Economy: Understanding the New Currency of Business*. Boston: Harvard Business School Press.

Davis, A. (2000) 'Public relations, news production and changing patterns of source access in the British national media', *Media, Culture and Society*, 22(1): 39–59.

Davis, J. (2008) *The Olympic Games Effect: How Sports Marketing Builds Strong Brands*. London: John Wiley.

Davis, S. (2000) *Brand Asset Management*. New Jersey: Jossey-Bass.

Dawson, N. and Hall, M. (2005) 'That's brand entertainment!', *Admap*, February (458).

DCMS (2005) 'United Kingdom Government response to issues paper on commercial communications', Department for Culture, Media and Sport. (Available at: http://ec.europa.eu/avpolicy/reg/history/consult/consultation_2005/contributions/index_en.htm.)

—— (2008a) Speech by Secretary of State to the convergence think tank, 11 June. (Available at: www.culture.gov.uk/reference_library/minister_speeches.)

—— (2008b) 'Public consultation on implementing the EU audiovisual media services directive'. (Available at: www.culture.gov.uk/reference_library/consultations/5309.aspx.)

Delaney, K.J. (2007) 'Yahoo expands online-ad reach', *Wall Street Journal*, 6 September, B3.

Department of Health (2004) 'Choosing health', Cm 6374, London: The Stationery Office.

Dermody, J. and Scullion, R. (2001) 'An exploration of the advertising ambitions and comparative advertising', *Journal of Advertising*, 20(2): 53–70.

—— and —— (2003) 'Exploring the consequences of negative political advertising for liberal democracy', *Journal of Political Marketing*, 2(1): 77–100.

Dewdney, A. and Ride, P. (2006) *The New Media Handbook*. London: Routledge.

Dill-Scott, W. (1908/1998) *The Psychology of Advertising*. New York: Arno Press.

Donaghy, J. (2008) 'Tough times for Howard of Halifax', *The Guardian*, 7 August. (Available at: www.guardian.co.uk/culture/tvandradioblog/2008/aug/07/toughtimesforhowardbrown, accessed 18 September 2008.)

Donaton, S. (2004) *Madison & Vine*. New York: McGraw-Hill.

Douglas, M. (2002) *Purity and Danger: An Analysis of Concepts of Pollution and Taboo*. London: Routledge.

Dunn, T. (1998) 'ARF/AMA marketing research industry survey: a tracking survey of marketing researchers and marketers', *Research Study Series*.

Du Plessis, E. (2005) *The Advertised Mind: Ground Breaking Insights into How our Brains Respond to Advertising*. London: Kogan Page.

Dye, R. (2000) 'The buzz on buzz', *Harvard Business Review* (November–December): 139–46.

EAA (2005) 'European sponsorship association policy statement on sponsorship by alcohol brands'. (Available at: www.sponsorship.org/freePapers/alcoSpons06.pdf.)

EASA (2005) *Advertising Self-regulation in Europe*. Brussels: EASA.

Eckert, C. (1991) 'Carole Lombard in Macy's window' in C. Herzog and J.M. Gaines (eds) *Fabrications: Costume and the Female Body*. London: Routledge.

The Economist (2005) 'The rapid growth of product placement', 27 October.

The Economist (2008) 'Everywhere and nowhere', 19 March.

Edwards, T. (1997) *Men in the Mirror: Men's Fashion, Masculinity and Consumer Society*. London: Cassell.

Ehrenberg, A. (1972) *Repeat Buying: Theory and Application*. Amsterdam and London: North-Holland Publishing Co.

Ehrenberg, A. and Hammond, K. (2001) 'The case against price-related promotions', *Admap*, June.

Elliott, S. (2007) 'Now the clicking is to watch the ads, not skip them', *New York Times*, 17 August.

Erdogan, B.Z. and Baker, M.J. (2000) 'Towards a practitioner-based model of selecting celebrity endorsers', *International Journal of Advertising*, 19(1). (Available at: www.warc.com.)

ESOMAR (2006) 'Global trends', *Highlights 2006*, ESOMAR World Research. (Available at: www.esomar.org/uploads/pdf/ESOMAR_highlights_2006.pdf.)

European Commission (2006) *Self-Regulation in the EU Advertising Sector*. Health and Consumer Protection Directorate General, Brussels: EC.

European Professional Women's Network in partnership with Egon Zehnder International and BoardEx, 'Third bi-annual European PWN board women monitor 2008 (Available at: www.europeanpwn.net/files/3rd_bwm_2008_press_release_1.pdf, accessed 15 September 2008.)

Evans, M. (2004) *Killing Thinking: The Death of the Universities.* London: Continuum.

Evans, C. and Gamman, L. (1995) 'The gaze revisited, or reviewing queer viewing' in P. Burston and C. Richardson *A Queer Romance: Lesbians, Gay Men and Popular Culture.* London and New York: Routledge.

Evans, M. (2007) 'Campus fashions follow haute couture model', *Times Higher Education Supplement*, 12 January.

Ewen, S. (1998) *PR! A Social History of Spin.* New York: Basic Books.

Farrell, M. (2007) 'Media in transition. Culture in transition', *Brand Papers*. (Available at: www.brandchannel.com, accessed 14 March.)

Fearn, H. (2008) 'Makeover mania', *Times Higher Education Supplement*, 6 March.

Federal Trade Commission (2005) Letter from Mary K. Engle, Associate Director for Advertising Practices, FTC to Gary Ruskin, Executive Director, Commercial Alert, 10 February. (Available at: www.ftc.gov/os/closings/staff/050210productplacemen.pdf.)

Feldwick, P. (2002) *What is Brand Equity Anyway?.* Henley-on-Thames: NTC Publications.

Fendley, A. (1995) *Commercial Break: The Inside Story of Saatchi & Saatchi.* London: Hamish Hamilton.

Fennell, B. (1999) 'Advertising in an accelerated culture', *Account Planning Group (UK)*, Creative Planning Awards. (Available at: www.apg.org.uk, accessed 20 April 2008.)

Field, P. (2008) 'How TV sponsorship can work harder', *Admap*, 496 (July/August): 17–18.

Fill, C. (2002) *Marketing Communications: Contexts, Strategies and Applications*. London: Prentice Hall.

Findlaw (2002) http://news.findlaw.com/hdocs/docs/mcdonalds/pelmanmcds21203acmp.pdf. (Access no longer available.)

Fisher, F. (2008) 'Should we ditch the pitch?', *Campaign*, 6 June, pp. 24–5.

Fletcher, W. (2008) *Powers of Persuasion: The Inside Story of British Advertising*. Oxford: Oxford University Press.

Florida, R. (2003) *The Rise of the Creative Class and How It's Transforming Work, Leisure and Everyday Life*. New York: Basic Books.

Fox, K. (2004) *Watching the English: The Hidden Rules of English Behaviour*. London: Hodder & Stoughton.

Franzen, G. *et al.* (1999) *Brands and Advertising: How Advertising Effectiveness Influences Brand Equity*. Henley-on-Thames: Admap Publications.

Freud, S. (1914/2001) 'On narcissism: an introduction' in *The Standard Edition of the Complete Psychological Works of Sigmund Freud: Early Psycho-analytic Publications. Vol. 14, 1914–1916*. (Trans. J. Strachey). London: Vintage.

Frith, K. and Mueller, B. (eds) (2003) *Advertising and Societies: Global Issues*. New York: Peter Lang.

Galician, M.L. (ed.) (2004) *Handbook of Product Placement in the Mass Media: New Strategies in Marketing Theory, Practice, Trends, and Ethics*. Philadelphia, PA: Haworth Press.

Gibbins, J. and Reimer, B. (1999) *The Politics of Postmodernity: An Introduction to Contemporary Politics and Culture*. London: Sage.

Gibbon, T. and Hawkes, R. (2006) 'What's next for viral marketing?', *Admap*, May (472): 53–5.

Gill, R. (2007) *Gender and the Media*. Cambridge: Polity Press.

Gilmore, J. and Pine, J. (2007) *Authenticity: What Consumers Really Want*. Boston, MA: Harvard Business School Press.

Gladwell, M. (2002) *The Tipping Point: How Little Things Can Make a Big Difference*. New York: Back Bay Books, Times Warner.

Glaister, D. (2008) 'Spot the difference: "L'Oreal denies 'whitening' Beyoncé Knowles' skin in cosmetics ad"', *The Guardian*, 9 August.

Goffman, E. (1979) *Gender Advertisements*. New York: Harper Collins.

Grant, I. and McLeod, C. (2007) 'Advertising agency planning: conceptualising network relationships', *Journal of Marketing Management*, 23(5–6): 425–42.

Gray, R. (2008) 'Google turns 10', *Marketing*, 17 September, pp. 28–31.

Green, L. (ed.) (2005) *Advertising Works and How: Winning Communications Strategies for Business*. Henley-on-Thames: World Advertising Research Centre.

Grey, J. (2008) *Television Entertainment*. London: Routledge.

Griffith University (2004) 'Griffith University: smarter campaign'. Advertising Federation of Australia.

Hackley, C. (2003) 'From consumer insight to advertising strategy: the account planner's integrative role in creating advertising development', *Marketing Intelligence and Planning*, 21: 446–52.

Haig, M. (2005) *Brand Failures: The Truth About the 100 Biggest Branding Mistakes of All Time*. New York: Kogan Page.

Hall, M. (2004) 'Broadcast sponsorship: how does it work?', *Admap*, 449 (April): 19–22.

Hansen, F. and Christensen, L.B. (eds) (2003) *Branding and Advertising*. Denmark: Copenhagen Business School Press.

Harris, I. (2002) 'Fwd: have you seen this?', *The Guardian*, 4 November.

Hartman, K. (2000) 'Studies of negative political advertising: an annotated bibliography', *Reference Services Review*, 28(3): 248–61.

Harvey, F. (2002) 'Ads may have to keep it real', *Financial Times: Creative Business*, 19 March, p. 3.

Hau, L. (2007a) 'A few truths about online video'. (Available at: www.forbes.com, accessed 28 August.)

—— (2007b) 'Web ad spending to eclipse radio in 2007'. (Available at www.forbes.com, accessed 29 August.)

Heath, R. (2001) *The Hidden Power of Advertising*. Henley-on-Thames: NTC Publications.

Hennion, A. and Meadel, C. (1989) 'The artisans of desire: the mediation of advertising between product and consumer', *Sociological Theory*, 7: 191–209.

Hodess, R., Tedesco, J. and Kaid, L. (2000) 'British party election broadcasts. A comparison of 1992 and 1997', *Harvard International Journal of Press/Politics*, 5(4): 55–70.

Hollis, N. (2007) 'To pass or to pass it on: that is the viral question', *Millward Brown's POV*, April. (Available at: www.wpp.com/wpp/marketing/digital/topassortopassiton.htm.)

Holt, D. (2002) 'Why do brands cause trouble? A dialectical theory of consumer culture and branding', *Journal of Consumer Research*, 29: 70–88.

Holt, D. (2004) *How Brands Became Icons: The Principles of Cultural Branding*. Boston: Harvard Business School Press.

Hopkins, C.C. (1910/1966) *Scientific Advertising*. New York: Crown Publishers.

Howell, N. (2003) 'Catching the bug', *New Media Age*, 4 October, pp. 31–2. (Available at: www.guardian.co.uk/technology/2002/nov/04/internetnews.mondaymediasection.)

IAS (2007) 'Alcohol and advertising: IAS factsheet'. London: The Institute of Alcohol Studies.

Ind, N. (1997) *The Corporate Brand*. Houndsmills: Macmillan Press.

IOC (2008a) *Olympic Marketing Fact File*. Lausanne: IOC.

—— (2008b) *IOC Marketing Media Guide: Beijing*. Lausanne: IOC.

IPA (2003) *The Client Brief: A Best Practice Guide to Briefing Communications Agencies*. (Available at: www.ipa.co.uk.)

——— and Future Foundation (2006) *The Future of Advertising and Agencies: A 10-year Perspective*. London: IPA.

———, DMA, ISBA, MCCA and PRCA (2006) *Finding an Agency: A Best Practice Guide to Agency Search and Selection*. (Available at: www.ipa.co.uk.)

ITV (2004) *Response to Ofcom Consultation on the Proposed Broadcasting Code*. (Available at: www.ofcom.org.uk/consult/condocs/Broadcasting_code/responses/.)

Jack, L. (2008) 'Sweet smell of innovation', *Marketing Week*, 17 January. (Available at: www.marketingweek.co.uk, accessed 15 September 2008.)

Jackson, N. and Lilleker, D. (2008) 'Politicians and Web 2.0: the current bandwagon or a changing mindset?', paper presented to the Web 2.0 Conference, April, Royal Holloway, University of London.

Jaffe, J. (2005) *Life After the 30-second Spot: Energize Your Brand with a Bold Mix of Alternatives to Traditional Advertising*. New York: John Wiley.

——— (2007) *Join the Conversation: How to Engage Marketing-weary Consumers with the Power of Community, Dialogue, and Partnership*. New York: John Wiley.

James, K. and Hensel, P. (1991) 'Negative advertising: the malicious strain of comparative advertising', *Journal of Advertising*, 20(2): 53–70.

Jenkins, H. (2006) *Convergence Culture: Where Old and New Media Collide*. New York: New York University Press.

Journal of Marketing Management (2001) 'Strategies of the 2001 British General Election', special edition, 'The marketing campaign: the 2001 British general election', 17(9–10): 969–87.

Jurvetson, S. (2000) 'What is viral marketing?'. (Available at: www.dfj.com/cgibin/artman/ublish/steve_may00.shtml.)

Kaid, L. (2004) 'Political advertising' in L. Kaid (ed.) *Handbook of Political Communication*. London: Lawrence Erlbaum Associates.

——— and Johnston, A. (2001) *Videostyle in Presidential Campaigns. Style and Content of Television Political Advertising*. Westport, CT: Praeger.

Kasapi, E. (2007) *Rethinking Humorous Advertising in a Global Setting: Advertising Practitioners' and Audiences' Views*. PhD thesis, UEL.

Kemp, G. (2007) 'Adwatch of the year: the work that worked, 2007', *Marketing*, 19 December, 6–7.

Kemper, S. (2003) 'How advertising makes its object' in T.M. Moeran (ed.) *Advertising Cultures*. Oxford: Berg.

Kent, J. and Calcroft, S. (1999) 'Batchelor's SuperNoodles' in N. Kendall (ed.) *Advertising Works 10*. Henley-on-Thames: World Advertising Research Centre. (Available at www.warc.com.).

King, S. (2007) 'What is a brand?' in J. Lannon and M. Baskin (eds) *A Master Class in Brand Planning: The Timeless Works of Stephen King*. Chichester: John Wiley.

Kirby, J. (2004) 'Using "word of mouse" in brand marketing', *Admap*, October (454): 134.

Kjeldgaard, D. and Askegaard, S. (2006) 'The globalization of youth culture: the global youth segment as structures of common difference', *Journal of Consumer Research*, 33: 231–47.

Klaassen, A. (2007) 'Video report: the role of user-generated content', *Advertising Age*, 6 June.

——— and Mcilroy, M. (2007) 'Why web video is the new 30-second spot', *Advertising Age*, 20 August.

Klein, D. (2000) *Women in Advertising: Ten Years On*. London: IPA.

Klein, N. (2000) *No Logo: Taking Aim at the Brand Bullies*. New York and London: Picador/Flamingo.

——— (2002) *No Logo: No Space, No Choice, No Jobs*. London: Flamingo.

Kline, S. (2004a) 'Sedentary lifestyle or fast food culture? Lessons from the battle of the bulge' in T.P. Madhav (ed.) *Food Industry and Health Concerns*. India: ICFAI University Press, Hyderabad.

——— (2004b) 'Fast food, sluggish kids'. (Accessed at: www.consume.bbk.ac.uk/publications.html.)

Knapton, S. (2008) 'Halifax's Howard dropped as downturn bites', *Daily Telegraph*, 7 August.

Kotler, P. and Calder, B.J. (2008) *Kellogg on Advertising and Media*. Hoboken, NJ: John Wiley.

Kumar, S. (2003) 'The intrigues and challenges of global advertising', *The Advertiser*, June: 16–22.

Lammiman, J. and Syrett, M. (2004) 'Advertising and millennials', *Young Consumers*, 5(4): 62–73.

Lance, S. and Woll, J. (2006) *The Little Blue Book of Advertising*. London: Portfolio Penguin.

Lang, T. and Heasman, M. (2004) *Food Wars: The Global Battle for Mouths, Minds and Markets*. London: Earthscan.

Law, A. (1998) *Open Minds: 21st Century Business Lessons and Innovations from St. Luke's*. London: Orion Business Books.

Lears, J. (1995) *Fables of Abundance: A Cultural History of Advertising in America*. New York: Basic Books.

Leiss, W., Kline, S., Jhally, S. and Botterill, J. (2005) *Social Communication in Advertising: Consumption in the Mediated Marketplace* (3rd edn). New York: Routledge.

Lewis, D. and Bridger, D. (2001) *The Soul of the New Consumer*. London: Nicholas Brearley.

Linn, S. (2003) *Consuming Kids: The Hostile Takeover of Childhood*. New York: The New Press.

Livingstone, S. (2005) 'Assessing the research base for the policy debate over the effects of food advertising to children', *International Journal of Advertising*, 24(3): 273–96.

—— (2006) *New Research on Advertising Foods to Children: An Updated Review of the Literature*. (Available at: www.ofcom.org.uk/consult/condocs/foodads/foodadsprint/annex9.pdf.)

—— and Helsper, E. (2004) *Advertising 'Unhealthy' Foods to Children: Understanding Promotion in the Context of Children's Daily Lives*. Report to Ofcom, London, April. (Available at: www.ofcom.org.uk/research/tv/reportsfood_ads/appendix2.pdf.)

LOCOG (2006) Information on London 2012's UK statutory marketing rights under the London Olympic games and Paralympic games Act 2006 (the '2006 Act') and the Olympic symbol etc (protection) Act 1995 ('OSPA')

—— (2007a) *Brand Protection: Businesses – What You Need to Know*. London: LOCOG.

—— (2007b) *Brand Protection: Non-Commercial Organisations – What You Need to Know*. London: LOCOG.

Love, J.F. (1986) *McDonald's Behind the Arches*. New York: Bantam Books.

Lury, C. (2004) *Brands: The Logos of Global Economy*. London: Routledge.

Madden, T.J. and Weinberger, M.G. (1984) 'Humour in advertising: a practitioner's view', *Journal of Advertising Research*, 24: 23–9.

Malefyt, T.D. (2003) 'Models, metaphors and client relations: the negotiated meanings of advertising' in T.D. Malefyt and B. Moeran (eds) *Advertising Cultures*. Oxford: Berg.

—— and Brian, M. (eds) (2003) *Advertising Cultures*. Oxford: Berg.

Marchand, R. (1985) *Advertising and the American Dream: Making way for modernity, 1920–1940*. Berkeley: University of California Press.

—— (1998) *Creating the Corporate Soul: The Rise of Public Relations and Corporate Imagery in American Big Business*. Berkeley, CA: University of California Press.

Martin, R. (2007) *The Psychology of Humour: An Integrative Approach*. London: Elsevier Academic Press.

Mayer, M. (1958) *Madison Avenue USA*. Middlesex: Penguin.

Mazzarella, W. (2003). *Shoveling Smoke: Advertising and Globalization in Contemporary India*. Durham, NC: Duke University Press.

McChesney, R. (2004) *The Problem of the Media: US Communication Politics in the 21st Century*. New York: Monthly Review Press.

McCracken, G. (2005) *Culture and Consumption II: Markets, Meaning and Brand Management*. Bloomington: Indiana University Press.

—— (2006) *Flock and Flow: Predicting and Managing Change in a Dynamic Marketplace*. Bloomington: Indiana University Press.

McCusker, G. (2004) *Tailspin: Public Relations Disasters*. New York: Kogan Page.

McDonald, C. and King, S. (1995) *Sampling the Universe: The Growth, Development and Influence of Market Research in Britain Since 1945*. Henley-on-Thames: NTC Books.

McDonald's (2008) Various press releases. (Available at: www.mcdonalds.co.uk/pages/global/uniform.html.)

McFall, L. (2004) *Advertising: A Cultural Economy*. London: Sage.

McGhee, G., Kiely, D., Gilmour, N. and Baskin, M. (2007) 'Subway – on a roll: how the regional trial of a repositioned and re-branded existing product for UK sandwich chain Subway led to a fully integrated global communications success story', bronze award winner at the IPA Effectiveness Awards.

McGowan, P. (2000) 'All the young dudes', *Admap*, November (411).

McGrath, M.-A., Sherry, J.F. Jr., Sidney, J. and Levy, J.L. (1993) 'Giving voice to the gift: the use of projective techniques to recover lost meanings', *Journal of Consumer Psychology*, 2.

MacLean, G. (2008) 'Is *Mad Men* misogynistic?', *The Guardian*, 21 May (Available at: www.guardian.co.uk/culture/garethmcleanblog/2008/may/21/inresponsetowilliamleiths.)

MacRury, I. (2007) 'Psychodynamic practice: individuals, groups and organisations', *Institutional Creativity and Pathologies of Potential Space Journal*, May, 13(2): 119–40.

—— (2008) 'The airport next door: London City airport – places and non-places' in M. Rustin and P. Cohen (eds) *London's Turning: The Prospect of Thames Gateway*. Farnham: Ashgate.

—— (2009a) *Advertising*. London: Routledge.

—— (2009b) 'Advertising and the new media environment'(updated/rewritten) in L. Albertazzi and P. Cobley (eds) *The Media: An Introduction* (3rd edn). London: Pearson.

Micheletti, M., Follesdal, A. and Stolle, D. (eds) (2003) *Politics, Products, and Markets: Exploring Political Consumerism Past and Future*. New Jersey: Transaction Press.

Millar, A., Fawcus, J. and Bloor, A. (2006) 'Axe "Click" – a global communication strategy', presented at the ESOMAR Annual Congress, September, London. (Available at: www.esomar.org, accessed 25 April 2008.)

Milligan, A. (2004) *Brand it Like Beckham: The Story of How Brand Beckham was Built*. London: Cyan.

Mintel (2008) 'iPod generation – UK April 2007'. (Available at: http://oxygen.mintel.com/sinatra/oxygen/display/id=273617.)

Mintel Special Report (2001) 'Men's grooming habits', February. (Available at: http://academic.mintel.com.)

Miracle, G.E. and Nevett, T.R. (1988) 'A comparative history of advertising self-regulation in the UK and the US', *European Journal of Marketing*, 22(4): 7–23.

Mitchell, V., Macklin, J. and Paxman, J. (2007) 'Social uses of advertising: an example of young male adults', *International Journal of Advertising*, 26(2): 199–222.

Mort, F. (1988) 'Boy's own? Masculinity, style and popular culture' in R. Chapman and J. Rutherford (eds) *Male Order: Unwrapping Masculinity*. London: Lawrence & Wishart, pp. 193–224.

—— (1996) *Cultures of Consumption: Commerce, Masculinities and Social Space*. London & New York: Routledge.

Mulkay, M.J. (1988) *On Humour: Its Nature and its Place in Modern Society*. Cambridge: Polity Press.

Murdock, G. (1992) 'Embedded persuasions: The fall and rise of integrated advertising' in D. Strinati and S. Wagg (eds) *Come on Down? Popular Media Culture in Post-war Britain*. London: Routledge.

—— (2000) 'Digital futures: European television in the age of convergence' in J. Wieten, G. Murdock and P. Dahlgren (eds) *Television Across Europe*. London: Sage.

NEF (2008) *Fool's Gold: How the 2012 Olympics is Selling East London Short, and a 10 Point Plan for a More Positive Local Legacy*. London: New Economics Foundation.

Nevett, T.R. (1982) *Advertising in Britain: A History*. London: Heinemann.

Newell, J., Salmon, C.T. and Chang, S. (2006) 'The hidden history of product placement', *Journal of Broadcasting & Electronic Media*, 50(4): 575–94.

Nicholls, W. and Raillard, G. (2004) 'Lynx pulse: proving the value of integration', silver winner at the IPA Effectiveness Awards. (Available at: www.warc.com, accessed 20 April 2008.)

Nixon, B. (2004) 'Advertising and marketing to children–everybody's business', *Advertising and Marketing to Children*, April/June: 19–25.

Nixon, S. (2003) *Advertising Cultures. Gender, Commerce, Creativity*. London: Sage.

Nyren, C. (2005) *Advertising to Baby Boomers*. Ithaca, NY: Paramount Market Publishing.

O'Dell, S. and Pajunen, J. (2000) *The Butterfly Customer: Capturing the Loyalty of Today's Elusive Customer*. Toronto: John Wiley.

O'Donohoe, S. (1994) 'Advertising uses and gratifications', *European Journal of Marketing*, 28: 52–75.

—— (1997) 'Raiding the postmodern pantry: advertising intertextuality and the young adult audience', *European Journal of Marketing*, 31: 234.

—— and Tynan, C. (1998) 'Beyond sophistication: dimensions of advertising literacy', *International Journal of Advertising*, 17: 467–82.

Ofcom (2004a) *Childhood Obesity: Food Advertising in Context*. London: Ofcom.

—— (2004b) *The Future Regulation of Broadcast Advertising*. London: Ofcom.

—— (2005a) *Young People and Alcohol Advertising*. London: Ofcom.

—— (2005b) *Television Promotions: What the Viewers Think*. London: Ofcom.

—— (2005c) *Broadcasting Code*. London: Ofcom.

—— (2007) *The International Communications Market 2007*. London: Ofcom.

—— (2008) *The UK Communications Market 2008*. London: Ofcom.

Offer, A. (1996) *In Pursuit of the Quality of Life*. Oxford: Oxford University Press.

Office for National Statistics (ONS) (2001) *National Food Survey*. London: ONS.

OFT (2004) *Misleading Advertisements*. London: OFT.

Packard, V. (1957) *The Hidden Persuaders*. London: Pelican.

Palmer, S. (2006) *Television Disrupted: The Transition from Network to Networked TV*. Burlington, MA: Focal Press.

Parsley, D. (2008) 'Storm clouds gather over media sector', *MediaWeek*, 22–9 April, pp. 26–8.

Parsons, A. (1997) 'The impact of Internet advertising: new medium of new marketing paradigm?', *Advertising Research Foundation, Online Media and its Measurement*, July.

Phelps, J., Lewis, R., Mobilio, L., Perry, D. and Raman, N. (2004) 'Viral marketing or electronic word-of-mouth advertising: examining consumer responses and motivations to pass along email', *Journal of Advertising Research*, 44 (December): 333–48.

Pidd, H. (2007) 'Food manufacturers target children on Internet after regulator's TV advertising clampdown', *The Guardian*, 31 July. (Available at: www.guardian.co.uk/media/2007/jul/31/newmedia.advertising1.)

Pine, J. and Gilmore, J. (1999) *The Experience Economy*. Cambridge, MA: Harvard University Press.

Poon, D. and Prendergast, G. (2006) 'A new framework for evaluating sponsorship opportunities', *International Journal of Advertising*, 35 (Autumn): 169–81.

Porter, L. and Golan, G. (2006) 'From subservient chickens to brawny men: a comparison of viral advertising to television advertising', *Journal of Interactive Advertising*, 6(2).

Powell, C. (1998) 'The role of labour's advertising in the 1997 General Election' in I. Crewe, B. Gosschalk and J. Bartle (eds) *Why Labour Won the General Election of 1997*. London: Frank Cass Publishers.

Presbrey, F. (1929) *The History and Development of Advertising*. New York: Doubleday.

Price, V., Cappella, J. and Nir, L. (2002) 'Does disagreement contribute to more deliberative opinion?', *Political Communications*, 19(1): 95–112.

Pringle, H. (2004a) *Celebrity Sells*. Chichester: John Wiley/IPA.

—— (2004b) 'Star gazing', *Creative Review*, August: 58–60.

Pringle, H. and Thompson, M. (1999) *Brand Spirit: How Cause Related Marketing Builds Brands*. London: John Wiley.

Rajan, A. (2008) 'L'Oréal under fire for "whitewashing" Beyoncé', *The Independent*, 8 August.

Rees, E. (2005) 'Getting to know the youth market', *Admap*, September (464): 20–2.

Reeves, R. (1961) *Reality in Advertising*. New York: Alfred A. Knopf.

Reid, A. (2005) 'Viral advertising campaigns', *Campaign*, 2 April.

—— (2008) 'Adland's digital fightback', *Campaign*, 23 May, pp. 20–1.

Revolution (2008) 'The online advertising report', April.

Ries, A. and Trout, J. (2001) *Positioning: The Battle for Your Mind*. New York: McGraw-Hill.

—— and Ries, L. (2002) *The Fall of Advertising and the Rise of PR*. London: Harper Collins.

Riffe, D., Lacy, S. and Fico, F. (1998) *Analysing Media Messages using Quantitative Content Analysis in Research*. London: Lawrence Erlbaum Associates.

Ritson, M. and Elliot, R. (1999) 'The social uses of advertising: an ethnographic study of adolescent advertising audiences', *Journal of Consumer Research*, 26: 260–78.

Ritzer, G. (2004) *The McDonaldization of Society* (revised New Century edn). Thousand Oaks, CA: Pine Forge Press.

Roberts, K. (2004) *Lovemarks: The Future Beyond Brands*. New York: PowerHouseBooks.

Roche, M. (2000). *Mega-events and Modernity: Olympics and Expos in the Growth of Global Culture*. New York: Routledge.

Said, E. (1993) *Culture and Imperialism*. New York: Knopf.

Sampson, H. (1874/1974) *A History of Advertising from the Earliest Times*. Detroit: Gale Research Co.

Sandison, N. (2008) 'Ryanair fined for using images of French president and wife in ads'. (Available at: www.brandrepublic.com, accessed 5 February 2008.)

Savigny, H. (2005) 'Labour, political marketing and the 2005 election: a campaign of two halves', *Journal of Marketing Management*, 21 (9/10): 925–42.

Saxton, G. (2005) 'Collections of cool', *Young Consumers*, 6(2): 18–27.

Scammell, M. (1999) *Designer Politics*. London: Macmillan.

Schlosser, E. (2001) *Fast Food Nation*. New York: Houghton Mifflin.

Schwartz, B. (2004) *The Paradox of Choice: Why Less is More*. New York: Harper Collins.

Scott, B. and Raillard, G. (2003) 'Lynx pulse: making tracks for Lynx', Account Planning Group (UK), silver award winner at the Creative Planning Awards 2003. (Available at: www.warc.com, accessed 25 April 2008.)

Scott, W.D. (1908/1988) *The Psychology of Advertising: A Simple Exposition of the Principles of Psychology in their Relation to Successful Advertising*. Boston: Thoemmes Continuum.

Scullion, R. and Dermody, J. (2005) 'The value of party election broadcasts for electoral engagement: a content analysis of the 2001 British General Election campaign', *International Journal of Advertising*, 24(3): 345–72.

Shaw, R. and Merrick, D. (2005) *Marketing Payback: Is Your Marketing Profitable?*. London: Prentice Hall/FT.

Shiota, M.N., Campos, B., Keltner, D. and Herenstein, M.J. (2004) 'Positive emotion and the regulation of interpersonal relationships' in P. Philoppot and R.S. Feldman (eds) *The Regulation of Emotion*. Mahwah, NJ: Lawrence Erlbaum Associates.

Silverman, G. (2006) 'How Jamie Oliver is blurring the lines between advertising and entertainment', *Financial Times*, 17 March, p. 10.

Smart, B. (1999) *Resisting McDonaldization*. Thousand Oaks, CA: Sage.

Smith, D. (2008) 'Food suppliers poised to cash in on the new "Delia effect"', *The Observer*, 10 February. (Accessed at: http://lifeandhealth.guardian.co.uk/food/story/0,,2255349,00.html.)

Sorrell, M. (2007) 'Exciting times', *Admap*, China supplement, February: 8–9.

Souza, M. and Quintanilha, S. (2006) 'Does fame always lead to fortune? Using celebrities in advertising', presented at the ESOMAR Latin American conference, October, Rio de Janeiro. (Accessed at: www.warc.com.)

Spicer, K. (2006) 'Celebrity: who's got the power?', *Sunday Times: Style Magazine*, 8 October, pp. 24–5.

Spigel, L. and Olsson, J. (eds) (2004) *Television After TV: Essays on a Medium in Transition*. Durham, NC: Duke University Press.

Spurgeon, C. (2008) *Advertising and New Media*. London: Routledge.

Stafford, M.R. and Faber, R.J. (eds) (2005) *Advertising, Promotion and New Media*. New York and London: M.E. Sharpe.

Staff Reporter (2008) 'Ad revenue tied to streams rises', *Wall Street Journal*, 17 January, B5.

Steel, E. (2007a) 'Advertising's brave new world', *Wall Street Journal*, 25 May, B1.

—— (2007b) 'YouTube to start selling ads in videos', *Wall Street Journal*, 22 August, B3.

Stengel, J. (2002) 'Life on the other side', *Campaign*, 17 May, p. 5.

Sternthal, B. and Craig, C.S. (1973) 'Humour in advertising', *Journal of Marketing*, 37: 12–18.

Sunderland, R. (2008) 'We lost sight of the true worth of things', *The Guardian*, 19 October. (Available at: www.guardian.co.uk/commentisfree/2008/oct/19/comment-consumeraffairs-creditcrunch, accessed 20 October 2008.)

Sustain (2001) *TV Dinners: What's Being Served up by the Advertisers?*. London: Sustain.

—— (2008) 'Junk food marketing'. (Available at: www.sustainweb.org/page.php?Id=117.)

Sunderland, P.L. and Denny, R.M. (2007) *Doing Anthropology in Consumer Research*. Walnut Creek, CA: Left Coast Press.

Swasy, A. (1993) *Soap Opera: The Inside Story of Proctor & Gamble*. New York: Times Books.

Tahir, T. (2008) 'Post-92 websites fail on the basics', *Times Higher Education Supplement*, 4 January.

Tan, E. (2007) 'Media usage per person drops for first time in a decade', *Advertising Age*, 7 August.

Tapscott, D. and Williams, A.D. (2006) *Wikinomics: How Mass Collaboration Changes Everything*. New York: Portfolio.

Thackeray, A. and Pinto, V.S. (2005) 'McCann-Erickson's ex-VP claims Rs 1.61 cr for sexual harassment'. (Available at: www.commercial-archive.com, accessed 18 September 2008.)

Tipper, H., Hollingworth, H., Hotchkiss, G. and Parsons, F. (1920) *The Principles of Advertising*. New York: Ronald Press.

Trout, J. (2001) *Big Brands Big Trouble*. New York: John Wiley.

—— and Rivkin, S. (2008) *Differentiate or Die: Survival in Our Era of Killer Competition* (2nd edn). Chichester: John Wiley.

Tungate, M. (2007) *Ad Land: A Global History of Advertising*. London: Kogan Page.

—— (2008) *Branded Male: Marketing to Men*. London and Philadelphia: Kogan Page.

Turner, Graeme (2004) *Understanding Celebrity*. London: Sage.

Turner, Graham (2008) *The Credit Crunch: Housing Bubbles, Globalisation and the Worldwide Economic Crisis*. London: Pluto.

Tylee, J. (2007a) 'Why pitching will remain a necessary evil', *Campaign*, 22 June. (Available at: www.brandrepublic.com, accessed 14 March 2008.)

—— (2007b) 'That was the year that was: Adland's 2007', *Campaign: The Annual*, 14 December.

Umarji, M.I.M. (2005) *Ethnic Representation in Agencies*. London: IPA.

Upton, F.H. (1860) *A Treatise on the Law of Trade Marks*. Albany, NY: Weare C. Little.

Vollmer, C. (2008) *Always On: Advertising and Marketing in the Era of Consumer Control*. New York: McGraw-Hill.

Vranica, S. (2007) 'Omnicom's super bowl ad buyer calls the plays', *Wall Street Journal*, 14 November, B4.

Wald, J. (2003) 'McDonald's obesity suit tossed US judge says complaint fails to prove chain is responsible for kids' weight gain'. (Accessed at: http://money.cnn.com/2003/01/22/news/companies/mcdonalds/.)

Walker, R. (2006) 'Free advertising', *New York Times Magazine*, 28 May.

WARC Reports (2008) 'The top viral marketing campaigns of 2007'.

Wareman, S. (2008) 'Sponsorship: is it worth it?', *Admap*, February.

Warren, M. (2007) 'Do celebrity endorsements still work?', *Campaign*, 2 November. (Accessed at: www. Brandrepublic.com.)

Watkins, S. (2005) 'The power of influence in the youth market', *Admap*, September (464): 23–5.

Weed, K. (2000) 'Elida Faberge: keeping a winning company winning', *Market Leader*, 11.

Wernick, A. (1991) *Promotional Culture*. London: Sage.

Which? (2007) *Marketing of Unhealthy Foods to Children*. London: Which?

White, R. (2006) 'Communicating with youth', *WARC Best Practice*, April. (Available at: www.warc.com, accessed 20 April 2008.)

—— (2007) ESOMAR supplement, *Admap*, September.

Whitehead, J. (2008) 'IPA backs ads in the face of downturn', *Marketing*, 9 January, p. 4.

Williams, R. (1980) 'Advertising: the magic system' in *Problems in Materialism and Culture*. London: Verso, pp. 170–95.

Williamson, J. (1978) *Decoding Advertisements*. London: Marion Boyars.

Wolburg, J.M. and Pokrywczynski, J. (2001) 'A psychographic analysis of "Generation Y"', *Journal of Advertising Research*, 41(5): 33–53.

Wolf, M.J. (2000) *The Entertainment Economy*. London: Penguin.

Wood, K. and Broadbent, T. (1999) 'Colgate: the science behind the smile' in N. Kendall (ed.) *Advertising Works 10*. Henley-on-Thames: World Advertising Research Centre.

World Advertising Research Center (2006) *The European Advertising and Media Forecast*, July, 20(5). Henley-on-Thames: World Advertising Research Center.

—— (2007) *The European Advertising and Media Forecast*, September, 21(6). Henley-on-Thames: World Advertising Research Center.

WPP (2006) 'WPP annual report'. (Available at: www.wpp.com/AnnualReports/2007/index.html.)

Wright, D.E. and Snow, R.E. (1980) 'Consumption as ritual in the high society' in R.B. Browne (ed.) *Rituals and Ceremonies in Popular Culture*. Ohio: Bowling Green University Popular Press.

Wright, R. (2000) *Advertising*. Harlow: FT/Prentice Hall.

Yohn, D.L. (2006) 'Do consumers always know best?', *Brandchannel*, 6 July.

Yum Chums (2008) (Available at: www.mcdonalds.co.uk/pages/global/yumchums.html.)

Zyman, S. (2002) *The End of Advertising as We Know It*. New York: John Wiley.

Websites

Ad Brands	www.adbrands.net
Ad Forum	www.adforum.com
Account Planning Group	www.apg.org.uk

Adbusters	www.adbusters.org
Advertising Age	www.adage.com
Advertising Association	www.adassoc.org.uk
Advertising Standards Authority	www.asa.org.uk
Brand Channel	www.brandchannel.com
Brand Republic	www.brandrepublic.com
British Interactive Media Association	www.bima.co.uk
Clearcast	www.clearcast.co.uk
Committee of Advertising Practice	www.cap.org.uk
DDB	www.ddb.com
Direct Marketing Association	www.the-dma.org
European Advertising Standards Alliance	www.easa-alliance.org
History of Advertising Trust	www.hatads.org.uk
Incorporated Society of British Advertisers	www.isba.org.uk
Institute of Practitioners in Advertising	www.ipa.co.uk
IPA Effectiveness Awards	www.ipaeffectivenessawards.co.uk
Institute of Sales Promotion	www.isp.org.uk
Internet Advertising Bureau	www.iabuk.net
Interbrand	www.interbrand.com
Interpublic	www.interpublic.com
Market Research Society	www.mrs.org.uk
Office of Communications	www.ofcom.org.uk
Publicis	www.publicis.com
Radio Advertising Bureau	www.rab.co.uk
World Advertising Research Centre	www.warc.com
WPP	www.wpp.com
Zenith Optimedia Marketers Portal	www.marketersportal.com

Index

Printed in the USA/Agawam, MA
September 29, 2010

544389.064